MODELS FOR WRITERS

SHORT ESSAYS FOR COMPOSITION

Fourth

Editors

Alfred Rosa
Paul Eschholz
University of Vermont

ST. MARTIN'S PRESS   NEW YORK

Senior Editor: Mark Gallaher
Project Management: Omega Publishing Services, Inc.
Cover Design: Keithley & Associates
Cover Art: Susan Sargent, *Abstract/Grey and Blue* (Tapestry)

For information, write:
St. Martin's Press, Inc.
175 Fifth Avenue
New York, NY 10010

ISBN: 0-312-04836-X

Acknowledgments

It is a violation of the law to reproduce these selections by any means
whatsoever without the written permission of the copyright holder.

Page 28, "Give Us Jobs, Not Admiration" by Eric Bigler. From *Newsweek.*
Reprinted by permission of the author.

Page 33, "Anxiety: Challenge by Another Name" by James Lincoln Collier.
Reprinted with permission from the December 1986 *Reader's Digest.*

Page 40, "Be Kind to Commuters" by Christopher M. Bellitto. From *Newsweek.*
Reprinted by permission of the author.

Page 45, "Students of Success" by Lynne V. Cheney. From *Newsweek.* Reprinted
by permission of the author.

Page 50, "Don't Let Stereotypes Warp Your Judgments" by Robert L. Heilbroner. Reprinted by permission of the author.

Page 58, "Reach Out and Write Someone" by Lynne Wenzel. From *Newsweek.*
Reprinted by permission of the author.

Page 62, "So That Nobody Has to Go to School If They Don't Want To" by Roger
Sipher. Copyright © 1977 by The New York Times Company. Reprinted by
permission.

Page 66, "The Corner Store" by Eudora Welty. Original title "The Little Store."
From *The Eye of the Story: Selected Essays and Reviews* by Eudora Welty.
Copyright © 1975 by Eudora Welty. Reprinted by permission of Random
House, Inc.

Acknowledgments and copyrights are continued at the back of the book on
pages 456–58, which constitute an extension of the copyright page.

 The text of this book has been printed on recycled paper.

Preface

Models for Writers offers seventy-four short, lively essays that represent particularly appropriate models for use by beginning college writers. Most of our selections are comparable in length to the essays students will write themselves, and each clearly illustrates a basic rhetorical element, principle, or pattern. Just as important, the essays deal with subjects that we know from our own classroom experience will spark the interest of most college students. In making our selections, we have sought a level of readability that is neither so easy as to be condescending nor so difficult as to distract the reader's attention from the rhetorical issue under study. And, although we have included a few older classics, most of the essays have been written in the last ten years. Drawn from a wide range of sources, they represent a variety of contemporary prose styles.

This fourth edition of *Models for Writers* has been revised in a manner that is based on our own recent experiences and on the many suggestions made by instructors who adopted and liked the first three editions. The introduction, which explains the purpose of the text and shows students how it can be used to improve their writing, now includes a third student essay. The new student essay "Why Are You Here?" is a personal narrative; another new student essay, "Where Is Le Bathroom?" is an argumentative essay calling for an increase in the teaching of foreign languages, especially in early elementary grades. We've retained, from the third edition, the expository student essay which explains the main reasons for the cockroach's durability. These three essays demonstrate the types of writing students will be doing at the beginning of the semester as well as later in the term. The chapter on "Comparison and Contrast" has been expanded to include a discussion as well as a model essay of the definition and use of analogy. Finally, well over one-third of the essays in this edition are new, many of them written in the last three to five years. At the suggestion of past users and reviewers, we have replaced selections with ones that we believe will prove even more workable, being careful in every case that the new essays meet the essential qualifications of brevity, clarity, and suitability for student writers.

As in the third edition, the essays in *Models for Writers, Fourth Edition,* are grouped into eighteen chapters, each devoted to a particular element or pattern. Chapters 1–7 focus on the concepts of thesis, unity, organization, beginnings and endings, paragraphs, transitions, and effective sentences. Next, Chapters 8 and 9 illustrate some aspects of language: the effects of diction and tone and the uses of figurative language. Finally, Chapters 10–18 explore the various types of writing most often required of college students: illustration, narration, description, process analysis, definition, division and classification, comparison and contrast (including analogy), cause and effect, and argument. The arrangement of the chapters suggests a logical teaching sequence, moving from the elements of the essay to its language to the different types of essays. An alternative teaching strategy might be to structure the course around Chapters 10–18, bringing in earlier chapters as necessary to illustrate various individual elements. Each chapter is self-contained, so that instructors may easily devise their own sequences, omitting or emphasizing certain chapters according to the needs of a particular group of students. Whatever sequence is followed, thematic comparisons among the selections will be facilitated by the alternate *Thematic Table of Contents* at the beginning of the book.

The chapters all follow a similar pattern. Each opens with an explanation of the element or principle to be considered, many including paragraph-length examples. We then present three or four essays, each of which has its own brief introduction providing information about the author and directing the student's attention to specific rhetorical features. Every essay is followed by study materials in three parts: *Questions for Study and Discussion, Vocabulary,* and *Suggested Writing Assignments.*

The *Questions for Study and Discussion* focus on the content, the author's purpose, and the rhetorical strategy used to achieve that purpose. Some questions allow brief answers, but most are designed to stimulate more searching analysis and to promote lively classroom discussion. In order to reinforce the lessons of other chapters and remind students that good writing is never one-dimensional, at least one question at the end of each series focuses on a writing concern other than the one highlighted in the chapter at hand. Whenever it seemed helpful, we have referred students to the *Glossary of Useful Terms,* which provides concise definitions of rhetorical and other terms. The *Vocabulary* exercise draws from each reading several words that students will find worth adding to their vocabularies. The exercise asks them to define each word as it is used in the context of the selection and then to use the word in a new sentence of their own.

The *Suggested Writing Assignments* provide two writing assignments for each essay. The first calls for an essay closely related to the content and style of the essay it follows, in effect encouraging the use of the reading selection as a direct model. The second writing assignment, while ranging a little further afield in subject, gives the student yet another opportunity to practice the particular rhetorical element or principle being illustrated.

We are indebted to many people for their criticism and advice as we prepared this fourth edition of *Models for Writers.* We are especially grateful to:

Charlotte Alexander, College of Staten Island; Cheryl Allen-Pfitzner, Fullerton College; Charles E. Beckwith, California State University-Los Angeles; Beverly Carmo, Community College of Allegheny County; Gloria de Blasio, The Santa Rosa Junior College; James Dlugos, Washington and Jefferson College; Susan Eggly, Wayne State University; Susan Frantz, La-Roche College; A. Gargano, Long Beach City College/LAC Campus; Maxine Gibson, Washtenaw Community College; Susan Gill, Chabot College; Susan Harless, Butte College; Judy Hathcock, Amarillo College; Elaine L. Horne, Manchester Community College; Judith Johnson, The Ohio State University at Newark; Phyllis Katz, University of Hartford; Jane Maher, Nassau Community College; Michael McKenna, SUNY-Delhi; Lynne Meng, Union County College; Clara Metzmeier, Campbellsville College; Renate Muendel, West Chester University; Linda L. Olson, California Polytechnical University at Pomona; Bruce I. Orton, San Diego State University; Mary Rehwald, Northland College; Richard Sanzenbacher, Embry Riddle University; Phyllis Scharner, Milwaukee Area Technical College; David Selke, Southern Ohio College-North Kentucky Branch; Alice Snelgrove, College of DuPage; Susan Stann, De Anza College; Ronald Sudol, Oakland University; Molly Abel Travis, Tulane University; Maria S. Vidale, De Anza College; Julie Wosk, SUNY Maritime College; Fadia A. Zannad, University of Nevada-Las Vegas.

It was once again our good fortune to have the editorial guidance of Julie Nord and Mark Gallaher of St. Martin's Press as we worked on this new edition. Our greatest debt, as always, is to our students, for all that they have taught us.

Alfred Rosa
Paul Eschholz

Contents

vii

II. The Language of the Essay   163

Thematic Contents

The Female Experience

The Minority Experience

Nature and Science

Controversies

Language and Thought

Enduring Issues

Health and Medicine

INTRODUCTION

Models for Writers is designed to help you learn to write by providing you with a collection of model essays, essays that are examples of good writing. We know that one of the best ways to learn to write and to improve our writing is to read. By reading we can begin to see how other writers have communicated their experiences, ideas, thoughts, and feelings. We can study how they have used the various elements of the essay—words, sentences, paragraphs, organizational patterns, transitions, examples, evidence, and so forth—and thus learn how we might effectively do the same. When we see, for example, how a writer like James Lincoln Collier develops an essay from a strong thesis statement, we can better appreciate the importance of having a clear thesis statement in our writing. When we see the way Lisa Brown uses transitions to link key phrases and important ideas so that readers can recognize clearly how the parts of her essay are meant to fit together, we have a better idea of how to achieve such clarity in our own writing.

But we do not learn only by observing, by reading. We also learn by doing, by writing, and in the best of all situations we engage in these two activities in conjunction with one another. *Models for Writers* encourages you, therefore, to write your essays, to practice what you are learning, as you are actually reading and analyzing the model essays in the text.

The kind of composition that you will be asked to write for your college writing instructor is most often referred to as an essay—a relatively short piece of nonfiction in which a writer attempts to develop one or more closely related points or ideas. An effective essay has a clear purpose, often provides useful information, has an effect on the reader's thoughts and feelings, and is usually a pleasure to read.

All well-written essays also share a number of structural and stylistic features that are illustrated by the various essays in *Models for Writers*. One good way to learn what these features

1

are and how you can incorporate them in your own writing is to look at each of them in isolation. For this reason we have divided *Models for Writers* first into three major sections and, within these sections, into eighteen chapters, each with its own particular focus and emphasis.

"The Elements of an Essay," the first section, includes chapters on the following subjects: thesis, unity, organization, beginnings and endings, paragraphs, transitions, and effective sentences. All these elements are essential to a well-written essay, but the concepts of thesis, unity, and organization underlie all the others and so come first in our sequence.

Briefly, "Thesis" shows how authors put forth or state the main ideas of their essays and how they use such statements to develop and control content; "Unity," how authors achieve a sense of wholeness in their essays; and "Organization," some important patterns that authors use to organize their thinking and writing. "Beginnings and Endings" offers advice and models of ways to begin and conclude essays, while "Paragraphs" concentrates on the importance of well-developed paragraphs and what is necessary to achieve them. "Transitions" concerns the various devices that writers use to move from one idea or section of an essay to the next. Finally, "Effective Sentences" focuses on techniques to make sentences powerful and create stylistic variety.

"The Language of the Essay," the second major section of the text, includes a chapter on diction and tone and one on figurative language. "Diction and Tone" shows how carefully writers choose words either to convey exact meanings or to be purposefully suggestive. In addition, this chapter shows how the words a writer uses can create a particular tone or relationship between the writer and the reader—one of irony, for example, or humor or great seriousness. "Figurative Language" concentrates on the usefulness of the special devices of language—such as simile, metaphor, and personification—that add richness and depth to one's writing.

The final section of *Models for Writers*, "Types of Essays," includes chapters on the various types of writing most often required of college writing students: "Illustration" (how to use examples to illustrate a point or idea); "Narration" (how to tell a story or give an account of an event); "Description" (how to present a verbal picture); "Process Analysis" (how to explain how something is done or happens); "Definition" (how to explain what something is); "Division and Classification" (how to divide a subject into its parts and place items into appropriate categories); "Comparison and Contrast" (how to demonstrate likenesses and differences); "Cause and Effect" (how to explain the causes of an event or the effects of an action); and, finally, "Argument" (how to use reason and logic to persuade someone to your way of thinking). These types of writing are referred to as *rhetorical modes*.

Studying the rhetorical modes and practicing using them is very important in any effort to broaden one's writing skills. In *Models for Writers* we look at each mode separately, one at a time; we believe this is the simplest and most effective way to introduce them. However this does not mean that a well-written essay is necessarily one that chooses a single mode and sticks to it exclusively and rigidly. Confining oneself to comparison and contrast throughout an entire essay, for instance, might prove impractical and may yield a strained, unnatural piece of writing. In fact, it is often best to use a single mode to organize your essay, and then to use the other modes as your material dictates. When you read the student essays that follow, notice how, for example, Laura LaPierre's essay is basically organized as a narrative, but also includes a good deal of description and even some comparison and contrast. Jon Clancy's essay is an argumentative one that makes its point with strong illustrations, and vivid narrative examples. As you read the model essays included throughout this text, you will find that in the service of the dominant mode a good many of them utilize a combination of rhetorical modes.

Combining rhetorical modes probably is not something you want to think about or even plan when you first tackle a writing assignment. Rather, it should develop naturally as you organize, draft, and revise your materials. As long as your essay remains clear and logical, this combining process will only enhance the interest, impact, and persuasiveness of your writing.

All of the chapters are organized in the same way. Each opens with an explanation of the element or principle under consideration. These introductions are intended to be brief, clear, and memorable. Here you will also usually find one or more short examples of the feature or principle being studied. Following the introduction, we present three or four model essays, each with a brief introduction of its own providing information about the author and directing your attention to the highlighted rhetorical features. Every essay is followed by study materials in three parts: *Questions for Study and Discussion*, *Vocabulary*, and *Suggested Writing Assignments*.

Models for Writers, then, provides information, instruction, and practice in writing essays. By reading carefully and thoughtfully and by applying what you learn, you can begin to have more and more control over your own writing. Laura LaPierre, Courtney Smith, and Jon Clancy, three of our own writing students at the University of Vermont, found this to be true, and their work is a good example of what can be achieved from studying models.

Three Model Student Essays

After reading several personal narratives—Helen Keller's "The Most Important Day" and Dick Gregory's "Shame" in particular—Laura LaPierre decided to write one of her own. Only weeks prior to writing this essay Laura had received some very bad news. It was the experience of living with this news that she decided to write about. It was painful, and not everyone would feel comfortable with a similar task, but Laura welcomed the opportunity because she came to a better understanding of her own fears and feelings as she moved from one draft to the next. What follows is the final draft of Laura's essay.

Why are you here?

Laura LaPierre

BEGINNING SETS CONTEXT: when, where, to whom   Balancing between a crutch on one side and an I.V. pole with wheels on the other, I dragged my stiff leg along the smooth, sterile floor of the hospital hall. All around me nurses, orderlies, and doctors bustled about, dodging well-meaning visitors laden with flowers and candy. The fluorescent lights glared down with a brightness so sharp that I squinted and thought that sunglasses might be in order. Sticking close to the wall, I rounded the corner and paused to rest for a moment. I breathed in the hot, antiseptic-smelling air which I had grown accustomed to and sighed angrily.

SELECTION OF DETAILS: harsh hospital environment
POINT OF VIEW: first person

Tears of hurt and frustration pricked at the corner of my eyes as the now familiar pain seared my leg. I tugged my bathrobe closer around my shoulder and, hauling my I.V. pole with me, I continued down the hall. One, two--second door on the left, she had said. I opened the heavy metal door, entered, and realized that I must be a little early because no one else was there yet. After glancing at my watch, I sat down and looked around the room, noting with disgust the prevalence of beige. Beige walls, beige ceiling, shiny beige floor tiles. A small cot stood in one corner with a beige bedspread, and in the opposite corner there was a sink, mirror, and beige waste basket. The only relief from the monotony was the circle of six or seven chairs where I sat. They were a vivid rust color and helped to brighten the dull room. The shades were drawn and the lights were much dimmer than they had been in the hall, and my eyes gradually relaxed as I waited.

ORGANIZATION: chronological sequence of events

SELECTION OF DETAILS: dull, uninviting room (dominant impression)

ORGANIZATION: time reference

People began to drift in until five of the seats were filled. A nurse was the head of the odd-looking group. Three of us were attached by long tubes to I.V. poles, and then there was a social worker. The man to my left wore a slightly faded, royal blue robe. He had a shock of unruly gray hair above an angular face with deeply sunken cheeks. His eyes were sunken, too, and glassy with pain. Yet he smiled and appeared untroubled by his I.V. pole.

Wearing a crisp white uniform and a pretty sweater, the nurse, a pleasant-looking woman in her late twenties, appeared friendly and sympathetic, though not to the point of being sappy. My impressions were confirmed as she began to speak.

DIALOGUE

``Okay. I guess we can begin. Welcome to our group, we meet every Monday at....'' She went on, but I wasn't paying attention anymore. I looked around the group and my eyes came to rest on the man sitting next to the nurse. In contrast to the other man's shriveled appearance, this man was robust. He was tall, with a protruding belly and a ruddy complexion. Unlike the other man, he seemed at war with his I.V. pole. He constantly fiddled with the tube and with the tape that held the needle in his arm. Eyes darting around the room, he nervously watched everyone.

COMPARISON AND CONTRAST: points to differences between men

I heard the nurse continue, ``So, let's all introduce ourselves and tell why

ECHO OF TITLE

we are here.'' We went around the circle
clockwise, starting with the nurse, and
when we got to the social worker, I looked
up and surveyed her while she talked. Aside
from contributing to the beige monotony
with her pants, she was agreeable both in
appearance and disposition.

    When it was my turn, I took a deep
breath and with my voice quivering began,
``My name is Laura an--''
    ``Hi, Laura!'' interrupted the
cheerful man on my left. I turned and
smiled weakly at him.

    Fighting back the tears, I continued,
``And I have bone cancer.''

SELECTION OF DETAILS: reinforces earlier description of room

DIALOGUE: shows instead of tells

ENDING: moment of truth

For an assignment following one of the readings in the chapter on unity, Courtney Smith was inspired by a television commercial to choose an unusual topic: cockroaches. In order to develop a thesis about these creatures, Courtney did some preliminary reading in the library, spoke to her biology professor who had some interesting exhibits to show her, and surveyed the roach control products available at her local supermarket. In sorting through the information she gathered, she was particularly surprised by the ability of cockroaches to survive under almost any circumstances. This ability seemed to her to provide a suitably narrow focus for a short, unified essay, so she began to analyze the various reasons for the insects' resiliency. By first making lists of the points she wanted to include in her essay, Courtney discovered that she could cluster the reasons into three groups. She was then able to formulate the following thesis: "Cockroaches are remarkably resilient creatures for three basic reasons." This thesis, in turn, helped Courtney to map her organization; she decided that her essay would have three major paragraphs to discuss each of the basic reasons cockroaches are so durable and that she would also need an introductory paragraph and a concluding paragraph.

This five-paragraph pattern provided the basis for her first draft.

What follows is the final draft of Courtney's essay, which incorporates a number of changes she made based on a critical evaluation of her first draft.

Cockroaches

Courtney Smith

BEGINNING: captures readers' attention

Have you ever tried to get rid of cockroaches? Those stupid little bugs refuse to go. You can chase them, starve them, spray them, and even try to squash them. But no matter what you do, they always come back. I have heard they are the only creatures that can survive a nuclear explosion. What do cockroaches have that enables them to be such extremely resilient insects?

THESIS

The answer is simple. Cockroaches have survived in even the most hostile environments because they possess several unique physical features, an amazing reproductive process, and an immune system that has frustrated even the best efforts of exterminators to get rid of them.

FIRST POINT: "physical features"

Cockroaches are thin, torpedo-shaped insects. Their body shape allows them to squeeze into small cracks or holes in walls and ceilings or dart into drains, thus

DESCRIPTION

avoiding all dangers. Their outer shell is extremely hard, making them almost impossible to crush. Cockroaches have sticky pads on their claws that enable them to climb walls or crawl upside down on

ceilings. They also have two little tails
called ``cerci'' to alert them to danger.
These cerci are covered with tiny hairs
that, like antennae, are sensitive to
things as small as a speck of dust or as
seemingly innocent as a puff of air.
Finally, if cockroaches can't find food,
they can sustain themselves for up to a
month without food, as long as they have
water. Combined with their other physical
features, this ability to go for long
periods without food has made the cockroach
almost invincible.

TOPIC SENTENCE: PARAGRAPH UNITY

Cockroaches give credence to the old
adage that there is safety in numbers. They
reproduce at a truly amazing rate. About
two months after mating, a new generation
of cockroaches is born. One cockroach can
produce about two dozen offspring each time
it mates. To get some idea of their
reproductive power, imagine that you start
with three pairs of cockroaches that mate.
Approximately three weeks after mating the
females lay their eggs, which hatch some
forty-five days later. If we assume two
dozen eggs from each female, the first
generation would number seventy-two
offspring. These roaches would continue to
multiply geometrically so that by year's
end the colony's population would total
more than 10,000 cockroaches. Stopping this
process is almost impossible because, even
if we were successful in annihilating the
adult population, it is more than likely

SECOND POINT: "reproductive process"

ILLUSTRATION: hypothetical example

that a new generation would already be on the way.

THIRD POINT: "immune system"

Finally, cockroaches have frustrated scientists with their ability to immunize themselves against drugs, poison, and bomb gases. The cockroaches then pass this new immunity on to the next generation quicker than a new poison can be made. Although scientists have studied the cockroach for a long time, they have not discovered the biological mechanism that enables them to develop immunity quickly. It is only natural, therefore, that many scientists have been at work on a ``birth control'' solution for cockroaches. By rendering at least some portion of the adult population sterile, scientists hope to gain a measure of control over the pesty creatures.

ENDING: prediction for the future

Today there are 3,500 different species of cockroaches. They have survived on this planet since the time of the dinosaurs some 350 million years ago. Whether or not scientists are successful in their latest efforts to rid us of cockroaches is yet to be determined. Odds are that they won't succeed. Given the cockroach's amazing record of survivability, it is not likely to turn up on the world's list of endangered species.

Jon Clancy's paper grew out of his reading the essays in Chapter 18. His assignment was to write an argument and, like Laura and Courtney, he was free to choose his own topic. He knew from past experience that in order to write a good essay he would have to write on a topic he cared about. He also knew that he should allow himself a reasonable amount of time to find such a topic and gather his ideas. After studying Russian four years and French for six, Jon had begun to wonder why he wasn't learning the languages as quickly and as well as other people. Then, after meeting a Soviet couple and their eight-year-old daughter, he understood. The girl, after only a few months in the United States, spoke English with only a slight accent while her mother was not progressing nearly as quickly. Never before did he realize how the difference in age affected the attainment of fluency. This gave Jon the idea to write an essay on the need to teach languages at an early age rather than only at the secondary and post-secondary levels, something that would have helped him, as well as many others, he thought.

Jon began by brainstorming about the topic. He made lists of all the ideas, facts, issues, arguments, opposing arguments, and refutations that came to mind as a result of his own reflections on the topic, as well as ideas he had gathered from several educators he interviewed about the teaching of foreign languages. Once he was confident that he had amassed enough information to begin writing, he made a rough outline of an organizational pattern he felt would work well for him. Keeping this pattern in mind, Jon wrote a first draft of his essay, then went back and examined it carefully, assessing how it could be improved.

Jon was writing this particular essay in the second half of the semester, after he had read a number of essays and had learned the importance of such matters as good paragraphing, unity, and transitions. In rereading his first draft, he realized that his organizational pattern could be clearer if he did not mix the reasons why Americans need to learn foreign languages with his suggestion for how we should actually go about teaching and learning them. He also found places where phrases and even whole sentences could be added to make his meaning clearer. He repositioned some sentences, added some key transitions, and changed a number of words to create a more forceful effect.

The final draft of Jon's paper illustrates that he has learned how the parts of a well-written essay fit together, and how to make revisions that emulate some of the qualities of the model

essays he has read and studied. The following is the final draft
of Jon's essay.

Where is Le Bathroom?

Jon Clancy

**BEGINNING: a
problem is
announced**

An American in Paris. To the French,
this is a most hideous thought. Thousands
of travellers from Boston to Boise head for
the city of lights each year, and very few
know enough French to ask for directions to
the nearest metro stop, police station, or
bathroom. Americans think that knowing the
language of a foreign country is not
necessary. The basic, arrogant assumption
is, ``Not to worry! The whole world knows
English.''

**ILLUSTRATION:
hypothetical
example**

The typical traveller is in for a rude
awakening when it is 3 a.m. on a remote
European road and suddenly the engine
overheats. The last gas station is 10
kilometers back, and there's not one
English-speaking Austrian to be found.
Quickly now! Refer to that dime store
phrase book and attempt to say, ``My car is
broken.'' Too bad. What actually came out

THESIS

was, ``My! Look at all the hedgehogs!'' We
Americans just do not have a strong
knowledge of languages, and something
should be done to change this.

**RHETORICAL
QUESTION**

But why should we begin emphasizing
foreign language study? Actually, the

**ORGANIZATION:
first argument**

benefits are great. For example, the
knowledge of a second language helps in

learning others. Strong similarities exist
within linguistic groups, such as the
Romance and Slavic families. Of course it's
not possible for Americans to know every
language, but once someone understands the
concepts of verb conjugation, noun cases, **ORGANIZATION:**
and noun gender, a foreign tongue will seem **second**
less intimidating. **argument**

We deal with many foreign speakers
right here in the United States. For
instance, those areas of the United States
which are near French-speaking parts of
Canada, such as New England, and those near
Mexico, are often visited by our foreign
neighbors. However, many Americans who
often deal with them do not know the most
basic French or Spanish phrases. People
will argue that those travelling in the
United States should know English. Fine.
But when we travel to Quebec, what do we
speak? That's right . . . ``Garkon, I'd
like un coca-cola, seel voos plate.''

Also, most urban areas in the U.S., **ORGANIZATION:**
especially those in the southern states, **third argument**
are home to Mexican, Cuban, and other Latin
American immigrants. These people have made
Spanish our second language, yet most
people do not bother to learn it at all.
Wouldn't it be beneficial if these
Hispanics and Americans who work and live
with each other took the time to learn each
other's native tongue, thus taking a big
step in bettering the understanding between
these two different but inevitably

inseparable cultures? Latin Americans are
making the more sincere effort in this
case, and as usual, the arrogant, lazy
Americans cannot be bothered broadening
their horizons beyond ``America's Funniest
Home Videos'' and ``Wheel of Fortune.''

ORGANIZATION:
fourth
argument

Linguistically, politically, and
economically, the world is growing closer
each year. According to Senator Paul Simon

QUOTATION:
supporting
opinion

of Illinois, ``Cultural isolation is a
luxury the United States can no longer
afford'' (qtd. in Seligmann 37). Places
like China and the Soviet Union do not seem
quite as far as they used to, and
international business is on the rise. With
the advent of international companies and a
global economy, we need to enhance inter-
nation communication. How can we expect to
understand these new neighbors and business
partners without knowing their language?
Each culture has its own, distinct
vocabulary which reflects its way of life.

EVIDENCE:
example used as
illustration

For example, the Russian word ``blat,''
which is the highly developed system of
favors between merchant and consumer, does
not have a direct English translation, but
it has significant economic, social, and
political ramifications in the U.S.S.R. One
surely cannot appreciate the importance and
beauty of foreign cultures by reading such
classics as Arabic at a Glance and Just
Enough Serbo-Croat.

RHETORICAL
QUESTION

But exactly how should we go about
making the United States more aware of the

world and the languages it speaks? Because
a person's cognitive learning skills are at
their peak at an early age, the first grade
would be an excellent place to begin
foreign language instruction. At birth,
according to noted brain surgeon Wilder
Penfield, there is a large area of the
brain, known as the uncommitted cortex,
which is not used. This part of the brain
becomes a perfect tool for learning a
second language in the early years--
especially before the age of 12 (789).

    Some would argue that the most
efficient way of solving the language
problem would be to work on the existing
programs at the junior high and high school
levels. However, these programs have been
in effect for many years, and the results
have been anything but promising. A high
school student will study a language for
two, three, or even four years and
afterwards will not have attained fluency.

    It should come as no surprise that
students in the teenage years do not excel
in the area of language study. On the other
hand, younger children are still learning
English in the first grade, so the teaching
of a second tongue would not be a
hindrance, but rather a complement. The
children surely will not protest this
addition, for if it is incorporated as part
of their learning from day one, they will
always associate French, Spanish, or even
Russian, with math and English, as part of

**SOLUTION TO
PROBLEM**

**EVIDENCE:
paraphrase of
scientific
authority**

**ORGANIZATION:
opposing
argument**

**REFUTATION OF
OPPOSING
ARGUMENT**

the school day. Also, there is a good chance that children would consider learning a foreign language fun.

Children all over the world begin to study English as a second language at a very early age, and despite its complexity,

EVIDENCE: personal experience

do amazingly well. For example, I just met the eight-year-old daughter of a Soviet family now living in the United States who participated in an intensive English instruction program. After only a few months, she learned the language so well that she was able to enter the fourth grade, speaking English with only a slight accent. On the other hand, her mother is taking much longer; she still has a strong accent and often stumbles over vocabulary. Young children have a clear advantage in learning languages.

EVIDENCE: examples of effective programs

Young children have little difficulty switching between two languages. Many schools, such as those in Montreal and in Gates County, North Carolina, have instituted bilingual school days. The morning lessons are taught in French, and the afternoon lessons in English. The direct method, when a parent speaks to a child in a second language from day one, is the best way to create proficient speakers.

ENDING: argument summarized

In order for Americans to better understand the world, we must be able to expand and grow with the world. The best way is through a second language. The present system of beginning instruction in junior high school does not create effective speakers and listeners. At this stage, the ability to learn a second language is severely diminished. However, starting in the primary years of a child's education, as has already been shown, will create a group of adept, bilingual people who will have no problems communicating and learning from other cultures. Let's not raise another generation of ignorant Americans who can't communicate with their foreign neighbors and are forced to walk the streets of Europe in agony because they can't find le bathroom.

ENDING: concluding sentence echoes title

WORKS CITED

Penfield, Wilder. ``Conditioning the Uncommitted Cortex for Language Learning.'' <u>Brain</u> 88.4 (1965): 387-398.

Seligmann, Jean. ``Speaking in Tongues.'' <u>Newsweek</u> Fall/Winter Special Edition, 1990: 36-37.

I

THE
ELEMENTS
OF THE
ESSAY

1

THESIS

The *thesis* of an essay is its main idea, the point it is trying to make. The thesis is often expressed in a one- or two-sentence statement, although sometimes it is implied or suggested rather than stated directly. The thesis statement controls and directs the content of the essay: everything that the writer says must be logically related to the thesis statement.

Usually the thesis is presented early in an essay, sometimes in the first sentence. Here are some thesis statements that begin essays:

> New York is a city of things unnoticed.
>
> Gay Talese

> Most Americans are in terrible shape.
>
> James F. Fixx

> One of the most potent elements in body language is eye behavior.
>
> Flora Davis

Each of these sentences does what a good thesis statement should do—it identifies the topic and makes an assertion about it.

Often writers prepare readers for a thesis statement with one or several sentences that establish a context. Notice, in the following example, how the author eases the reader into his thesis about television instead of presenting it abruptly in the first sentence:

> With the advent of television, for the first time in history, all aspects of animal and human life and death, of societal and individual behavior have been condensed on the average to a 19 inch diagonal screen and a 30 minute time slot. Television, a unique medium, claiming to be neither a reality nor art, has become reality for many of us, particularly for our children who are growing up in front of it.
>
> Jerzy Kosinski

21

On occasion a writer may even purposefully delay the presentation of a thesis until the middle or end of an essay. If the thesis is controversial or needs extended discussion and illustration, the writer might present it later to make it easier for the reader to understand and accept it. Appearing near or at the end of an essay, a thesis also gains prominence.

Some kinds of writing do not need thesis statements. These include descriptions, narratives, and personal writing such as letters and diaries. But any essay that seeks to explain or prove a point has a thesis that is usually set forth in a thesis statement.

THE MOST IMPORTANT DAY

Helen Keller

Helen Keller (1880–1968) was afflicted by a dis-
ease that left her blind and deaf at the age of
eighteen months. With the aid of her teacher,
Anne Sullivan, she was able to overcome her se-
vere handicaps, to graduate from Radcliffe Col-
lege, and to lead a productive and challenging
adult life. In the following selection from her au-
tobiography, The Story of My Life *(1902), Keller*
tells of the day she first met Anne Sullivan, a day
she regarded as the most important in her life.
Notice that Keller states her thesis in the first
paragraph and that it serves to focus and unify
the remaining paragraphs.

The most important day I remember in all my life is the 1
one on which my teacher, Anne Mansfield Sullivan, came
to me. I am filled with wonder when I consider the immea-
surable contrast between the two lives which it connects. It
was the third of March, 1887, three months before I was seven
years old.

On the afternoon of that eventful day, I stood on the porch, 2
dumb, expectant. I guessed vaguely from my mother's signs and
from the hurrying to and fro in the house that something
unusual was about to happen, so I went to the door and waited
on the steps. The afternoon sun penetrated the mass of honeysuckle that covered the porch and fell on my upturned face. My
fingers lingered almost unconsciously on the familiar leaves
and blossoms which had just come forth to greet the sweet
southern spring. I did not know what the future held of marvel
or surprise for me. Anger and bitterness had preyed upon me
continually for weeks and a deep languor had succeeded this
passionate struggle.

Have you ever been at sea in a dense fog, when it seemed as   3
if a tangible white darkness shut you in, and the great ship,
tense and anxious, groped her way toward the shore with plummet and sounding-line, and you waited with beating heart for
something to happen? I was like that ship before my education
began, only I was without compass or sounding-line, and had
no way of knowing how near the harbor was. "Light! give me
light!" was the wordless cry of my soul, and the light of love
shone on me in that very hour.

I felt approaching footsteps. I stretched out my hand as I sup-   4
posed to my mother. Someone took it, and I was caught up and
held close in the arms of her who had come to reveal all things
to me, and, more than all things else, to love me.

The morning after my teacher came she led me into her room   5
and gave me a doll. The little blind children at the Perkins Institution had sent it and Laura Bridgman had dressed it; but I did
not know this until afterward. When I had played with it a little
while, Miss Sullivan slowly spelled into my hand the word
"d-o-l-l." I was at once interested in this finger play and tried to
imitate it. When I finally succeeded in making the letters correctly I was flushed with childish pleasure and pride. Running
downstairs to my mother I held up my hand and made the letters for doll. I did not know that I was spelling a word or even
that words existed; I was simply making my fingers go in mon-
keylike imitation. In the days that followed I learned to spell in
this uncomprehending way a great many words, among them
pin, hat, cup and a few verbs like *sit, stand* and *walk*. But my
teacher had been with me several weeks before I understood
that everything has a name.

One day, while I was playing with my new doll, Miss Sullivan   6
put my big rag doll into my lap also, spelled "d-o-l-l" and tried
to make me understand that "d-o-l-l" applied to both. Earlier in
the day we had had a tussle over the words "m-u-g" and
"w-a-t-e-r." Miss Sullivan had tried to impress it upon me that
"m-u-g" is *mug* and that "w-a-t-e-r" is *water*, but I persisted in
confounding the two. In despair she had dropped the subject
for the time, only to renew it at the first opportunity. I became
impatient at her repeated attempts and, seizing the new doll, I
dashed it upon the floor. I was keenly delighted when I felt the

fragments of the broken doll at my feet. Neither sorrow nor regret followed my passionate outburst. I had not loved the doll. In the still, dark world in which I lived there was no strong sentiment or tenderness. I felt my teacher sweep the fragments to one side of the hearth, and I had a sense of satisfaction that the cause of my discomfort was removed. She brought me my hat, and I knew I was going out into the warm sunshine. This thought, if a wordless sensation may be called a thought, made me hop and skip with pleasure.

We walked down the path to the well-house, attracted by the fragrance of the honeysuckle with which it was covered. Some one was drawing water and my teacher placed my hand under the spout. As the cool stream gushed over one hand she spelled into the other the word *water*, first slowly, then rapidly. I stood still, my whole attention fixed upon the motions of her fingers. Suddenly I felt a misty consciousness as of something forgotten—a thrill of returning thought; and somehow the mystery of language was revealed to me. I knew then that "w-a-t-e-r" meant the wonderful cool something that was flowing over my hand. The living word awakened my soul, gave it light, hope, joy, set it free! There were barriers still, it is true, but barriers that could in time be swept away. 7

I left the well-house eager to learn. Everything had a name, and each name gave birth to a new thought. As we returned to the house every object which I touched seemed to quiver with life. That was because I saw everything with the strange, new sight that had come to me. On entering the door I remembered the doll I had broken. I felt my way to the hearth and picked up the pieces. I tried vainly to put them together. Then my eyes filled with tears; for I realized what I had done, and for the first time I felt repentance and sorrow. 8

I learned a great many new words that day. I do not remember what they all were; but I do know that *mother, father, sister, teacher* were among them—words that were to make the world blossom for me, "like Aaron's rod, with flowers." It would have been difficult to find a happier child than I was as I lay in my crib at the close of that eventful day and lived over the joys it had brought me, and for the first time longed for a new day to come. 9

Questions for Study and Discussion

1. What is Helen Keller's thesis in this essay?
2. What is Helen Keller's purpose in this essay? (Glossary: *Purpose*)
3. What was Helen Keller's state of mind before Anne Sullivan arrived to help her? To what does she compare herself?
4. Why was the realization that everything has a name important to Helen Keller?
5. How was the "mystery of language" (7) revealed to Helen Keller? What were the consequences of this new understanding of the nature of language for her?
6. Helen Keller narrates the events of the day Anne Sullivan arrived (2–4), the morning after she arrived (5), and one day several weeks after her arrival (6–9). Describe what happens on each day, and explain how these separate incidents support her thesis.

Vocabulary

Refer to your dictionary to define the following words as they are used in this selection. Then use each word in a sentence of your own.

dumb (2)   plummet (3)
preyed (2)   tussle (6)
languor (2)   vainly (8)
passionate (2)

Suggested Writing Assignments

1. Think about an important day in your own life. Using the thesis statement "The most important day of my life was _____," write an essay in which you show the significance of that day by recounting and explaining the events that took place.
2. For many people around the world, the life of Helen Keller stands as the symbol of what can be achieved by an individual despite seemingly insurmountable handicaps. Her

achievements have also had a tremendous impact upon those who are not afflicted with handicaps, leading them to believe that they can accomplish more than they ever thought possible. Consider the role of handicapped people in our society, develop an appropriate thesis, and write an essay on the topic.

GIVE US JOBS, NOT ADMIRATION

Eric Bigler

Eric Bigler was born in Powhatan Point, Ohio, in 1958. Despite a diving accident while he was in high school that left him paralyzed from the chest down, Bigler went on to earn his bachelor's degree in social work and his master's degree in business and industrial counseling management at Wright State University in Dayton, Ohio. Eric now works part-time in the Augmentative Communications Research Laboratory at Wright State, where he does research on using state-of-the-art computer technology to help the disabled work with computers. When he wrote this essay, however, he was still looking for full-time employment, still waiting to hear the words, "You're hired."

Tuesday I have another job interview. Like most I have had so far, it will probably end with the all-too-familiar words, "We'll let you know of our decision in a few days."

Many college graduates searching for their first career job might simply accept that response as, "Sorry, we're not interested in you," and blame the rejection on inexperience or bad chemistry. For myself and other disabled people, however, this response often seems to indicate something more worrisome: a reluctance to hire the handicapped even when they're qualified. I have been confined to a wheelchair since 1974, when a high-school diving accident left me paralyzed from the chest down. But that didn't prevent me from earning a bachelor's in social work in 1983, and I am now finishing up a master's degree in business and industrial management, specializing in employee relations and human-resource development.

Our government spends a great deal of money to help the handicapped, but it does not necessarily spend it all wisely. For example, in 1985 Ohio's Bureau of Vocational Rehabilitation (BVR) spent more than $4 million in tuition and other expenses so that disabled students could obtain a college education. BVR's philosophy is that the amount of money spent educating students will be repaid in disabled employees' taxes. The agency assists graduates by offering workshops on résumé writing and interviewing techniques, skills many already learned in college. BVR also maintains files of résumés that are matched with help-wanted notices from local companies and employs placement specialists to work directly with graduates during their job search.

Even with all this assistance, however, graduates still have 4 trouble getting hired. Such programs might do better if they concentrated on the perceptions of employers as well as the skills of applicants. More important, improving contacts with prospective employers might encourage them to actively recruit the disabled.

Often, projects that *do* show promise don't get the chance to 5 thrive. I was both a client and an informal consultant to one program, Careers for the Disabled in Dayton, which asked local executives to make a commitment to hire disabled applicants whenever possible. I found this strategy to be on target, since support for a project is more likely when it is ordered from the top. The program also offered free training seminars to corporations on how they can work effectively with the disabled candidate. In April of 1986—less than a year after it was started and after only three disabled people were placed—the program was discontinued because, according to the director, they had "no luck at getting [enough] corporations to join the program."

Corporations need to take a more independent and active 6 part in hiring qualified handicapped persons. Today's companies try to show a willingness to innovate, and hiring people like myself would enhance that image. Madison Avenue has finally recognized that the disabled are also consumers; more and more often, commercials include them. But advertisers could break down even more stereotypes. I would like to see one of those Hewlett-Packard commercials, for instance, show an employee racing down the sidewalk in his wheelchair, pulling alongside a pay phone and calling a colleague to ask "What if . . .?"

Corporate recruiters also need to be better prepared for 7 meeting with disabled applicants. They should be ready to answer queries about any barriers that their building's design may pose, and they should be forthright about asking their own questions. It's understandable that employers are afraid to mention matters that are highly personal and may prove embarassing—or, even worse, discriminatory. There's nothing wrong, however, with an employer reassuring him or herself about whether an applicant will be able to reach files, operate computers or even get into the bathroom. Until interviewers change their style, disabled applicants need to initiate discussion of disability-related issues.

Government has tried to improve hiring for the disabled 8 through Affirmative Action programs. The Rehabilitation Act of 1973 says institutions or programs receiving substantial amounts of federal money can't discriminate on the basis of handicap. Yet I was saddened and surprised to discover how many companies spend much time and money writing great affirmative-action and equal-opportunity guidelines but little time following them. Then there are the cosmetic acts, such as the annual National Employ the Handicapped Week every October. If President Reagan (or anyone else) wants to help the disabled with proclamations, more media exposure is necessary. I found out about the last occasion in 1985 from a brief article on the back of a campus newspaper—a week after it had happened.

As if other problems were not enough, the disabled who 9 search unsuccessfully for employment often face a loss of self-esteem and worth. In college, many disabled people I have talked to worked hard toward a degree so they would be prepared for jobs after graduation. Now they look back on their four or more years as wasted time. For these individuals, the days of earning good grades and accomplishing tough tasks fade away, leaving only frustrating memories. Today's job market is competitive enough without prejudice adding more "handicaps."

About that interview . . . five minutes into it, I could feel the 10 atmosphere chill. The interviewer gave me general information instead of trying to find out if I was right for the job. I've been there before. Then the session closed with a handshake, and those same old words: "We'll let you know." They said I should be so proud of myself for doing what I am doing. That's what they always say. I'm tired of hearing how courageous I am. So are other disabled people. We need jobs, and we want to work like anyone else.

But still, I remain an optimist. I know someday soon a company will be smart enough to realize how much I have to offer them in both my head and my heart. 11

Maybe then I'll hear the words so many of us really want to hear: "You're hired." 12

Questions for Study and Discussion

1. What does Bigler feel is wrong with government programs aimed at helping the disabled? What does he suggest be done to improve the situation?

2. What is Bigler's thesis in this essay? Where in the essay is his thesis most clearly presented?

3. Does Bigler give his readers any reasons why the disabled are not being hired as often as they should be? Does the success of his thesis depend upon his providing such reasons? Explain.

4. Bigler frames his essay with references to a particular job interview. Discuss the way Bigler connects the beginning and ending of his essay. Has he employed an effective strategy in this regard? Explain.

5. What are the "cosmetic acts" that Bigler refers to in paragraph 8? Why does he use this particular term? (Glossary: *Diction*)

6. What audience(s) would seem to be most interested in what Bigler has to say in his essay? Explain.

Vocabulary

Refer to your dictionary to define the following words as they are used in this selection. Then use each word in a sentence of your own.

worrisome (2)   forthright (7)
seminars (5)   proclamations (8)
enhance (6)   self-esteem (9)

Suggested Writing Assignments

1. Write an essay in which you use as your thesis the formula "Give us _____, not _____." You may use one of the following topics or create one of your own:

   Give us peace, not more arms.

   Give us results, nor more red tape.

   Give us action, not talk.

   Give us jobs, not welfare.

   Give us choices, not rules.

   Give us answers, not excuses.

   Give us opportunities, not promises.

   Give us better government, not more taxes.

2. One year after Eric Bigler's essay was published, he was still not employed in a full-time position. Develop a thesis and write an essay of your own as to why the disabled have a difficult time gaining employment despite their personal talents and educational backgrounds.

ANXIETY: CHALLENGE BY ANOTHER NAME

James Lincoln Collier

*James Lincoln Collier is a free-lance writer with
over six hundred articles to his credit. He was
born in New York in 1928 and graduated from
Hamilton College in 1950. Among his many
books are* Rock Star *(1970),* It's Murder at St.
Basket's *(1972),* My Brother Sam Is Dead *(1974),*
Rich and Famous *(1975),* Give Dad My Best
(1976), and Duke Ellington *(1987). Collier's best-
known book is* The Making of Jazz: A Compre-
hensive History *(1978), still regarded as the best
general history of the subject. As you read the
following essay, pay particular attention to Collier's thesis, where it is placed in the essay, and
how well he supports it.*

Between my sophomore and junior years at college, a   1
chance came up for me to spend the summer vacation
working on a ranch in Argentina. My roommate's father was in
the cattle business, and he wanted Ted to see something of it.
Ted said he would go if he could take a friend, and he chose me.

The idea of spending two months on the fabled Argentine   2
Pampas was exciting. Then I began having second thoughts. I
had never been very far from New England, and I had been
homesick my first few weeks at college. What would it be like in
a strange country? What about the language? And besides, I
had promised to teach my younger brother to sail that summer.
The more I thought about it, the more the prospect daunted me.
I began waking up nights in a sweat.

In the end I turned down the proposition. As soon as Ted   3
asked somebody else to go, I began kicking myself. A couple of
weeks later I went home to my old summer job, unpacking car-
tons at the local supermarket, feeling very low. I had turned

down something I wanted to do because I was scared, and had ended up feeling depressed. I stayed that way for a long time. And it didn't help when I went back to college in the fall to discover that Ted and his friend had had a terrific time.

In the long run that unhappy summer taught me a valuable 4 lesson out of which I developed a rule for myself: *do what makes you anxious; don't do what makes you depressed.*

I am not, of course, talking about severe states of anxiety or 5 depression, which require medical attention. What I mean is that kind of anxiety we call stage fright, butterflies in the stomach, a case of nerves—the feelings we have at a job interview, when we're giving a big party, when we have to make an important presentation at the office. And the kind of depression I am referring to is that downhearted feeling of the blues, when we don't seem to be interested in anything, when we can't get going and seem to have no energy.

I was confronted by this sort of situation toward the end of 6 my senior year. As graduation approached, I began to think about taking a crack at making my living as a writer. But one of my professors was urging me to apply to graduate school and aim at a teaching career.

I wavered. The idea of trying to live by writing was scary—a 7 lot more scary than spending a summer on the Pampas, I thought. Back and forth I went, making my decision, unmaking it. Suddenly, I realized that every time I gave up the idea of writing, that sinking feeling went through me; it gave me the blues.

The thought of graduate school wasn't what depressed me. It 8 was giving up on what deep in my gut I really wanted to do. Right then I learned another lesson. To avoid that kind of depression meant, inevitably, having to endure a certain amount of worry and concern.

The great Danish philosopher Søren Kierkegaard believed 9 that anxiety always arises when we confront the possibility of our own development. It seems to be a rule of life that you can't advance without getting that old, familiar, jittery feeling.

Even as children we discover this when we try to expand our- 10 selves by, say, learning to ride a bike or going out for the school play. Later in life we get butterflies when we think about having that first child, or uprooting the family from the old hometown to find a better opportunity halfway across the country. Any time, it seems, that we set out aggressively to get something we want, we meet up with anxiety. And it's going to be our traveling companion, at least part of the way, into any new venture.

When I first began writing magazine articles, I was frequently required to interview big names—people like Richard Burton, Joan Rivers, sex authority William Masters, baseball-great Dizzy Dean. Before each interview I would get butterflies and my hands would shake. 11

At the time, I was doing some writing about music. And one person I particularly admired was the great composer Duke Ellington. Onstage and on television, he seemed the very model of the confident, sophisticated man of the world. Then I learned that Ellington still got stage fright. If the highly honored Duke Ellington, who had appeared on the bandstand some 10,000 times over 30 years, had anxiety attacks, who was I to think I could avoid them? 12

I went on doing those frightening interviews, and one day, as I was getting onto a plane for Washington to interview columnist Joseph Alsop, I suddenly realized to my astonishment that I was looking forward to the meeting. What had happened to those butterflies? 13

Well, in truth, they were still there, but there were fewer of them. I had benefited, I discovered, from a process psychologists call "extinction." If you put an individual in an anxiety-provoking situation often enough, he will eventually learn that there isn't anything to be worried about. 14

Which brings us to a corollary to my basic rule: *you'll never eliminate anxiety by avoiding the things that caused it.* I remember how my son Jeff was when I first began to teach him to swim at the lake cottage where we spent our summer vacations. He resisted, and when I got him into the water he sank and sputtered and wanted to quit. But I was insistent. And by summer's end he was splashing around like a puppy. He had "extinguished" his anxiety the only way he could—by confronting it. 15

The problem, of course, is that it is one thing to urge somebody else to take on those anxiety-producing challenges; it is quite another to get ourselves to do it. 16

Some years ago I was offered a writing assignment that 17

would require three months of travel through Europe. I had been abroad a couple of times on the usual "If it's Tuesday this must be Belgium" trips, but I hardly could claim to know my way around the continent. Moreover, my knowledge of foreign languages was limited to a little college French.

I hesitated. How would I, unable to speak the language, to-   18
tally unfamiliar with local geography or transportation sys-
tems, set up interviews and do research? It seemed impossible, and with considerable regret I sat down to write a letter beg-ging off. Halfway through, a thought—which I subsequently made into another corollary to my basic rule—ran through my mind: *you can't learn if you don't try.* So I accepted the assign-ment.

There were some bad moments. But by the time I had fin-   19
ished the trip I was an experienced traveler. And ever since, I have never hesitated to head for even the most exotic of places, without guides or even advanced bookings, confident that somehow I will manage.

The point is that the new, the different, is almost by definition   20
scary. But each time you try something, you learn, and as the learning piles up, the world opens to you.

I've made parachute jumps, learned to ski at 40, flown up the   21
Rhine in a balloon. And I know I'm going to go on doing such things. It's not because I'm braver or more daring than others. I'm not. But I don't let the butterflies stop me from doing what I want. Accept anxiety as another name for challenge and you can accomplish wonders.

Questions for Study and Discussion

1. What is Collier's thesis in this essay? Based on your own experiences, do you think that Collier's thesis is a valid one? Explain.

2. What is the process known to psychologists as "extinc-tion"?

3. Collier provides some rules for himself. What are these rules? He says that his second and third rules are corol-laries to a basic rule. What does Collier mean?

4. What do you think Collier's purpose was in writing this essay? (Glossary: *Purpose*) Explain.
5. Identify the figure of speech that Collier uses toward the end of paragraph 10. (Glossary: *Figures of Speech*)
6. Explain how paragraphs 17–19 function within the context of Collier's essay. (Glossary: *Illustration*)

Vocabulary

Refer to your dictionary to define the following words as they are used in this selection. Then use each word in a sentence of your own.

daunted (2)	butterflies (5)
proposition (3)	crack (6)
anxiety (5)	venture (10)
depression (5)	corollary (15)

Suggested Writing Assignments

1. Building on your own experiences and the reading you have done, write an essay in which you use as your thesis either Collier's basic rule or one of his corollaries to that basic rule.
2. Write an essay in which you use any of the following as your thesis:

   Good manners are a thing of the past.

   We need rituals in our lives.

   To tell a joke well is an art.

   We are a drug-dependent society.

   Losing weight is a breeze.

2

UNITY

A well-written essay should be unified; that is, everything in it should be related to its thesis, or main idea. The first requirement for unity is that the thesis itself be clear, either through a direct statement, called the *thesis statement,* or by implication. The second requirement is that there be no digressions, no discussion or information that is not shown to be logically related to the thesis. A unified essay stays within the limits of its thesis.

Here, for example, is a short essay called "Over-Generalizing" about the dangers of making generalizations. As you read, notice how carefully author Stuart Chase sticks to his point.

One swallow does not make a summer, nor can two or three cases often support a dependable generalization. Yet all of us, including the most polished eggheads, are constantly falling into this mental peopletrap. It is the commonest, probably the most seductive, and potentially the most dangerous, of all the fallacies.

You drive through a town and see a drunken man on the sidewalk. A few blocks further on you see another. You turn to your companion: "Nothing but drunks in this town!" Soon you are out in the country, bowling along at fifty. A car passes you as if you were parked. On a curve a second whizzes by. Your companion turns to you: "All the drivers in this state are crazy!" Two thumping generalizations, each built on two cases. If we stop to think, we usually recognize the exaggeration and the unfairness of such generalizations. Trouble comes when we do not stop to think—or when we build them on a prejudice.

This kind of reasoning has been around for a long time. Aristotle was aware of its dangers and called it "reasoning by example," meaning too few examples. What it boils down to is failing to count your swallows before announcing that summer is here. Driving from my home to New Haven the other day, a distance of about forty miles, I caught myself saying: "Every time I look around I see a new ranch-type house going up." So on the return trip I counted them; there were exactly five under construction. And how many times had I "looked around"? I suppose I had glanced to right and left—as one must at side roads and so forth in driving—several hundred times.

In this fallacy we do not make the error of neglecting 4 facts altogether and rushing immediately to the level of opinion. We start at the fact level properly enough, but *we do not stay there.* A case of two and up we go to a rousing over-simplification about drunks, speeders, ranch-style houses—or, more seriously, about foreigners, Negroes, labor leaders, teen-agers.

Why do we over-generalize so often and sometimes so 5 disastrously? One reason is that the human mind is a generalizing machine. We would not be people without this power. The old academic crack: "All generalizations are false, including this one," is only a play on words. We *must* generalize to communicate and to live. But we should beware of beating the gun; of not waiting until enough facts are in to say something useful. Meanwhile it is a plain waste of time to listen to arguments based on a few hand-picked examples.

Everything in the essay relates to Chase's thesis statement, which is included in the essay's first sentence: ". . . nor can two or three cases often support a dependable generalization." Paragraphs 2 and 3 document the thesis with examples; paragraph 4 explains how over-generalizing occurs; paragraph 5 analyzes why people over-generalize; and, for a conclusion, Chase restates his thesis in different words. An essay may be longer, more complex, and more wide-ranging than this one, but to be effective it must also avoid digressions and remain close to the author's main idea.

BE KIND TO COMMUTERS

Christopher M. Bellitto

Christopher M. Bellitto was born in the Bronx, New York, in 1965. Admitted to New York University as a University Scholar, he graduated Phi Beta Kappa with a degree in journalism and politics. Among his other honors are scholarships in journalism from Gannett and from Scripps-Howard, and the prestigious Time Inc. College Achievement Award for being one of the twenty top college students in the country. After graduation, he worked for Newsweek On Campus. *He currently teaches at a New York City high school. As you read his essay, notice the way Bellitto has ensured that all of his information relates to his thesis that college students who commute don't have it as easy as you might think. This essay first appeared in the October 1986 issue of* Newsweek on Campus.

You may think that those of us who live at home and commute to school have it easy. There's a washing machine with no wait, a new tube of toothpaste in the medicine cabinet and, most important, a fridge stocked with food someone else has paid for. Not only that, but the phone bill is usually taken care of and dinner's sitting in the microwave even late at night. That's not college, you sneer—that's permanent adolescence.

So maybe we look like pampered kids, but it's not that simple. The college student living at home leads a paradoxical life. Like you, we came to college to learn about ourselves; self-exploration is as much a part of our education as organic chem. Yet it's hard to maintain our independence when Mom or Dad can't shake the parental instincts for surveillance. Nor can family obligations be avoided easily. What do I do, for example, when my parents' anniversary falls the day before my finals? The truth is, being a student who hasn't left the nest can be just

40

as difficult as trying to get along with a roommate you don't like.

Our problems can be complex. To some extent, we're second-class citizens in the social world: it's tough to enjoy clubs, frat parties and dances when you have to drive back home or catch the last bus. Ditto when you realize you can't make the only review class for business law because it ends late. But that's not the critical issue: after all, everybody's got standing invites to crash with friends in the dorm. The real problem is that we lose out on the results of those activities: a sense of camaraderie that springs from nights spent cramming for industrial psychology, gossiping about who's sleeping with whom and, after most of the favorite topics of both George Will and Dear Abby are exhausted, sharing the heart-to-heart realization that graduation is closer than we think. True, we commuters can join in every now and again, but we can't fall into the day-and-night rhythm of collegial introspection. There's a whole group of us who'll never be able to appreciate the lifetime bonds of "The Big Chill" as much as our dorming peers.

Then there's the issue of budgeting time. Commuters have much more structured days than dormers; we have to. Many of us live as we do to save money, and we devote a lot of hours to jobs that can help defray tuition. Of course, working out our convoluted schedules may teach more about efficiency than all the freshman workshops on note-taking. Who else but a commuter could perfect the art of plotting discreet-probability distribution on a train hurtling through a dark tunnel while some sleaze with Mick Belker breath hulks down over your textbook? And sharing one bathroom with parents preparing for work, little brothers late for school and a sister rinsing stockings in the sink makes the three-minute shower sprint a useful skill that rivals almost anything gleaned from a class. True, all this planning becomes moot when the 40-minute trip takes two hours because of a track fire and a wino who gets caught in the door.

There's a myth that commuters are lucky because they can leave the jungle of school and go home. Actually, you dormers may have it easier here: at least you can get away with screaming out of the window and working off tension at a party that's never hard to find. When we have a bad stretch, there's no escape; the end of a frustrating day is just the beginning. First there's the long ride home where, on public transportation, the heaters and air conditioners seem to operate on Argentina's schedule of seasons. Then there are the reminders from parents which, however well intentioned, are still nagging. How can we feel "on our own" when we're constantly told: "*Call* if you'll be late"? And of course there's Grandma, who starts heating up the leftovers when we're three blocks away, sits to watch us eat them and then clucks that we're too skinny and not getting enough sleep. Even if the lasagna is major league, it might be even nicer just to be left ALONE sometimes.

And when the breakaway point does come, leave-taking is more painful for those of us who've never really left. Students who move out of the house for college can enjoy a separate peace; they build another base of operations on campus. True, all families have a hard time saying goodbye to the child who goes off to school at 18, but by graduation they've gotten over it and come to view you as an adult with your own life. Commuters are not nearly so detached. There are some family situations we can't ignore. It's the difference between returning for Thanksgiving to discover how old Grandpa has gotten and living with him, watching him die a little more each day. That makes the parting at graduation even more poignant—for both families *and* students.

The living arrangement is hard on our elders, too, since they're torn between stepping back to allow us autonomy and jumping in where they always have before. When school is miles away, parents can't *see* their kids staying up until 6 a.m. to type a paper or letting loose with a keg—though I'm sure both situations are vividly imagined during many a late night's insomnia. Naturally, at home your movement is watched. I can appreciate that my mother worries if I don't make it home by a certain hour, but I build up some tense moments myself if I can't stay late at the library doing research for tomorrow's oral presentation. "I don't even know you anymore," is a frustrated parent's response to a student who, of necessity, sometimes uses home like a boarding house. But we're supposed to get to know our profs, make new friends and be exposed to new fields—and that can only be accomplished when we're on our own.

We are a special breed: young adults who are enthusiastic   8
about the independence of being in college yet remain to some
degree children in our family's eyes—and to some extent, perhaps, in our own. I still believe that I'm receiving a top-notch
education, though I'll be the first to admit—and lament—that
I'm also missing out on some of the traditional collegiate experiences. So don't think of commuters as lesser beings or as soft-
ies who are taking the easy way out. We're just caught between
the rock of academia and the sometimes hard place of home,
struggling with the age-old problem of serving two masters.

Questions for Study and Discussion

1. What is Bellitto's thesis? (Glossary: *Thesis*) Where is it
   stated? What relationship does Bellitto's title have to his
   thesis?
2. According to Bellitto, what are some of the problems that
   commuters face while at school? While at home? What, if
   anything, does he want from us as readers of his essay?
3. One student who has read this essay thought that the examples Bellitto uses are very practical and good ones.
   What is your assessment of his examples? If you, too, find
   them effective, explain why. (Glossary: *Examples*)
4. How effective is Bellitto's use of transitions to link paragraphs? (Glossary: *Transitions*)
5. Bellitto's style in this essay is informal. It is smooth, easy
   to read, but nevertheless controlled and detailed. What is
   there about the author's choice of words that contributes
   to his informal style? (Glossary: *Diction*)
6. Explain in your own words the meaning of the following
   phrases from this selection:
   a. permanent adolescence (1)
   b. parental instincts for surveillance (2)
   c. standing invites to crash (3)
   d. collegial introspection (3)
   e. convoluted schedules (4)

f. Argentina's schedule of seasons (5)
g. letting loose with a keg (7)
h. the rock of academia and the sometimes hard place of home (8)

Vocabulary

Refer to your dictionary to define the following words as they are used in this selection. Then use each word in a sentence of your own.

sneer (1)	defray (4)
pampered (2)	sleaze (4)
ditto (3)	moot (4)
camaraderie (3)	autonomy (7)

Suggested Writing Assignments

1. What general impression do you think most students have of commuters? If you are a commuter yourself, what do you feel is the general impression that other students have of you? What relationship do these impressions have to reality? Are commuters "second-class citizens in the social world," as Bellitto claims? Write a unified essay that relies on your experiences as well as the experiences of your friends in exploring this topic.

2. Bellitto says that "being a student who hasn't left the nest can be just as difficult as trying to get along with the roommate you don't like" (2). How difficult is it to get along with a roommate? What concessions have to be made? What kind of communication is necessary for one to live in the confines of a dorm room? What lessons have to be learned? Write an essay that is well unified on living with a roommate. Be sure that your examples are well chosen and illustrate the thesis you establish.

STUDENTS OF SUCCESS

Lynne V. Cheney

Lynne V. Cheney was born in Casper, Wyoming. She holds a doctorate in English from the University of Wisconsin and has taught at George Washington University and the University of Wyoming. Cheney was serving as director of the National Endowment for the Humanities in 1986 when this article appeared in Newsweek. *Note the author's skillful organization of evidence not only to support her thesis but also to enhance the unity of her essay.*

Not long ago, my college-age daughter read about a software genius who became a multimillionaire before he was 30. "That does it," she said, "I'm going into computers."

This daughter, who has never met a political science course she didn't like, was only joking. But a study conducted by the Carnegie Foundation shows that many young people do think seriously along these lines. Instead of choosing college majors—and careers—according to their interests, they are channeling themselves into fields that promise to be profitable: business, engineering, computer science, allied health programs.

Given the high cost of a college education, this trend is not surprising. A bachelor's degree now costs $40,000 at an average independent college. Can we expect students to major in the liberal arts when their starting salaries will be significantly lower than they are for business and professional majors? Shouldn't they get the best possible return on their investment?

They should, but I would suggest that there are better ways to calculate profit and loss than by looking at starting salaries. Consider, first of all, that very few people stay in the same line of work over a lifetime. They switch jobs, even change professions, and what is crucial for advancement is not specialized training but the ability to think critically and judge wisely. Given the difficulty of predicting which skills will be in demand even five years from now, let along over a lifetime, a student's best career preparation is one that emphasizes general understanding and intellectual curiosity: a knowledge of how to learn and the desire to do it. Literature, history, philosophy and the social sciences—majors that students avoid today—are the ones traditionally believed to develop such habits of mind.

I recently conducted an informal survey of successful Americans, and while several dozen phone calls aren't proof of the value of a liberal-arts major, the results are suggestive. The communications world, for example, is dominated by liberal-arts majors. Thomas H. Wyman, chairman of CBS, majored in English, as did Cathleen Black, publisher of USA Today. Washington Post columnist William Raspberry studied history; NBC News anchorman Tom Brokaw, political science.

In public life, too, leaders more often than not were students of the liberal arts. They form a majority in the president's cabinet. Secretary of State George Shultz and Secretary of Energy John Herrington majored in economics. Interior Secretary Donald Hodel majored in government, and Transportation Secretary Elizabeth Dole, political science. Secretary of the Treasury James Baker read history with a minor in classics; Secretary of Education William Bennett studied philosophy.

The president himself majored in economics and sociology. His communications director, Pat Buchanan, majored in English and philosophy. White House chief of staff (and former treasury secretary) Donald Regan was an English major and before he came to government had a remarkably successful business career as the head of Merrill Lynch. Secretary of Commerce Malcolm Baldrige headed Scovill Manufacturing, and now the former English major is leading a campaign for clear writing in government.

Executives like Regan and Baldrige are not unusual. According to a recent report in Fortune magazine, 38 percent of today's CEO's majored in the liberal arts, and a close reading of The New York Times shows that 9 of the top 13 executives at IBM are liberal-arts majors. At AT&T, a study showed social-science and humanities graduates moving into middle management faster than engineers and doing at least as well as their business and engineering counterparts in reaching top management levels.

For several years now, corporate executives have extolled the 9 wide range of knowledge and interests that a study of the liberal arts encourages. And now under Tom Wyman's direction, CBS has funded an organization that investigates exactly why it is that liberal-arts training is valuable to the American corporation. "In an increasingly competitive, internationally oriented and technologically innovative society," Wyman recently wrote, "successful executives will be those who can understand—and interpret—complex relationships and who are capable of continually reconsidering assumptions underlying old operating practices."

In the past, such top-level views did not always filter down to 10 where entry-level hiring is done. But reports from that front are encouraging. A study by Northwestern University shows that many major companies plan to increase their hiring of liberal-arts graduates by some 20 percent in 1986. Or as one employer recently told "Today" show viewers, "Those that are involved in recruiting people to the company are looking for . . . broader skills . . . Then we will worry about teaching them terminology, specifics of the jobs."

I don't mean to argue that liberal arts is the only road to suc- 11 cess. The average starting salary for engineers remains impressively high, almost $30,000 compared to $21,000 for a liberal-arts graduate. In fact, my informal survey also shows that engineers are doing well in a variety of fields. Chrysler chairman Lee Iacocca was an engineering major, as was former Delaware Gov. Pete du Pont. My point is that there are many paths to success and students shouldn't force themselves down any single one if their true interests lie elsewhere. College should be a time for intellectual enthusiasm, for trying to read one's way through the library, for heated debate with those who see the world differently. College should be a time for learning to enjoy the life of the mind rather than for learning to tolerate what one doesn't find interesting.

Students who follow their hearts in choosing majors will 12 most likely end up laboring at what they love. They're the ones who will put in the long hours and intense effort that achievement requires. And they're the ones who will find the sense of purpose that underlies most human happiness.

Questions for Study and Discussion

1. In the first paragraph of her essay, Cheney relates the tale of her daughter's reaction to a computer genius's good fortune. In paragraph 2 she asks two rhetorical questions. Her thesis is not stated until paragraph three (Glossary: *Thesis*) How well do the opening paragraphs serve as a lead to her thesis? (Glossary: *Beginnings*) Explain.

2. Explain in your own words the difference between a liberal arts and a technical education.

3. On what evidence does Cheney base her argument that a liberal arts education might be preferable to a technical one? Can you think of any other points she might have included? In what ways might paragraph 11 be considered a contradiction of her thesis?

4. Whom do you think Cheney intends as her audience? (Glossary: *Audience*) What in her essay led you to this conclusion? Explain.

5. Make a brief outline of Cheney's essay. How does her organization contribute to the overall unity of her essay? (Glossary: *Organization*)

6. Explain in your own words what a corporate executive might mean by "critical thinking."

7. Cheney has a somewhat different definition of the word "success" than most college students do. How does she define it? What concessions to their definition does she make in her own?

Vocabulary

Refer to your dictionary to define the following words as they are used in this selection. Then use each word in a sentence of your own.

critically (4)   extolled (9)
counterparts (8)   innovative (9)

Suggested Writing Assignments

1. What does Cheney find wrong with today's technical education? In an essay describe the changes you would suggest for curriculum reform in technical education so as to satisfy Cheney's reservations about it. Be sure to state your thesis clearly and organize your evidence so that it supports your thesis.

2. In presenting her thesis, Cheney makes no allowance for any other factors besides financial success that might be contributing to students' choices of technical majors. Some scholars have pointed out that we are not a nation of thinkers and readers; others will insist rightly that some students genuinely prefer the technical courses which happen to promise higher pay. In an essay of your own, explore some of the reasons besides economics that might contribute to a student's decision to pursue a technical career.

DON'T LET STEREOTYPES
WARP YOUR JUDGMENTS

Robert L. Heilbroner

The economist Robert L. Heilbroner was educated at Harvard and at the New School for Social Research, where he has been the Norman Thomas Professor of Economics since 1972. He has written The Future as History *(1960),* A Primer of Government Spending: Between Capitalism and Socialism *(1970), and* An Inquiry into the Human Prospect *(1974). "Don't Let Stereotypes Warp Your Judgments" first appeared in* Reader's Digest, *and it is a particularly timely essay for people who are seeking understanding and respect for all in a culturally diverse, pluralistic society. As you read this essay, pay specific attention to its unity—the relationships of the paragraphs to the thesis.*

Is a girl called Gloria apt to be better-looking than one called 1
Bertha? Are criminals more likely to be dark than blond?
Can you tell a good deal about someone's personality from
hearing his voice briefly over the phone? Can a person's nationality be pretty accurately guessed from his photograph? Does
the fact that someone wears glasses imply that he is intelligent?

The answer to all these questions is obviously, "No." 2

Yet, from all the evidence at hand, most of us believe these 3
things. Ask any college boy if he'd rather take his chances with
a Gloria or a Bertha, or ask a college girl if she'd rather blind-
date a Richard or a Cuthbert. In fact, you don't have to ask:
college students in questionnaires have revealed that names
conjure up the same images in their minds as they do in yours—
and for as little reason.

Look into the favorite suspects of persons who report "suspi- 4
cious characters" and you will find a large percentage of them
to be "swarthy" or "dark and foreign-looking"—despite the tes-

timony of criminologists that criminals do *not* tend to be dark, foreign or "wild-eyed." Delve into the main asset of a telephone stock swindler and you will find it to be a marvelously confidence-inspiring telephone "personality." And whereas we all think we know what an Italian or a Swede looks like, it is the sad fact that when a group of Nebraska students sought to match faces and nationalities of 15 European countries, they were scored wrong in 93 percent of their identifications. Finally, for all the fact that horn-rimmed glasses have now become the standard television sign of an "intellectual," optometrists know that the main thing that distinguishes people with glasses is just bad eyes.

Stereotypes are a kind of gossip about the world, a gossip 5
that makes us prejudge people before we ever lay eyes on them. Hence it is not surprising that stereotypes have something to do with the dark world of prejudice. Explore most prejudices (note that the word means prejudgment) and you will find a cruel stereotype at the core of each one.

For it is the extraordinary fact that once we have typecast the 6
world, we tend to see people in terms of our standardized pictures. In another demonstration of the power of stereotypes to affect our vision, a number of Columbia and Barnard students were shown 30 photographs of pretty but unidentified girls, and asked to rate each in terms of "general liking," "intelligence," "beauty" and so on. Two months later, the same group were shown the same photographs, this time with fictitious Irish, Italian, Jewish and "American" names attached to the pictures. Right away the ratings changed. Faces which were now seen as representing a national group went down in looks and still farther down in likability, while the "American" girls suddenly looked decidedly prettier and nicer.

Why is it that we stereotype the world in such irrational and 7
harmful fashion? In part, we begin to type-cast people in our childhood years. Early in life, as every parent whose child has watched a TV Western knows, we learn to spot the Good Guys from the Bad Guys. Some years ago, a social psychologist showed very clearly how powerful these stereotypes of childhood vision are. He secretly asked the most popular youngsters in an elementary school to make errors in their morning gym exercises. Afterwards, he asked the class if anyone had noticed

any mistakes during gym period. Oh, yes, said the children. But it was the *unpopular* members of the class—the "bad guys"— they remembered as being out of step.

We not only grow up with standardized pictures forming inside of us, but as grown-ups we are constantly having them thrust upon us. Some of them, like the half-joking, half-serious stereotypes of mothers-in-law, or country yokels, or psychiatrists, are dinned into us by the stock jokes we hear and repeat. In fact, without such stereotypes, there would be a lot fewer jokes. Still other stereotypes are perpetuated by the advertisements we read, the movies we see, the books we read.   8

And finally, we tend to stereotype because it helps us make sense out of a highly confusing world, a world which William James once described as "one great, blooming, buzzing confusion." It is a curious fact that if we don't *know* what we're looking at, we are often quite literally unable to *see* what we're looking at. People who recover their sight after a lifetime of blindness actually cannot at first tell a triangle from a square. A visitor to a factory sees only noisy chaos where the superintendent sees a perfectly synchronized flow of work. As Walter Lippmann has said, "For the most part we do not first see, and then define; we define first, and then we see."   9

Stereotypes are one way in which we "define" the world in order to see it. They classify the infinite variety of human beings into a convenient handful of "types" towards whom we learn to act in stereotyped fashion. Life would be a wearing process if we had to start from scratch with each and every human contact. Stereotypes economize on our mental effort by covering up the blooming, buzzing confusion with big recognizable cut-outs. They save us the "trouble" of finding out what the world is like—they give it its accustomed look.   10

Thus the trouble is that stereotypes make us mentally lazy. As S. I. Hayakawa, the authority on semantics, has written: "The danger of stereotypes lies not in their existence, but in the fact that they become for all people some of the time, and for some people all the time, *substitutes for observation.*" Worse yet, stereotypes get in the way of our judgment, even when we do observe the world. Someone who has formed rigid preconceptions of all Latins as "excitable," or all teenagers as "wild," doesn't alter his point of view when he meets a calm and delib-   11 erate Genoese, or a serious-minded high school student. He brushes them aside as "exceptions that prove the rule." And, of course, if he meets someone true to type, he stands triumphantly vindicated. "They're all like that," he proclaims, having encountered an excited Latin, an ill-behaved adolescent.

Hence, quite aside from the injustice which stereotypes do to others, they impoverish ourselves. A person who lumps the world into simple categories, who type-casts all labor leaders as "racketeers," all businessmen as "reactionaries," all Harvard men as "snobs," and all Frenchmen as "sexy," is in danger of becoming a stereotype himself. He loses his capacity to be himself—which is to say, to see the world in his own absolutely unique, inimitable and independent fashion. 12

Instead, he votes for the man who fits his standardized picture of what a candidate "should" look like or sound like, buys the goods that someone in his "situation" in life "should" own, lives the life that others define for him. The mark of the stereotype person is that he never surprises us, that we do indeed have him "typed." And no one fits this strait-jacket so perfectly as someone whose opinions about *other people* are fixed and inflexible. 13

Impoverishing as they are, stereotypes are not easy to get rid of. The world we type-cast may be no better than a Grade B movie, but at least we know what to expect of our stock characters. When we let them act for themselves in the strangely unpredictable way that people do act, who knows but that many of our fondest convictions will be proved wrong? 14

Nor do we suddenly drop our standardized pictures for a blinding vision of the Truth. Sharp swings of ideas about people often just substitute one stereotype for another. The true process of change is a slow one that adds bits and pieces of reality to the pictures in our heads, until gradually they take on some of the blurriness of life itself. Little by little, we learn not that Jews and Negroes and Catholics and Puerto Ricans are "just like everybody else"—for that, too, is a stereotype—but that each and every one of them is unique, special, different and individual. Often we do not even know that we have let a stereotype lapse until we hear someone saying, "all so-and-so's are like such-and-such," and we hear ourselves saying, "Well—maybe." 15

Can we speed the process along? Of course we can. 16

First, we can become *aware* of the standardized pictures in 17
our heads, in other people's heads, in the world around us.

Second, we can become suspicious of all judgments that we 18
allow exceptions to "prove." There is no more chastening
thought than that in the vast intellectual adventure of science,
it takes but one tiny exception to topple a whole edifice of
ideas.

Third, we can learn to be chary of generalizations about peo- 19
ple. As F. Scott Fitzgerald once wrote: "Begin with an individual, and before you know it you have created a type; begin with
a type, and you find you have created—nothing."

Most of the time, when we type-cast the world, we are not in 20
fact generalizing about people at all. We are only revealing the
embarrassing facts about the pictures that hang in the gallery
of stereotypes in our own heads.

Questions for Study and Discussion

1. What is Heilbroner's main point, or thesis, in this essay?
   (Glossary: *Thesis*)
2. Study paragraphs 6, 8, and 15. Each paragraph illustrates
   Heilbroner's thesis. How? What does each paragraph contribute to support the thesis?
3. Transitional devices indicate relationships between paragraphs and thus help to unify the essay. Identify three
   transitions in this essay. Explain how they help to unify
   the essay. (Glossary: *Transitions*)
4. What are the reasons Heilbroner gives for why we stereotype individuals? What are some of the dangers of stereotypes, according to Heilbroner? How does he say we can
   rid ourselves of stereotypes?
5. Heilbroner uses the word *picture* in his discussion of stereotypes. Why is this an appropriate word in this discussion? (Glossary: *Diction*)

Vocabulary

Refer to your dictionary to define the following words as they are used in this selection. Then use each word in a sentence of your own.

irrational (7)   impoverish (12)
perpetuated (8)   chastening (18)
infinite (10)   edifice (18)
preconceptions (11)   chary (19)
vindicated (11)

Suggested Writing Assignments

1. Write an essay in which you attempt to convince your readers that it is not in their best interests to perform a particular act—for example, smoke, take stimulants to stay awake, go on a crash diet, or make snap judgments. In writing your essay, follow Heilbroner's lead: first identify the issue; then explain why it is a problem; and, finally, offer a solution or some advice. Remember to unify the various parts of your essay.

2. Have you ever been considered as a stereotype—a student, or a member of a particular sex, class, ethnic, national, or racial group? Write a unified essay that examines how stereotyping has affected you, how it has perhaps changed you, and how you regard the process.

3

ORGANIZATION

In an essay, ideas and information cannot be presented all at once; they have to be arranged in some order. That order is the essay's organization.

The pattern of organization in an essay should be suited to the writer's subject and purpose. For example, if you are writing about your experience working in a fast-food restaurant, and your purpose is to tell about the activities of a typical day, you might present those activities in chronological order. If, on the other hand, you wish to argue that working in a bank is an ideal summer job, you might proceed from the least rewarding to the most rewarding aspect of this job; this is called "climactic" order.

Some often-used patterns of organization are time order, space order, and logical order. Time order, or chronological order, is used to present events as they occurred. A personal narrative, a report of a campus incident, or an account of a historical event can be most naturally and easily related in chronological order. The description of a process, such as the refinishing of a table, the building of a stone wall, or the way to serve a tennis ball, almost always calls for a chronological organization. Of course, the order of events can sometimes be rearranged for special effect. For example, an account of an auto accident may begin with the collision itself and then go back in time to tell about the events leading up to it. One essay that is a model of chronological order is Dick Gregory's "Shame" (pp. 238–42).

Space order is used when describing a person, place, or thing. This organizational pattern begins at a particular point and moves in some direction, such as left to right, top to bottom, east to west, outside to inside, front to back, near to far, around, or over. In describing a house, for example, a writer could move from top to bottom, from outside to inside, or in a circle around the outside. Gilbert Highet's "Subway Station" (pp. 263–65) is an essay in which space is used as the organizing principle.

Logical order can take many forms depending on the writer's purpose. These include: general to specific, most familiar to least familiar, and smallest to biggest. Perhaps the most common type of logical order is order of importance. Notice how the writer uses this order in the following paragraph:

> The Egyptians have taught us many things. They were excellent farmers. They knew all about irrigation. They built temples which were afterwards copied by the Greeks and which served as the earliest models for the churches in which we worship nowadays. They invented a calendar which proved such a useful instrument for the purpose of measuring time that it has survived with a few changes until today. But most important of all, the Egyptians learned how to preserve speech for the benefit of future generations. They invented the art of writing.

By organizing the material according to the order of increasing importance, the writer places special emphasis on the final sentence. In writing a descriptive essay you can move from the least striking to the most striking detail, so as to keep your reader interested and involved in the description. In an explanatory essay you can start with the point that readers will find least difficult to understand and move on to the most difficult; that's how teachers organize many courses. Or, in writing an argumentative essay, you can move from your least controversial point to the most controversial, preparing your reader gradually to accept your argument.

REACH OUT AND WRITE SOMEONE

Lynn Wenzel

*Lynn Wenzel has been published in many ma-
jor newspapers and magazines, including* Newsweek, *the* New York Times, Newsday, *and* Down
East: The Magazine of Maine. *She is currently
music reviewer for* New Directions for Women.
Her book Just a Song at Twilight: The Story of
American Popular Sheet Music *appeared in
1989. Wenzel was graduated magna cum laude
from William Paterson College and makes her
home in Maywood, New Jersey. As you read her
essay, pay particular attention to the way she has
organized her examples to illustrate the importance of letter writing.*

E veryone is talking about the breakup of the telephone   1
company. Some say it will be a disaster for poor people
and a bonanza for large companies while others fear a personal
phone bill so exorbitant that—horror of horrors—we will all
have to start writing letters again.

It's about time. One of the many talents lost in this increas-   2
ingly technological age is that of putting pen to paper in order
to communicate with family, friends and lovers.

Reading, and enjoying it, may not be the strong suit of our   3
young but writing has truly become a lost art. I am not talking
about creative writing because this country still has its full
share of fine fiction and poetry writers. There will always be
those special few who need to transform experiences into short
stories or poetry.

No, the skill we have lost is that of letter writing. When was   4
the last time the mailbox contained anything more than bills,
political and fund-raising appeals, advertisements, catalogs,
magazines or junk mail?

Once upon a time, the only way to communicate from a dis-   5
tance was through the written word. As the country expanded

and people moved west, they knew that when they left mother, father, sister, brother, it was very probably the last time they would see them again. So daughters, pioneering in Indiana or Michigan, wrote home with the news that their first son had been born dead, but the second child was healthy and growing and they also had a house and barn. By the time the letter reached east, another child might have been born, yet it was read over and again, then smoothed out and slipped into the family Bible or keepsake box.

Letters were essential then. Imagine John Adams fomenting revolution and forming a new government without Abigail's letters to sustain him. Think of Elizabeth Barrett and Robert Browning without their written declarations of love; of all the lovers who, parted against their will, kept hope alive through letters often passed by hand or mailed in secret.   6

And what of history? Much of our knowledge of events and of the people who lived them is based on such commonplace communication. Harry Truman's letters to Bess, Mamie and Ike's correspondence and Eleanor Roosevelt's letters to some of her friends all illuminate actions and hint at intent. F. Scott Fitzgerald's letters to his daughter, Scottie, which were filled with melancholy over his wife's mental illness, suggest in part the reason why his last years were so frustratingly uncreative. Without letters we would have history—dry facts and dates of wars, treaties, elections, revolutions. But the causes and effects might be left unclear.   7

We would also know little about women's lives. History, until recently, neglected women's contributions to events. Much of what we now know about women in history comes from letters found, more often than not, in great-grandmother's trunk in the attic, carefully tied with ribbon, or stored, yellowed and boxed, in a carton in the archives of a "women's college." These letters have helped immensely over the past ten years to create a verifiable women's history which is now taking its rightful place alongside weighty tomes about men's contributions to the changing world.   8

The story of immigration often begins with a letter. Millions of brave souls, carrying their worldly possessions in one bag, stepped off a ship and into American life on the strength of a note saying, "Come. It's better here."   9

To know how important the "art" of letter writing was, we   10
have only to look at the accouterments our ancestors treasured
and considered necessary: inkstands of silver, gold or glass,
crafted to occupy a prominent place on the writing table; hot
wax for a personal seal; the seals themselves, sometimes or-
nately carved in silver; quills, and then fountain pens. These
were not luxuries but necessities.

Perhaps most important of all, letter writing required *think-*   11
ing before putting pen to paper. No hurried telephone call can
ever replace the thoughtful, intelligent correspondence between
two people, the patching up of a friendship, the formal request
for the pleasure of someone's company, or a personal apology.
Once written and sent, the writer can never declare, "But I
never said that." Serious letter writing demands thought, logic,
organization and sincerity because words, once written, cannot
be taken back. These are qualities we must not lose, but ones
we should polish and bring to luster.

What, after all, will we lose: our lover's letters tied with an   12
old hair ribbon, written from somewhere far away; our children's first scribbled note from summer camp; the letters
friends sent us as we scattered after college; letters we sent our
parents telling them how much they meant to us? Without letters, what will we save, laugh about, read out loud to each other
20 years from now on a snowy afternoon in front of a fire?

Telephone bills.   13

And that is the saddest note of all.   14

Questions for Study and Discussion

1. What is Wenzel's thesis in this essay? Where is it stated?
   (Glossary: *Thesis*)
2. Why does Wenzel concentrate on letter writing in her essay and not on other kinds of writing?
3. What role has letter writing played in our understanding
   of history, according to Wenzel?
4. In what ways is writing a letter different from making a
   phone call? What can letter writing do to help us develop
   as human beings?

chron/hist.

5. Which of the three patterns of organization has Wenzel used in presenting her examples of the importance of letter writing? Support your answer with examples.

6. How effective do you find the beginning and ending of Wenzel's essay? Explain. (Glossary: *Beginnings and Endings*)

Vocabulary

Refer to your dictionary to define the following words as they are used in this selection. Then use each word in a sentence of your own.

exorbitant (1)   accouterments (10)
fomenting (6)   seal (10)
tomes (8)

Suggested Writing Assignments

1. Write a personal letter to a friend or relative with whom you haven't been in contact for some while. Draft and redraft the letter carefully, making it as thoughtful and interesting as you can. Send the letter and report back to your class or instructor on the response that the letter elicited.

2. Think of a commonplace subject that people might take for granted but that you find interesting. Write an essay on that subject, using one of the following types of logical order:

   least important to most important
   most familiar to least familiar
   smallest to biggest
   oldest to newest
   easiest to understand to most difficult to understand
   good news to bad news
   general to specific

SO THAT NOBODY HAS TO GO TO SCHOOL IF THEY DON'T WANT TO

Roger Sipher

Roger Sipher is an associate professor of history at the State University of New York at Cortland. In the following essay, which first appeared in the New York Times *on December 22, 1977, Sipher offers a radical solution to the failure of public schools to provide an adequate education to those who desire it. As you read his essay, notice how Sipher makes clear the logical connections of his points as he develops his argument.*

A decline in standardized test scores is but the most recent indicator that American education is in trouble.

One reason for the crisis is that present mandatory-attendance laws force many to attend school who have no wish to be there. Such children have little desire to learn and are so antagonistic to school that neither they nor more highly motivated students receive the quality education that is the birthright of every American.

The solution to this problem is simple: Abolish compulsory-attendance laws and allow only those who are committed to getting an education to attend.

This will not end public education. Contrary to conventional belief, legislators enacted compulsory-attendance laws to legalize what already existed. William Landes and Lewis Solomon, economists, found little evidence that mandatory-attendance laws increased the number of children in school. They found, too, that school systems have never effectively enforced such laws, usually because of the expense involved.

There is no contradiction between the assertion that compulsory attendance has had little effect on the number of children attending school and the argument that repeal would be a positive step toward improving education. Most parents want a high school education for their children. Unfortunately, compulsory attendance hampers the ability of public school officials to enforce legitimate educational and disciplinary policies and thereby make the education a good one.

Private schools have no such problem. They can fail or dis- 6 miss students, knowing such students can attend public school. Without compulsory attendance, public schools would be freer to oust students whose academic or personal behavior undermines the educational mission of the institution.

Has not the noble experiment of a formal education for every- 7 one failed? While we pay homage to the homily, "You can lead a horse to water but you can't make him drink," we have pretended it is not true in education.

Ask high school teachers if recalcitrant students learn any- 8 thing of value. Ask teachers if these students do any homework. Ask if the threat of low grades motivates them. Quite the contrary, these students know they will be passed from grade to grade until they are old enough to quit or until, as is more likely, they receive a high school diploma. At the point when students could legally quit, most choose to remain since they know they are likely to be allowed to graduate whether they do acceptable work or not.

✓ Abolition of archaic attendance laws would produce enor- 9 mous dividends.

First, it would alert everyone that school is a serious place 10 where one goes to learn. Schools are neither day-care centers nor indoor street corners. Young people who resist learning should stay away; indeed, an end to compulsory schooling would require them to stay away.

Second, students opposed to learning would not be able to 11 pollute the educational atmosphere for those who want to learn. Teachers could stop policing recalcitrant students and start educating.

Third, grades would show what they are supposed to: how 12 well a student is learning. Parents could again read report cards and know if their children were making progress.

Fourth, public esteem for schools would increase. People 13 would stop regarding them as way stations for adolescents and start thinking of them as institutions for educating America's youth.

Fifth, elementary schools would change because students would find out early that they had better learn something or risk flunking out later. Elementary teachers would no longer have to pass their failures on to junior high and high school.   14

Sixth, the cost of enforcing compulsory education would be eliminated. Despite enforcement efforts, nearly 15 percent of the school-age children in our largest cities are almost permanently absent from school.   15

Communities could use these savings to support institutions to deal with young people not in school. If, in the long run, these institutions prove more costly, at least we would not confuse their mission with that of schools.   16

Schools should be for education. At present, they are only tangentially so. They have attempted to serve an all-encompassing social function, trying to be all things to all people. In the process they have failed miserably at what they were originally formed to accomplish.   17

Questions for Study and Discussion

1. What, according to Sipher, is the chief flaw in the compulsory attendance law?

2. Has Sipher used the principle of space, time, or logic to organize his essay? Explain.

3. Sipher's essay divides neatly into three main parts. Identify those parts and discuss the function or purpose of each.

4. What is Sipher's attitude toward those children whom he describes as not wanting an education? Choose examples of his diction to support your answer. (Glossary: *Diction*)

5. Sipher lists six "dividends" resulting from the elimination of compulsory attendance. Which did you find the most appealing? The least appealing? Can you add any potential benefits to his list? Explain.

6. Cite examples of Sipher's use of parallelism in his essay, and explain how it strengthens his argument. (Glossary: *Parallelism*)

Vocabulary

Refer to your dictionary to define the following words as they are used in this selection. Then use each word in a sentence of your own.

compulsory (6)   archaic (9)
homily (7)   tangentially (17)
recalcitrant (8)

Suggested Writing Assignments

1. Sipher believes that "Schools should be for education," but concludes that currently "they are only tangentially so" (17). Based upon your own experiences with public education, write an essay in which you support or attack Sipher's assessment. Be sure to use detailed examples to illustrate your thesis.

2. Sipher says little about the fate of students who would be ousted for failure to conform to public school standards of behavior. What is your reaction to this part of his plan? Does it seem reasonable to you, or do you see any fundamental problems with it? In an essay, explain what you think ought to happen to recalcitrant students who undermine "the educational mission of the institution."

THE CORNER STORE

Eudora Welty

Eudora Welty is perhaps one of the most honored and respected writers at work today. She was born in 1909 in Jackson, Mississippi, where she has lived most of her life. Her published works include many short stories, now available as her Collected Stories *(1980); five novels; a collection of her essays,* The Eye of the Story *(1975); and a memoir,* One Writer's Beginnings *(1987). In 1973 her novel* The Optimist's Daughter *won the Pulitzer prize for fiction. Welty's description of the corner store, taken from an essay about growing up in Jackson, will recall for many readers the neighborhood store where they grew up.*

Our Little Store rose right up from the sidewalk; standing   1
in a street of family houses, it alone hadn't any yard in
front, any tree or flower bed. It was a plain frame building covered over with brick. Above the door, a little railed porch ran across on an upstairs level and four windows with shades were looking out. But I didn't catch on to those.

Running in out of the sun, you met what seemed total obscu-   2
rity inside. There were almost tangible smells—licorice recently sucked in a child's cheek, dill pickle brine that had leaked through a paper sack in a fresh trail across the wooden floor, ammonia-loaded ice that had been hoisted from wet croker sacks and slammed into the icebox with its sweet butter at the door, and perhaps the smell of still untrapped mice.

Then through the motes of cracker dust, cornmeal dust, the   3
Gold Dust of the Gold Dust Twins that the floor had been swept out with, the realities emerged. Shelves climbed to high reach all the way around, set out with not too much of any one thing but a lot of things—lard, molasses, vinegar, starch, matches, kerosene, Octagon soap (about a year's worth of octagon-shaped coupons cut out and saved brought a signet ring ad-

dressed to you in the mail). It was up to you to remember what you came for, while your eye traveled from cans of sardines to tin whistles to ice cream salt to harmonicas to flypaper (over your head, batting around on a thread beneath the blades of the ceiling fan, stuck with its testimonial catch).

Its confusion may have been in the eye of its beholder. En- 4
chantment is cast upon you by all those things you weren't supposed to have need for, to lure you close to wooden tops you'd
outgrown, boys' marbles and agates in little net pouches, small
rubber balls that wouldn't bounce straight, frail, frazzly kite
string, clay bubble pipes that would snap off in your teeth, the
stiffest scissors. You could contemplate those long narrow
boxes of sparklers gathering dust while you waited for it to be
the Fourth of July or Christmas, and noisemakers in the shape
of tin frogs for somebody's birthday party you hadn't been invited to yet, and see that they were all marvelous.

You might not have even looked for Mr. Sessions when he 5
came around his store cheese (as big as a doll's house) and in
front of the counter looking for you. When you'd finally asked
him for, and received from him in its paper bag, whatever single
thing it was that you had been sent for, the nickel that was left
over was yours to spend.

Down at a child's eye level, inside those glass jars with 6
mouths in their sides through which the grocer could run his
scoop or a child's hand might be invited to reach for a choice,
were wineballs, all-day suckers, gumdrops, peppermints. Making a row under the glass of a counter were the Tootsie Rolls,
Hershey bars, Goo Goo Clusters, Baby Ruths. And whatever
was the name of those pastilles that came stacked in a cardboard cylinder with a cardboard lid? They were thin and dry,
about the size of tiddledy-winks, and in the shape of twisted
rosettes. A kind of chocolate dust came out with them when you
shook them out in your hand. Were they chocolate? I'd say,
rather, they were brown. They didn't taste of anything at all,
unless it was wood. Their attraction was the number you got for
a nickel.

Making up your mind, you circled the store around and 7
around, around the pickle barrel, around the tower of Cracker-
jack boxes; Mr. Sessions had built it for us himself on top of a
packing case like a house of cards.

If it seemed too hot for Crackerjacks, I might get a cold   8
drink. Mr. Sessions might have already stationed himself by the
cold-drinks barrel, like a mind reader. Deep in ice water that
looked black as ink, murky shapes—that would come up as
Coca-Colas, Orange Crushes, and various flavors of pop—were
all swimming around together. When you gave the word, Mr.
Sessions plunged his bare arm in to the elbow and fished out
your choice, first try. I favored a locally bottled concoction
called Lake's Celery. (What else could it be called? It was made
by a Mr. Lake out of celery. It was a popular drink here for years
but was not known universally, as I found out when I arrived in
New York and ordered one in the Astor bar.) You drank on the
premises, with feet set wide apart to miss the drip, and gave
him back his bottle and your nickel.

But he didn't hurry you off. A standing scales was by the   9
door, with a stack of iron weights and a brass slide on the balance arm, that would weigh you up to three hundred pounds.
Mr. Sessions, whose hands were gentle and smelled of carbolic,
would lift you up and set your feet on the platform, hold your
loaf of bread for you, and taking his time while you stood still
for him, he would make certain of what you weighed today. He
could even remember what you weighed the last time, so you
could subtract and announce how much you'd gained. That was
goodbye.

Questions for Study and Discussion

1. Which of the three patterns of organization has Welty
   used in this essay: chronological, spatial, or logical? If she
   has used more than one, where precisely has she used
   each type?

2. What is the dominant impression that Welty creates in
   her description of the corner store? (Glossary: *Dominant
   Impression*) How does Welty create this dominant impression?

3. What does Welty mean when she writes that the store's
   "confusion may have been in the eye of its beholder" (4)?
   What factors might lead one to become confused?

4. What impression of Mr. Sessions does Welty create? What details contribute to this impression?

5. Welty places certain pieces of information in parentheses in this essay. Why are they in parentheses? What, if anything, does this information add to our understanding of the corner store? Might this information be left out? Explain.

6. Comment on Welty's ending. Is it too abrupt? Why or why not? (Glossary: *Beginnings and Endings*)

Vocabulary

Refer to your dictionary to define the following words as they are used in this selection. Then use each word in a sentence of your own.

frame (1)	signet (3)
tangible (2)	agates (4)
brine (2)	concoction (8)
motes (3)	scales (9)

Suggested Writing Assignments

1. Describe your neighborhood store or supermarket. Gather a large quantity of detailed information from memory and from an actual visit to the store if that is still possible. Once you have gathered your information, try to select those details that will help you create a dominant impression of the store. Finally, organize your examples and illustrations according to some clear organizational pattern.

2. Write an essay on one of the following topics:

   local restaurants
   reading materials
   television shows
   ways of financing a college education
   types of summer employment

   Be sure to use an organizational pattern that is well thought out and suited to both your material and your purpose.

4

Beginnings and Endings

"Begin at the beginning and go on till you come to the end: then stop," advised the King of Hearts in *Alice in Wonderland*. "Good advice, but more easily said than done," you might be tempted to reply. Certainly, no part of writing essays can be more daunting than coming up with effective beginnings and endings. In fact, many writers feel these are the most important parts of any piece of writing regardless of its length. Even before coming to your introduction proper, your readers will usually know something about your intentions from your title. Titles like "The Case against Euthanasia," "How to Buy a Used Car," or "What Is a Migraine Headache?" indicate both your subject and approach and prepare your readers for what is to follow.

But what makes for an effective beginning? Not unlike a personal greeting, a good beginning should catch a reader's interest and then hold it. The experienced writer realizes that most readers would rather do almost anything than make a commitment to read, so the opening or "lead," as journalists refer to it, requires a lot of thought and much revising to make it right and to keep the reader's attention from straying. The inexperienced writer knows that the beginning is important but tries to write it first and to perfect it before moving on to the rest of the essay. Although there are no "rules" for writing introductions, we can offer one bit of general advice: wait until the writing process is well underway or almost completed before focusing on your lead. Following this advice will keep you from spending too much time on an introduction that you will probably revise. More importantly, once you actually see how your essay develops, you will know better how to introduce it to your reader.

In addition to capturing your reader's attention, a good beginning frequently introduces your thesis and either suggests or actually reveals the structure of the composition. Keep in mind that the best beginning is not necessarily the most catchy or the most shocking but the one most appropriate for the job you are trying to do.

Beginnings

The following examples from published essays show you some effective beginnings:

Short Generalization

It is a miracle that New York works at all.

E. B. White

Startling Claim

It is possible to stop most drug addiction in the United States within a very short time.

Gore Vidal

Rhetorical Questions

Just how interconnected *is* the animal world? Is it true that if we change any part of that world we risk unduly damaging life in other, larger parts of it?

Matthew Douglas

Humor/Apt Quotation

The right to pursue happiness is issued to Americans with their birth certificates, but no one seems quite sure which way it ran. It may be we are issued a hunting license but offered no game. Jonathan Swift seemed to think so when he attacked the idea of happiness as "the possession of being well-deceived," the felicity of being "a fool among knaves." For Swift saw society as Vanity Fair, the land of false goals.

John Ciardi

Startling Fact

Charles Darwin and Abraham Lincoln were born on the same day—February 12, 1809. They are also linked in another curious way—for both must simultaneously play, and for similar reasons, the role of man and legend.

Stephen Jay Gould

Dialogue

"This would be excellent, to go in the ocean with this thing," says Dave Gembutis, fifteen.

He is looking at a $170 Sea Cruiser raft.

"Great," says his companion, Dan Holmes, also fifteen.

This is at Herman's World of Sporting Goods, in the middle of the Woodfield Mall in Schaumburg, Illinois.

Bob Greene

Statistics/Question

In the 40 years from 1939 to 1979 white women who work full time have with monotonous regularity made slightly less than 60 percent as much as white men. Why?

Lester C. Thurow

Irony

In Moulmein, in lower Burma, I was hated by large numbers of people—the only time in my life that I have been important enough for this to happen to me.

George Orwell

There are many more excellent ways to begin an essay, but there are also some ways of beginning that should be avoided. Some of these follow:

Apology

I am a college student and do not consider myself an expert on the computer industry, but I think that many computer companies make false claims about just how easy it is to learn to use a computer.

Complaint

I'd rather write about a topic of my own choice than the one that is assigned, but here goes.

Webster's Dictionary

Webster's New Collegiate Dictionary defines the verb *to snore* as follows: "to breathe during sleep with a rough hoarse noise due to vibration of the soft palate."

Platitude

America is the land of opportunity and no one knows it better than Madonna.

Reference to Title

As you can see from my title, this essay is about why we should continue to experiment with human heart transplants.

Endings

An effective ending does more than simply indicate where the writer stopped writing. A conclusion may summarize; may inspire the reader to further thought or even action; may return to the beginning by repeating key words, phrases, or ideas; or may surprise the reader by providing a particularly convincing example to support a thesis. Indeed, there are, as with beginnings, many ways to write a conclusion, but the effectiveness of any choice really must be measured by how appropriately it fits what has gone before it. In the following conclusion to a long chapter on weasel words, a form of deceptive advertising language, writer Paul Stevens summarizes the points that he has made:

A weasel word is a word that's used to imply a meaning that cannot be truthfully stated. Some weasels imply meanings that are not the same as their actual definition, such as "help," "like," or "fortified." They can act as qualifiers and/ or comparatives. Other weasels, such as "taste" and "flavor," have no definite meanings, and are simply subjective opinions offered by the manufacturer. A weasel of omission is one that implies a claim so strongly that it forces you to supply the bogus fact. Adjectives are weasels used to convey feelings and emotions to a greater extent than the product itself can.

In dealing with weasels, you must strip away the innuendos and try to ascertain the facts, if any. To do this, you need to ask questions such as: How? Why? How many? How much? Stick to basic definitions of words. Look them up if you have to. Then, apply the strict definition to the text of the advertisement or commercial. "Like" means similar to, but not the same as. "Virtually" means the same in essence, but not in fact.

Above all, never underestimate the devious qualities of a weasel. Weasels twist and turn and hide in dark shadows. You must come to grips with them, or advertising will rule you forever.

My advise to you is: Beware of weasels. They are nasty and untrainable, and they attack pocketbooks.

If you are having trouble with your conclusion—and this is not an uncommon problem—it may be because of problems with your essay itself. Frequently, writers do not know when to end because they are not sure about their overall purpose in the first place. For example, if you are taking a trip and your purpose is to go to Chicago, you'll know when you get there and will stop. But if you don't really know where you are going, it's very difficult to know when to stop.

It's usually a good idea in your conclusion to avoid such over-worked expressions as "In conclusion," "In summary," "I hope I have shown," or "Finally." Your conclusion should also do more than simply repeat what you've said in your opening paragraph. The most satisfying essays are those in which the conclusion provides an interesting way of wrapping up ideas introduced in the beginning and developed throughout.

YOU ARE HOW YOU EAT

Enid Nemy

*Born in Winnipeg, Canada, Enid Nemy has had
an active career in journalism. She worked as a
reporter and an editor for Canadian newspapers
before joining the* New York Times *in 1963. At
the* Times *she writes "New Yorkers, Etc.," an
award-winning column devoted to New York
City's people and events. Notice how Nemy's beginning establishes her thesis and sets up her
examples and how her ending reverberates back
through the essay.*

There's nothing peculiar about a person walking along a   1
Manhattan street, or any other street for that matter, eating an ice cream cone. It's the approach that's sometimes a little strange—ice-cream-cone-eating is not a cut-and-dried, standardized, routine matter. It is an accomplishment with infinite
variety, ranging from methodical and workmanlike procedures
to methods that are visions of delicacy and grace.

The infinite variety displayed in eating ice cream isn't by any   2
means unique; it applies to all kinds of food. The fact is that although a lot of research has been done on what people eat and
where they eat it, serious studies on the way food is eaten have
been sadly neglected.

Back to ice cream, as an example. If five people leave an ice   3
cream store with cones, five different methods of eating will
likely be on view. There are people who stick out their tongues
on top of a scoop, but don't actually eat the ice cream. They
push it down into the cone—push, push, push—then take an in-
termission to circle the perimeter, lapping up possible drips.

After this, it's again back to pushing the ice cream farther   4
into the cone. When the ice cream has virtually disappeared
into the crackly cone, they begin eating. These people obviously
don't live for the moment; they plan for the future, even if the
future is only two minutes away. Gobble up all the ice cream on

top and be left with a hollow cone? Forget it. Better to forgo immediate temptation and then enjoy the cone right to the end.

On the other hand, there are the "now" types who take great 5 gobby bites of the ice cream. Eventually, of course, they get down to an empty cone, which they might eat and, then again, they might throw away (if the latter, one wonders why they don't buy cups rather than cones, but no point in asking).

The most irritating of all ice cream eaters are the elegant 6 creatures who manage to devour a whole cone with delicate little nibbles and no dribble. The thermometer might soar, the pavement might melt, but their ice cream stays as firm and as rounded as it was in the scoop. No drips, no minor calamities— and it's absolutely not fair, but what can you do about it?

Some of the strangest ice cream fans can be seen devouring 7 sundaes and banana splits. They are known as "layer by layer" types. First they eat the nuts and coconut and whatever else is sprinkled on top. Then they eat the sauce; then the banana, and finally the ice cream, flavor by flavor. Some might feel that they are eating ingredients and not a sundae or a split, but what do they care?

As for chocolate eaters, there are three main varieties, at least 8 among those who like the small individual chocolates. A certain percentage pop the whole chocolate into their mouths, crunch once or twice and down it goes. Others pop the whole chocolate into their mouths and let it slowly melt. A smaller number hold the chocolate in hand while taking dainty little bites.

Peanuts and popcorn are a completely different matter. Of 9 course, there are always one or two souls who actually pick up single peanuts and popcorn kernels, but the usual procedure is to scoop up a handful. But even these can be subdivided into those who feed them in one at a time and those who sort of throw the handful into the open mouth, then keep on throwing in handfuls until the plate, bag or box is empty. The feeders-in-one-at-a-time are, needless to say, a rare breed with such iron discipline that they probably exercise every morning and love it.

Candies like M & M's are treated by most people in much the 10 same way as peanuts or popcorn. But there are exceptions, among them those who don't start eating until they have separated the colors. Then they eat one color at a time, or one of each color in rotation. Honestly.

A sandwich cookie is a sandwich cookie, and you take bites of 11 it, and so what? So what if you're the kind who doesn't take bites until it's pulled apart into two sections. And if you're this kind of person, and an amazing number are, the likelihood is that the plain part will be eaten first, and the one with icing saved for last. Watch Oreo eaters.

A woman who seems quite normal in other respects said that 12 although she considers her eating habits quite run-of-the-mill, she has been told that they are, in fact, peculiar.

"If I have meat or chicken and a couple of vegetables on a 13 plate, I go absolutely crazy if they don't come out even," she said. "I like to take a piece of meat and a little bit of each vegetable together. If, as I'm eating I end up with no meat and a lot of broccoli, or no potatoes and a piece of chicken, it drives me mad."

A man listening to all this rolled his eyes in disbelief. Pecu- 14 liar is putting it mildly, he said. He would never eat like that.

How does he eat? 15

"One thing at a time," he said. "First I eat the meat, then one 16 of the vegetables, then the other. How else would you eat?"

Questions for Study and Discussion

1. Study the beginning of Nemy's essay. How does it serve Nemy's purpose? (Glossary: *Purpose*)
2. What is Nemy's thesis in this essay? (Glossary: *Thesis*)
3. Nemy has written an essay of classification. (Glossary: *Division and Classification*) How does classification serve her purpose?
4. What connection does Nemy make between paragraphs 7 and 8? Where in the essay does Nemy prepare you for the change in subject from ice cream to chocolate?
5. Is this essay merely an attempt to be humorous, or is there something more to its subject than we might sus-

pect? You might wish to reconsider the title in determining your response to this question. (Glossary: *Title*)

6. How fitting is Nemy's conclusion for the essay she has written? Would it have been better if the essay ended with a different paragraph—say, paragraph 11 or 13? Explain.

Vocabulary

Refer to your dictionary to define the following words as they are used in this selection. Then use each word in a sentence of your own.

infinite (1)	irritating (6)
methodical (1)	dainty (8)
unique (2)	iron (9)
perimeter (3)	icing (11)

Suggested Writing Assignments

1. Enid Nemy's discussion of the various ways people eat is by no means exhaustive. Much remains to observe and report. Write an essay modeled on hers in which you report on what you have observed of people's eating habits. Try, as Nemy has done, to suggest the importance of what you have observed, perhaps even spending more time in your essay developing a theory on the relationship between eating and behavior or personality.

2. How we say "Hello" and "Goodbye" can be extremely important in interpersonal relationships. Write an essay using your own experiences to examine the importance of the various kinds of greetings and farewells. Your essay should have an effective opening and a fitting conclusion.

HOW TO TAKE A JOB INTERVIEW

Kirby W. Stanat

*A former personnel recruiter and placement offi-
cer at the University of Wisconsin—Milwaukee,
Kirby W. Stanat has helped thousands of people
get jobs.* His book Job Hunting Secrets and Tactics *(1977) tells readers what they need to know
in order to get the jobs they want. In this selection Stanat analyzes the campus interview, a
process that hundreds of thousands of college
students undergo each year as they seek to enter
the job market. Notice how Stanat begins and
how the "snap" of his ending echoes back
through his essay.*

To succeed in campus job interviews, you have to know   1
where that recruiter is coming from. The simple answer is
that he is coming from corporate headquarters.

That may sound obvious, but it is a significant point that too   2
many students do not consider. The recruiter is not a free spirit
as he flies from Berkeley to New Haven, from Chapel Hill to
Boulder. He's on an invisible leash to the office, and if he is
worth his salary, he is mentally in corporate headquarters all
the time he's on the road.

If you can fix that in your mind—that when you walk into that   3
bare-walled cubicle in the placement center you are walking
into a branch office of Sears, Bendix or General Motors—you
can avoid a lot of little mistakes and maybe some big ones.

If, for example, you assume that because the interview is on   4
campus the recruiter expects you to look and act like a student,
you're in for a shock. A student is somebody who drinks beer,
wears blue jeans and throws a Frisbee. No recruiter has jobs
for student Frisbee whizzes.

A cool spring day in late March, Sam Davis, a good recruiter   5
who has been on the college circuit for years, is on my campus

talking to candidates. He comes out to the waiting area to meet the student who signed up for an 11 o'clock interview. I'm standing in the doorway of my office taking in the scene.

Sam calls the candidate: "Sidney Student." There sits Sidney. He's at a 45 degree angle, his feet are in the aisle, and he's almost lying down. He's wearing well-polished brown shoes, a tasteful pair of brown pants, a light brown shirt, and a good looking tie. Unfortunately, he tops off this well-coordinated outfit with his Joe's Tavern Class A Softball Championship jacket, which has a big woven emblem over the heart. 6

If that isn't bad enough, in his left hand is a cigarette and in his right hand is a half-eaten apple. 7

When Sam calls his name, the kid is caught off guard. He ditches the cigarette in an ashtray, struggles to his feet, and transfers the apple from the right to the left hand. Apple juice is everywhere, so Sid wipes his hand on the seat of his pants and shakes hands with Sam. 8

Sam, who by now is close to having a stroke, gives me that what-do-I-have-here look and has the young man follow him into the interviewing room. 9

The situation deteriorates even further—into pure Laurel and Hardy. The kid is stuck with the half-eaten apple, doesn't know what to do with it, and obviously is suffering some discomfort. He carries the apple into the interviewing room with him and places it in the ashtray on the desk—right on top of Sam's freshly lit cigarette. 10

The interview lasts five minutes. . . . 11

Let us move in for a closer look at how the campus recruiter operates. 12

Let's say you have a 10 o'clock appointment with the recruiter from the XYZ Corporation. The recruiter gets rid of the candidate in front of you at about 5 minutes to 10, jots down a few notes about what he is going to do with him or her, then picks up your résumé or data sheet (which you have submitted in advance). . . . 13

Although the recruiter is still in the interview room and you are still in the lobby, your interview is under way. You're on. The recruiter will look over your sheet pretty carefully before he goes out to call you. He develops a mental picture of you. 14

He thinks, "I'm going to enjoy talking with this kid," or "This 15 one's going to be a turkey." The recruiter has already begun to make a screening decision about you.

His first impression of you, from reading the sheet, could 16 come from your grade point. It could come from misspelled words. It could come from poor erasures or from the fact that necessary information is missing. By the time the recruiter has finished reading your sheet, you've already hit the plus or minus column.

Let's assume the recruiter got a fairly good impression from 17 your sheet.

Now the recruiter goes out to the lobby to meet you. He al- 18 most shuffles along, and his mind is somewhere else. Then he calls your name, and at that instant he visibly clicks into gear. He just went to work.

As he calls your name he looks quickly around the room, 19 waiting for somebody to move. If you are sitting on the middle of your back, with a book open and a cigarette going, and if you have to rebuild yourself to stand up, the interest will run right out of the recruiter's face. You, not the recruiter, made the appointment for 10 o'clock, and the recruiter expects to see a young professional come popping out of that chair like today is a good day and you're anxious to meet him.

At this point, the recruiter does something rude. He doesn't 20 walk across the room to meet you halfway. He waits for you to come to him. Something very important is happening. He wants to see you move. He wants to get an impression about your posture, your stride, and your briskness.

If you slouch over to him, sidewinderlike, he is not going to be 21 impressed. He'll figure you would probably slouch your way through your workdays. He wants you to come at him with lots of good things going for you. If you watch the recruiter's eyes, you can see the inspection. He glances quickly at shoes, pants, coat, shirt; dress, blouse, hose—the whole works.

After introducing himself, the recruiter will probably say, 22 "Okay, please follow me," and he'll lead you into his interviewing room.

When you get to the room, you may find that the recruiter 23 will open the door and gesture you in—with him blocking part of the doorway. There's enough room for you to get past him, but it's a near thing.

As you scrape past, he gives you a closeup inspection. He 24 looks at your hair; if it's greasy, that will bother him. He looks at your collar; if it's dirty, that will bother him. He looks at your shoulders; if they're covered with dandruff, that will bother him. If you're a man, he looks at your chin. If you didn't get a close shave, that will irritate him. If you're a woman, he checks your makeup. If it's too heavy, he won't like it.

Then he smells you. An amazing number of people smell bad. 25 Occasionally a recruiter meets a student who smells like a canal horse. That student can expect an interview of about four or five minutes.

Next the recruiter inspects the back side of you. He checks 26 your hair (is it combed in front but not in back?), he checks your heels (are they run down?), your pants (are they baggy?), your slip (is it showing?), your stockings (do they have runs?).

Then he invites you to sit down. 27

At this point, I submit, the recruiter's decision on you is 75 to 28 80 percent made.

Think about it. The recruiter has read your résumé. He 29 knows who you are and where you are from. He knows your marital status, your major and your grade point. And he knows what you have done with your summers. He has inspected you, exchanged greetings with you and smelled you. There is very little additional hard information that he must gather on you. From now on it's mostly body chemistry.

Many recruiters have argued strenuously with me that they 30 don't make such hasty decisions. So I tried an experiment. I told several recruiters that I would hang around in the hall outside the interview room when they took candidates in.

I told them that as soon as they had definitely decided not to 31 recommend (to department managers in their companies) the candidate they were interviewing, they should snap their fingers loud enough for me to hear. It went like this.

First candidate: 38 seconds after the candidate sat down: 32 Snap!

Second candidate: 1 minute, 42 seconds: Snap! 33

Third candidate: 45 seconds: Snap! 34

One recruiter was particularly adamant, insisting that he 35
didn't rush to judgment on candidates. I asked him to participate in the snapping experiment. He went out in the lobby,
picked up his first candidate of the day, and headed for an interview room.

As he passed me in the hall, he glared at me. And his fingers 36
went "Snap!"

Questions for Study and Discussion

1. Explain the appropriateness of the beginning and ending of Stanat's essay.
2. What are Stanat's purpose and thesis in telling the reader how the recruitment process works? (Glossary: *Purpose* and *Thesis*)
3. In paragraphs 12–29 Stanat explains how the campus recruiter works. Make a list of the steps in that process.
4. Why do recruiters pay so much attention to body language when they interview job candidates?
5. What specifically have you learned from reading Stanat's essay? Do you feel that the essay is useful in preparing someone for a job interview? Explain.
6. Stanat's tone—his attitude toward his subject and audience—in this essay is informal. What in his sentence structure and diction creates this informality? Cite examples. How might the tone be made more formal for a different audience?

Vocabulary

Refer to your dictionary to define the following words as they are used in this selection. Then use each word in a sentence of your own.

cubicle (3)   résumé (13)
deteriorates (10)   adamant (35)

Suggested Writing Assignments

1. Stanat's purpose is to offer practical advice to students interviewing for jobs. Determine a subject about which you could offer advice to a specific audience. Present your advice in the form of an essay, being careful to provide an attention-grabbing beginning and a convincing conclusion.

2. Stanat gives us an account of the interview process from the viewpoint of the interviewer. If you have ever been interviewed and remember the experience well, write an essay on your feelings and thoughts as the interview took place. What were the circumstances of the interview? What questions were asked of you, how did you feel about them, and how comfortable was the process? How did the interview turn out? What precisely, if anything, did you learn from the experience? What advice would you give anyone about to be interviewed?

HUGH TROY: PRACTICAL JOKER

Alfred Rosa and Paul Eschholz

*Alfred Rosa and Paul Eschholz are both profes-
sors of English at the University of Vermont,
where they teach courses in composition, the
English language, and American literature. In
the following article, which first appeared in
The People's Almanac #2 in 1978, Rosa and
Eschholz draw a portrait of a man who believed
that in the hands of an expert a practical joke
was more than just a good laugh. As you read,
notice how the opening serves to build interest
and how the conclusion works to reflect the
point of the essay.*

Nothing seemed unusual. In fact, it was a rather common 1
occurrence in New York City. Five men dressed in over-
alls roped off a section of busy Fifth Avenue in front of the old
Rockefeller residence, hung out MEN WORKING signs, and began
ripping up the pavement. By the time they stopped for lunch,
they had dug quite a hole in the street. This crew was different,
however, from all the others that had descended upon the
streets of the city. It was led by Hugh Troy—the world's greatest
practical joker.

For lunch, Troy led his tired and dirty crew into the dining 2
room of a fashionable Fifth Avenue hotel that was nearby. When
the headwaiter protested, Troy took him into his confidence.
"It's a little gag the manager wants to put over," he told the
waiter. The men ate heartily and seemed not to notice that
indignant diners were leaving the premises. After lunch Troy
and his men returned to their digging, and by late afternoon
they had greatly enlarged the hole in the avenue. When quitting
time arrived, they dutifully hung out their red lanterns, left the
scene, and never returned. City officials discovered the hoax
the next day, but they never learned who the pranksters were.

Hugh Troy was born in Ithaca, N.Y., where his father was a 3 professor at Cornell University. After graduating from Cornell, Troy left for New York City, where he became a successful illustrator of children's books. When W.W. II broke out, he went into the army and eventually became a captain in the 21st Bomber Command, 20th Air Force, under Gen. Curtis LeMay. After the war he made his home in Garrison, N.Y., for a short while before finally settling in Washington, D.C., where he lived until his death.

As a youngster Troy became a friend of the painter Louis 4 Agassiz Fuertes, who encouraged Troy to become an artist and may have encouraged the boy to become a practical joker as well. While Fuertes and Troy were out driving one day, Fuertes saw a JESUS SAVES sign and swiped it. Many a good laugh was had when several days later people saw the sign firmly planted in front of the Ithaca Savings Bank. The boy put up a few signs of his own. Fascinated by the word *pinking*, he posted a sign in front of his house: PINKING DONE. No one needed pinking done, but curiosity got the best of some, who stopped to ask what pinking was. "It's a trade secret," Troy quipped. The boy was also a member of a skating club, and when he needed some pocket money, he tacked an old cigar box near the entrance of the clubhouse, along with a PLEASE HELP sign. People naturally began dropping change into the box, change which Troy routinely pocketed.

The fun for Troy really began when he entered Cornell. Some 5 of his celebrated antics involved a phony plane crash, reports on the campus radio station of an enemy invasion, an apparent ceiling collapse, and a cherry tree which one year miraculously bore apples. Troy's most successful stunt at Cornell concerned a rhinoceros. Using a wastebasket made from the foot of a rhinoceros, which he borrowed from his friend Fuertes, Troy made tracks across the campus and onto the frozen reservoir, stopping at the brink of a large hole in the ice. Nobody knew what to make of the whole thing until campus zoologists confirmed the authenticity of the tracks. Townspeople then began to complain that their tap water tasted of rhinoceros. Not until the truth surfaced did the complaints subside.

Troy's antics did not stop when he graduated from Cornell. 6 Shortly after moving to New York, he purchased a park bench, an exact duplicate of those used by the city. With the help of a friend, he hauled it into Central Park. As soon as Hugh and his cohort spied a policeman coming down the path, they picked up the bench and started off with it. In no time the mischievous pair were in the local hoosegow. At that point the clever Troy produced his bill of sale, forcing the embarrassed police to release him and his pal. The two men repeated the caper several times before the entire force finally caught on.

Often Troy's pranks were conceived on the spur of the moment. For example, on a whim Troy bought a dozen copies of the 1932 election-night extra announcing Roosevelt's victory. The papers remained in mothballs until New Year's Eve, 1935, when Hugh and a group of merrymakers rode the city's subways, each with a copy of the newspaper. Other passengers, most of whom were feeling no pain, did a double take at the bold headline: ROOSEVELT ELECTED. 7

When the Museum of Modern Art sponsored the first American showing of Van Gogh's work in 1935, Hugh was on the scene again. The exhibit attracted large crowds of people who Troy suspected were more interested in the sensational aspects of the artist's life than in his paintings. To test his theory, Troy fashioned a replica of an ear out of chipped beef and had it neatly mounted in a blue velvet display case. A small card telling the grisly story was attached: "This was the ear which Vincent Van Gogh cut off and sent to his mistress, a French prostitute, Dec. 24, 1888." The "chipped beef ear" was then placed on a table in the gallery where Van Gogh's paintings were displayed. Troy got immediate results. New York's "art lovers" flocked to the ear, which, as Troy suspected, was what they really wanted to see after all. 8

Hugh Troy's pranks were never vindictive, but once, when irked by the operator of a Greenwich Village movie theater, he got the last laugh. One evening he took a jar full of moths into the theater and released them during the show. The moths flew directly for the light from the projector and made it impossible for anyone to see the picture. While the manager tried to appease the angry moviegoers, Hugh looked on with satisfaction. 9

To protest the tremendous amount of paperwork in the army during W.W. II, Troy invented the special "flypaper report." Each day he sent this report to Washington to account for the number of flies trapped on the variously coded flypaper ribbons hanging in the company's mess hall. Soon the Pentagon, as might be expected, was asking other units for their flypaper 10 reports. Troy was also responsible for "Operation Folklore." While stationed in the South Pacific, he and two other intelligence officers coached an island youngster in fantastic Troy-devised folktales, which the child then told to a gullible visiting anthropologist.

While some of his practical jokes were pure fun, many were designed to expose the smugness and gullibility of the American public. Annoyed by a recently announced course in ghostwriting at American University, Troy placed the following ad in the *Washington Post:* "Too Busy to Paint? Call on The Ghost Artists. We Paint It—You Sign It!! Why Not Give an Exhibition?" The response was more than he had bargained for. The hundreds of letters and phone calls only highlighted the fact that Americans' pretentiousness about art and their attempts to buy their way into "arty circles" had not waned since the Van Gogh escapade. 11

Whether questioning the values of American society or simply relieving the monotony of daily life, Hugh Troy always managed to put a little bit of himself into each of his stunts. One day he attached a plaster hand to his shirt sleeve and took a trip through the Holland Tunnel. As he approached the tollbooth, with his toll ticket between the fingers of the artificial hand, Troy left both ticket and hand in the grasp of the stunned tollbooth attendant and sped away. 12

Questions for Study and Discussion

1. Reread the first two paragraphs of this essay. Are they a fitting introduction to the essay? Why, or why not? What would be gained or lost if the essay began with paragraph 3?
2. Reread the last paragraph of the essay. Is this paragraph a fitting conclusion? Why, or why not?
3. What in particular made Hugh Troy the world's greatest practical joker; that is, what put him in a different league than the ordinary prankster?
4. Briefly describe the organization of Rosa and Eschholz's essay. Would the essay be as effective if the paragraphs

were rearranged in a different order? Explain. (Glossary: *Organization*)

5. Rosa and Eschholz write that many of Troy's jokes "were designed to expose the smugness and gullibility of the American public" (11). What do they mean by that statement? Choose several of Troy's jokes and explain how they accomplished this particular purpose.

6. Are people today as smug and gullible as they used to be or less or more so? Explain.

Vocabulary

Refer to your dictionary to define the following words as they are used in this selection. Then use each word in a sentence of your own.

hoax (2)	vindictive (9)
pinking (4)	irked (9)
hoosegow (6)	appease (9)
caper (6)	smugness (11)
whim (7)	waned (11)

Suggested Writing Assignments

1. If you yourself are a practical joker, or if you have ever known one, write an essay modeled after Rosa and Eschholz's "Hugh Troy." Try to recount in detail the pranks that have been carried out and, most importantly, try to assess their significance. Give extra time and attention to the opening and concluding portions of your essay, making sure they do their jobs well.

2. Write an essay in which you discuss the need for humor in our lives. Draw upon your experiences, as well as those of classmates, to recount humorous situations, events, and statements in order to analyze how they have served to ease tensions, tone down aggressive behavior, or lighten an otherwise dark moment. Be sure that the beginning of your essay grabs and holds the reader's attention and that the ending provides a conclusion rather than just a stopping point.

EVEN YOU CAN GET IT

Bruce Lambert

Bruce Lambert was born in 1943, in Albany, New York, and attended Hamilton College, where he prepared for a career in journalism. Lambert covered government and political issues for several New York newspapers until 1984 when he began to focus on the issue of AIDS. In 1988 the New York Times *assigned Lambert to cover the AIDS story exclusively. He first published the following article on March 11 and 12, 1989. In it he alerts heterosexuals that they should not become complacent about protecting themselves from the dangers of AIDS. Notice how Lambert catches our attention with his surprising opening line and how his conclusion captures the "determined optimism" of Alison's struggle.*

A lison L. Gertz wasn't supposed to get AIDS.   1

She has never injected drugs or had a blood transfusion, and   2
she describes herself as "not at all promiscuous." But she does
say she had a single sexual encounter—seven years ago—with a
male acquaintance who, she has since learned, has died of AIDS.

Though AIDS has hit hardest among gay men and poor intra-   3
venous drug users. It also afflicts people like Ms. Gertz.

"People think this can't happen to them," she said in an inter- 4
view at her Manhattan apartment. "I never thought I could have
AIDS."

Going Public

She is 23 years old, affluent, college-educated and a profes-   5
sional from a prominent family. She grew up on Park Avenue.

Now Ms. Gertz and her family are going public because they   6
have a message. A message for heterosexuals who could make a
potentially fatal mistake if they dismiss the threat of AIDS. A

message for doctors who may miss a diagnosis; she spent three weeks undergoing exhaustive hospital tests for all other conceivable causes of her illness before AIDS was discovered. And a message asking for greater public support on AIDS issues.

"I decided when I was in the hospital I would give as much   7
time as I can to help people who are going through this, and warn others of the danger," she said. "I want to make a condom commercial, do speaking engagements, whatever I can.

"All the AIDS articles are about homosexuals or poor people   8
on drugs, and unfortunately a lot of people just flip by them," she said. "They think it doesn't apply to them."

But she added: "They can't turn the page on me. I could be   9
one of them, or their daughter. They have to deal with this."

Statistics show that the number of AIDS cases is rising   10
alarmingly among heterosexuals who get the virus by sharing needles for drugs and then pass it to their sex partners and babies.

Although there is no evidence that AIDS is spreading rampantly among other heterosexuals in this country—as it is in   11
Haiti and parts of Africa—cases like Ms. Gertz's do exist. About four percent of all newly reported AIDS cases stem from heterosexual intercourse, and that rate has been remaining steady.

New York City has recorded 524 cases in which women got   12
acquired immune deficiency syndrome through sexual intercourse. The men they were with were infected through either drug use or sexual contact with other men. Another 83 cases were of women from Haiti or Africa.

"It Took Only One Time for Me"

"I want to talk to these kids who think they're immortal," Ms.   13
Gertz said. "I want to tell them: I'm heterosexual, and it took only one time for me."

Ms. Gertz is certain how it happened. "It was one romantic   14
night," she said. "There were roses and champagne and everything. That was it. I only slept with him once."

Ms. Gertz has since learned that the man was bisexual and   15
that he has died of AIDS. Had she known his past then, she said, she doubts it would have made a difference. "At that point they weren't publicizing AIDS," she said. "It wasn't an issue then."

AIDS is no respecter of wealth or social status. Ms. Gertz is a   16
granddaughter of a founder of the old Gertz department stores
in Queens and on Long Island. Her father, Jerrold E.
Gertz, is a real-estate executive; her mother, Carol, is the co-founder of
Tennis Lady, a national chain of high-fashion shops. Ms. Gertz
went to Horace Mann, an exclusive private school in the Bronx,
then studied art at Parsons School of Design in Manhattan.

"Probably Just a Bug"

When AIDS struck, Ms. Gertz said, "I was just, as they say,   17
starting out in life." Her goals had been simple: "I wanted a
house and kids and animals and to paint my paintings.

She had recently signed on with an art agent, embarking on   18
a career as an illustrator. She had also quit her pack-a-day
smoking habit and joined a health club "to get really healthy,"
she said.

Then fever and a spell of diarrhea hit last summer. A doctor   19
told her it was "probably just a bug," she said. But the symptoms persisted, so she checked into Lenox Hill Hospital.

When her doctor told her the diagnosis, he had tears in his   20
eyes. "I said 'Oh, my God. I'm going to die,'" she recalled. "And
as I said it, I thought to myself, 'No I'm not. Why am I saying
this?' I thought my life was over. 'I'm 22, I'm never going to have
sex again. I'm never going to have children.'"

Determined to Keep Going

From that initial shock, Ms. Gertz bounced back with the   21
ebullience so well known to her friends—they call her Ali for
short—and with the fervor of activism that runs in the family.
Recovering from her first treatment, she returned to her apartment, her pets (a dog, Saki; a cat, Sambucca, and tropical fish)
and a new course in life.

"It's a dreadful disease, but it's also a gift," she said. "I've   22
always been positive, optimistic. I thought, 'What can I do with
it? I like to think I'm here for a purpose. If I die, I would like to
have left something, to make the world a little bit better before
I go, to help people sick like me and prevent others from getting
this. It would make it all worthwhile."

She and friends are organizing a fall theater performance   23

and dinner-dance to raise money for an AIDS newsletter and other AIDS services. Her parents and their friends are planning a spring benefit for an organization they are forming called Concerned Parents and Friends for AIDS Research. To keep her functioning normally, Ms. Gertz each day takes   24
AZT, Acyclovir and Bactrim pills, which fight the virus and opportunistic diseases. "We just have to keep her healthy until there's a breakthrough and they find a cure," her mother said.

"I Started to Cry Softly"

"I'm not afraid of death, but I am afraid of pain," Ms. Gertz   25
said. She is learning psychological and behavioral techniques to withstand it, and doctors have promised medication if she needs it. "As far as dying goes, it's okay," she said. "There's no point in thinking about it now."

But her frequent high spirits do not erase her pain. While   26
watching a soap opera love scene one day, she said, "I started to cry softly."

"I've made a conscious effort not to cry in front of people,"   27
she added. "But I do give myself a certain amount of time each month to be miserable, to cry and to vent."

Ms. Gertz is an only child. Her illness "was an enormous   28
shock," her father said. "AIDS was the furthest thing from my mind. I used to suspect they magnified the statistics to get research money." Now he's giving and raising money himself and feels "anger at AIDS happening to anyone."

"It certainly turned our lives around," Mrs. Gertz said. "It   29
changes your perspective on what's important." For her, every day starts with a morning call to her daughter's apartment, a block away.

One of Ms. Gertz's first concerns was not for herself. "I was   30
worried about my previous boyfriends." she said. "I didn't want them to be sick." Two past boyfriends have been tested, she said and "both of them are O.K."

Her current boyfriend "is wonderful," she said. "He's stood   31
by me." But AIDS has changed their relationship. "Yes, you can have safe sex. I know all the facts, and so does he. But still, in the back of his mind, he is scared, so we don't sleep together any more, and that's rough."

Ms. Gertz has not felt ostracized as many AIDS patents have.   32
But there have been a few exceptions.

"The nurses told me this one resident doctor, a woman, in-   33
sisted that I must have used IV drugs or must have had anal
sex," Ms. Gertz said. She interprets the doctor's own possible
risk by regarding the patient as different.

Loss of a Friend

"And one friend I lost," Ms. Gertz said. "She left. She deserted   34
me." That, too, she understands. "She was with me at Studio 54
during those earlier years, and she was much more sexually active than I was. It wasn't my mortality she was facing; it was her
own. She just couldn't handle it."

Health insurance is a problem that has made her financially   35
dependent on her parents. "I think the insurance company
owes me about $50,000," she said. "I haven't gotten one dime.
They're trying to prove I knew I had this before I signed up for
the policy two years before."

That angers Ms. Gertz because of the dozens of exhaustive,   36
sometimes painful, tests she underwent to find what was wrong.

The Gertz family praises the hospital staff and their doctors,   37
but it does regret that AIDS wasn't checked earlier, Mrs. Gertz
said, "Because of her background, nobody thought this was a
possibility."

"It stands to reason you're going to see more people like Ali,"   38
her mother said, since AIDS symptoms may not show up for 10
or 12 years.

Indeed, such cases are appearing.   39

Dr. Jody Robinson, an internist in Washington who has writ-   40
ten on AIDS, said that other cases like Ms. Gertz's are "out there."

"How many is a tremendous unknown," he said. "It may not   41
be an overwhelming number, but what will it be five or six
years from now?"

The danger, he said, is that because experts have said there   42
has not been an explosive outbreak among heterosexuals, people have become complacent.

"The common wisdom has gone back to the idea that AIDS is   43
really the gay plague and disease of IV drug users that it was
set out to be in the first place, and the warning on heterosexual
spread was a false alarm," he said.

Alison Gertz struggles against AIDS with the benefit of a   44
number of factors unknown to most patients—she has a determined optimism bolstered by the love of family and friends,
financial aid and first-class medical care.

Gathered on a sofa for photographs, the Gertz family was all   45
hugs and smiles. "I never felt from the beginning that this was
anything to be hidden or ashamed of," Mrs. Gertz said. After a
few pictures were taken, she wondered aloud. "Should we be
looking so happy for such a serious subject?"

For a few seconds the family managed sober expressions for   46
the camera. But soon, for at least one more day, the smiles broke
through again.

Questions for Study and Discussion

1. How would you describe Lambert's beginning? How did
   you react to it? Did you think his beginning was effective?
   Why or why not?

2. How did Alison Gertz get AIDS? Did it surprise you that a
   heterosexual female contracted AIDS?

3. In paragraph 22 Alison Gertz says, "It's a dreadful disease, but its also a gift." What does Alison mean by this?

4. Who is Alison Gertz' audience? (Glossary: *Audience*) What
   is her message for this audience? How likely is her audience to hear her message? Explain.

5. What is Lambert's attitude towards AIDS? What in his
   essay led you to this conclusion?

6. How has Lambert organized his essay? What function do
   the running titles serve with his overall organizational plan?

Vocabulary

Refer to your dictionary to define the following words as they
are used in this selection. Then use each word in a sentence of
your own.

promiscuous (2)	embark (18)
affluent (5)	ebullience (21)
rampant (11)	fervor (21)

optimistic (22)   ostracized (32)
opportunistic (24)   bolster (44)

Suggested Writing Assignments

1. How knowledgeable is the American public about AIDS? Do you think we know all the facts? How has the media worked to inform society of hazards and untruths about AIDS? Write an essay in which you discuss what responsibility you believe the media has to keep the public informed.

2. American pop-singer Madonna has recently come under fire for the "lurid" content of some of her videos and stage shows. Madonna explains that her sexual overtones will encourage children to go to their parents and discuss things such as safe sex and premarital sex. How do you react to her reasoning? Is her approach for bringing these topics into the open a reasonable one? Write an essay in which you discuss the role of sex education in our fight against AIDS.

5

PARAGRAPHS

Within an essay, the paragraph is the most important unit of thought. Like the essay, it has its own main idea, often stated directly in a topic sentence. Like a good essay, a good paragraph is unified: it avoids digressions and develops its main idea. Paragraphs use many of the rhetorical techniques that essays use, techniques such as classification, comparison and contrast, and cause and effect. In fact, many writers find it helpful to think of the paragraph as a very small, compact essay.

Here is a paragraph from an essay on testing:

> Multiple-choice questions distort the purposes of education. Picking one answer among four is very different from thinking a question through to an answer of one's own, and far less useful in life. Recognition of vocabulary and isolated facts makes the best kind of multiple-choice questions, so these dominate the tests, rather than questions that test the use of knowledge. Because schools want their children to perform well, they are often tempted to teach the limited sorts of knowledge most useful on the tests.

This paragraph, like all well-written paragraphs, has several distinguishing characteristics: it is unified, coherent, and adequately developed. It is unified in that every sentence and every idea relate to the main idea, stated in the topic sentence, "Multiple-choice questions distort the purposes of education." It is coherent in that the sentences and ideas are arranged logically and the relationships among them are made clear by the use of effective transitions. Finally, the paragraph is adequately developed in that it presents a short but persuasive argument supporting its main idea.

How much development is "adequate" development? The answer depends on many things: how complicated or controversial the main idea is; what readers already know and believe; how much space the writer is permitted. Everyone, or nearly everyone, agrees that the earth circles around the sun; a single sentence would be enough to make that point. A writer trying to argue that affirmative action has outlived its usefulness, however, would need many sentences, indeed many paragraphs, to develop that idea convincingly.

Here is another model of an effective paragraph. As you read this paragraph about the resourcefulness of pigeons in evading attempts to control them, pay particular attention to its controlling idea, unity, development, and coherence.

> Pigeons [and their human friends] have proved remarkably resourceful in evading nearly all the controls, from birth-control pellets to carbide shells to pigeon apartment complexes, that pigeon-haters have devised. One of New York's leading museums once put large black rubber owls on its wide ledges to discourage the large number of pigeons that roosted there. Within the day the pigeons had gotten over their fear of owls and were back perched on the owls' heads. A few years ago San Francisco put a sticky coating on the ledges of some public buildings, but the pigeons got used to the goop and came back to roost. The city then tried trapping, using electric owls, and periodically exploding carbide shells outside a city building, hoping the noise would scare the pigeons away. It did, but not for long, and the program was abandoned. More frequent explosions probably would have distressed the humans in the area more than the birds. Philadelphia tried a feed that makes pigeons vomit, and then, they hoped, go away. A New York firm claimed it had a feed that made a pigeon's nervous system send "danger signals" to the other members of its flock.

The controlling idea is stated at the beginning in a topic sentence. Other sentences in the paragraph support the controlling idea with examples. Since all the separate examples illustrate how pigeons have evaded attempts to control them, the paragraph is unified. Since there are enough examples to convince the reader of the truth of the topic statement, the paragraph is adequately developed. Finally, the regular use of transitional words and phrases such as *once, within the day, a few years ago,* and *then,* lends the paragraph coherence.

How long should a paragraph be? In modern essays most paragraphs range from 50 to 250 words, but some run a full page or more and others may be only a few words long. The best answer is that a paragraph should be long enough to develop its main idea adequately. Some authors, when they find a paragraph running very long, may break it into two or more paragraphs so that readers can pause and catch their breath. Other writers forge ahead, relying on the unity and coherence of their paragraph to keep their readers from getting lost.

Articles and essays that appear in magazines and newspapers often have relatively short paragraphs, some of only one or two sentences. The reason is that they are printed in very narrow columns, which make paragraphs of average length appear very long. But often you will find that these journalistic "paragraphs" could be joined together into a few longer, more normal paragraphs. Longer, more normal paragraphs are the kind you should use in all but journalistic writing.

SIMPLICITY

William Zinsser

*William Zinsser was born in New York City in
1922. After graduating from Princeton University, he worked for the* New York Herald Tribune, *first as a feature writer and later as its
drama editor and film critic. Currently the executive editor of the Book-of-the-Month Club, Zinsser has written a number of books, including*
Pop Goes America *(1966),* The Lunacy Boom
(1970), Writing with a Word Processor *(1983),*
Willie and Dwike: An American Profile *(1984),
and* Writing to Learn *(1988), as well as other
social and cultural commentaries. In this selection from his popular book* On Writing Well,
*Zinsser, reminding us of Thoreau before him,
exhorts the writer to "Simplify, simplify." Notice
that Zinsser's paragraphs are unified and logically developed, and consequently work well
together to support his thesis.*

Clutter is the disease of American writing. We are a society   1
strangling in unnecessary words, circular constructions,
pompous frills and meaningless jargon.

Who can understand the viscous language of everyday Amer-   2
ican commerce and enterprise: the business letter, the interof-
fice memo, the corporation report, the notice from the bank explaining its latest "simplified" statement? What member of an
insurance or medical plan can decipher the brochure that describes what the costs and benefits are? What father or mother
can put together a child's toy—on Christmas Eve or any other
eve—from the instructions on the box? Our national tendency
is to inflate and thereby sound important. The airline pilot who
announces that he is presently anticipating experiencing considerable precipitation wouldn't dream of saying that it may

rain. The sentence is too simple—there must be something wrong with it.

But the secret of good writing is to strip every sentence to its cleanest components. Every word that serves no function, every long word that could be a short word, every adverb that carries the same meaning that's already in the verb, every passive construction that leaves the reader unsure of who is doing what—these are the thousand and one adulterants that weaken the strength of a sentence. And they usually occur, ironically, in proportion to education and rank.

During the late 1960s, the president of a major university wrote a letter to mollify the alumni after a spell of campus unrest. "You are probably aware," he began, "that we have been experiencing very considerable potentially explosive expressions of dissatisfaction on issues only partially related." He meant that the students had been hassling them about different things. I was far more upset by the president's English than by the students' potentially explosive expressions of dissatisfaction. I would have preferred the presidential approach taken by Franklin D. Roosevelt when he tried to convert into English his own government's memos, such as this blackout order of 1942:

> Such preparations shall be made as will completely obscure all Federal buildings and non-Federal buildings occupied by the Federal government during an air raid for any period of time from visibility by reason of internal or external illumination.

"Tell them," Roosevelt said, "that in buildings where they have to keep the work going to put something across the windows."

Simplify, simplify. Thoreau said it, as we are so often reminded, and no American writer more consistently practiced what he preached. Open *Walden* to any page and you will find a man saying in a plain and orderly way what is on his mind:

> I went to the woods because I wished to live deliberately, to front only the essential facts of life, and see if I could not learn what it had to teach, and not, when I came to die, discover that I had not lived. I did not wish to live what was not life, living is so dear; nor did I wish to practice resignation, unless it was quite necessary. I wanted to live deep and suck out all the marrow of life, to live so sturdily

and Spartan-like as to put to rout all that was not life, to cut a broad swath and shave close, to drive life into a corner, and reduce it to its lowest terms, and, if it proved to be mean, why then to get the whole and genuine meanness of it, and publish its meanness to the world; or if it were sublime, to know it by experience, and be able to give a true account of it.

How can the rest of us achieve such enviable freedom from clutter? The answer is to clear our heads of clutter. Clear thinking becomes clear writing; one can't exist without the other. It's impossible for a muddy thinker to write good English. You may get away with it for a paragraph or two, but soon the reader will be lost, and there's no sin so grave, for the reader will not easily be lured back.   7

Who is this elusive creature, the reader? The reader is someone with an attention span of about sixty seconds—a person assailed by forces competing for the minutes that might otherwise be spent on a magazine or a book. At one time these forces weren't so numerous or so possessive: newspapers, radio, spouse, home, children. Today they also include a "home entertainment center" (TV, VCR, video camera, tapes and CDs), pets, a fitness program, a lawn and a garden and all the gadgets that have been bought to keep them spruce, and that most potent of competitors, sleep. The person snoozing in a chair, holding a magazine or a book, is a person who was being given too much unnecessary trouble by the writer.   8

It won't do to say that the reader is too dumb or too lazy to keep pace with the train of thought. If the reader is lost, it's usually because the writer hasn't been careful enough. The carelessness can take any number of forms. Perhaps a sentence is so excessively cluttered that the reader, hacking through the verbiage, simply doesn't know what it means. Perhaps a sentence has been so shoddily constructed that the reader could read it in any of several ways. Perhaps the writer has switched pronouns in midsentence, or has switched tenses, so the reader loses track of who is talking or when the action took place. Perhaps Sentence B is not a logical sequel to Sentence A—the writer, in whose head the connection is clear, hasn't bothered to provide the missing link. Perhaps the writer has used an important word incorrectly by not taking the trouble to look it up. The writer may think that "sanguine" and "sanguinary"   9 mean the same thing, but the difference is a bloody big one. The reader can only infer (speaking of big differences) what the writer is trying to imply.

Faced with such obstacles, readers are at first remarkably tenacious. They blame themselves—they obviously missed something, and they go back over the mystifying sentence, or over the whole paragraph, piecing it out like an ancient rune, making guesses and moving on. But they won't do this for long. The writer is making them work too hard, and they will look for one who is better at the craft.   10

Writers must therefore constantly ask: What am I trying to say? Surprisingly often they don't know. Then they must look at what they have written and ask: Have I said it? Is it clear to someone encountering the subject for the first time? If it's not, that's because some fuzz has worked its way into the machinery. The clear writer is someone clearheaded enough to see this stuff for what it is: fuzz.   11

I don't mean that some people are born clearheaded and are therefore natural writers, whereas others are naturally fuzzy and will never write well. Thinking clearly is a conscious act that writers must force upon themselves, just as if they were embarking on any other project that requires logic: adding up a laundry list or doing an algebra problem. Good writing doesn't come naturally, though most people obviously think it does. The professional writer is constantly being bearded by strangers who say they'd like to "try a little writing sometime"— meaning when they retire from their real profession, like insurance or real estate. Or they say, "I could write a book about that." I doubt it.   12

Writing is hard work. A clear sentence is no accident. Very few sentences come out right the first time, or even the third time. Remember this as a consolation in moments of despair. If you find that writing is hard, it's because it *is* hard. It's one of the hardest things that people do.   13

Questions for Study and Discussion

1. What exactly does Zinsser mean by clutter? How does Zinsser feel that we can free outselves of clutter?

2. In paragraph 3 Zinsser lists a number of "adulterants" that weaken English sentences and claims that "they usually occur, ironically, in proportion to education and rank." Why do you suppose this is true?
3. What is the relationship between thinking and writing for Zinsser?
4. In paragraph 11, Zinsser says that writers must constantly ask themselves some questions. What are these and why are they important?
5. How do Zinsser's first and last paragraphs serve to introduce and conclude his essay? (Glossary: *Beginnings and Endings*.)
6. What is the function of paragraphs 4–6 in the context of the essay?
7. How do the questions in paragraph 2 further Zinsser's purpose? (Glossary: *Rhetorical Question*)

Vocabulary

Refer to your dictionary to define the following words as they are used in this selection. Then use each word in a sentence of your own.

pompous (1)	enviable (7)
decipher (2)	tenacious (10)
adulterants (3)	bearded (12)
mollify (4)	

Suggested Writing Assignments

1. The following pages show a passage from the final manuscript for Zinsser's essay. Carefully study the manuscript and Zinsser's changes, and then write several well-developed paragraphs analyzing the ways he has eliminated clutter.

is too dumb or too lazy to keep pace with the ~~writer's~~ train
of thought. My sympathies are ~~entirely~~ with him.) ~~He's not~~
~~so dumb.~~ (If the reader is lost, it is generally because the
writer ~~of the article~~ has not been careful enough to keep
him on the ~~proper~~ path.

This carelessness can take any number of ~~different~~ forms.
Perhaps a sentence is so excessively ~~long and~~ cluttered that
the reader, hacking his way through ~~all~~ the verbiage, simply
doesn't know what it ~~the writer~~ means. Perhaps a sentence has
been so shoddily constructed that the reader could read it in
any of several ~~two or three different~~ ways. ~~He thinks he knows what~~
~~the writer is trying to say, but he's not sure.~~ Perhaps the
writer has switched pronouns in mid-sentence, or ~~perhaps he~~
has switched tenses, so the reader loses track of who is
talking ~~to whom~~ or ~~exactly~~ when the action took place. Perhaps Sentence B is not a logical sequel to Sentence A -- the
writer, in whose head the connection is ~~perfectly~~ clear, has
not bothered to provide ~~given enough thought to providing~~ the missing link. Perhaps the writer has used an important word incorrectly by not
taking the trouble to look it up ~~and make sure.~~ He may think
that "sanguine" and "sanguinary" mean the same thing, but)
~~I can assure you that~~ (the difference is a bloody big one ~~to the~~
~~reader.~~ The reader ~~He~~ can only ~~try to~~ infer ~~what~~ (speaking of big differences) what the writer is trying to imply.

Faced with these ~~such a variety of~~ obstacles, the reader
is at first a remarkably tenacious bird. He ~~tends to~~ blames
himself. ~~He~~ obviously missed something, ~~he thinks,~~ and he goes
back over the mystifying sentence, or over the whole paragraph,
piecing it out like an ancient rune, making guesses and moving

on. But he won't do this for long. ~~He will soon run out of~~ ~~patience.~~ (The writer is making him work too hard ~~-->harder~~ ~~than he should have to work --~~ and the reader will look for ~~a writer~~ **one** who is better at his craft.

The writer must therefore constantly ask himself: What am I trying to say ~~in this sentence?~~ (Surprisingly often, he doesn't know.) ~~And~~ Then he must look at what he has ~~just~~ written and ask: Have I said it? Is it clear to someone **encountering** ~~who is coming upon~~ the subject for the first time? If it's not**,** ~~clear,~~ it is because some fuzz has worked its way into the machinery. The clear writer is a person ~~who is~~ clear-headed enough to see this stuff for what it is: fuzz.

I don't mean ~~to suggest~~ that some people are born clear-headed and are therefore natural writers, whereas **others** ~~other people~~ are naturally fuzzy and will ~~therefore~~ never write well. Thinking clearly is ~~an entirely~~ conscious act that the writer must **force** ~~keep forcing~~ upon himself, just as if he were **embarking** ~~starting out~~ on any other ~~kind of~~ project that **requires** ~~calls for~~ logic: adding up a laundry list or doing an algebra problem ~~or playing chess.~~ Good writing doesn't ~~just~~ come naturally, though most people obviously think **it does.** ~~it's as easy as walking.~~ The professional

2. If what Zinsser writes about clutter is an accurate assessment, we should easily find numerous examples of clutter all around us. During the next few days, make a point of looking for clutter in the written materials you come across. Choose one example that you find—an article, an essay, a form letter, or a chapter from a textbook, for example—and write an extended analysis explaining how it might have been written more simply. Develop your paragraphs well, make sure they are coherent, and try not to "clutter" your own writing.

OLD AT SEVENTEEN

David Vecsey

David Vecsey was born in Port Washington, New York, in 1969. When the following essay was published in the "About Men" column of the New York Times Magazine, David Vecsey was an eighteen-year-old freshman at Bradley University in Peoria, Illinois. Vecsey loves all sports, but out of his particular interest in baseball he is at work on a novel that is, he says, "half fiction and half fact interweaving events in the narrator's life with those of a baseball team's season from opening day to the World Series." Vecsey says that the theme of "Old at Seventeen" is very important and has enduring interest for him. As you read his account of the many signs of his "aging," pay particular attention to the way he composes his paragraphs.

There are signs that say you're getting older. Getting a driver's license, needing a shave every morning, going to college and reading the front page of a paper before the sports section—these all say a person is getting older. Any man who says getting older comes later, that it's a matter of balding and middle-aged spread, just can't remember, I say.

The most major signal up to now that I was getting old happened late last winter when Richie and Micah appeared at my front door early in the morning. School had been canceled because of a foot of snow. They asked me if I wanted to go on the golf course for a little while. I actually asked them, "For what?"

In the summer, the Plandome Country Club golf course is a haven for doctors and lawyers who like to wear plaid pants and hit a defenseless white ball. It's also good for catching some rays. But in the winter, it has traditionally been a haven for children who soar down "Old Glory" hill as fast as they can on a flimsy piece of wood or plastic. When I was younger, friends and I spent every waking moment out on the golf course, sledding. Now I was asking them why they wanted to go out there. Soon I'll be calling pants "trousers" and reading the *Reader's Digest* on a regular basis.

I agreed to go with them, and I put on jeans and a sweatshirt, 4 as opposed to the snowsuit my mother used to bundle me up in when I was 8 or 9. I wisely decided to wear boots instead of sneakers. Old Glory is the most popular hill on the course, and is literally 50 yards from my house, so we were there in no time. I helped Richie carry the toboggan; I no longer own a sled.

When we reached the top of Old Glory, my first thought was 5 that it must have shrunk, because it is no longer the mountain it used to be. It looked more like a fairway with snow on it. I watched the little kids zooming down the hill at top speeds, and I noticed something: they no longer ride Flexible Flyers or Yankee Clippers. They own sleds of the 1980's, plastic structures that look like bikes and cars and boats and things. I think some even have power steering and shocks.

Richie dropped the toboggan, and we figured out the best 6 route to take down to the bottom. I suggested that we take a side way, so we wouldn't hit the bumps in the middle. I was greeted with sour looks of disgust. Hitting all the bumps was the idea. I was berated into going first—taking the middle path. My knees cracked and my back ached as I crouched into a sitting position on the toboggan. Micah pushed me off, and I slowly started to descend the hill. "This isn't so bad," I said, "I used to do this all the time."

Then I picked up speed. The nightmare began. Snow flew into 7 my face as I hit about 60 miles an hour. I screamed at the top of my lungs, only to be greeted by a mouthful of snow. Out of control, I screamed at people to get out of the way. Bodies jumped and dodged aside. Up ahead, a snow bank headed right toward me. I was engulfed in it. Snow was everywhere—down my shoes, down my pants, about a gallon of it down my throat.

I ached and was freezing to death. There's no way, I thought, 8 that I used to do this every day, all day. That was another little kid, a masochist, not me. I stood up and turned around to see two sleds, each containing a small child of about 12. They were going too fast, and they collided. The two children lay there motionless. I ran to help, and I noticed that the reason they were motionless was because they were laughing too hard to move. "That was awesome, Jimmy. Let's do it again," one yelled, and they grabbed their sleds and ran up the hill.

I decided to do the same, and headed up the hill. That is when   9
it finally looked like the massive mountain I remembered. Each step I took became heavier and heavier. I dragged the toboggan of death behind me as I trudged up the hill. I reached the top, where Richie and Micah anxiously awaited their turns. They wanted to try it standing up.

I told them that, from then on, I'd prefer to observe. More   10
sour looks. They disappeared into the crowd, and I looked around. One father was yelling at his son for going too fast, and another scolded his son for not beating his friend in a race. A crowd of mothers huddled together over a steaming thermos, talking about what idiots their husbands were, always excited about last week's football game. "Who are they playing in the Super Bowl?" one woman asked. "I think they already played it," her friend said. "Who won?" "CBS, I think." Their conversation rolled on, and I walked away.

A group of children formed a train by hanging onto one an-   11
other's ankles. It reminded me of when we used to play "hijack the sled." We'd all start within five feet of one another at the top of the hill, but once we picked up speed, the object was to crash into the other players, knock them off, and take their empty sleds down the hill. The man who got to the bottom first won. Ah, those were the days. But I'm civilized now. I'd rather play "negotiation," in which we sit on the sleds at the top of the hill and discuss life.

A boy of about 11 sat on his sled, holding snow up to his   12
bloody nose. His friends called him a wimp because he wouldn't go down again. A little girl punched out a little boy for touching her sled, and he went crying to his mom, who was busy listening to her other son complain about the cold. The mom's face turned red, partially because of the cold, but mostly because of her wrath. She grabbed both kids' wrists and dragged them to the car. Their day is history now. Never complain to a cold mother, it's bad news.

I came to the conclusion that leaving the golf course wasn't   13
such a bad idea. I'm no longer the weatherproof tot I used to be. Instead, I'm a teen-ager who would rather read or watch a

movie than wrap my body around a tree while sledding. If the me of my Old Glory days met the me of my teen-age years, he would call me a lame-o and find someone else to sled with. He would be right, too, but sledding is for the younger crowd, not for us ancient 17-year-olds.

I miss that wiry little kid who used to daredevil on sleds to   14
impress his friends. Fear was no object then. But today the thought of coasting down ice and snow isn't my idea of Eden. I'll watch, thanks, with the other old people.

Questions for Study and Discussion

1. Vecsey realized that he was getting old when he went sledding. What in particular made him realize that he was not as young as he used to be?
2. Identify the topic sentences in paragraphs 1, 2, and 7. (Glossary: *Topic Sentence*) How does Vecsey develop these topic sentences?
3. What transitions, if any, has Vecsey used between paragraphs 10 and 11 and between paragraphs 11 and 12? (Glossary: *Transitions*)
4. In the context of the whole essay what is the function of paragraph 10? Of paragraph 12?
5. Much of Vecsey's essay is a narrative. (Glossary: *Narration*) Where does the narrative proper begin? What is the nature of the material that precedes the narrative proper?
6. What is Vecsey's tone in this essay? (Glossary: *Tone*) What in particular leads you to your assessment?

Vocabulary

Refer to your dictionary to define the following words as they are used in this selection. Then use each word in a sentence of your own.

haven (3)   engulfed (7)
berated (6)   masochist (8)

trudged (9)   wiry (14)
wimp (12)

Suggested Writing Assignments

1. Write an essay modeled on Vecsey's in which you consider signs that you, too, are growing older. Support your thesis with small, insightful examples and then with one more detailed extended example. Pay particular attention to the way in which your topic sentences are established and positioned within the paragraphs as well as the way the paragraphs themselves are developed.

2. Select one of the following statements as the thesis for a short essay. Make sure that each paragraph of your essay is unified, coherent, and adequately developed.

    Car pooling is beneficial but makes demands of people.

    Social activities for first-year college students are limited.

    A college should be a community not merely a collection of people.

    College is expensive.

DEATH AND JUSTICE: HOW CAPITAL PUNISHMENT AFFIRMS LIFE

Edward I. Koch

Democrat Edward I. Koch was mayor of New York City from 1978 to 1990. A New Yorker by birth, Koch quickly established himself as a no-holds-barred, nothing-left-unsaid, tough-guy spokesman for the people he served. He led his city through a period of economic and social change characterized by labor strikes, a rise in violent street crime, and unemployment. In the following article, which first appeared in the New Republic *in March 1985, Koch argues in favor of the death penalty. Using a technique in keeping with his personality, Koch sets up his opponents' arguments like so many cans on a fence and then attempts to shoot them full of holes. As you read his essay, notice how he uses facts, statistics, quotations, and numerous examples to develop his paragraphs.*

L ast December a man named Robert Lee Willie, who had   1
been convicted of raping and murdering an 18-year-old woman, was executed in the Louisiana state prison. In a statement issued several minutes before his death, Mr. Willie said: "Killing people is wrong. . . . It makes no difference whether it's citizens, countries, or governments. Killing is wrong." Two weeks later in South Carolina, an admitted killer named Joseph Carl Shaw was put to death for murdering two teenagers. In an appeal to the governor for clemency, Mr. Shaw wrote: "Killing is wrong when I did it. Killing is wrong when you do it. I hope you have the courage and moral strength to stop the killing."

It is a curiosity of modern life that we find ourselves being   2
lectured on morality by cold-blooded killers. Mr. Willie previously had been convicted of aggravated rape, aggravated kidnapping, and the murders of a Louisiana deputy and a man

from Missouri. Mr. Shaw committed another murder a week before the two for which he was executed, and admitted mutilating the body of the 14-year-old girl he killed. I can't help wondering what prompted these murderers to speak out against killing as they entered the deathhouse door. Did their newfound reverence for life stem from the realization that they were about to lose their own?

Life is indeed precious, and I believe the death penalty helps to affirm this fact. Had the death penalty been a real possibility in the minds of these murderers, they might well have stayed their hand. They might have shown moral awareness before their victims died, and not after. Consider the tragic death of Rosa Velez, who happened to be home when a man named Luis Vera burglarized her apartment in Brooklyn. "Yeah, I shot her," Vera admitted. "She knew me, and I knew I wouldn't go to the chair."

During my twenty-two years in public service, I have heard the pros and cons of capital punishment expressed with special intensity. As a district leader, councilman, congressman, and mayor, I have represented constituencies generally thought of as liberal. Because I support the death penalty for heinous crimes of murder, I have sometimes been the subject of emotional and outraged attacks by voters who find my position reprehensible or worse. I have listened to their ideas. I have weighed their objections carefully. I still support the death penalty. The reasons I maintain my position can be best understood by examining the arguments most frequently heard in opposition.

1. *The death penalty is "barbaric."* Sometimes opponents of capital punishment horrify with tales of lingering death on the gallows, of faulty electric chairs, or of agony in the gas chamber. Partly in response to such protests, several states such as North Carolina and Texas switched to execution by lethal injection. The condemned person is put to death painlessly, without ropes, voltage, bullets, or gas. Did this answer the objections of death penalty opponents? Of course not. On June 22, 1984, the *New York Times* published an editorial that sarcastically attacked the new "hygienic" method of death by injection, and stated that "execution can never be made humane through science." So it's not the method that really troubles opponents. It's the death itself they consider barbaric.

Admittedly, capital punishment is not a pleasant topic. How-   6
ever, one does not have to like the death penalty in order to support it any more than one must like radical surgery, radiation,
or chemotherapy in order to find necessary these attempts at
curing cancer. Ultimately we may learn how to cure cancer with
a simple pill. Unfortunately, that day has not yet arrived. Today
we are faced with the choice of letting the cancer spread or trying to cure it with the methods available, methods that one day
will almost certainly be considered barbaric. But to give up and
do nothing would be far more barbaric and would certainly delay the discovery of an eventual cure. The analogy between cancer and murder is imperfect, because murder is not the "disease" we are trying to cure. The disease is injustice. We may not
like the death penalty, but it must be available to punish crimes
of cold-blooded murder, cases in which any other form of
punishment would be inadequate and, therefore, unjust. If we
create a society in which injustice is not tolerated, incidents of
murder—the most flagrant form of injustice—will diminish.

2. *No other major democracy uses the death penalty.* No other   7
major democracy—in fact, few other countries of any description—are plagued by a murder rate such as that in the United
States. Fewer and fewer Americans can remember the days when
unlocked doors were the norm and murder was a rare and ter-
rible offense. In America the murder rate climbed 122 percent
between 1963 and 1980. During that same period, the murder
rate in New York City increased by almost 400 percent, and the
statistics are even worse in many other cities. A study at M.I.T.
showed that based on 1970 homicide rates a person who lived in
a large American city ran a greater risk of being murdered than
an American soldier in World War II ran of being killed in combat. It is not surprising that the laws of each country differ according to differing conditions and traditions. If other countries had our murder problem, the cry for capital punishment
would be just as loud as it is here. And I daresay that any other
major democracy where 75 percent of the people supported the
death penalty would soon enact it into law.

3. *An innocent person might be executed by mistake.* Consider   8
the work of Hugo Adam Bedau, one of the most implacable foes
of capital punishment in this country. According to Mr. Bedau,
it is "false sentimentality to argue that the death penalty should

be abolished because of the abstract possibility that an innocent person might be executed." He cites a study of the 7,000 executions in this country from 1893 to 1971, and concludes that the record fails to show that such cases occur. The main point, however, is this. If government functioned only when the possibility of error didn't exist, government wouldn't function at all. Human life deserves special protection, and one of the best ways to guarantee that protection is to assure that convicted murderers do not kill again. Only the death penalty can accomplish this end. In a recent case in New Jersey, a man named Richard Biegenwald was freed from prison after serving 18 years for murder; since his release he has been convicted of committing four murders. A prisoner named Lemuel Smith, who, while serving four life sentences for murder (plus two life sentences for kidnapping and robbery) in New York's Green Haven Prison, lured a woman corrections officer into the chaplain's office and strangled her. He then mutilated and dismembered her body. An additional life sentence for Smith is meaningless. Because New York has no death penalty statute, Smith has effectively been given a license to kill.

But the problem of multiple murder is not confined to the nation's penitentiaries. In 1981, 91 police officers were killed in the line of duty in this country. Seven percent of those arrested in the cases that have been solved had a previous arrest for murder. In New York City in 1976 and 1977, 85 persons arrested for homicide had a previous arrest for murder. Six of these individuals had two previous arrests for murder, and one had four previous murder arrests. During those two years the New York police were arresting for murder persons with a previous arrest for murder on the average of one every 8.5 days. This is not surprising when we learn that in 1975, for example, the median time served in Massachusetts for homicide was less than two and a half years. In 1976 a study sponsored by the Twentieth Century Fund found that the average time served in the United States for first-degree murder is ten years. The median time served may be considerably lower.

4. Capital punishment cheapens the value of human life. On the contrary, it can be easily demonstrated that the death penalty strengthens the value of human life. If the penalty for rape were lowered, clearly it would signal a lessened regard for the victims' suffering, humiliation, and personal integrity. It would cheapen their horrible experience, and expose them to an increased danger of recurrence. When we lower the penalty for murder, it signals a lessened regard for the value of the victim's life. Some critics of capital punishment, such as columnist Jimmy Breslin, have suggested that a life sentence is actually a harsher penalty for murder than death. This is sophistic nonsense. A few killers may decide not to appeal a death sentence, but the overwhelming majority make every effort to stay alive. It is by exacting the highest penalty for the taking of human life that we affirm the highest value of human life.

5. *The death penalty is applied in a discriminatory manner.* 11 This factor no longer seems to be the problem it once was. The appeals process for a condemned prisoner is lengthy and painstaking. Every effort is made to see that the verdict and sentence were fairly arrived at. However, assertions of discrimination are not an argument for ending the death penalty but for extending it. It is not justice to exclude everyone from the penalty of the law if a few are found to be so favored. Justice requires that the law be applied equally to all.

6. *Thou Shalt Not Kill.* The Bible is our greatest source of 12 moral inspiration. Opponents of the death penalty frequently cite the sixth of the Ten Commandments in an attempt to prove that capital punishment is divinely proscribed. In the original Hebrew, however, the Sixth Commandment reads "Thou Shalt Not Commit Murder," and the Torah specifies capital punishment for a variety of offenses. The biblical viewpoint has been upheld by philosophers throughout history. The greatest thinkers of the 19th century—Kant, Locke, Hobbes, Rousseau, Montesquieu, and Mill—agreed that natural law properly authorizes the sovereign to take life in order to vindicate justice. Only Jeremy Bentham was ambivalent. Washington, Jefferson, and Franklin endorsed it. Abraham Lincoln authorized executions for deserters in wartime. Alexis de Tocqueville, who expressed profound respect for American institutions, believed that the death penalty was indispensable to the support of social order. The United States Constitution, widely admired as one of the seminal achievements in the history of humanity, condemns cruel and inhuman punishment, but does not condemn capital punishment.

7. The death penalty is state-sanctioned murder. This is the 13 defense with which Messrs. Willie and Shaw hoped to soften the resolve of those who sentenced them to death. By saying in effect, "You're no better than I am," the murderer seeks to bring his accusers down to his own level. It is also a popular argument among opponents of capital punishment, but a transparently false one. Simply put, the state has rights that the private individual does not. In a democracy, those rights are given to the state by the electorate. The execution of a lawfully condemned killer is no more an act of murder than is legal imprisonment an act of kidnapping. If an individual forces a neighbor to pay him money under threat of punishment, it's called extortion. If the state does it, it's called taxation. Rights and responsibilities surrendered by the individual are what give the state its power to govern. This contract is the foundation of civilization itself.

Everyone wants his or her rights, and will defend them 14 jealously. Not everyone, however, wants responsibilities, especially the painful responsibilities that come with law enforcement. Twenty-one years ago a woman named Kitty Genovese was assaulted and murdered on a street in New York. Dozens of neighbors heard her cries for help but did nothing to assist her. They didn't even call the police. In such a climate the criminal understandably grows bolder. In the presence of moral cowardice, he lectures us on our supposed failings and tries to equate his crimes with our quest for justice.

The death of anyone—even a convicted killer—diminishes us 15 all. But we are diminished even more by a justice system that fails to function. It is an illusion to let ourselves believe that doing away with capital punishment removes the murderer's deed from our conscience. The rights of society are paramount. When we protect guilty lives, we give up innocent lives in exchange. When opponents of capital punishment say to the state, "I will not let you kill in my name," they are also saying to murderers: "You can kill in your *own* name as long as I have an excuse for not getting involved."

It is hard to imagine anything worse than being murdered 16 while neighbors do nothing. But something worse exists. When those same neighbors shrink back from justly punishing the murderer, the victim dies twice.

Questions for Study and Discussion

1. In your own words, what is Koch's thesis, and where does he present it?

2. Is Koch's argument in favor of capital punishment based more on his desire for punishment or on his belief that it functions as a deterrent? Cite references from the text to support your answer.

3. How do paragraphs 1–3 function in the context of Koch's essay? Could Koch have made his argument just as effectively without them? Explain.

4. What kinds of evidence does Koch use to support his arguments for the death penalty? How does Koch organize his evidence within each paragraph? Which kinds of evidence did you find the most convincing? Why?

5. Koch begins paragraphs 5, 7, 8, 10, 11, 12 and 13 with his opponent's argument against capital punishment. How well does this strategy work? Did you find Koch's refutation of each of these arguments convincing? Explain why or why not.

6. Identify the analogy that Koch uses in paragraph 6. (Glossary: *Analogy*) Explain how the analogy works in the context of Koch's argument?

7. Explain the meaning of Koch's title. In what ways can the death penalty actually affirm that which it so blatantly snuffs out?

Vocabulary

Refer to your dictionary to define the following words as they are used in this selection. Then use each word in a sentence of your own.

clemency (1)	median (9)
constituencies (4)	sophistic (10)
heinous (4)	proscribed (12)
reprehensible (4)	ambivalent (12)
lethal (5)	seminal (12)
implacable (8)	extortion (13)

Suggested Writing Assignments

1. Koch supports the death penalty for what he calls "heinous crimes of murder." What do you suppose Koch means by "heinous crimes of murder"? If a society can decide in favor of the death penalty, how does it then decide which crimes will be so punished? Write an essay in which you present your thinking on this issue.

2. In a letter to the editor, argue against Koch's proposal. What materials in Koch's essay can you turn to your own use? What kinds of appeals will you make to your audience? Can it be argued that the death penalty is nothing more than legalized murder?

6

TRANSITIONS

Transitions are words and phrases that are used to signal the relationships between ideas in an essay and to join the various parts of an essay together. Writers use transitions to relate ideas within sentences, between sentences, and between paragraphs. Perhaps the most common type of transition is the so-called transitional expression. Following is a list of transitional expressions categorized according to their functions.

ADDITION: and, again, too, also, in addition, further, furthermore, moreover, besides

CAUSE AND EFFECT: therefore, consequently, thus, accordingly, as a result, hence, then, so

COMPARISON: similarly, likewise, by comparison

CONCESSION: to be sure, granted, of course, it is true, to tell the truth, certainly, with the exception of, although this may be true, even though, naturally

CONTRAST: but, however, in contrast, on the contrary, on the other hand, yet, nevertheless, after all, in spite of

EXAMPLE: for example, for instance

PLACE: elsewhere, here, above, below, farther on, there, beyond, nearby, opposite to, around

RESTATEMENT: that is, as I have said, in other words, in simpler terms, to put it differently, simply stated

SEQUENCE: first, second, third, next, finally

SUMMARY: in conclusion, to conclude, to summarize, in brief, in short

TIME: afterward, later, earlier, subsequently, at the same time, simultaneously, immediately, this time, until now, before, meanwhile, shortly, soon, currently, when, lately, in the meantime, formerly

Besides transitional expressions, there are two other important ways to make transitions: by using pronoun reference and by repeating key words and phrases. This paragraph begins with the phrase "Besides transitional expressions": the phrase contains the transitional word *besides* and also repeats an earlier idea. Thus the reader knows that this discussion is moving toward a new but related idea. Repetition can also give a word or idea emphasis: "Foreigners look to America as a land of freedom. Freedom, however, is not something all Americans enjoy."

Pronoun reference avoids monotonous repetition of nouns and phrases. Without pronouns, these two sentences are wordy and tiring to read: "Jim went to the concert, where he heard some of Beethoven's music. Afterwards, Jim bought a recording of some of Beethoven's music." A more graceful and readable passage results if two pronouns are substituted in the second sentence: "Afterwards, he bought a recording of it." The second version has another advantage in that it is now more tightly related to the first sentence. The transition between the two sentences is smoother.

In the following example, notice how Rachel Carson uses transitional expressions, repetition of words and ideas, and pronoun reference:

> Under primitive agricultural conditions the farmer had few insect problems. *These* arose with the intensification of agriculture—the devotion of immense acreages to a single crop. *Such a system* set the stage for explosive increases in specific insect populations. Single-crop farming does not take advantage of the principles by which nature works; *it* is agriculture as an engineer might conceive it to be. Nature has introduced great variety into the landscape, but man has displayed a passion for

pronoun reference

repeated key idea

pronoun reference

pronoun reference

repeated key word

repeated key idea

simplifying *it. Thus he* undoes the built-in checks and balances by which nature holds the species within bounds. One important natural *check* is a limit on the amount of suitable habitat for each species. *Obviously then,* an insect that lives on wheat can build up its population to much higher levels on a farm devoted to wheat than on one in which wheat is intermingled with other crops to which the insect is not adapted.

The same thing happens in other situations. A generation or more ago, the towns of large areas of the United States lined their streets with the noble elm tree. *Now* the beauty *they* hopefully created is threatened with complete destruction as disease sweeps through the elms, carried by a beetle that would have only limited chance to build up large populations and to spread from tree to tree if the elms were only occasional trees in a richly diversified planting.

transitional expression; pronoun reference

transitional expression

transitional expression; pronoun reference

Carson's transitions in this passage enhance its *coherence*— that quality of good writing that results when all sentences, paragraphs and longer divisions of an essay are effectively and naturally connected.

WHY I WANT TO HAVE A FAMILY

Lisa Brown

When she wrote the following essay, Lisa Brown was a junior majoring in American Studies at the University of Texas. In her essay, which was published as a "My Turn" column in the October 1984 issue of Newsweek on Campus, *she uses a variety of transitional devices to put together a coherent argument that many women in their drive to success have overlooked the potential for fulfillment inherent in good relationships and family life.*

For years the theory of higher education operated something like this: men went to college to get rich, and women went to college to marry rich men. It was a wonderful little setup, almost mathematical in its precision. To disturb it would have been to rock an American institution.

During the '60s, though, this theory lost much of its luster. As the nation began to recognize the idiocy of relegating women to a secondary role, women soon joined men in what once were male-only pursuits. This rebellious decade pushed women toward independence, showed them their potential and compelled them to take charge of their lives. Many women took the opportunity and ran with it. Since then feminine autonomy has been the rule, not the exception, at least among college women.

That's the good news. The bad news is that the invisible push has turned into a shove. Some women are downright obsessive about success, to the point of becoming insular monuments to selfishness and fierce bravado, the condescending sort that hawks: "I don't need *anybody*. So there." These women dismiss children and marriage as unbearably outdated and potentially harmful to their up-and-coming careers. This notion of independence smacks of egocentrism. What do these women fear? Why can't they slow down long enough to remember that relationships and a family life are not inherently awful things?

Granted that for centuries women were on the receiving end   4
of some shabby treatment. Now, in an attempt to liberate college women from the constraints that forced them almost
exclusively into teaching or nursing as a career outside the
home—always subject to the primary career of motherhood—
some women have gone too far. Any notion of motherhood
seems to be regarded as an unpleasant reminder of the past,
when homemakers were imprisoned by husbands, tots and
household chores. In short, many women consider motherhood
a time-consuming obstacle to the great joy of working outside
the home.

The rise of feminism isn't the only answer. Growing up has   5
something to do with it, too. Most people find themselves in a
bind as they hit their late 20s: they consider the ideals they
grew up with and find that these don't necessarily mix with the
ones they've acquired. The easiest thing to do, it sometimes
seems, is to throw out the precepts their parents taught. Growing up, my friends and I were enchanted by the idea of starting
new traditions. We didn't want self-worth to be contingent upon
whether there was a man or child around the house to make us
feel wanted.

I began to reconsider my values after my sister and a friend   6
had babies. I was entertained by their pregnancies and fascinated by the births; I was also thankful that I wasn't the one
who had to change the diapers every day. I was a doting aunt
only when I wanted to be. As my sister's and friend's lives
changed, though, my attitude changed. I saw their days flip-
flop between frustration and joy. Though these two women lost
the freedom to run off to the beach or to a bar, they gained
something else—an abstract happiness that reveals itself when
they talk about Jessica's or Amanda's latest escapade or vocabulary addition. Still in their 20s, they shuffle work and motherhood with the skill of poker players. I admire them, and I marvel at their kids. Spending time with the Jessicas and Amandas
of the world teaches us patience and sensitivity and gives us a
clue into our own pasts. Children are also reminders that there
is a future and that we must work to ensure its quality.

Now I feel challenged by the idea of becoming a parent. I   7
want to decorate a nursery and design Halloween costumes; I

want to answer my children's questions and help them learn to read. I want to be unselfish. But I've spent most of my life working in the opposite direction: toward independence, no emotional or financial strings attached. When I told a friend—one who likes kids but never, ever wants them—that I'd decided to accommodate motherhood, she accused me of undermining my career, my future, my life. "If that's all you want, then why are you even in college?" she asked.

The answer's simple: I want to be a smart mommy. I have solid career plans and look forward to working. I make a distinction between wanting kids and wanting nothing but kids. And I've accepted that I'll have to give up a few years of full-time work to allow time for being pregnant and buying Pampers. As for undermining my life, I'm proud of my decision because I think it's evidence that the women's movement is working. While liberating women from the traditional childbearing role, the movement has given respectability to motherhood by recognizing that it's not a brainless task like dishwashing. At the same time, women who choose not to have children are not treated as oddities. That certainly wasn't the case even 15 years ago. While the graying, middle-aged bachelor was respected, the female equivalent—tagged a spinster—was automatically suspect. 8

Today, women have choices: about careers, their bodies, children. I am grateful that women are no longer forced into motherhood as a function of their biology; it's senseless to assume that having a uterus qualifies anyone to be a good parent. By the same token, it is ridiculous for women to abandon all maternal desire because it might jeopardize personal success. Some women make the decision to go childless without ever analyzing their true needs or desires. They forget that motherhood can add to personal fulfillment. 9

I wish those fiercely independent women wouldn't look down upon those of us who, for whatever reason, choose to forgo much of the excitement that runs in tandem with being single, liberated and educated. Excitement also fills a family life; it just comes in different ways. 10

I'm not in college because I'll learn how to make tastier pot roast. I'm a student because I want to make sense of the world 11 and of myself. By doing so, I think I'll be better prepared to be a mother to the new lives that I might bring into the world. I'll also be a better me. It's a package deal I don't want to turn down.

Questions for Study and Discussion

1. What is Brown arguing for in this essay? What does she say prompted a change in her attitude? (Glossary: *Attitude*)
2. Against what group is Brown arguing? What does she find wrong with the beliefs of that group?
3. What reasons does she provide for wanting to have a family?
4. Identify Brown's use of transitions in paragraphs 2, 3, 4, 6, 8, and 9. How do these help you as a reader to follow her point?
5. What are the implications for you of Brown's last two sentences in paragraph 6: "Spending time with the Jessicas and Amandas of the world teaches us patience and sensitivity and gives us a clue into our pasts. Children are also the reminders that there is a future and that we must work to ensure its quality"?
6. For what audience do you think this essay is intended? Do you think men would be as interested as women in the author's viewpoint? Explain. (Glossary: *Audience*)

Vocabulary

Refer to your dictionary to define the following words as they are used in this selection. Then use each word in a sentence of your own.

relegating (2)	precepts (5)
autonomy (2)	contingent (5)
insular (3)	doting (6)
bravado (3)	tandem (10)

Suggested Writing Assignments

1. Write an essay in which you argue any one of the following positions with regard to the women's movement: it has gone too far; it is out of control; it is misdirected; it hasn't gone far enough or done enough; it needs to reach more women and men; it should lower its sights; a position of your own different from the above. Whichever position you argue, be sure that you provide sufficient evidence to support your point of view.

2. Fill in the following statement and write an argument in support of it:

   The purpose of a college education is to _____

   _____ .

How I Got Smart

Steve Brody

Steve Brody is a retired high-school English teacher who enjoys writing about the lighter side of teaching. He was born in Chicago in 1915 and received his bachelor's degree in English from Columbia University. In addition to his articles in educational publications, Brody has published many newspaper articles on travel and a humorous book about golf, How to Break Ninety Before You Reach It *(1979). As you read his account of how love made him smart, notice the way he uses transitional words and expressions to unify his essay and make it a seamless whole.*

A common misconception among youngsters attending school is that their teachers were child prodigies. Who else but a bookworm, prowling the libraries and disdaining the normal youngster's propensity for play rather than study, would grow up to be a teacher anyway?

I tried desperately to explain to my students that the image they had of me as an ardent devotee of books and homework during my adolescence was a bit out of focus. Au contraire! I hated compulsory education with a passion. I could never quite accept the notion of having to go to school while the fish were biting.

Consequently, my grades were somewhat bearish. That's how my father, who dabbled in the stock market, described them, Presenting my report card for my father to sign was like serving him a subpoena. At midterm and other sensitive periods, my father kept a low profile.

But in my sophomore year, something beautiful and exciting happened. Cupid aimed his arrow and struck me squarely in the heart. All at once, I enjoyed going to school, if only to gaze at the lovely face beneath the raven tresses in English II. My princess sat near the pencil sharpener, and that year I ground up enough pencils to fuel a campfire.

Alas, Debbie was far beyond my wildest dreams. We were 5 separated not only by five rows of desks, but by about 50 I.Q. points. She was the top student in English II, the apple of Mrs. Larrivee's eye. I envisioned how eagerly Debbie's father awaited her report card.

Occasionally, Debbie would catch me staring at her, and she 6 would flash a smile—an angelic smile that radiated enlightenment and quickened my heartbeat. It was a smile that signaled hope and made me temporarily forget the intellectual gulf that separated us.

I schemed desperately to bridge that gulf. And one day, as I 7 was passing the supermarket, an idea came to me.

A sign in the window announced that the store was offering 8 the first volume of a set of encyclopedias at the introductory price of 29 cents. The remaining volumes would cost $2.49 each, but it was no time to be cynical.

I purchased Volume I—Aardvark to Asteroid—and began my 9 venture into the world of knowledge. I would henceforth become a seeker of facts. I would become chief egghead in English II and sweep the princess off her feet with a surge of erudition. I had it all planned.

My first opportunity came one day in the cafeteria line. I 10 looked behind me and there she was.

"Hi," she said. 11

After a pause, I wet my lips and said, "Know where anchovies 12 come from?"

She seemed surprised. "No, I don't." 13

I breathed a sigh of relief. "The anchovy lives in salt water 14 and is rarely found in fresh water." I had to talk fast, so that I could get all the facts in before we reached the cash register. "Fishermen catch anchovies in the Mediterranean Sea and along the Atlantic coast near Spain and Portugal."

"How fascinating," said Debbie. 15

"The anchovy is closely related to the herring. It is thin and 16 silvery in color. It has a long snout and a very large mouth."

"Incredible." 17

"Anchovies are good in salads, mixed with eggs, and are often 18 used as appetizers before dinner, but they are salty and cannot be digested too rapidly."

Debbie shook her head in disbelief. It was obvious that I had made quite an impression.   19

A few days later, during a fire drill, I sidled up to her and asked, "Ever been to the Aleutian Islands?"   20

"Never have," she replied.   21

"Might be a nice place to visit, but I certainly wouldn't want to live there," I said.   22

"Why not?" said Debbie, playing right into my hands.   23

"Well, the climate is forbidding. There are no trees on any of the 100 or more islands in the group. The ground is rocky and very little plant life can grow on it."   24

"I don't think I'd even care to visit," she said.   25

The fire drill was over and we began to file into the building, so I had to step it up to get the natives in. "The Aleuts are short and sturdy and have dark skin and black hair. They subsist on fish, and they trap blue fox, seal and otter for their valuable fur."   26

Debbie's hazel eyes widened in amazement. She was undoubtedly beginning to realize that she wasn't dealing with an ordinary lunkhead. She was gaining new and valuable insights instead of engaging in the routine small talk one would expect from most sophomores.   27

Luck was on my side, too. One day I was browsing through the library during my study period. I spotted Debbie sitting at a table, absorbed in a crossword puzzle. She was frowning, apparently stumped on a word. I leaned over and asked if I could help.   28

"Four-letter word for Oriental female servant," Debbie said.   29

"Try *amah*," I said, quick as a flash.   30

Debbie filled in the blanks, then turned to stare at me in amazement. "I don't believe it," she said. "I just don't believe it."   31

And so it went, that glorious, amorous, joyous sophomore year. Debbie seemed to relish our little conversations and hung on my every word. Naturally, the more I read, the more my confidence grew. I expatiated freely on such topics as adenoids, air brakes, and arthritis.   32

In the classroom, too, I was gradually making my presence felt. Among my classmates, I was developing a reputation as a wheeler-dealer in data. One day, during a discussion of Coleridge's "The Ancient Mariner," we came across the word *albatross.*

"Can anyone tell us what an albatross is?" asked Mrs. Larrivee.

My hand shot up. "The albatross is a large bird that lives mostly in the ocean regions below the equator, but may be found in the north Pacific as well. The albatross measures as long as four feet and has the greatest wingspread of any bird. It feeds on the surface of the ocean, where it catches shellfish. The albatross is a very voracious eater. When it is full it has trouble getting into the air again."

There was a long silence in the room. Mrs. Larrivee couldn't quite believe what she had just heard. I sneaked a peek at Debbie and gave her a big wink. She beamed proudly and winked back.

It was a great feeling, having Debbie and Mrs. Larrivee and my peers according me respect and paying attention when I spoke.

My grades edged upward and my father no longer tried to avoid me when I brought home my report card. I continued reading the encyclopedia diligently, packing more and more into my brain.

What I failed to perceive was that Debbie all this while was going steady with a junior from a neighboring school—a hockey player with a C + average. The revelation hit me hard, and for a while I felt like disgorging and forgetting everything I had learned. I had saved enough money to buy Volume II—Asthma to Bullfinch—but was strongly tempted to invest in a hockey stick instead.

How could she lead me on like that—smiling and concurring and giving me the impression that I was important?

I felt not only hurt, but betrayed. Like Agamemnon, but with less dire consequences, thank God.

In time I recovered from my wounds. The next year Debbie moved from the neighborhood and transferred to another school. Soon she became no more than a fleeting memory.

Although the original incentive was gone, I continued pour- 43
ing over the encyclopedias, as well as an increasing number of
other books. Having savored the heady wine of knowledge, I
could not now alter my course. For:

> "A little knowledge is a dangerous thing:
> Drink deep, or taste not the Pierian spring."

So wrote Alexander Pope, Volume XIV, Paprika to Ptero- 44
dactyl.

Questions for Study and Discussion

1. Why didn't Brody stop reading the volumes of the encyclopedias when he discovered that Debbie had a steady boyfriend?
2. If you find Brody's narrative humorous, try to explain the
   sources of his humor. For example, what humor resides in
   the choice of examples Brody uses?
3. How are paragraphs 2 and 3, 3 and 4, 5 and 6, 31 and 32,
   and 43 and 44 linked? Identify the transitions that Brody
   uses in paragraph 35.
4. Brody refers to Coleridge's "The Ancient Mariner" in
   paragraph 33 and Agamemnon in paragraph 41, and he
   quotes Alexander Pope in paragraph 43. Use an encyclopedia to explain Brody's allusions. (Glossary: *Allusion*)
5. Comment on the effectiveness of the beginning and ending
   of Brody's essay. (Glossary: *Beginnings and Endings*)
6. Brody could have told his story using far less dialogue
   than he did. What, in your opinion, would have been
   gained or lost had he done so? (Glossary: *Dialogue*)

Vocabulary

Refer to your dictionary to define the following words as they
are used in this selection. Then use each word in a sentence of
your own.

misconception (1)
prodigies (1)
devotee (2)
bearish (3)
dabbled (3)
surge (9)
erudition (9)
snout (16)
sidled (20)

forbidding (24)
subsist (26)
amorous (32)
expatiated (32)
adenoids (32)
voracious (35)
disgorging (39)
savored (43)

Suggested Writing Assignments

1. One serious thought that arises as a result of reading Brody's essay is that perhaps we learn best when we are sufficiently motivated to do so. And once motivated, the desire to learn seems to feed on itself: "Having savored the heady wine of knowledge, I could not now alter my course" (43). Write an essay in which you explore this same subject using your own experiences.

2. In *The New York Times Complete Manual of Home Repair,* Bernard Gladstone gives directions for applying blacktop sealer to a driveway. His directions appear below in scrambled order. First, carefully read all of Gladstone's sentences. Next, arrange the sentences in what seems to you the correct sequence, paying attention to transitional devices. Be prepared to explain the reasons for your particular arrangement of the sentences.

   1. A long-handled pushbroom or roofing brush is used to spread the coating evenly over the entire area.
   2. Care should be taken to make certain the entire surface is uniformly wet, though puddles should be swept away if water collects in low spots.
   3. Greasy areas and oil slicks should be scraped up, then scrubbed thoroughly with a detergent solution.
   4. With most brands there are just three steps to follow.
   5. In most cases one coat of sealer will be sufficient.
   6. The application of blacktop sealer is best done on a day when the weather is dry and warm, preferably while the sun is shining on the surface.

7. This should not be applied until the first coat is completely dry.
8. First sweep the surface absolutely clean to remove all dust, dirt and foreign material.
9. To simplify spreading and to assure a good bond, the surface of the driveway should be wet down thoroughly by sprinkling with a hose.
10. However, for surfaces in poor condition a second coat may be required.
11. The blacktop sealer is next stirred thoroughly and poured on while the surface is still damp.
12. The sealer should be allowed to dry overnight (or longer if recommended by the manufacturer) before normal traffic is resumed.

FACING VIOLENCE

Michael T. Kaufman

Warsaw Bureau Chief of the New York Times,
*Michael T. Kaufman was born in 1938 in Paris
and grew up in the United States. He studied at
the* Bronx High School of Science, City College
of New York, *and* Columbia University. *He began
his career at the* New York Times *as a reporter
and feature writer and before assuming his
present position, served as bureau chief in Ot-
tawa, Canada. The following article appeared in
the* New York Times Magazine. *In it Kaufman
reflects on our reluctance to deal with the realities of violence, preferring instead the superficial
and vicarious version we get on television. As
you read Kaufman's essay, notice how he makes
smooth transitions from one paragraph to the
next with transitional expressions, pronoun references, and the repetition of key ideas.*

A lmost 20 years ago, when my oldest son was very young, I 1
tried to shield the boy from violence and aggression, these
alleged attributes of manliness. My wife and I had agreed to
raise our children in an atmosphere of nonviolence, without
playthings that simulated weapons. Then my uncle came to
visit us from Israel. My uncle, unlike his wife and children, had
survived Auschwitz, and he was surprised that my son had no
toy guns. I tried to explain, but, asserting the moral authority
of a war victim and survivor, he took my son off to Macy's to
buy the biggest, noisiest toy machine gun he could find. My
uncle said that if people do not go bang bang when they are
young they go bang bang when they grow up.

Since then, we have lived in Africa and in Asia and I have seen 2
and heard bang bang. I am not sure I fully understand what my
uncle meant, but I no longer think that exposure to the symbols

135

of death and violence causes little boys to grow up ethically impaired. In fact, now that I am living in North American civilization, where enormous energies are spent rendering death and violence either fictional or abstract, I think the greatest moral pitfall is not that we witness too much bang bang, but that, for the most part, we perceive it vicariously. We shield ourselves from real death and pain while paying to see these same things, sanitized and stylized, in the movies.

This idea crystallized in my mind after a conversation I had a   3 short while ago with Jack Troake, a thoughtful man who, like his father, grandfather and great-grandfather, makes his living by fishing from his home port of Twillingate, Newfoundland. Like his ancestors and neighbors, he also used to spend the ice-bound winter months hunting gray skin seals, but he does so no longer. The market for seal pelts in Europe and the United States has been destroyed because of protests launched abroad by animal-rights groups. The original protests were against the clubbing of baby white-furred seal pups, a hunt that Jack Troake never joined. Then the outcry spread to include all seals. Last year, a British supermarket chain declared it would no longer stock Canadian fish because of someone's belief that some fishermen either now hunt seals or once did.

As we sat on Mr. Troake's radar-equipped boat watching his   4 sons mend nets, he made it clear that he was flabbergasted and insulted by what he assumed to be the view of some foreigners that he and his neighbors were barbarians. "Look old boy, there's no doubt about it, I make my living killing things. We kill mackerel and cod and we used to kill seals. Now, there seems to be a bunch of people who do not like that. I imagine them sitting eating lamb chops and steak and chicken, thinking they all come neatly wrapped in plastic from some food factory. I wonder whether they have ever seen anything die or anything born, except on television and in the movies. But, to tell you the truth, old boy, I really feel sorry for those people who are so upset about this old Christian."

Me too. I left Twillingate, and in a motel that night I watched   5 the footage from Beirut. As I remember now, it contained what have become the current visual clichés of violence. Men firing bazookas around a corner at something. Smoke and rubble.

Women with shopping bags walking fast across a street. Adolescent gunmen smiling into the camera from the backs of trucks. It conveyed a sense of destruction, but it stopped short of being horrible. I knew the images were authentic, but they did not seem real. They blurred into an already crowded memory bank of two-dimensional violence: Dirty Harry, the A Team, Beirut, Belfast, El Salvador, car crashes. And I thought how I, bombarded with such pictures of death, had, two years ago, backed away from the real drama of death when it touched me as something more than a witness. I had sent my own mother to die in a nursing home, among death specialists. I did not hold her as her life ebbed. Later, I consoled myself with the thought that this is what people do in a technological culture, and that, anyway, the room was clean and the doctors said she did not suffer greatly.

I recall how we used to hear that the images of the Vietnam War, shown on television, sensitized the nation. Perhaps. I can recall the naked little girl running from napalm, and the man being shot by a police official in Saigon. But everything else has been jumbled in memory, and what remains are mostly recollections of what I now think of as my skin-deep shock and my pious responses. There were too many images. The only people I hear talking about Vietnam now are the ones who were there. 6

What I do remember is the first dead man I ever saw, a man shot and bleeding on dirty stairs in New York. I remember victims of massacres in Zaire and Rhodesia, and I can recall where each of those bodies lay. I remember an Afghan freedom fighter in a hospital in Peshawar, his leg lost in a land-mine explosion. He had his rifle with him, and his 7-year-old son was on his bed touching the man's stump. The father was talking about returning to fight Soviet forces; he hoped that his son would continue the fight. For that small boy, perhaps, the moment was indeed too much bang bang, but I am no longer sure. 7

As for little boys playing with toy guns, I don't think it matters much, one way or the other. What does matter, it seems to me, is that at some time in their formative years, maybe in high school, our children should bear witness to the everyday violence they could see, say, in an emergency ward of a big city hospital. I know it sounds extreme, but maybe our children 8 could learn something valuable if they were taken for a day or two to visit a police station or an old-age home. It might serve as an antidote for the unreal violence on all our screens.

What would be learned, I think, is that, up close and in three dimensions, the dead, the dying and the suffering are always to some extent "us." On the screens they always seem to be "them." I don't understand it, really, any more than my uncle's view of bang bang, but I know that as long as men die and men kill it is wrong to turn away too much. Also, I am certain that I would prefer to be judged by the hunter Jack Troake than by anyone who would judge him harshly.

9

Questions for Study and Discussion

1. What is Kaufman's thesis? (Glossary *Thesis*) Where is it stated? Is it stated in more than one place?
2. What did Kaufman's uncle have to say about guns? Why do you suppose Kaufman has difficulty understanding him? Do you? Explain.
3. Does Kaufman develop his thesis using emotional appeals or thoughtful examples? Cite examples from the text to support your answer.
4. What exactly are the "visual clichés" Kaufman refers to in paragraph 5? Why do you suppose he thinks they fall short of being "horrible"?
5. In paragraph 5, Kaufman relates the deeply personal tale of his mother's death. What is the effect of this incident on the you? What would have been gained or lost had he left it out?
6. Reread the first sentences in paragraphs 1–7. What do they have in common? How do they work to make the transition from paragraph to paragraph?
7. Why do you suppose Kaufman would "prefer to be judged by the hunter Jack Troake than by anyone who would judge him harshly"? Explain.

Vocabulary

Refer to your dictionary to define the following words as they are used in this selection. Then use each word in a sentence of your own.

alleged (1) flabbergasted (4)
impaired (2) sensitized (6)
vicariously (2) antidote (8)

Suggested Writing Assignments

1. Kaufman believes that "We shield ourselves from real death and pain while paying to see these same things, sanitized and stylized, in the movies." Using examples from your own experience or observation, write an essay in which you agree or disagree with Kaufman's assessment of civilization in America.

2. In paragraph 8, Kaufman offers a solution to the problem of un-faced violence. How realistic is his solution? How necessary is it? In your own words, defend or attack Kaufman's solution.

7

EFFECTIVE SENTENCES

Each of the following paragraphs describes the city of Vancouver. Although the content of both paragraphs is essentially the same, the first paragraph is written in sentences of nearly the same length and pattern and the second paragraph in sentences of varying length and pattern.

Water surrounds Vancouver on three sides. The snow-crowned Coast Mountains ring the city on the northeast. Vancouver has a floating quality of natural loveliness. There is a curved beach at English Bay. This beach is in the shape of a half moon. Residential high rises stand behind the beach. They are in pale tones of beige, blue, and ice-cream pink. Turn-of-the-century houses of painted wood frown upward at the glitter of office towers. Any urban glare is softened by folds of green lawns, flowers, fountains, and trees. Such landscaping appears to be unplanned. It links Vancouver to her ultimate treasure of greenness. That treasure is thousand-acre Stanley Park. Surrounding stretches of water dominate. They have image-evoking names like False Creek and Lost Lagoon. Sailboats and pleasure craft skim blithely across Burrard Inlet. Foreign freighters are out in English Bay. They await their turn to take on cargoes of grain.

Surrounded by water on three sides and ringed to the northeast by the snow-crowned Coast Mountains, Vancouver has a floating quality of natural loveliness. At English Bay, the half-moon curve of beach is backed by high rises in pale tones of beige, blue, and ice-cream pink. Turn-of-the-century houses of painted wood frown upward at the glitter of office towers. Yet any urban glare is quickly softened by folds of green lawns, flowers, fountains, and trees that in a seemingly unplanned fashion link Vancouver to her ultimate treasure of greenness—thousand-acre Stanley Park. And always it is the surrounding stretches of water that dominate, with their image-evoking names like False Creek and Lost Lagoon. Sailboats and pleasure craft skim blithely across Burrard Inlet, while out in English Bay foreign freighters await their turn to take on cargoes of grain.

The difference between these two paragraphs is dramatic. The first is monotonous because of the sameness of the sentences and because the ideas are not related to one another in a meaningful way. The second paragraph is much more interesting and readable; its sentences vary in length and are structured to clarify the relationships among the ideas. Sentence variety, an important aspect of all good writing, should not be used for its own sake, but rather to express ideas precisely and to emphasize the most important ideas within each sentence. Sentence variety includes the use of subordination, the periodic and loose sentence, the dramatically short sentence, the active and passive voice, and coordination.

Subordination, the process of giving one idea less emphasis than another in a sentence, is one of the most important characteristics of an effective sentence and a mature prose style. Writers subordinate ideas by introducing them either with subordinating conjunctions (*because, if, as though, while, when, after, in order that*) or with relative pronouns (*that, which, who, whomever, what*). Subordination not only deemphasizes some ideas, but also highlights others that the writer feels are more important.

Of course, there is nothing about an idea—*any* idea—that automatically makes it primary or secondary in importance. The writer decides what to emphasize, and he or she may choose to emphasize the less profound or noteworthy of two ideas. Consider, for example, the following sentence: "Jane was reading a novel the day that Mount St. Helens erupted." Everyone, including the author of the sentence, knows that the Mount St. Helens eruption is a more noteworthy event than Jane's reading a novel. But the sentence concerns Jane, not the volcano, and so her reading is stated in the main clause, while the eruption is subordinated in a dependent clause.

Generally, writers place the ideas they consider important in main clauses, and other ideas go into dependent clauses. For example:

When she was thirty years old, she made her first solo flight across the Atlantic.

When she made her first solo flight across the Atlantic, she was thirty years old.

The first sentence emphasizes the solo flight; in the second, the emphasis is on the pilot's age.

Another way to achieve emphasis is to place the most important words, phrases, and clauses at the beginning or end of a sentence. The ending is the most emphatic part of a sentence; the beginning is less emphatic; and the middle is the least emphatic of all. The two sentences about the pilot put the main clause at the end, achieving special emphasis. The same thing occurs in a much longer kind of sentence, called a *periodic sentence*. Here is an example from John Updike:

> On the afternoon of the first day of spring, when the gutters were still heaped high with Monday's snow but the sky itself had been swept clean, we put on our galoshes and walked up the sunny side of Fifth Avenue to Central Park.

By holding the main clause back, Updike keeps his readers in suspense and so puts the most emphasis possible on his main idea.

A *loose sentence*, on the other hand, states its main idea at the beginning and then adds details in subsequent phrases and clauses. Rewritten as a loose sentence, Updike's sentence might read like this:

> We put on our galoshes and walked up the sunny side of Fifth Avenue to Central Park on the afternoon of the first day of spring, when the gutters were still heaped high with Monday's snow but the sky itself had been swept clean.

The main idea still gets plenty of emphasis, since it is contained in a main clause at the beginning of the sentence. Yet a loose sentence resembles the way people talk: it flows naturally and is easy to understand.

Another way to create emphasis is to use a *dramatically short sentence*. Especially following a long and involved sentence, a short declarative sentence helps drive a point home. Here are two examples, the first from Edwin Newman and the second from David Wise:

Meaning no disrespect, I suppose there is, if not general rejoicing, at least some sense of relief when the football season ends. It's a long season.

The executive suite on the thirty-fifth floor of the Columbia Broadcasting System skyscraper in Manhattan is a tasteful blend of dark wood paneling, expensive abstract paintings, thick carpets, and pleasing colors. It has the quiet look of power.

Finally, since the subject of a sentence is automatically emphasized, writers may choose to use the *active voice* when they want to emphasize the doer of an action and the *passive voice* when they want to downplay or omit the doer completely. Here are two examples:

High winds pushed our sailboat onto the rocks, where the force of the waves tore it to pieces.

Our sailboat was pushed by high winds onto the rocks, where it was torn to pieces by the force of the waves.

The first sentence emphasizes the natural forces that destroyed the boat, while the second sentence focuses attention on the boat itself. The passive voice may be useful in placing emphasis, but it has important disadvantages. As the examples show, and as the terms suggest, active-voice verbs are more vigorous and vivid than the same verbs in the passive voice. Then, too, some writers use the passive voice to hide or evade responsibility. "It has been decided" conceals who did the deciding, whereas "I have decided" makes all clear. So the passive voice should be used only when necessary—as it is in this sentence.

Often, a writer wants to place equal emphasis on several facts or ideas. One way to do this is to give each its own sentence. For example:

Nancy Lopez selected her club. She lined up her shot. She chipped the ball to within a foot of the pin.

But a long series of short, simple sentences quickly becomes tedious. Many writers would combine these three sentences by using *coordination.* The coordinating conjunctions *and, but, or, nor, for, so,* and *yet* connect words, phrases, and clauses of equal importance:

> Nancy Lopez selected her club, lined up her shot, *and*
> chipped the ball to within a foot of the pin.

By coordinating three sentences into one, the writer not only makes the same words easier to read, but also shows that Lopez's three actions are equally important parts of a single process.

When parts of a sentence are not only coordinated but also grammatically the same, they are *parallel.* Parallelism in a sentence is created by balancing a word with a word, a phrase with a phrase, or a clause with a clause. Parallelism is often used in speeches—for example, in the last sentence of Lincoln's *Gettysburg Address* ("government of the people, by the people, for the people, shall not perish from the . . ."). Here is another example, from the beginning of Mark Twain's *The Adventures of Huckleberry Finn:*

> Persons attempting to find a motive in this narrative will be
> prosecuted; persons attempting to find a moral in it will be
> banished; persons attempting to find a plot in it will be
> shot.

AN EYE-WITNESS ACCOUNT OF THE SAN FRANCISCO EARTHQUAKE

Jack London

Jack London (1876–1916) was born in San Francisco and attended school only until the age of fourteen. A prolific and popular fiction writer, he is perhaps best remembered for his novels The Call of the Wild *(1903),* The Sea Wolf *(1904), and* White Fang *(1906). London was working near San Francisco when the great earthquake hit that city in the early morning of April 16, 1906. In the aftermath of the 1989 earthquake in San Francisco, many people recalled London's account of the earlier disaster. Notice how, in this account of the quake's aftermath, London uses a variety of sentence structures to capture the feelings that this disaster evoked in him.*

The earthquake shook down in San Francisco hundreds of thousands of dollars' worth of walls and chimneys. But the conflagration that followed burned up hundreds of millions of dollars' worth of property. There is no estimating within hundreds of millions the actual damage wrought. Not in history has a modern imperial city been so completely destroyed. San Francisco is gone! Nothing remains of it but memories and a fringe of dwelling houses on its outskirts. Its industrial section is wiped out. Its social and residential section is wiped out. The factories and warehouses, the great stores and newspaper buildings, the hotels and the palaces of the nabobs, are all gone. Remains only the fringe of dwelling houses on the outskirts of what was once San Francisco.

Within an hour after the earthquake shock the smoke of San Francisco's burning was a lurid tower visible a hundred miles away. And for three days and nights this lurid tower swayed in the sky, reddening the sun, darkening the day, and filling the land with smoke.

On Wednesday morning at a quarter past five came the earth-   3
quake. A minute later the flames were leaping upward. In a
dozen different quarters south of Market Street, in the working-
class ghetto, and in the factories, fires started. There was no
opposing the flames. There was no organization, no communication. All the cunning adjustments of a twentieth-century
city had been smashed by the earthquake. The streets were
humped into ridges and depressions and piled with debris of
fallen walls. The steel rails were twisted into perpendicular and
horizontal angles. The telephone and telegraph systems were
disrupted. And the great water mains had burst. All the shrewd
contrivances and safeguards of man had been thrown out of
gear by thirty seconds' twitching of the earth's crust.

By Wednesday afternoon, inside of twelve hours, half the   4
heart of the city was gone. At that time I watched the vast conflagration from out on the bay. It was dead calm. Not a flicker
of wind stirred. Yet from every side wind was pouring in upon
the city. East, west, north, and south, strong winds were blowing upon the doomed city. The heated air rising made an enormous suck. Thus did the fire of itself build its own colossal
chimney through the atmosphere. Day and night, this dead
calm continued, and yet, near to the flames, the wind was often
half a gale, so mighty was the suck. . . .

Wednesday night saw the destruction of the very heart of the   5
city. Dynamite was lavishly used, and many of San Francisco's
proudest structures were crumbled by man himself into ruins,
but there was no withstanding the onrush of the flames. Time
and again successful stands were made by the fire fighters, and
every time the flames flanked around on either side, or came up
from the rear, and turned to defeat the hard-won victory.

An enumeration of the buildings destroyed would be a direc-   6
tory of San Francisco. An enumeration of the buildings unde-
stroyed would be a line and several addresses. An enumeration
of the deeds of heroism would stock a library and bankrupt the
Carnegie medal fund.* An enumeration of the dead—will never
be made. All vestiges of them were destroyed by the flames. The
number of the victims of the earthquake will never be known.

---

*Fund established by the philanthropist Andrew Carnegie in 1905 for the rec-
ognition of heroic deeds.

Questions for Study and Discussion

1. In this short passage London draws contrasts between the forces of nature and those of humans. Why do you think London draws these contrasts? What is their effect?
2. In paragraph 4 London says that "the fire of itself [built] its own colossal chimney through the atmosphere." What does he mean?
3. From what vantage point does London describe the destruction of the city? Where does he tell us where he is?
4. What is the effect of the short sentences "San Francisco is gone!" and "It was dead calm" in paragraphs 1 and 4?
5. Why do you suppose London uses the passive voice instead of the active voice in paragraph 3? (Glossary: *Voice*)
6. Point out examples of parallelism in paragraphs 1, 2, and 6. How does London add emphasis through the use of this rhetorical device? (Glossary: *Parallelism*)

Vocabulary

Refer to your dictionary to define the following words as they are used in this selection. Then use each word in a sentence of your own.

conflagration (1)   contrivances (3)
nabobs (1)   vestiges (6)
lurid (2)

Suggested Writing Assignments

1. If you have ever been an eyewitness to a disaster, either natural or man-made, write an account similar to London's of its consequences. Give special attention to the variety of your sentences according to the advice provided in the introduction to "Effective Sentences."
2. Write a brief essay using one of the following sentences to focus and control the descriptive details you select. Place the sentence in the essay wherever it will have the greatest emphasis.

It was a strange party.
He was nervous.
I was shocked.
Music filled the air.
Dirt was everywhere.

PLAYING TO WIN

Margaret A. Whitney

Margaret A. Whitney, a doctoral candidate in technical communications at Rensselaer Poly-technic Institute, is a writer by profession. In the following article, first published in 1988 in the New York Times Magazine, *Whitney describes how her daughter overcame sexual stereotypes in the face of social resistance towards women in sports. As you read Whitney's account of her daughter Ann's love for sports, notice how the varied structures of Whitney's sentences enhance her descriptions of those experiences.*

My daughter is an athlete. Nowadays, this statement won't strike many parents as unusual, but it does me. Until her freshman year in high school, Ann was only marginally interested in sport of any kind. When she played, she didn't swing hard, often dropped the ball, and had an annoying habit of tittering on field or court.

Indifference combined with another factor that did not bode well for a sports career. Ann was growing up to be beautiful. By the eighth grade, nature and orthodontics had produced a 5-foot-8-inch, 125-pound, brown-eyed beauty with a wonderful smile. People told her, too. And, as many young women know, it is considered a satisfactory accomplishment to be pretty and stay pretty. Then you can simply sit still and enjoy the unconditional positive regard. Ann loved the attention too, and didn't consider it demeaning when she was awarded "Best Hair," female category, in the eighth-grade yearbook.

So it came as a surprise when she became a jock. The first indication that athletic indifference had ended came when she joined the high-school cross-country team. She signed up in early September and ran third for the team within three days. Not only that. After one of those 3.1-mile races up hill and down dale on a rainy November afternoon, Ann came home muddy and bedraggled. Her hair was plastered to her head, and the mascara she had applied so carefully that morning ran in dark circles under her eyes. This is it, I thought. Wait until Lady Astor sees herself. But the kid with the best eighth-grade hair went on to finish the season and subsequently letter in cross-country, soccer, basketball and softball.

I love sports, she tells anyone who will listen. So do I, though 4 my midlife quest for a doctorate leaves me little time for either playing or watching. My love of sports is bound up with the goals in my life and my hopes for my three daughters. I have begun to hear the message of sports. It is very different from many messages that women receive about living, and I think it is good.

My husband, for example, talked to Ann differently when he 5 realized that she was a serious competitor and not just someone who wanted to get in shape so she'd look good in a prom dress. Be aggressive, he'd advise. Go for the ball. Be intense.

Be intense. She came in for some of the most scathing criticism from her dad, when, during basketball season, her intensity waned. You're pretending to play hard, he said. You like it on the bench? Do you like to watch while your teammates play?

I would think, how is this kid reacting to such advice? For 7 years, she'd been told at home, at school, by countless advertisements, "Be quiet, Be good, Be still." When teachers reported that Ann was too talkative, not obedient enough, too flighty. When I dressed her up in frilly dresses and admonished her not to get dirty. When ideals of femininity are still, quiet, cool females in ads whose vacantness passes for sophistication. How can any adolescent girl know what she's up against? Have you ever really noticed intensity? It is neither quiet nor good. And it's definitely not pretty.

In the end, her intensity revived. At half time, she'd look for 8 her father, and he would come out of the bleachers to discuss tough defense, finding the open player, squaring up on her jump shot. I'd watch them at the edge of the court, a tall man and a tall girl, talking about how to play.

Of course I'm particularly sensitive at this point in my life to 9 messages about trying hard, being active, getting better through individual and team effort. Ann, you could barely handle a basketball two years ago. Now you're bringing the ball up against the press. Two defenders are after you. You must dribble, stop, pass. We're depending on you. We need you to help us. I wonder if my own paroxysms of uncertainty would be eased had more people urged me—be active, go for it!

Not that dangers don't lurk for the females of her generation. I occasionally run this horror show in my own mental movie theater: an unctuous but handsome lawyer-like drone of a young man spies my Ann. Hmmm, he says unconsciously to himself, good gene pool, and wouldn't she go well with my BMW and the condo? Then I see Ann with a great new hairdo kissing the drone goodbyehoney and setting off to the nearest mall with splendid-looking children to spend money. 10

But the other night she came home from softball tryouts at 6 in the evening. The dark circles under her eyes were from exhaustion, not makeup. I tried too hard today, she says. I feel like I'm going to puke. 11

After she has revived, she explains. She wants to play a particular position. There is competition for it. I can't let anybody else get my spot, she says, I've got to prove that I can do it. Later we find out that she has not gotten the much-wanted third-base position, but she will start with the varsity team. My husband talks about the machinations of coaches and tells her to keep trying. You're doing fine, he says. She gets that I-am-going-to-keep-trying look on her face. The horror-show vision of Ann-as-Stepford-Wife fades. 12

Of course, Ann doesn't realize the changes she has wrought, the power of her self-definition. I'm an athlete, Ma, she tells me when I suggest participation in the school play or the yearbook. But she has really caused us all to rethink our views of existence: her younger sisters who consider sports a natural activity for females, her father whose advocacy of women has increased, and me. Because when I doubt my own abilities, I say to myself, Get intense, Margaret. Do you like to sit on the bench? 13

And my intensity revives. 14

I am not suggesting that participation in sports is the answer for all young women. It is not easy—the losing, jealousy, raw competition and intense personal criticism of performance. 15

And I don't wish to imply that the sports scene is a morality 16 play either. Girls' sports can be funny. You can't forget that out on that field are a bunch of people who know the meaning of the word cute. During one game, I noticed that Ann had a blue ribbon tied on her ponytail, and it dawned on me that every girl on the team had an identical bow. Somehow I can't picture the Celtics gathered in the locker room of the Boston Garden agreeing to wear the same color sweatbands.

No, what has struck me, amazed me and made me hold my breath in wonder and in hope is both the ideal of sport and the reality of a young girl not afraid to do her best. 17

I watch her bringing the ball up the court. We yell encouragement from the stands, though I know she doesn't hear us. Her face is red with exertion, and her body is concentrated on the task. She dribbles, draws the defense to her, passes, runs. A teammate passes the ball back to her. They've beaten the press. She heads toward the hoop. Her father watches her, her sisters watch her, I watch her. And I think, drive, Ann, drive. 18

Questions for Study and Discussion

1. Why was Whitney surprised that Ann became interested in sports? What social attitudes worked against Ann's becoming a good athlete? How does the author feel about these attitudes? How do you feel about these attitudes?

2. In paragraph 7 Whitney says, "ideals of femininity are still, quiet, cool females in ads whose vacantness passes for sophistication." Do you agree? Find some ads to support your answer.

3. Why does the author wish she had been told to "go for it" when she was younger? How does Whitney believe this would have changed her life? Do you agree with her reasoning?

4. Would you describe Whitney's tone (Glossary: *Tone*) as angry, frustrated, resigned or something else? Is her tone different at different points in the essay or does it remain consistent? Cite examples of her diction (Glossary: *Diction*) to support your answer.

5. Whitney mixes short, dramatic sentences with longer, more detailed ones. Choose several instances of this and comment on the possible reasons for this strategy. (Glossary: *Emphasis*)

Vocabulary

Refer to your dictionary to define the following words as they are used in this selection. Then use each word in a sentence of your own.

marginally (1)	admonish (7)
titter (1)	paroxysm (9)
bode (2)	unctuous (10)
bedraggled (3)	machinations (12)
scathing (6)	wrought (13)
wane (6)	

Suggested Writing Assignments

1. Read or reread Langston Hughes essay, "Salvation" (pp. 159–62). Write an essay in which you compare and contrast Whitney's variety of sentence structures with that of Hughes.

2. Without changing the meaning, rewrite the following paragraph using a variety of sentence structures to add interest and emphasis. When you have finished, add another paragraph to finish the idea, again paying attention to sentence structure.

   The score was 8 to 10. Allied was down. Allied was at bat. It was the bottom of the seventh inning. The bases were loaded. There were two strikes. There were two outs. Ronson's pitcher was throwing all strikes. Sweat was pouring from the batter's forehead. It was hot. The batter was nervous. This game determined the state champs. The state champs would go to the national tournament. The national tournament was in Washington, D.C. The batter took some practice swings. The batter pivoted the ball of her foot into the ground. The dirt was dusty. Dust flew into the umpire's face. The batter was ready. The batter nodded to the pitcher.

A BROTHER'S MURDER

Brent Staples

Brent Staples was born in 1951 in Chester, Pennsylvania, an industrial city southwest of Philadelphia. He studied at Widener University in Chester and at the University of Chicago. Formerly a teacher, Staples began his newspaper career as a reporter for the Chicago Sun-Times. *He later became an editor of the* New York Times Book Review *and now serves as assistant metropolitan editor of the* New York Times. *The following essay first appeared in the* New York Times Magazine. *In it Staples mourns the tragic death of his younger brother, a victim of the male machismo that stalks its prey in the African-American ghettos of large cities. Listen to Staples's sentences as you read this essay. Notice how they add interest, readability, and drama to the story he is telling.*

It has been more than two years since my telephone rang with the news that my younger brother Blake—just twenty-two years old—had been murdered. The young man who killed him was only twenty-four. Wearing a ski mask, he emerged from a car, fired six times at close range with a massive .44 Magnum, then fled. The two had once been inseparable friends. A senseless rivalry—beginning, I think, with an argument over a girlfriend—escalated from posturing, to threats, to violence, to murder. The way the two were living, death could have come to either of them from anywhere. In fact, the assailant had already survived multiple gunshot wounds from an accident much like the one in which my brother lost his life.

As I wept for Blake I felt wrenched backward into events and circumstances that had seemed light-years gone. Though a decade apart, we both were raised in Chester, Pennsylvania, an angry, heavily black, heavily poor, industrial city southwest of

Philadelphia. There, in the 1960s, I was introduced to mortality, not by the old and failing, but by beautiful young men who lay wrecked after sudden explosions of violence. The first, I remembered from my fourteenth year—Johnny, brash lover of fast cars, stabbed to death two doors from my house in a fight over a pool game. The next year, my teenage cousin, Wesley, whom I loved very much, was shot dead. The summers blur. Milton, an angry young neighbor, shot a crosstown rival, wounding him badly. William, another teenage neighbor, took a shotgun blast to the shoulder in some urban drama and displayed his bandages proudly. His brother, Leonard, severely beaten, lost an eye and donned a black patch. It went on.

I recall not long before I left for college, two local Vietnam   3 veterans—one from the Marines, one from the Army—arguing fiercely, nearly at blows about which outfit had done the most in the war. The most killing, they meant. Not much later, I read a magazine article that set that dispute in a context. In the story, a noncommissioned officer—a sergeant, I believe— said he would pass up any number of affluent, suburban-born recruits to get hard-core soldiers from the inner city. They jumped into the rice paddies with "their manhood on their sleeves," I believe he said. These two items—the veterans arguing and the sergeant's words—still characterize for me the circumstances under which black men in their teens and twenties kill one another with such frequency. With a touchy paranoia born of living battered lives, they are desperate to be *real* men. Killing is only machismo taken to the extreme. Incursions to be punished by death were many and minor, and they remain so: they include stepping on the wrong toe, literally; cheating in a drug deal; simply saying "I dare you" to someone holding a gun; crossing territorial lines in a gang dispute. My brother grew up to wear his manhood on his sleeve. And when he died, he was in that group—black, male and in its teens and early twenties—that is far and away the most likely to murder or be murdered.

I left the East Coast after college, spent the mid- and late   4 1970s in Chicago as a graduate student, taught for a time, then became a journalist. Within ten years of leaving my hometown, I was over-educated and "upwardly mobile," ensconced on a quiet, tree-lined street where voices raised in anger were scarcely ever heard. The telephone, like some grim umbilical, kept me connected to the old world with news of deaths, imprisonings and misfortune. I felt emotionally beaten up. Perhaps to protect myself, I added a psychological dimension to the physical distance I had already achieved. I rarely visited my hometown. I shut it out.

As I fled the past, so Blake embraced it. On Christmas of   5 1983, I traveled from Chicago to a black section of Roanoke, Virginia, where he then lived. The desolate public housing projects, the hopeless, idle young men crashing against one another—these reminded me of the embittered town we'd grown up in. It was a place where once I would have been comfortable, or at least sure of myself. Now, hearing of my brother's forays into crime, his scrapes with police and street thugs, I was scared, unsteady on foreign terrain.

I saw that Blake's romance with the street life and the hustler   6 image had flowered dangerously. One evening that late December, standing in some Roanoke dive among drug dealers and grim, hair-trigger losers, I told him I feared for his life. He had affected the image of the tough he wanted to be. But behind the dark glasses and the swagger, I glimpsed the baby-faced toddler I'd once watched over. I nearly wept. I wanted desperately for him to live. The young think themselves immortal, and a dangerous light shone in his eyes as he spoke laughingly of making fools of the policemen who had raided his apartment looking for drugs. He cried out as I took his right hand. A line of stitches lay between the thumb and index finger. Kickback from a shotgun, he explained, nothing serious. Gunplay had become part of his life.

I lacked the language simply to say: Thousands have lived   7 this for you and died. I fought the urge to lift him bodily and shake him. This place and the way you are living smells of death to me, I said. Take some time away, I said. Let's go downtown tomorrow and buy a plane ticket anywhere, take a bus trip, anything to get away and cool things off. He took my alarm casually. We arranged to meet the following night—an appointment he would not keep. We embraced as though through glass. I drove away.

As I stood in my apartment in Chicago holding the receiver   8 that evening in February 1984, I felt as though part of my soul had been cut away. I questioned myself then, and I still do. Did I not reach back soon enough or earnestly enough for him? For weeks I awoke crying from a recurrent dream in which I chased him, urgently trying to get him to read a document I had, as though reading it would protect him from what had happened in waking life. His eyes shining like black diamonds, he smiled and danced just beyond my grasp. When I reached for him, I caught only the space where he had been.

Questions for Study and Discussion

1. Staples opens with a jarring account of his brother's death. How effective is this opening? (Glossary: *Beginnings and Endings*) How well does it set the tone of the essay? (Glossary: *Tone*)

2. When and where does Staples first encounter "mortality"? What is unusual about his encounter?

3. In paragraph 3, Staples relates the story of the Vietnam veterans and the sergeant. Why does he use these incidents to illustrate his point? How helpful are they to an understanding of his point? What does Staples mean when he writes that "killing is only machismo taken to the extreme"?

4. Staples is almost poetic in his use of language to capture feelings. Cite examples of his diction (Glossary: *Diction*), and discuss how his choice of words heightens the emotionalism and drama of his essay.

5. Staples alternates sentences of great length and detail with short sentences of five words or less. What is the effect of each kind of sentence? What is the effect of juxtaposing them?

6. Staples goes to great pains to contrast his life and that of his brother. What are some of the points of contrast? (Glossary: *Comparison and Contrast*) What does it reveal about his attitude toward his brother's fate?

7. What is the meaning of Staples's last line? Who or what does Staples "blame" for his brother's death?

Vocabulary

Refer to your dictionary to define the following words as they are used in this selection. Then use each word in a sentence of your own.

escalated (1)	umbilical (4)
affluent (3)	forays (5)
machismo (3)	hustler (6)
incursions (3)	swagger (6)
ensconced (4)	

Suggested Writing Assignments

1. Staples suggests that his getting out of the ghetto was his salvation. However, for many poor African-Americans living in the inner city, the solution is not so simple. Taking your cues from circumstances Staples mentions in his essay and your own knowledge of the problems facing the inner cities, write an essay in which you discuss what society and the law can do to help young men like Blake.

2. Just what is "machismo" and how much do you think it contributed to Blake's death? Was it only harmful when added to the other conditions of life in the ghetto? Is it less harmful and perhaps even desirable in any other situation you can think of? Write an essay in which you define "machismo" and discuss its positive and/or negative effects within American society today.

SALVATION

Langston Hughes

*Born in Joplin, Missouri, Langston Hughes
(1902–1967), an important figure in the black cultural movement of the 1920s known as the Harlem Renaissance, wrote poetry, fiction, and plays,
and contributed a column to the* New York Post.
He is best known for The Weary Blues *(1926) and
other books of poetry that express his racial
pride, his familiarity with African-American traditions, and his understanding of jazz rhythms.
As you read the following selection from his
autobiography* The Big Sea *(1940), notice how
Hughes varies the lengths and types of sentences
he uses for the sake of emphasis.*

I was saved from sin when I was going on thirteen. But not   1
really saved. It happened like this. There was a big revival at
my Auntie Reed's church. Every night for weeks there had been
much preaching, singing, praying, and shouting, and some very
hardened sinners had been brought to Christ, and the member-
ship of the church had grown by leaps and bounds. Then just
before the revival ended, they held a special meeting for children, "to bring the young lambs to the fold." My aunt spoke of
it for days ahead. That night I was escorted to the front row and
placed on the mourners' bench with all the other young sinners,
who had not yet been brought to Jesus.

My aunt told me that when you were saved you saw a light,   2
and something happened to you inside! And Jesus came into
your life! And God was with you from then on! She said you
could see and hear and feel Jesus in your soul. I believed her. I
have heard a great many old people say the same thing and it
seemed to me they ought to know. So I sat there calmly in the
hot, crowded church, waiting for Jesus to come to me.

The preacher preached a wonderful rhythmical sermon, all   3
moans and shouts and lonely cries and dire pictures of hell, and

then he sang a song about the ninety and nine safe in the fold, but one little lamb was left out in the cold. Then he said: "Won't you come? Won't you come to Jesus? Young lambs, won't you come?" And he held out his arms to all us young sinners there on the mourners' bench. And the little girls cried. And some of them jumped up and went to Jesus right away. But most of us just sat there.

A great many old people came and knelt around us and   4
prayed, old women with jet-black faces and braided hair, old men with work-gnarled hands. And the church sang a song about the lower lights are burning, some poor sinners to be saved. And the whole building rocked with prayer and song.

Still I kept waiting to *see* Jesus.   5

Finally all the young people had gone to the altar and were   6
saved, but one boy and me. He was a rounder's son named Westley. Westley and I were surrounded by sisters and deacons praying. It was very hot in the church, and getting late now. Finally Westley said to me in a whisper: "God damn! I'm tired o' sitting here. Let's get up and be saved." So he got up and was saved.

Then I was left all alone on the mourners' bench. My aunt   7
came and knelt at my knees and cried, while prayers and songs swirled all around me in the little church. The whole congregation prayed for me alone, in a mighty wail of moans and voices. And I kept waiting serenely for Jesus, waiting, waiting—but he didn't come. I wanted to see him, but nothing happened to me. Nothing! I wanted something to happen to me, but nothing happened.

I heard the songs and the minister saying: "Why don't you   8
come? My dear child, why don't you come to Jesus? Jesus is waiting for you. He wants you. Why don't you come? Sister Reed, what is this child's name?"

"Langston," my aunt sobbed.   9

"Langston, why don't you come? Why don't you come and be   10
saved? Oh, Lamb of God! Why don't you come?"

Now it was really getting late. I began to be ashamed of my-   11
self, holding everything up so long. I began to wonder what God thought about Westley, who certainly hadn't seen Jesus either, but who was now sitting proudly on the platform, swinging his knickerbockered legs and grinning down at me, surrounded by

deacons and old women on their knees praying. God had not struck Westley dead for taking his name in vain or for lying in the temple. So I decided that maybe to save further trouble, I'd better lie, too, and say that Jesus had come, and get up and be saved.

So I got up. 12

Suddenly the whole room broke into a sea of shouting, as 13 they saw me rise. Waves of rejoicing swept the place. Women leaped in the air. My aunt threw her arms around me. The minister took me by the hand and led me to the platform.

When things quieted down, in a hushed silence, punctuated 14 by a few ecstatic "Amens," all the new young lambs were blessed in the name of God. Then joyous singing filled the room.

That night, for the last time in my life but one—for I was a big 15 boy twelve years old—I cried. I cried, in bed alone, and couldn't stop. I buried my head under the quilts, but my aunt heard me. She woke up and told my uncle I was crying because the Holy Ghost had come into my life, and because I had seen Jesus. But I was really crying because I couldn't bear to tell her that I had lied, that I had deceived everybody in the church, that I hadn't seen Jesus, and that now I didn't believe there was a Jesus any more, since he didn't come to help me.

Questions for Study and Discussion

1. What is salvation? Is it important to young Langston Hughes that he be saved? Why is it important to Langston's aunt that he be saved?

2. Why does young Langston expect to be saved at the revival meeting? Once the children are in church, what appeals are made to them to encourage them to seek salvation?

3. Why does young Langston cry on the night of his being "saved"? Why is the story of his being saved so ironic? (Glossary: *Irony*)

4. What would be gained or lost if the essay began with the first two sentences combined as follows: "I was saved

from sin when I was going on thirteen, but I was not really saved"?

5. Identify the coordinating conjunctions in paragraph 3. Rewrite the paragraph without them. Compare your paragraph with the original, and explain what Hughes gains by using coordinating conjunctions. (Glossary: *Coordination*)

6. Identify the subordinating conjunctions in paragraph 15. What is it about the ideas in this last paragraph that makes it necessary for Hughes to use these subordinating conjunctions?

7. How does Hughes's choice of words, or diction, help to establish a realistic atmosphere for a religious revival meeting? (Glossary: *Diction*)

Vocabulary

Refer to your dictionary to define the following words as they are used in this selection. Then use each word in a sentence of your own.

dire (3)   punctuated (14)
gnarled (4)   ecstatic (14)
vain (11)

Suggested Writing Assignments

1. Like the young Langston Hughes, we sometimes find ourselves in situations in which, for the sake of conformity, we do things we do not believe in. Consider one such experience you have had, and write an essay about it. What is it about human nature that makes us occasionally act in ways that contradict our inner feelings? As you write, pay particular attention to your sentence variety.

2. Reread the introduction to this chapter. Then review one of the essays that you have written, paying particular attention to sentence structure. Recast sentences as necessary in order to make your writing more interesting and effective.

II

THE
LANGUAGE
OF THE
ESSAY

8

DICTION AND TONE

Diction

Diction refers to a writer's choice and use of words. Good diction is precise and appropriate—the words mean exactly what the writer intends, and the words are well suited to the writer's subject, purpose, and intended audience.

For careful writers it is not enough merely to come close to saying what they want to say; they select words that convey their exact meaning. Perhaps Mark Twain put this best when he said, "The difference between the right word and the almost right word is the difference between lightning and the lightning bug." Inaccurate, imprecise, or inappropriate diction not only fails to convey the writer's intended meaning but also may cause confusion and misunderstanding for the reader.

Connotation and Denotation

Both connotation and denotation refer to the meanings of words. Denotation is the dictionary meaning of a word, the literal meaning. Connotative meanings are the associations or emotional overtones that words have acquired gradually. For example, the word *home* denotes a place where someone lives, but it connotes warmth, security, family, comfort, affection, and other more private thoughts and images. The word *residence* also denotes a place where someone lives, but its connotations are colder and more formal.

Many words in English have synonyms, words with very similar denotations—for example, *mob, crowd, multitude,* and *bunch.* Deciding which to use depends largely on the connotations that each synonym has and the context in which the word is to be used. For example, you might say, "There was a crowd at the lecture," but not "There was a mob at the lecture." Good writers are sensitive to both the denotations and the connotations of words.

Abstract and Concrete Words

Abstract words name ideas, conditions, emotions—things nobody can touch, see, or hear. Some abstract words are *love, wisdom, cowardice, beauty, fear,* and *liberty.* People often disagree about abstract things. You may find a forest beautiful, while someone else might find it frightening, and neither of you would be wrong. Beauty and fear are abstract ideas; they exist in your mind, not in the forest along with the trees and the owls. Concrete words refer to things we can touch, see, hear, smell, and taste, such as *sandpaper, soda, birch trees, smog, cow, sailboat, rocking chair,* and *pancake.* If you disagree with someone on a concrete issue—say, you claim that the forest is mostly birch trees, while the other person says it is mostly pine—only one of you can be right, and both of you can be wrong; what kinds of trees grow in the forest is a concrete fact, not an abstract idea.

Good writing balances ideas and facts, and it also balances abstract and concrete diction. If the writing is too abstract, with too few concrete facts and details, it will be unconvincing and tiresome. If the writing is too concrete, devoid of ideas and emotions, it can seem pointless and dry.

General and Specific Words

General and *specific* do not necessarily refer to opposites. The same word can often be either general or specific, depending on the context: *Dessert* is more specific than *food*, but more general than *chocolate cream pie*. Being very specific is like being concrete: *chocolate cream pie* is something you can see and taste. Being general, on the other hand, is like being abstract. *Food, dessert,* and even *pie* are general classes of things that bring no particular taste or image to mind.

Good writing moves back and forth from the general to the specific. Without specific words, generalities can be unconvincing and even confusing: the writer's idea of "good food" may be very different from the reader's. But writing that does not relate specifics to each other by generalization often lacks focus and direction.

Clichés

Some words, phrases, and expressions have become trite through overuse. Let's assume your roommate has just returned from an evening out. You ask her "How was the concert?" She responds, "The concert was okay, but they had us *packed in* there *like sardines*. How was your evening?" And you reply, "Well, I finished my term paper, but the noise here is enough to *drive me crazy*. The dorm is a real *zoo*." At one time the italicized expressions were vivid and colorful, but through constant use they have grown stale and ineffective. The experienced writer always tries to avoid such clichés as *believe it or not, doomed to failure, hit the spot, let's face it, sneaking suspicion, step in the right direction,* and *went to great lengths.*

Jargon

Jargon, or technical language, is the special vocabulary of a trade or profession. Writers who use jargon do so with an awareness of their audience. If their audience is a group of coworkers or professionals, jargon may be used freely. If the audience is a more general one, jargon should be used sparingly and carefully so that readers can understand it. Jargon becomes inappropriate when it is overused, used out of context, or used pretentiously. For example, computer terms such as *input, output,* and *feedback* are sometimes used in place of *contribution, result,* and *response* in other fields, especially in business. If you think about it, the terms suggest that people are machines, receiving and processing information according to a program imposed by someone else.

Formal and Informal Diction

Diction is appropriate when it suits the occasion for which it is intended. If the situation is informal—a friendly letter, for example—the writing may be colloquial; that is, its words may be chosen to suggest the way people talk with each other. If, on the other hand, the situation is formal—a term paper or a research report, for example—then the words should reflect this formality. Informal writing tends to be characterized by slang, contractions, references to the reader, and concrete nouns. Formal writing tends to be impersonal, abstract, and free of contractions and references to the reader. Formal writing and informal writing are, of course, the extremes. Most writing falls between these two extremes and is a blend of those formal and informal elements that best fit the context.

Tone

Tone is the attitude a writer takes toward the subject and the audience. The tone may be friendly or hostile, serious or humorous, intimate or distant, enthusiastic or skeptical.

As you read the following paragraphs, notice how each writer has created a different tone and how that tone is supported by the diction—the writer's particular choice and use of words.

Nostalgic

My generation is special because of what we missed rather than what we got, because in a certain sense we are the first and the last. The first to take technology for granted. (What was a space shot to us, except an hour cut from Social Studies to gather before a TV in the gym as Cape Canaveral counted down?) The first to grow up with TV. My sister was 8 when we got our set, so to her it seemed magic and always somewhat foreign. She had known books already and would never really replace them. But for me, the TV set was, like the kitchen sink and the telephone, a fact of life.

Joyce Maynard, "An 18-Year-Old Looks Back on Life"

Angry

Cans. Beer cans. Glinting on the verges of a million miles of roadways, lying in scrub, grass, dirt, leaves, sand, mud, but never hidden. Piels, Rheingold, Ballantine, Schaefer, Schlitz, shining in the sun or picked by moon or the beams of headlights at night; washed by rain or flattened by wheels, but never dulled, never buried, never destroyed. Here is the mark of savages, the testament of wasters, the stain of prosperity.

Marya Mannes, "Wasteland"

Humorous

In perpetrating a revolution, there are two requirements: someone or something to revolt against and someone to actually show up and do the revolting. Dress is usually casual and both parties may be flexible about time and place but if either faction fails to attend the whole enterprise is likely to come off badly. In the Chinese Revolution of 1650 neither party showed up and the deposit on the hall was forfeited.

Woody Allen, "A Brief, Yet Helpful Guide to Civil Disobedience"

Resigned

I make my living humping cargo for Seaboard World Airlines, one of the big international airlines at Kennedy Airport. They handle strictly all cargo. I was once told that one of the Rockefellers is the major stockholder for the airline, but I don't really think about that too much. I don't get paid to think. The big thing is to beat that race with the time clock every morning of your life so the airline will be happy. The worst thing a man could ever do is to make suggestions about building a better airline. They pay people $40,000 a year to come up with better ideas. It doesn't matter that these ideas never work; it's just that they get nervous when a guy from South Brooklyn or Ozone Park acts like he has a brain.

Patrick Fenton, "Confessions of a Working Stiff"

Ironic

Once upon a time there was a small, beautiful, green and graceful country called Vietnam. It needed to be saved. (In later years no one could remember exactly what it needed to be saved from, but that is another story.) For many years Vietnam was in the process of being saved by France, but the French eventually tired of their labors and left. Then America took on the job. America was well equipped for country-saving. It was the richest and most powerful nation on earth. It had, for example, nuclear explosives on hand and ready to use equal to six tons of TNT for every man, woman, and child in the world. It had huge and very efficient factories, brilliant and dedicated scientists, and most (but not everybody) would agree, it had good intentions. Sadly, America had one fatal flaw—its inhabitants were in love with technology and thought it could do no wrong. A visitor to America during the time of this story would probably have guessed its outcome after seeing how its inhabitants were treating their own country. The air was mostly foul, the water putrid, and most of the land was either covered with concrete or garbage. But Americans were never much on introspection, and they didn't foresee the result of their loving embrace on the small country. They set out to save Vietnam with the same enthusiasm and determination their forefathers had displayed in conquering the frontier.

The Sierra Club, "A Fable for Our Times"

The diction and tone of an essay are subtle forces, but they exert a tremendous influence on readers. They are instrumental in determining how we will feel while reading the essay and what attitude we will have toward its argument or the points that it makes. Of course, readers react in a variety of ways. An essay written informally but with a largely angry tone may make one reader defensive and unsympathetic; another may feel the author is being unusually honest and courageous, and may admire this and feel moved by it. Either way, the diction and tone of the piece have made a strong emotional impression. As you read the essays in this chapter and throughout this book, see if you can analyze how the word choice (diction) and tone are shaping your reactions.

On Being 17, Bright, and Unable to Read

David Raymond

When the following article appeared in the New
York Times *in 1976, David Raymond was a high-
school student in Connecticut. In his essay he
poignantly discusses his great difficulty in reading because of dyslexia and the many problems
he experienced in school as a result. As you read,
pay attention to the naturalness of the author's
diction.*

One day a substitute teacher picked me to read aloud from 1
the textbook. When I told her "No, thank you," she came
unhinged. She thought I was acting smart, and told me so. I
kept calm, and that got her madder and madder. We must have
spent 10 minutes trying to solve the problem, and finally she
got so red in the face I thought she'd blow up. She told me she'd
see me after class.

Maybe someone like me was a new thing for that teacher. But 2
she wasn't new to me. I've been through scenes like that all my
life. You see, even though I'm 17 and a junior in high school, I
can't read because I have dyslexia. I'm told I read "at a fourth-
grade level," but from where I sit, that's not reading. You can't
know what that means unless you've been there. It's not easy to
tell how it feels when you can't read your homework assignments or the newspaper or a menu in a restaurant or even notes
from your own friends.

My family began to suspect I was having problems almost 3
from the first day I started school. My father says my early
years in school were the worst years of his life. They weren't so
good for me, either. As I look back on it now, I can't find the
words to express how bad it really was. I wanted to die. I'd
come home from school screaming, "I'm dumb. I'm dumb—I
wish I were dead!"

I guess I couldn't read anything at all then—not even my own   4
name—and they tell me I didn't talk as good as other kids. But
what I remember about those days is that I couldn't throw a
ball where it was supposed to go, I couldn't learn to swim, and
I wouldn't learn to ride a bike, because no matter what anyone
told me, I knew I'd fail.

Sometimes my teachers would try to be encouraging. When I   5
couldn't read the words on the board they'd say, "Come on,
David, you know that word." Only I didn't. And it was embarrassing. I just felt dumb. And dumb was how the kids treated
me. They'd make fun of me every chance they got, asking me to
spell "cat" or something like that. Even if I knew how to spell
it, I wouldn't; they'd only give me another word. Anyway, it was
awful, because more than anything I wanted friends. On my
birthday when I blew out the candles I didn't wish I could learn
to read; what I wished for was that the kids would like me.

With the bad reports coming from school, and with me moan-   6
ing about wanting to die and how everybody hated me, my parents began looking for help. That's when the testing started.
The school tested me, the child-guidance center tested me, private psychiatrists tested me. Everybody knew something was
wrong—especially me.

It didn't help much when they stuck a fancy name onto it. I   7
couldn't pronounce it then—I was only in second grade—and I
was ashamed to talk about it. Now it rolls off my tongue, because I've been living with it for a lot of years—dyslexia.

All through elementary school it wasn't easy. I was always   8
having to do things that were "different," things the other kids
didn't have to do. I had to go to a child psychiatrist, for instance.

One summer my family forced me to go to a camp for chil-   9
dren with reading problems. I hated the idea, but the camp
turned out pretty good, and I had a good time. I met a lot of kids
who couldn't read and somehow that helped. The director of
the camp said I had a higher I.Q. than 90 percent of the population. I didn't believe him.

About the worst thing I had to do in fifth and sixth grade was   10
go to a special education class in another school in our town. A
bus picked me up, and I didn't like that at all. The bus also

picked up emotionally disturbed kids and retarded kids. It was like going to a school for the retarded. I always worried that someone I knew would see me on that bus. It was a relief to go to the regular junior high school.

Life began to change a little for me then, because I began to feel better about myself. I found the teachers cared; they had meetings about me and I worked harder for them for a while. I began to work on the potter's wheel, making vases and pots that the teachers said were pretty good. Also, I got a letter for being on the track team. I could always run pretty fast.   11

At high school the teachers are good and everyone is trying to help me. I've gotten honors some marking periods and I've won a letter on the cross-country team. Next quarter I think the school might hold a show of my pottery. I've got some friends. But there are still some embarrassing times. For instance, every time there is writing in the class, I get up and go to the special education room. Kids ask me where I go all the time. Sometimes I say, "to Mars."   12

Homework is a real problem. During free periods in school I go into the special ed room and staff members read assignments to me. When I get home my mother reads to me. Sometimes she reads an assignment into a tape recorder, and then I go into my room and listen to it. If we have a novel or something like that to read, she reads it out loud to me. Then I sit down with her and we do the assignment. She'll write, while I talk my answers to her. Lately I've taken to dictating into a tape recorder, and then someone—my father, a private tutor or my mother—types up what I've dictated. Whatever homework I do takes someone else's time, too. That makes me feel bad.   13

We had a big meeting in school the other day—eight of us, four from the guidance department, my private tutor, my parents and me. The subject was me. I said I wanted to go to college, and they told me about colleges that have facilities and staff to handle people like me. That's nice to hear.   14

As for what happens after college, I don't know and I'm worried about that. How can I make a living if I can't read? Who will hire me? How will I fill out the application form? The only thing that gives me any courage is the fact that I've learned about well-known people who couldn't read or had other prob-   15 lems and still made it. Like Albert Einstein, who didn't talk until he was 4 and flunked math. Like Leonardo da Vinci, who everyone seems to think had dyslexia.

I've told this story because maybe some teacher will read it 16 and go easy on a kid in the classroom who has what I've got. Or, maybe some parent will stop nagging his kid, and stop calling him lazy. Maybe he's not lazy or dumb. Maybe he just can't read and doesn't know what's wrong. Maybe he's scared, like I was.

Questions for Study and Discussion

1. What is dyslexia? Is it essential for an understanding of the essay that we know more about dyslexia than Raymond tells us? Explain.

2. What does Raymond say his purpose is in telling his story?

3. What does Raymond's story tell us about the importance of our early childhood experiences, especially within our educational system?

4. Raymond uses many colloquial and idiomatic expressions, such as "she got so red in the face I thought she'd blow up" and "she came unhinged" (1). Identify other examples of such diction and tell how they affect the essay.

5. In the context of the essay, comment on the appropriateness of each of the following possible choices of diction. Which word is better in each case? Why?
   a. *selected* for *picked* (1)
   b. *experience* for *thing* (2)
   c. *speak as well* for *talk as good* (4)
   d. *negative* for *bad* (6)
   e. *important* for *big* (14)
   f. *failed* for *flunked* (15)
   g. *frightened* for *scared* (16)

6. How would you describe Raymond's tone in this essay?

Vocabulary

Refer to your dictionary to define the following words as they are used in this selection. Then use each word in a sentence of your own.

dyslexia (2)   psychiatrists (6)

Suggested Writing Assignments

1. Imagine that you are away at school. Recently you were caught in a radar speed trap—you were going 70 miles per hour in a 55-mile-per-hour zone—and have just lost your license; you will not be able to go home this coming weekend, as you had planned. Write two letters in which you explain why you will not be able to go home, one to your parents and the other to your best friend. Your audience is different in each case, so be sure to choose your diction accordingly.

2. Select an essay you have already completed in this course, and rewrite it in a different tone. If the essay was originally formal or serious, lighten it so that it is now informal and humorous. Pay special attention to diction. Actually think in terms of a different reader as your audience—not your instructor but perhaps your classmates, your clergyman, your sister, or the state environmental protection board. Reshape your essay as necessary.

EVERY 23 MINUTES

Linda Weltner

Boston Globe columnist Linda Weltner *was born in 1938 in Worcester, Massachusetts. She began her writing career after graduating from Wellesley College. She has written two novels for young adults,* Beginning to Feel the Magic *(1981) and* The New Voice *(1981), and a collection of her essays entitled* No Place Like Home *was published in 1989. The following essay first appeared in the* Globe *on June 6, 1986. In it Weltner draws profiles of victims to make a dramatic and emotional case against driving drunk. As you read her essay, notice how Weltner's diction underscores the restrained anger in her appeal against drinking and driving.*

M y husband and I went to a funeral a few weeks ago. The 1
man we honored had not been ill and will never grow
old. He was killed in his car on a Sunday night, driving home
along a divided highway.

It was an ordinary evening, no blacker than any other, when 2
a car coming in the other direction jumped the median strip,
broke through the guard rail, and hit two other cars before
smashing head on into his. According to the newspaper, the
driver, who was returning from a wedding, seemed puzzled.
"I only had two bottles of beer and two glasses of champagne,"
she is reported to have said.

A wedding. 3

Followed by a funeral. 4

I wish she could have been there to see all the lives her act has 5
changed forever, the wife, and four children, the extended family, the hundreds and hundreds of friends who sat in numbed
silence, listening to words which barely touched the depths of
their grief.

Strange to think that, according to the National Highway   6
Traffic Safety Administration, this happens in America every
23 minutes.

Somebody drinks.   7

Somebody drives.   8

Somebody dies.   9

And other lives are altered forever, though sometimes the   10
changes may be invisible to a casual observer. By chance, the
day before the funeral I ran into a longtime acquaintance while
shopping. He commented on my crutches. I asked if he had ever
broken his leg.

"Uh, I have a long rod in this thigh," he said, "from an auto-   11
mobile accident two weeks after I came back from Vietnam."

"That's ironic. To leave a war zone and get injured," I teased   12
him. "You're lucky it wasn't worse."

"Well, my wife was killed in the crash and so was the wife of   13
the driver," he said uncomfortably. "We were hit by a drunk."

I've known this man for years, yet suddenly realized there   14
was a whole chapter of his life he never mentioned. I asked and
discovered he'd remained in the hospital seven weeks, and that
all that time he'd known his wife was dead. It was hard to know
where to go from there, for there are questions you can't put to
someone in a casual conversation, like "How could you bear
it?" or "What did you do about wanting revenge?"

I wish I knew the answers to those questions. I wish I could   15
offer those answers to the woman who, overwhelmed by grief,
could barely walk as she followed her husband's coffin from
the synagogue.

My friend Lynn saw a movie at the high school where she   16
teaches in which the young male narrator recounted how he'd
killed someone while driving drunk. "He said he didn't know
how he'd stand it if he'd killed someone he loved," Lynn told me.
"That really bothered me. Isn't everyone someone that somebody loves?"

Every 23 minutes, who dies?   17

A mother who will never comfort the child who needs her. A   18
woman who will never know how very much her friends depended on her. A man whose contributions to his community
would have made a difference. A wife whose husband cannot
picture the future without her.

Every 23 minutes, who dies?   19
A son who involuntarily abandons his parents in their old   20
age. A father who can never acknowledge his children's accomplishments. A daughter who can never take back her angry
words in parting. A sister who will never be her sister's maid of
honor.
Every 23 minutes, who dies?   21
A brother who will not be there to hold his newborn nephew.   22
A friend whose encouragement is gone forever. A bride-to-be
who will never say her vows. An aunt whose family will fragment and fall apart.
Every 23 minutes, who dies?   23
A child who will never fulfill his early promise. An uncle who   24
leaves his children without guidance and support. A grandmother whose husband must now grow old alone. A lover who
never had a chance to say how much he cared.
Every 23 minutes.   25
A void opens.   26
Someone looks across the table at a vacant chair, climbs into   27
an empty bed, feels the pain of no voice, no touch, no love.
Where there was once intimacy and contact, now there is only
absence and despair.
Every 23 minutes.   28
A heart breaks.   29
Someone's pain shatters the confines of her body, leaking out   30
in tears, exploding in cries, defying the healing power of tranquilizers and Seconal. Sleep offers no escape from the nightmare of awakening. And morning brings only the irreversibility
of loss.
Every 23 minutes.   31
A dream ends.   32
Someone's future blurs and goes blank as anticipation fades   33
into nothingness. The phone will not ring, the car will not pull
into the driveway. The weight of tomorrow becomes unbearable
in a world in which all promises have been forcibly broken.
Every 23 minutes.   34
Somebody wants to run. Somebody wants to hide.   35
Someone is left with hate. Somebody wants to die.   36
And we permit this to go on.   37
Every 23 minutes.   38

Questions for Study and Discussion

1. How does Weltner feel about drinking? About drinking and driving? Explain.

2. Why do you suppose Weltner offers so little detail about the man who was the victim of the drunk driver? Does it help or hinder her argument?

3. Weltner makes liberal use of short sentences in her essay. Cite examples of these fragments and describe their overall effect on the reader. (Glossary: *Sentence*)

4. There are two ironies in the story of the Vietnam veteran. What are they? (Glossary: *Irony*) What point does Weltner make with this example? (Glossary: *Example*)

5. Beginning with paragraph 17, Weltner offers a litany of despair resulting from drunk driving. How did you react to Weltner's repeated use of the phrase, "Every 23 minutes"? Was it intrusive or did it effectively underscore the urgency of her position? How did you react to the numerous examples she uses? Were they realistic? Did they make her point? What would have been gained or lost had she made them more specific or detailed?

6. What is Weltner's tone in this essay? (Glossary: *Tone*) Is it angry, resigned, objective, or something else? Cite examples of her language to support your answer.

Vocabulary

Refer to your dictionary to define the following words as they are used in this selection. Then use each word in a sentence of your own.

median (2)   void (26)
fragment (22)   intimacy (27)

Suggested Writing Assignments

1. Almost everyone has been affected in one way or another by the tragedy of drunk driving. From your own experience or drawing upon that of a friend, explain how well

you think Weltner has described the feelings of anger and despair that come with the loss or injury of someone you love at the hands of a drunk driver. Attempt to answer the questions Weltner raises. "How could you bear it?" "What did you do about wanting revenge?"

2. Weltner concludes her essay with the discouraged cry that "we permit this to go on." What exactly can we do about it? What laws are in effect in your state? What kinds of solutions are being proposed? Laws can deal with people after they have driven drunk. What, if anything, can be done to encourage people not to drink and drive in the first place? Write an essay in which you present your views on this issue.

BITING THE BULLETS

Gerald Nachman

*Gerald Nachman was born in 1938 in Oakland,
California, and began his writing career at San
Jose State where he was a humorist and television critic for the* San Jose Mercury. *More recently Nachman wrote an entertainment column
for the* San Francisco Chronicle, *but he has also
written on a wide range of topics including politics, fashion and social issues. He is the author
of two books,* Playing House *(1977) and* Out on
a Whim: Some Very Close Brushes With Life
*(1983). His writing earned him the Page One
Award in 1965 and the Associated Press Feature-
Writing Award in 1974. In "Biting the Bullets,"
taken from* Out on a Whim, *Nachman makes
pointed use of satire as he enters the gun-control
debate and takes on all its participants.*

A fter a seventeen-year study, my sub-subcommittee on gun   1
control has come up with a compromise solution: bullet
control.

By banning the large-scale sale of bullets, gun owners may   2
keep their weapons, the average person (or squirrel) will be safe
and criminals won't have to go around empty-handed.

It will, of course, still be possible to get conked over the head   3
with a gun butt, but this is just a first step. The agreement
should satisfy everyone except perhaps the hard-to-please National Bullet Association and its 728 members.

The ban on bullets will work this way: Starting in 1984, all   4
cartridges fired by "Saturday-night specials" will be illegal—
however, so as not to annoy the powerful pro-ammo lobby and
collectors of antique bullets, all other ammunition will still be
readily available.

By 1990, all bullets fired by "Sunday-through-Tuesday-night   5
specials" will be outlawed (except in woodsy states).

181

Bullet control is designed to mollify the rifle groups whose 6
favorite slogan is "Guns don't kill people—people kill people."
When the committee looked into this, it found that, in actual
(target) practice, bullets kill people.

The committee also discovered that, to inflict any real dam- 7
age, the bullet should be inside a gun. To test this, several
marksmen tried to pick off a moving target by *throwing* bullets
at it. Results showed that the bullets merely ricocheted off the
man and he escaped with only a few nicks.

When the same test was tried using bullets fired from a gun, 8
however, the fellow died (presumably from the bullets). The
committee concluded that guns and bullets can be hazardous to
your health when "used in connection with each other," as our
report phrases it. To be on the safe side, though, the committee
temporarily recommends a twenty-minute "cooling off" period
for people purchasing bullets.

As it now stands, any nut can walk into a gun shop and buy 9
enough lead to wipe out a small town. Until the new law goes
into effect, a ruling will require "all nuts to be registered and
forced to cool their heels for half an hour."

Another popular riflemen's slogan—"When guns are out- 10
lawed, only outlaws will have guns"—is true enough, the committee agreed, but many outlaws who testified before the committee said they're willing to give bullet control a try.

"Look," said one gangster, "we hate to be unreasonable about 11
this, but we'd look pretty dumb wandering around the streets
without a gun. We can be every bit as terrifying with an empty
.38 and then at least we won't be booked for carrying a loaded
weapon."

Sub-subcommittee members foresee a day when Congress 12
may pass a measure banning guns with handles and, eventually,
triggers. Gradually, the entire gun will be phased out of existence, a part at a time. Remarks one congressman, "There's no
reason to rush into this gun-control thing helter-skelter."

Questions for Study and Discussion

1. What is Nachman's attitude toward gun-control? How do
   you know? What is his purpose in this essay? (Glossary:
   Purpose)

2. Satire is a literary form that uses wit, irony or sarcasm to expose vice or folly. Which of these elements does Nachman use in his satire? Why do you suppose he has chosen to treat so serious a subject in this way?
3. To whom is Nachman addressing his essay? The anti-gun lobby? The N.R.A.? A general audience or one that is politically aware? (Glossary: *Audience*) Cite examples of his diction that support your answer. (Glossary: *Diction*)
4. Exactly who are the participants in the gun-control debate? What fault does Nachman find in each of their positions?
5. Reread Nachman's essay paying attention to his use of humor. Which passages did you find particularly amusing? Why? What is the source of his humor?

Vocabulary

Refer to your dictionary to define the following words as they are used in this selection. Then use each word in a sentence of your own.

compromise (1)   ricocheted (7)
ban (4)   helter-skelter (12)
mollify (6)

Suggested Writing Assignments

1. Satire is seldom used merely to entertain the reader. Its purpose is to inform or bring about change. In his essay, Nachman wants his readers to consider the tactics used by participants in the gun-control debate. Through his use of satire Nachman suggests that they manipulate public sympathies with foolish, superficial arguments in order to achieve their ends. In an essay, consider the ways in which satire is a particularly effective means of arguing a serious subject. When is it most appropriate? When might it be inappropriate?
2. In an essay of your own use satire to inform or work for change on an issue you are familiar with, such as campus dress, coed dorms, Greeks on campus, or dining hall food.

THE MIDDLE-CLASS BLACK'S BURDEN

Leanita McClain

Leanita McClain, a voice for middle-class African-Americans, knows all too well that "as long as we are denigrated as a group, no one of us has made it." First published in Newsweek *in 1980, McClain's essay is a powerful appeal to whites and African-Americans alike to strive for true racial equality. For McClain, who committed suicide in 1984, racial equality was never more that a "hollow victory." As you read her essay, pay particular attention to the persuasive emotional appeal of her word choice.*

I am a member of the black middle-class who has had it with being patted on the head by white hands and slapped in the face by black hands for my success.

Here's a discovery that too many people still find startling: when given equal opportunities at white-collar pencil pushing, blacks want the same things from life that everyone else wants. These include the proverbial dream house, two cars, an above-average school and a vacation for the kids at Disneyland. We may, in fact, want these things more than other Americans because most of us have been denied them so long.

Meanwhile, a considerable number of the folks we left behind in the "old country," commonly called the ghetto, and the militants we left behind in their antiquated ideology can't berate middle-class blacks enough for "forgetting where we came from." We have forsaken the revolution, we are told, we have sold out. We are Oreos, they say, black on the outside, white within.

The truth is, we have not forgotten; we would not dare. We are simply fighting on different fronts and are no less war weary, and possibly more heartbroken, for we know the black and white worlds can meld, and that there can be a better world.

It is impossible for me to forget where I came from as long as I am prey to the jive hustler who does not hesitate to exploit my childhood friendship. I am reminded, too, when I go back to the old neighborhood in fear—and have my purse snatched—and when I sit down to a business lunch and have an old classmate wait on my table. I recall the girl I played dolls with who now rears five children on welfare, the boy from church who is in prison for murder, the pal found dead of a drug overdose in the alley where we once played tag.

My life abounds in incongruities. Fresh from a vacation in   6
Paris, I may, a week later, be on the milk-run Trailways bus to Deep South backcountry attending the funeral of an ancient uncle whose world stretched only 50 miles and who never learned to read. Sometimes when I wait at the bus stop with my attaché case, I meet my aunt getting off the bus with other cleaning ladies on their way to do my neighbors' floors.

But I am not ashamed. Black progress has surpassed our   7
greatest expectations; we never saw much hope for it, and the achievement has taken us by surprise.

In my heart, however, there is no safe distance from the   8
wretched past of my ancestors or the purposeless present of some of my contemporaries; I fear such a fate can reclaim me. I am not comfortably middle class; I am uncomfortably middle class.

I have made it, but where? Racism still dogs my people. There   9
are still communities in which crosses are burned on the lawns of black families who have the money and grit to move in.

What a hollow victory we have won when my sister, dressed   10
in her designer everything, is driven to the rear door of the luxury high rise in which she lives because the cab driver, noting only her skin color, assumes she is the maid, or the nanny, or the cook, but certainly not the lady of any house at this address.

I have heard the immigrants' bootstrap tales, the simplistic   11
reproach of "why can't you people be like us." I have fulfilled the entry requirements of the American middle class, yet I am left, at times, feeling unwelcome and stereotyped. I have overcome the problems of food, clothing and shelter, but I have not overcome my old nemesis, prejudice. Life is easier, being black is not.

I am burdened daily with showing whites that blacks are   12
people. I am, in the old vernacular, a credit to my race. I am my

brothers' keeper, and my sisters', though many of them have abandoned me because they think that I have abandoned them.

I run a gauntlet between two worlds, and I am cursed and so   13
blessed by both. I travel, observe and take part in both; I can also be used by both. I am a rope in a tug of war. If I am a token in my downtown office, so am I at my cousin's church tea. I assuage white guilt. I disprove black inadequacy and prove to my parents' generation that their patience was indeed a virtue.

I have a foot in each world, but I cannot fool myself about   14
either. I can see the transparent deceptions of some whites and the bitter hopelessness of some blacks. I know how tenuous my grip on one way of life is, and how strangling the grip of the other way of life can be.

Many whites have lulled themselves into thinking that race   15
relations are just grand because they were the first on their block to discuss crab grass with the new black family. Yet too few blacks and whites in this country send their children to school together, entertain each other or call each other friend. Blacks and whites dining out together draw stares. Many of my co-workers see no black faces from the time the train pulls out Friday evening until they meet me at the coffee machine Monday morning. I remain a novelty.

Some of my "liberal" white acquaintances pat me on the   16
head, hinting that I am a freak, that my success is less a matter of talent than of luck and affirmative action. I may live among them, but it is difficult to live with them. How can they be sincere about respecting me, yet hold my fellows in contempt? And if I am silent when they attempt to sever me from my own, how can I live with myself?

Whites won't believe I remain culturally different; blacks   17
won't believe I remain culturally the same.

I need only look in a mirror to know my true allegiance, and   18
I am painfully aware that, even with my off-white trappings, I am prejudged by my color.

As for the envy of my own people, am I to give up my career,   19
my standard of living, to pacify them and set my conscience at ease? No. I have worked for these amenities and deserve them, though I can never enjoy them without feeling guilty.

These comforts do not make me less black, nor oblivious to   20
the woe in which many of my people are drowning. As long as

we are denigrated as a group, no one of us has made it. Inasmuch as we all suffer for every one left behind, we all gain for every one who conquers the hurdle.

Questions for Study and Discussion

1. In paragraph 1, McClain says she "has had it with being patted on the head by white hands and slapped in the face by black hands for my success." Why do white people pat her head? Why do black people slap her face? Why do you suppose that this bothers McClain?
2. Other members of McClain's race think she has sold them out. Why do they think that way? Do you agree or disagree? How does McClain explain her role and behavior as a middle-class African-American?
3. Identify the rational and emotional appeals McClain makes to the reader. Which of these appeals is more effective?
4. Which paragraph in McClain's essay best captures her tone? (Glossary: *Tone*) What is that tone? Is it angry, resigned, humorous, frustrated or something else?
5. Reread the essay paying particular attention to McClain's use of pronouns. Particularly note the two senses in which she uses the word "we." What are they? What different feelings are they meant to evoke? Explain.

Vocabulary

Refer to your dictionary to define the following words as they are used in this selection. Then use each word in a sentence of your own.

proverbial (2)	vernacular (12)
militants (3)	gauntlet (13)
antiquated (3)	assuage (13)
meld (4)	denigrated (20)
incongruities (6)	

Suggested Writing Assignments

1. Take a letter or memorandum that you have received from your college administration or some other bureaucratic body, and rewrite it so as to avoid the deadly dull diction and tone of most official correspondence. Your revision should convey all the necessary information contained in the original, but should do so in a lively and entertaining way.

2. McClain's essay conveys a sense of "hollow victory." Think about the author's situation and how she feels. Describe a time when you have experienced a "hollow" sense of victory. Be sure your tone and your diction adequately convey your sense of emptiness.

9

FIGURATIVE LANGUAGE

Figurative language is language used in an imaginative rather than a literal sense. Although it is most often associated with poetry, figurative language is used widely in our daily speech and in our writing. Prose writers have long known that figurative language not only brings freshness and color to writing, but also helps to clarify ideas.

Two of the most commonly used figures of speech are the simile and the metaphor. A *simile* is an explicit comparison between two essentially different ideas or things that uses the words *like* or *as* to link them.

> Canada geese sweep across the hills and valleys like a formation of strategic bombers.
>
> Benjamin B. Bachman

> I walked toward her and hailed her as a visitor to the moon might salute a survivor of a previous expedition.
>
> John Updike

A *metaphor*, on the other hand, makes an implicit comparison between dissimilar ideas or things without using *like* or *as*.

> She was very old and small and she walked slowly in the dark pine shadows, moving a little from side to side in her steps, with the balanced heaviness and lightness of a pendulum in a grandfather clock.
>
> Eudora Welty

> Charm is the ultimate weapon, the supreme seduction, against which there are few defenses.
>
> Laurie Lee

In order to take full advantage of the richness of a particular comparison, writers sometimes use several sentences or even a whole paragraph to develop a metaphor. Such a comparison is called an *extended metaphor*.

The point is that you have to strip down your writing before you can build it back up. You must know what the essential tools are and what job they were designed to do. If I may belabor the metaphor on carpentry, it is first necessary to be able to saw wood neatly and to drive nails. Later you can bevel the edges or add elegant finials, if that is your taste. But you can never forget that you are practicing a craft that is based on certain principles. If the nails are weak, your house will collapse. If your verbs are weak and your syntax is rickety, your sentences will fall apart.

William Zinsser

Another frequently used figure of speech is *personification*. In personification the writer attributes human qualities to animals or inanimate objects.

Blond October comes striding over the hills wearing a crimson shirt and faded green trousers.

Hal Borland

Indeed, haste can be the assassin of elegance.

T. H. White

In the preceding examples, the writers have, through the use of figurative language, both livened up their prose and given emphasis to their ideas. Keep in mind that figurative language should never be used merely to "dress up" writing; above all, it should help you to develop your ideas and to clarify your meaning for the reader.

THE MISSISSIPPI RIVER

Mark Twain

Mark Twain (1835–1910), born in Hannibal, Missouri, created Huckleberry Finn *(1884),* Tom Sawyer *(1876),* The Prince and the Pauper *(1882), and* A Connecticut Yankee in King Arthur's Court *(1889), among other classics. One of America's most popular writers, Twain is generally regarded as the most important practitioner of the realistic school of writing, a style that emphasized observable details. As you read the following passage from* Life on the Mississippi, *notice how Twain makes use of figurative language to describe two quite different ways of seeing the great Mississippi River.*

Now when I had mastered the language of this water and had come to know every trifling feature that bordered the great river as familiarly as I knew the letters of the alphabet, I had made a valuable acquisition. But I had lost something, too. I had lost something which could never be restored to me while I lived. All the grace, the beauty, the poetry, had gone out of the majestic river! I still kept in mind a certain wonderful sunset which I witnessed when steamboating was new to me. A broad expanse of the river was turned to blood; in the middle distance the red hue brightened into gold, through which a solitary log came floating, black and conspicuous; in one place a long, slanting mark lay sparkling upon the water; in another the surface was broken by boiling, tumbling rings that were as many-tinted as an opal; where the ruddy flush was faintest was a smooth spot that was covered with graceful circles and radiating lines, ever so delicately traced; the shore on our left was densely wooded, and the somber shadow that fell from this forest was broken in one place by a long, ruffled trail that shone like silver; and high above the forest wall a clean-stemmed dead tree waved a single leafy bough that glowed like a flame in the unobstructed splendor that was flowing from the sun. There were graceful curves, reflected images, woody heights, soft distances, and over the whole scene, far and near, the dissolving lights drifted steadily, enriching it every passing moment with new marvels of coloring.

I stood like one bewitched. I drank it in, in a speechless rapture. The world was new to me and I had never seen anything like this at home. But as I have said, a day came when I began to cease from noting the glories and the charms which the moon and the sun and the twilight wrought upon the river's face; another day came when I ceased altogether to note them. Then, if that sunset scene had been repeated, I should have looked upon it without rapture and should have commented upon it inwardly after this fashion: "This sun means that we are going to have wind to-morrow; that floating log means that the river is rising, small thanks to it; that slanting mark on the water refers to a bluff reef which is going to kill somebody's steamboat one of these nights, if it keeps on stretching out like that; those tumbling 'boils' show a dissolving bar and a changing channel there; the lines and circles in the slick water over yonder are a warning that that troublesome place is shoaling up dangerously; that silver streak in the shadow of the forest is the 'break' from a new snag and he has located himself in the very best place he could have found to fish for steamboats; that tall dead tree, with a single living branch, is not going to last long, and then how is a body ever going to get through this blind place at night without the friendly old landmark?"

No, the romance and beauty were all gone from the river. All the value any feature of it had for me now was the amount of usefulness it could furnish toward compassing the safe piloting of a steamboat. Since those days, I have pitied doctors from my heart. What does the lovely flush in a beauty's cheek mean to a doctor but a "break" that ripples above some deadly disease? Are not all her visible charms sown thick with what are to him the signs and symbols of hidden decay? Does he ever see her beauty at all, or doesn't he simply view her professionally and comment upon her unwholesome condition all to himself? And doesn't he sometimes wonder whether he has gained most or lost most by learning his trade?

Questions for Study and Discussion

1. Twain's essay reveals that he has two attitudes toward the Mississippi River. What are those attitudes, and where are they presented in the essay? (Glossary: *Attitude*)
2. In his conclusion Twain says that since the days when he learned his profession, he has pitied doctors. Why does he say this?
3. Twain uses a number of similes and metaphors in his essay. Identify three of each, and explain what is being compared in each case.
4. What is Twain's tone in this essay? (Glossary: *Tone*)
5. What effect do the italicized words have in each of the following quotations from this selection? How do these words contribute to Twain's description? (Glossary: *Connotation/Denotation*)
   a. ever so *delicately* traced (1)
   b. shadow that *fell* from this forest (1)
   c. *wrought* upon the river's face (2)
   d. show a *dissolving* bar (2)
   e. to get through this *blind* place at night (2)
   f. lovely *flush* in a beauty's cheek (3)

Vocabulary

Refer to your dictionary to define the following words as they are used in this selection. Then use each word in a sentence of your own.

acquisition (1)   rapture (2)
hue (1)   romance (3)
opal (1)

Suggested Writing Assignments

1. Write an essay modeled on Twain's in which you offer your two different views of a particular scene, event, or issue. Describe how you once regarded your subject, and then describe how you now view the subject. For exam-

ple, you might wish to present the way you once viewed your home town or high school, and the way you now view it. Be sure to use at least one simile and one metaphor in your essay.

2. Write an essay describing one of the places listed below or any other place of your choice. Use at least one simile and one metaphor to clarify and enliven your description.

a factory
a place of worship
a fast-food restaurant
your dormitory
your college library
your favorite place on campus
your home town

CONVERSATIONAL BALLGAMES

Nancy Masterson Sakamoto

Born in the United States, Nancy Masterson Sakamoto became familiar with Japanese culture and attitudes after marrying a Japanese man and living for some time in Osaka where she taught English to native Japanese. Currently she teaches Buddhism at the University of Hawaii. The following essay is a chapter from her book Polite Fictions *(1982), a textbook for Japanese students learning conversational English. In it she uses the analogy of a ball game to help her readers understand the contrast between the Japanese and American styles of conversation.*

After I was married and had lived in Japan for a while, my 1
Japanese gradually improved to the point where I could take part in simple conversations with my husband and his friends and family. And I began to notice that often, when I joined in, the others would look startled, and the conversational topic would come to a halt. After this happened several times, it became clear to me that I was doing something wrong. But for a long time, I didn't know what it was.

Finally, after listening carefully to many Japanese conversa- 2
tions, I discovered what my problem was. Even though I was speaking Japanese, I was handling the conversation in a western way.

Japanese-style conversations develop quite differently from 3
western-style conversations. And the difference isn't only in the languages. I realized that just as I kept trying to hold western-style conversations even when I was speaking Japanese, so my English students kept trying to hold Japanese-style conversations even when they were speaking English. We were unconsciously playing entirely different conversational ballgames.

A western-style conversation between two people is like a 4

game of tennis. If I introduce a topic, a conversational ball, I expect you to hit it back. If you agree with me, I don't expect you simply to agree and do nothing more. I expect you to add some-thing—a reason for agreeing, another example, or an elabora-tion to carry the idea further. But I don't expect you always to agree. I am just as happy if you question me, or challenge me, or completely disagree with me. Whether you agree or disagree, your response will return the ball to me.

And then it is my turn again. I don't serve a new ball from my 5 original starting line. I hit your ball back again from where it has bounced. I carry your idea further, or answer your ques-tions or objections, or challenge or question you. And so the ball goes back and forth, with each of us doing our best to give it a new twist, an original spin, or a powerful smash.

And the more vigorous the action, the more interesting and 6 exciting the game. Of course, if one of us gets angry, it spoils the conversation, just as it spoils a tennis game. But getting excited is not at all the same as getting angry. After all, we are not trying to hit each other. We are trying to hit the ball. So long as we attack only each other's opinions, and do not attack each other personally, we don't expect anyone to get hurt. A good conversation is supposed to be interesting and exciting.

If there are more than two people in the conversation, then it 7 is like doubles in tennis, or like volleyball. There's no waiting in line. Whoever is nearest and quickest hits the ball, and if you step back, someone else will hit it. No one stops the game to give you a turn. You're responsible for taking your own turn.

But whether it's two players or a group, everyone does his 8 best to keep the ball going, and no one person has the ball for very long.

A Japanese-style conversation, however, is not at all like 9 tennis or volleyball. It's like bowling. You wait for your turn. And you always know your place in line. It depends on such things as whether you are older or younger, a close friend or a relative stranger to the previous speaker, in a senior or junior position, and so on.

When your turn comes, you step up to the starting line with 10 your bowling ball, and carefully bowl it. Everyone else stands back and watches politely, murmuring encouragement. Every-one waits until the ball has reached the end of the alley, and watches to see if it knocks down all the pins, or only some of them, or none of them. There is a pause, while everyone registers your score.

Then, after everyone is sure that you have completely finished 11
your turn, the next person in line steps up to the same starting line, with a different ball. He doesn't return your ball, and he does not begin from where your ball stopped. There is no back and forth at all. All the balls run parallel. And there is always a suitable pause between turns. There is no rush, no excitement, no scramble for the ball.

No wonder everyone looked startled when I took part in 12
Japanese conversations. I paid no attention to whose turn it was, and kept snatching the ball halfway down the alley and throwing it back at the bowler. Of course the conversation died. I was playing the wrong game.

This explains why it is almost impossible to get a western- 13
style conversation or discussion going with English students in Japan. I used to think that the problem was their lack of English language ability. But I finally came to realize that the biggest problem is that they, too, are playing the wrong game.

Whenever I serve a volleyball, everyone just stands back and 14
watches it fall, with occasional murmurs of encouragement. No one hits it back. Everyone waits until I call on someone to take a turn. And when that person speaks, he doesn't hit my ball back. He serves a new ball. Again, everyone just watches it fall.

So I call on someone else. This person does not refer to what 15
the previous speaker has said. He also serves a new ball. Nobody seems to have paid any attention to what anyone else has said. Everyone begins again from the same starting line, and all the balls run parallel. There is never any back and forth. Everyone is trying to bowl with a volleyball.

And if I try a simpler conversation, with only two of us, then 16
the other person tries to bowl with my tennis ball. No wonder foreign English teachers in Japan get discouraged.

Now that you know about the difference in the conversa- 17
tional ballgames, you may think that all your troubles are over. But if you have been trained all your life to play one game, it is no simple matter to switch to another, even if you know the rules. Knowing the rules is not at all the same thing as playing the game.

Even now, during a conversation in Japanese I will notice a   18
startled reaction, and belatedly realize that once again I have
rudely interrupted by instinctively trying to hit back the other
person's bowling ball. It is no easier for me to "just listen" during a conversation, than it is for my Japanese students to "just
relax" when speaking with foreigners. Now I can truly sym-
pathize with how hard they must find it to try to carry on a
western-style conversation.

If I have not yet learned to do conversational bowling in   19
Japanese, at least I have figured out one thing that puzzled me
for a long time. After his first trip to America, my husband complained that Americans asked him so many questions and made
him talk so much at the dinner table that he never had a chance
to eat. When I asked him why he couldn't talk and eat at the
same time, he said that Japanese do not customarily think that
dinner, especially on fairly formal occasions, is a suitable time
for extended conversation.

Since westerners think that conversation is an indispensable   20
part of dining, and indeed would consider it impolite not to
converse with one's dinner partner, I found this Japanese custom rather strange. Still, I could accept it as a cultural difference even though I didn't really understand it. But when my
husband added, in explanation, that Japanese consider it extremely rude to talk with one's mouth full, I got confused. Talking with one's mouth full is certainly not an American custom.
We think it very rude, too. Yet we still manage to talk a lot and
eat at the same time. How do we do it?

For a long time, I couldn't explain it, and it bothered me. But   21
after I discovered the conversational ballgames, I finally found
the answer. Of course! In a western-style conversation, you hit
the ball, and while someone else is hitting it back, you take a
bite, chew, and swallow. Then you hit the ball again, and then
eat some more. The more people there are in the conversation,
the more chances you have to eat. But even with only two of you
talking, you still have plenty of chances to eat.

Maybe that's why polite conversation at the dinner table has   22
never been a traditional part of Japanese etiquette. Your turn to
talk would last so long without interruption that you'd never
get a chance to eat.

Questions for Study and Discussion

1. What exactly is the problem Sakamoto addresses? Does she offer any solutions to the problem? Why or why not?
2. What differences between the Japanese and American cultures can you infer from the differences in their conversational styles?
3. This essay was written originally for Japanese students. What in her essay tells you that this is Sakamoto's intended audience? (Glossary: *Audience*)
4. The use of analogy is central to Sakamoto's argument. What three main analogies does she use? Where are they introduced? Explain how each analogy works. How well do they suit both Sakamoto's argument and her audience? Explain.
5. At the conclusion of her essay, Sakamoto offers a possible explanation of the differing conversational styles. Did you find this information useful? What would have been gained or lost had she left it out? Explain.

Vocabulary

Refer to your dictionary to define the following words as they are used in this selection. Then use each word in a sentence of your own.

vigorous (6)   indispensable (20)
belatedly (18)

Suggested Writing Assignments

1. Use an analogy of your own to clarify the differences between people in a social situation with which you are familiar. For instance, male and female styles of conversation, parent and child attitudes toward sex, or older sibling, younger sibling attitudes toward privacy. In choosing your diction and analogy be sure to consider your intended audience.

2. Getting an A in chemistry, asking someone out for the first time, quitting a job—all can be seen to have procedures or "rules." Imagine that a friend of yours faces one of these life situations or another of your choosing. What "rules" might you suggest he or she follow? In considering this assignment, what rules do you become aware of that you had not thought of before?

THE BARRIO

Robert Ramirez

*Robert Ramirez has worked as a cameraman,
reporter, anchorman, and producer for the news
team at KGBT-TV in Edinburg, Texas. Presently,
he works in the Latin American division of the
Northern Trust Bank in Chicago. In the following essay, notice how Ramirez uses figurative
language to awaken the reader's senses to the
sights, smells, and sounds that are the essense of
the barrio.*

The train, its metal wheels squealing as they spin along the 1
silvery tracks, rolls slower now. Through the gaps between
the cars blinks a streetlamp, and this pulsing light on a barrio
streetcorner beats slower, like a weary heartbeat, until the train
shudders to a halt, the light goes out, and the barrio is deep
asleep.

Throughout Aztlán (the Nahuatl term meaning "land to the 2
north"), trains grumble along the edges of a sleeping people.
From Lower California, through the blistering Southwest,
down the Rio Grande to the muddy Gulf, the darkness and
mystery of dreams engulf communities fenced off by railroads,
canals, and expressways. Paradoxical communities, isolated
from the rest of the town by concrete columned monuments of
progress, and yet stranded in the past. They are surrounded by
change. It eludes their reach, in their own backyards, and the
people, unable and unwilling to see the future, or even touch
the present, perpetuate the past.

Leaning from the expressway or jolting across the tracks, one 3
enters a different physical world permeated by a different
attitude. The physical dimensions are impressive. It is a large
section of town which extends for fifteen blocks north and
south along the tracks, and then advances eastward, thinning
into nothingness beyond the city limits. Within the invisible (yet

sensible) walls of the barrio, are many, many people living in too few houses. The homes, however, are much more numerous than on the outside.

Members of the barrio describe the entire area as their home.   4
It is a home, but it is more than this. The barrio is a refuge from the harshness and the coldness of the Anglo world. It is a forced refuge. The leprous people are isolated from the rest of the community and contained in their section of town. The stoical pariahs of the barrio accept their fate, and from the angry seeds of rejection grow the flowers of closeness between out- casts, not the thorns of bitterness and the mad desire to flee. There is no want to escape, for the feeling of the barrio is known only to its inhabitants, and the material needs of life can also be found here.

The *tortillería* [tortilla factory] fires up its machinery three   5
times a day, producing steaming, round, flat slices of barrio bread. In the winter, the warmth of the tortilla factory is a wool *sarape* [blanket] in the chilly morning hours, but in the summer, it unbearably toasts every noontime customer.

The *panadería* [bakery] sends its sweet messenger aroma   6
down the dimly lit street, announcing the arrival of fresh, hot sugary *pan dulce* [sweet rolls].

The small corner grocery serves the meal-to-meal needs of   7
customers, and the owner, a part of the neighborhood, willingly gives credit to people unable to pay cash for foodstuffs.

The barbershop is a living room with hydraulic chairs, radio,   8
and television, where old friends meet and speak of life as their salted hair falls aimlessly about them.

The pool hall is a junior level country club where '*chucos*,   9
[young men] strangers in their own land, get together to shoot pool and rap, while veterans, unaware of the cracking, popping balls on the green felt, complacently play dominoes beneath rudely hung *Playboy* foldouts.

The *cantina* [canteen or snackbar] is the night spot of the   10
barrio. It is the country club and the den where the rites of puberty are enacted. Here the young become men. It is in the taverns that a young dude shows his *machismo* through the quantity of beer he can hold, the stories of *rucas* [women] he has had, and his willingness and ability to defend his image against hardened and scarred old lions.

No, there is no frantic wish to flee. It would be absurd to leave 11
the familiar and nervously step into the strange and cold Anglo
community when the needs of the Chicano can be met in the
barrio.

The barrio is closeness. From the family living unit, familial 12
relationships stretch out to immediate neighbors, down the
block, around the corner, and to all parts of the barrio. The feeling of family, a rare and treasurable sentiment, pervades and
accounts for the inability of the people to leave. The barrio is
this attitude manifested on the countenances of the people, on
the faces of their homes, and in the gaiety of their gardens.

The color-splashed homes arrest your eyes, arouse your curi- 13
osity, and make you wonder what life scenes are being played
out in them. The flimsy, brightly colored, wood-frame houses
ignore no neon-brilliant color. Houses trimmed in orange, char-
treuse, lime-green, yellow, and mixtures of these and other hues
beckon the beholder to reflect on the peculiarity of each home.
Passing through this land is refreshing like Brubeck,* not nar-
coticizing like revolting rows of similar houses, which neither
offend nor please.

In the evenings, the porches and front yards are occupied 14
with men calmly talking over the noise of children playing
baseball in the unpaved extension of the living room, while the
women cook supper or gossip with female neighbors as they
water the *jardines* [gardens]. The gardens mutely echo the ex-
pressive verses of the colorful houses. The denseness of multi-
colored plants and trees gives the house the appearance of an
oasis or a tropical island hideaway, sheltered from the rest of
the world.

Fences are common in the barrio, but they are fences and not 15
the walls of the Anglo community. On the western side of town,
the high wooden fences between houses are thick, impenetrable
walls, built to keep the neighbors at bay. In the barrio, the
fences may be rusty, wire contraptions or thick green shrubs. In
either case you can see through them and feel no sense of in-
trusion when you cross them.

Many lower-income families of the barrio manage to main- 16
tain a comfortable standard of living through the communal

*Dave Brubeck, pianist, composer, and conductor of "cool" modern jazz.

action of family members who contribute their wages to the head of the family. Economic need creates interdependence and closeness. Small barefooted boys sell papers on cool, dark Sunday mornings, deny themselves pleasantries, and give their earnings to *mamá.* The older the child, the greater the responsibility to help the head of the household provide for the rest of the family.

There are those, too, who for a number of reasons have not   17 achieved a relative sense of financial security. Perhaps it results from too many children too soon, but it is the homes of these people and their situation that numbs rather than charms. Their houses, aged and bent, oozing children, are fissures in the horn of plenty. Their wooden homes may have brick-pattern asbestos tile on the outer walls, but the tile is not convincing.

Unable to pay city taxes or incapable of influencing the city   18 to live up to its duty to serve all the citizens, the poorer barrio families remain trapped in the nineteenth century and survive as best they can. The backyards have well-worn paths to the outhouses, which sit near the alley. Running water is considered a luxury in some parts of the barrio. Decent drainage is usually unknown, and when it rains, the water stands for days, an incubator of health hazards and an avoidable nuisance. Streets, costly to pave, remain rough, rocky trails. Tires do not last long, and the constant rattling and shaking grind away a car's life and spread dust through screen windows.

The houses and their *jardines,* the jollity of the people in an   19 adverse world, the brightly feathered alarm clock pecking away at supper and cautiously eyeing the children playing nearby, produce a mystifying sensation at finding the noble savage alive in the twentieth century. It is easy to look at the positive qualities of life in the barrio, and look at them with a distantly envious feeling. One wishes to experience the feelings of the barrio and not the hardships. Remembering the illness, the hunger, the feeling of time running out on you, the walls, both real and imagined, reflecting on living in the past, one finds his envy becoming more elusive, until it has vanished altogether.

Back now beyond the tracks, the train creaks and groans, the   20 cars jostle each other down the track, and as the light begins its pulsing, the barrio, with all its meanings, greets a new dawn with yawns and restless stretchings.

Questions for Study and Discussion

1. What is the barrio? Where is it? What does Ramirez mean that "There is no want to escape, the feeling of the barrio is known only to its inhabitants, and the material needs of life can also be found there"?
2. Ramirez uses Spanish phrases throughout his essay. Why do you suppose he uses them? What is their effect on the reader? He also uses the words "home," "refuge," "family," and "closeness." What do they connote in the context of this essay? (Glossary: *Connotation/Denotation*) In what ways, if any, are they essential to his purpose? (Glossary: *Purpose*)
3. Identify several of the metaphors Ramirez uses in his essay and explain why they are particularly appropriate for this essay?
4. Explain Ramirez's use of the imagery of walls and fences to describe a sense of cultural isolation. What might this imagery be symbolic of? (Glossary: *Symbol*)
5. Ramirez goes into some detail about the many groups in the barrio. Identify those groups. In what ways do they participate in the unity of life in the barrio?
6. Ramirez begins his essay with a relatively positive picture of the barrio, but ends on a more disheartening note. Why has he organized his essay this way? What might the effect have been if he had reversed these images? (Glossary: *Beginnings and Endings*)

Vocabulary

Refer to your dictionary to define the following words as they are used in this selection. Then use each word in a sentence of your own.

paradoxical (2)	Chicano (11)
eludes (2)	countenances (12)
permeated (3)	fissures (17)
stoical (4)	elusive (19)
pariahs (4)	adverse (19)
complacently (9)	

Suggested Writing Assignments

1. Write a brief essay in which you describe your own neighborhood.

2. In paragraph 19 of his essay Ramirez says, "One wishes to experience the feelings of the barrio and not the hardships." Explore his meaning in light of what you have just read and other experience or knowledge you may have of "ghetto" living. In what way can it be said that the hardships of such living are a necessary part of its "feelings"? How might barrio life change, for the good or the bad, if the city were to "live up to its duty to serve all the citizens"?

THE DEATH OF BENNY PARET

Norman Mailer

Norman Mailer, born in Long Branch, New Jersey, in 1923, graduated from Harvard University in 1943 with a degree in engineering. While at Harvard, he made the decision to become a writer and, with the publication of his first novel, The Naked and the Dead *(1948), based on his war experiences in the Pacific during World War II, Mailer established himself as a writer of note. Mailer's literary interests have ranged widely over the years, from novels to nonfiction and journalism; from politics, sports, feminism, and lunar exploration to popular culture, ancient Egyptian culture, and criminality. In this account of the welterweight championship fight between Benny Paret and Emile Griffith, we can experience what Mailer himself felt as he sat at ringside the fateful night of March 25, 1962, the night of Paret's last fight. As you read, notice the way Mailer uses figures of speech to evoke the scene for the reader.*

P aret was a Cuban, a proud club fighter who had become 1 welterweight champion because of his unusual ability to take a punch. His style of fighting was to take three punches to the head in order to give back two. At the end of ten rounds, he would still be bouncing, his opponent would have a headache. But in the last two years, over the fifteen-round fights, he had started to take some bad maulings.

This fight had its turns. Griffith won most of the early 2 rounds, but Paret knocked Griffith down in the sixth. Griffith had trouble getting up, but made it, came alive and was dominating Paret again before the round was over. Then Paret began to wilt. In the middle of the eighth round, after a clubbing punch had turned his back to Griffith, Paret walked three disgusted steps away, showing his hindquarters. For a champion, he took much too long to turn back around. It was the first hint of weakness Paret had ever shown, and it must have inspired a particular shame, because he fought the rest of the fight as if he were seeking to demonstrate that he could take more punishment than any man alive. In the twelfth, Griffith caught him. Paret got trapped in a corner. Trying to duck away, his left arm and his head became tangled on the wrong side of the top rope. Griffith was in like a cat ready to rip the life out of a huge boxed rat. He hit him eighteen right hands in a row, an act which took perhaps three or four seconds, Griffith making a pent-up whimpering sound all the while he attacked, the right hand whipping like a piston rod which has broken through the crankcase, or like a baseball bat demolishing a pumpkin. I was sitting in the second row of that corner—they were not ten feet away from me, and like everybody else, I was hypnotized. I had never seen one man hit another so hard and so many times. Over the referee's face came a look of woe as if some spasm had passed its way through him, and then he leaped on Griffith to pull him away. It was the act of a brave man. Griffith was uncontrollable. His trainer leaped into the ring, his manager, his cut man, there were four people holding Griffith, but he was off on an orgy, he had left the Garden, he was back on a hoodlum's street. If he had been able to break loose from his handlers and the referee, he would have jumped Paret to the floor and whaled on him there.

And Paret? Paret died on his feet. As he took those eighteen ³ punches something happened to everyone who was in psychic range of the event. Some part of his death reached out to us. One felt it hover in the air. He was still standing in the ropes, trapped as he had been before, he gave some little half-smile of regret, as if he were saying, "I didn't know I was going to die just yet," and then, his head leaning back but still erect, his death came to breathe about him. He began to pass away. As he passed, so his limbs descended beneath him, and he sank slowly to the floor. He went down more slowly than any fighter had ever gone down, he went down like a large ship which turns on end and slides second by second into its grave. As he went down, the sound of Griffith's punches echoed in the mind like a heavy ax in the distance chopping into a wet log.

Questions for Study and Discussion

1. What differentiated Paret and Griffith for Mailer? Who was the welterweight champion?
2. What are the implications of Griffith's actions in the twelfth round of the fight for the sport of boxing in general?
3. Identify at least three similes in this essay. Why do you think Mailer felt the need to use figures of speech in describing Paret's death?
4. Mailer starts paragraph 3 with a question. What effect does this question have on you as a reader? (Glossary: *Rhetorical Question*)
5. Does Mailer place the blame for Paret's death on anyone? Explain.
6. Explain how Mailer personifies death in paragraph 3.

Vocabulary

Refer to your dictionary to define the following words as they are used in this selection. Then use each word in a sentence of your own.

wilt (2)	psychic (3)
spasm (2)	hover (3)

Suggested Writing Assignments

1. The death of Benny Paret was neither the first nor the last death to occur in professional boxing. Should boxing, therefore, be banned? Write an essay arguing for or against the continuation of professional boxing. As you write, use several figures of speech to enliven your essay.
2. Sports commentators and critics have pointed to the role fans have played in the promotion of violence in sports. If you feel that fans promote violent behavior, what do you suggest can be done, if anything, to alleviate the negative effect fans have? Using examples from your own experience in attending sporting events, write an essay explaining your position on this subject. Enrich your descriptions with figures of speech.

III

TYPES
OF
ESSAYS

10

ILLUSTRATION

Illustration is the use of examples to make ideas more concrete and to make generalizations more specific and detailed. Examples enable writers not just to tell but to show what they mean. For example, an essay about recently developed alternative sources of energy becomes clear and interesting with the use of some examples—say, solar energy or the heat from the earth's core. The more specific the example, the more effective it is. Along with general statements about solar energy, the writer might offer several examples of how the home building industry is installing solar collectors instead of conventional hot water systems, or building solar greenhouses to replace conventional central heating.

In an essay a writer uses examples to clarify or support the thesis; in a paragraph, to clarify or support the main idea. Sometimes a single striking example suffices; sometimes a whole series of related examples is necessary. The following paragraph presents a single extended example—an anecdote, or story—that illustrates the author's point about cultural differences:

> Whenever there is a great cultural distance between two people, there are bound to be problems arising from differences in behavior and expectations. An example is the American couple who consulted a psychiatrist about their marital problems. The husband was from New England and had been brought up by reserved parents who taught him to control his emotions and to respect the need for privacy. His wife was from an Italian family and had been brought up in close contact with all the members of her large family, who were extremely warm, volatile and demonstrative. When the husband came home after a hard day at the office, dragging his feet and longing for peace and quiet, his wife would rush to him and smother him. Clasping his hands, rubbing his brow, crooning over his

weary head, she never left him alone. But when the wife was upset or anxious about her day, the husband's response was to withdraw completely and leave her alone. No comforting, no affectionate embrace, no attention—just solitude. The woman became convinced her husband didn't love her and, in desperation, she consulted a psychiatrist. Their problem wasn't basically psychological but cultural.

Edward T. Hall

This single example is effective because it is *representative*—that is, essentially similar to other such problems he might have described and familiar to many readers. Hall tells the story with enough detail that readers can understand the couple's feelings and so better understand the point he is trying to make.

In contrast, Edwin Way Teale supports his topic sentence about country superstitions with eleven examples:

In the folklore of the country, numerous superstitions relate to winter weather. Back-country farmers examine their corn husks—the thicker the husk, the colder the winter. They watch the acorn crop—the more acorns, the more severe the season. They observe where white-faced hornets place their paper nests—the higher they are, the deeper will be the snow. They examine the size and shape and color of the spleens of butchered hogs for clues to the severity of the season. They keep track of the blooming of dogwood in the spring—the more abundant the blooms, the more bitter the cold in January. When chipmunks carry their tails high and squirrels have heavier fur and mice come into country houses early in the fall, the superstitious gird themselves for a long, hard winter. Without any scientific basis, a wider-than-usual black band on a woolly-bear caterpillar is accepted as a sign that winter will arrive early and stay late. Even the way a cat sits beside the stove carries its message to the credulous. According to a belief once widely held in the Ozarks, a cat sitting with its tail to the fire indicates very cold weather is on the way.

Edwin Way Teale

Teale uses numerous examples because he is writing about various superstitions. Also, putting all those strange beliefs side by side in a kind of catalogue makes the paragraph fun to read as well as informative.

Illustration 215

Illustration is often found in effective writing; nearly every essay in this book contains one or more examples. Likewise this introduction has used examples to clarify its points about illustration.

A CRIME OF COMPASSION

Barbara Huttmann

Barbara Huttmann is a nurse, a teacher, and a writer. Her interest in the patients' rights issue is clearly evident in her two books, The Patient's Advocate *and* Code Blue. *In the following essay, which first appeared in* Newsweek *in 1983, Huttmann narrates the final months of the life of Mac, one of her favorite patients. By using emotional and graphic detail, Huttmann hopes her example of Mac will convince her audience of the need for new legislation which would permit terminally-ill patients to choose to die rather than suffer great pain and indignity.*

M urderer," a man shouted. "God help patients who get *you* for a nurse." 1

"What gives you the right to play God?" another one asked. 2

It was the Phil Donahue show where the guest is a fatted calf 3 and the audience a 200-strong flock of vultures hungering to pick at the bones. I had told them about Mac, one of my favorite cancer patients. "We resuscitated him 52 times in just one month. I refused to resuscitate him again. I simply sat there and held his hand while he died."

There wasn't time to explain that Mac was a young, witty, 4 macho cop who walked into the hospital with 32 pounds of attack equipment, looking as if he could single-handedly protect the whole city, if not the entire state. "Can't get rid of this cough," he said. Otherwise, he felt great.

Before the day was over, tests confirmed that he had lung 5 cancer. And before the year was over, I loved him, his wife, Maura, and their three kids as if they were my own. All the nurses loved him. And we all battled his disease for six months without ever giving death a thought. Six months isn't such a long time in the whole scheme of things, but it was long enough to see him lose his youth, his wit, his macho, his hair, his bowel

216

and bladder control, his sense of taste and smell, and his ability
to do the slightest thing for himself. It was also long enough to
watch Maura's transformation from a young woman into a
haggard, beaten old lady.

When Mac had wasted away to a 60-pound skeleton kept alive   6
by liquid food we poured down a tube, i.v. solutions we dripped
into his veins, and oxygen we piped to a mask on his face, he
begged us: "Mercy . . . for God's sake, please just let me go."

The first time he stopped breathing, the nurse pushed the   7
button that calls a "code blue" throughout the hospital and
sends a team rushing to resuscitate the patient. Each time he
stopped breathing, sometimes two or three times in one day, the
code team came again. The doctors and technicians worked
their miracles and walked away. The nurses stayed to wipe the
saliva that drooled from his mouth, irrigate the big craters of
bedsores that covered his hips, suction the lung fluids that
threatened to drown him, clean the feces that burned his skin
like lye, pour the liquid food down the tube attached to his
stomach, put pillows between his knees to ease the bone-on-
bone pain, turn him every hour to keep the bedsores from
getting worse, and change his gown and linen every two hours
to keep him from being soaked in perspiration.

At night I went home and tried to scrub away the smell of   8
decaying flesh that seemed woven into the fabric of my uniform. It was in my hair, the upholstery of my car—there was no
washing it away. And every night I prayed that Mac would die,
that his agonized eyes would never again plead with me to let
him die.

Every morning I asked his doctor for a "no-code" order.   9
Without that order, we had to resuscitate every patient who
stopped breathing. His doctor was one of several who believe
we must extend life as long as we have the means and knowledge to do it. To not do it is to be liable for negligence, at least
in the eyes of many people, including some nurses. I thought
about what it would be like to stand before a judge, accused of
murder, if Mac stopped breathing and I didn't call a code.

And after the fifty-second code, when Mac was still lucid   10
enough to beg for death again, and Maura was crumbled in my
arms again, and when no amount of pain medication stilled his
moaning and agony, I wondered about a spiritual judge. Was all

this misery and suffering supposed to be building character or infusing us all with the sense of humility that comes from impotence?

Had we, the whole medical community, become so arrogant 11
that we believed in the illusion of salvation through science? Had we become so self-righteous that we thought meddling in God's work was our duty, our moral imperative and our legal obligation? Did we really believe that we had the right to force "life" on a suffering man who had begged for the right to die?

Such questions haunted me more than ever early one morn- 12
ing when Maura went home to change her clothes and I was bathing Mac. He had been still for so long, I thought he at last had the blessed relief of coma. Then he opened his eyes and moaned, "Pain . . . no more . . . Barbara . . . do something . . . God, let me go."

The desperation in his eyes and voice riddled me with guilt. 13
"I'll stop," I told him as I injected the pain medication.

I sat on the bed and held Mac's hands in mine. He pressed his 14
bony fingers against my hand and muttered, "Thanks." Then there was one soft sigh and I felt his hands go cold in mine. "Mac?" I whispered, as I waited for his chest to rise and fall again.

A clutch of panic banded my chest, drew my finger to the 15
code button, urged me to do something, anything . . . but sit there alone with death. I kept one finger on the button, without pressing it, as a waxen pallor slowly transformed his face from person to empty shell. Nothing I've ever done in my 47 years has taken so much effort as it took *not* to press that code button.

Eventually, when I was as sure as I could be that the code 16
team would fail to bring him back, I entered the legal twilight zone and pushed the button. The team tried. And while they were trying, Maura walked into the room and shrieked, "No . . . don't let them do this to him . . . for God's sake . . . please, no more."

Cradling her in my arms was like cradling myself, Mac, and 17
all those patients and nurses who had been in this place before, who do the best they can in a death-denying society.

So a TV audience accused me of murder. Perhaps I am guilty. 18
If a doctor had written a no-code order, which is the only *legal* alternative, would he have felt any less guilty? Until there is

legislation making it a criminal act to code a patient who has requested the right to die, we will all of us risk the same fate as Mac. For whatever reason, we developed the means to prolong life, and now we are forced to use it. We do not have the right to die.

Questions for Study and Discussion

1. Why did people in the audience of the Phil Donahue Show call Huttmann a "murderer"? Is there any sense in which their accusation is justified? In what ways do you think Huttmann might agree with them?
2. In paragraph 15, Huttmann says, "Nothing I've ever done in my 47 years has taken so much effort as it took *not* to press that code button." How effectively does she illustrate her struggle against pressing the button? What steps led to her ultimate decision not to press the code button?
3. What, according to Huttmann, is the "only legal alternative" to her action? What does she find hypocritical about that choice?
4. Huttmann makes a powerfully emotional appeal for a patient's right to die. Some readers might even find some of her story shocking or offensive. Cite examples of some of the graphic scenes Huttmann describes and discuss their impact on you as a reader. Did they help persuade you to Huttmann's point of view or did you find them overly unnerving? What would have been gained or lost had she left them out?
5. The story in Huttmann's example covers a period of six months. In paragraphs 4–6, she describes the first five months of Mac's illness; in paragraphs 7–10, the sixth month; and in paragraphs 11–17, the final morning. In what ways does her use of time illustrate her point that a patient must be permitted to choose to die? Explain.
6. Huttmann concludes her essay with the statement, "We do not have the right to die." What does she mean by this? In your opinion, is she exaggerating, or simply stat-

ing the facts? Does her example of Mac adequately illustrate Huttman's concluding point?

Vocabulary

Refer to your dictionary to define the following words as they
are used in this selection. Then use each word in a sentence of
your own.

resuscitate (3)   imperative (11)
irrigate (7)   waxen (15)
lucid (10)   pallor (15)

Suggested Writing Assignments

1. Write a letter to the editor of *Newsweek* in which you respond to Huttmann's essay. Would you be for or against
   legislation that would give terminally ill patients the right
   to die? Give examples from your personal experience or
   from your reading to support your opinion.
2. Using one of the following sentences as your thesis statement, write an essay giving examples from personal experience or from reading to support your opinion.

   Consumers have more power than they realize.
   Most products do/do not measure up to the claims of
      their advertisements.
   Religion is/is not alive and well.
   Government works far better than its critics claim.
   Being able to write well is more than a basic skill.
   The seasons for professional sports are too long.
   Today's college students are serious minded when it
      comes to academics.

DARKNESS AT NOON

Harold Krents

Harold Krents prepared for a career as a lawyer at Harvard and Oxford and practiced law in Washington, D. C. until his death in 1986. He is the author of To Race the Wind *(1972). Krents, blind from birth, had long been interested in the plight of the handicapped. In the following essay, which first appeared in the* New York Times, *Krents draws on his own experiences to illustrate the idea that physical handicaps need not be disabling.*

Blind from birth, I have never had the opportunity to see myself and have been completely dependent on the image I create in the eye of the observer. To date it has not been narcissistic.

There are those who assume that since I can't see, I obviously also cannot hear. Very often people will converse with me at the top of their lungs, enunciating each word very carefully. Conversely, people will also often whisper, assuming that since my eyes don't work, my ears don't either.

For example, when I go to the airport and ask the ticket agent for assistance to the plane, he or she will invariably pick up the phone, call a ground hostess and whisper: "Hi, Jane, we've got a 76 here." I have concluded that the word "blind" is not used for one of two reasons: Either they fear that if the dread word is spoken, the ticket agent's retina will immediately detach or they are reluctant to inform me of my condition of which I may not have been previously aware.

On the other hand, others know that of course I can hear, but believe that I can't talk. Often, therefore, when my wife and I go out to dinner, a waiter or waitress will ask Kit if "*he* would like a drink" to which I respond that "indeed *he* would."

This point was graphically driven home to me while we were in England. I had been given a year's leave of absence from my

221

Washington law firm to study for a diploma in law degree at
Oxford University. During the year I became ill and was hospitalized. Immediately after admission, I was wheeled down to
the X-ray room. Just at the door sat an elderly woman—elderly
I would judge from the sound of her voice. "What is his name?"
the woman asked the orderly who had been wheeling me.

"What's your name?" the orderly repeated to me.   6

"Harold Krents," I replied.   7

"Harold Krents," he repeated.   8

"When was he born?"   9

"When were you born?"   10

"November 5, 1944," I responded.   11

"November 5, 1944," the orderly intoned.   12

This procedure continued for approximately five minutes at   13
which point even my saint-like disposition deserted me. "Look,"
I finally blurted out, "this is absolutely ridiculous. Okay,
granted I can't see, but it's got to have become pretty clear to
both of you that I don't need an interpreter."

"He says he doesn't need an interpreter," the orderly reported   14
to the woman.

The toughest misconception of all is the view that because I   15
can't see, I can't work. I was turned down by over forty law
firms because of my blindness, even though my qualifications
included a cum laude degree from Harvard College and a good
ranking in my Harvard Law School class.

The attempt to find employment, the continuous frustration   16
of being told that it was impossible for a blind person to practice law, the rejection letters, not based on my lack of ability but
rather on my disability, will always remain one of the most
disillusioning experiences of my life.

Fortunately, this view of limitation and exclusion is begin-   17
ning to change. On April 16, the Department of Labor issued
regulations that mandate equal-employment opportunities for
the handicapped. By and large, the business community's response to offering employment to the disabled has been enthusiastic.

I therefore look forward to the day, with the expectation that   18
it is certain to come, when employers will view their handicapped workers as a little child did me years ago when my
family still lived in Scarsdale.

I was playing basketball with my father in our backyard   19
according to procedures we had developed. My father would
stand beneath the hoop, shout, and I would shoot over his head
at the basket attached to our garage. Our next-door neighbor,
aged five, wandered over into our yard with a playmate. "He's
blind," our neighbor whispered to her friend in a voice that
could be heard distinctly by Dad and me. Dad shot and missed;
I did the same. Dad hit the rim: I missed entirely: Dad shot and
missed the garage entirely. "Which one is blind?" whispered
back the little friend.

I would hope that in the near future when a plant manager is   20
touring the factory with the foreman and comes upon a handicapped and nonhandicapped person working together, his
comment after watching them work will be, "Which one is
disabled?"

Questions for Study and Discussion

1. What is Krents's thesis, and where is it stated? (Glossary:
   Thesis)
2. What is the meaning of Krents's title?
3. How does Krents make use of anecdotes to support his
   thesis? Does he use inductive or deductive reasoning to
   make his point? (Glossary: *Induction, Deduction*)
4. Krents describes three commonly held misconceptions
   about handicapped people and provides an example to
   support each of them. How persuasive is each example?
   How has Krents organized the misconceptions he names?
   Would another method of organization have been more
   suitable? Explain (Glossary: *Organization*)
5. Krents relies on the use of irony throughout his essay.
   Identify several instances of irony and explain in what
   ways they contribute to the overall point of his essay.
   (Glossary: *Irony*)
6. In paragraph 16, Krents explains that he had been turned
   down for jobs "not based on my lack of ability, but rather
   on my disability." How does he distinguish between the

two and in what way is the distinction important? How does Krents's concluding anecdote function in the context of this distinction? Explain.

Vocabulary

Refer to your dictionary to define the following words as they are used in this selection. Then use each word in a sentence of your own.

narcissistic (1)   disposition (13)
enunciate (2)   disillusioning (16)
invariably (3)   mandate (17)

Suggested Writing Assignments

1. Krents tells of three experiences he had as a blind person in order to make his point that the handicapped are unfairly and unreasonably discriminated against. Draw from events in your own life as a woman, a man, a student, or a young person to demonstrate the ways in which we can be unfairly judged, not because of who we are, but because of what we are.

2. Using one of the following statements as your main idea, write an essay illustrating your thesis with examples from personal experience or from your reading.

    People show their intelligence in many different ways.

    If things can go wrong, they probably will.

    Many toys on the market today promote sexual stereotypes.

    School teaches us as many undesirable things as good things.

    Clothes do/do not make the man/woman.

WHAT MAKES A LEADER?

Michael Korda

Michael Korda is the author of such best sellers as Power *(1975),* Male Chauvinism *(1979),* Charmed Lives *(1979), and* Queenie *(1985). In this essay, which first appeared in* Newsweek, *Korda discusses the qualities that all good leaders have in common. Notice Korda's use of a variety of historic and contemporary examples to make his definition concrete.*

Not every President is a leader, but every time we elect a 1 President we hope for one, especially in times of doubt and crisis. In easy times we are ambivalent—the leader, after all, makes demands, challenges the status quo, shakes things up.

Leadership is as much a question of timing as anything else. 2 The leader must appear on the scene at a moment when people are looking for leadership, as Churchill did in 1940, as Roosevelt did in 1933, as Lenin did in 1917. And when he comes, he must offer a simple, eloquent message.

Great leaders are almost always great simplifiers, who cut 3 through argument, debate and doubt to offer a solution everybody can understand and remember. Churchill warned the British to expect "blood, toil, tears and sweat"; FDR told Americans that "the only thing we have to fear is fear itself"; Lenin promised the war-weary Russians peace, land and bread. Straightforward but potent messages.

We have an image of what a leader ought to be. We even rec- 4 ognize the physical signs: leaders may not necessarily be tall, but they must have bigger-than-life, commanding features— LBJ's nose and ear lobes; Ike's broad grin. A trademark also comes in handy: Lincoln's stovepipe hat, JFK's rocker. We expect our leaders to stand out a little, not to be like ordinary men. Half of President Ford's trouble lay in the fact that, if you closed your eyes for a moment, you couldn't remember his face, figure or clothes. A leader should have an unforgettable identity, instantly and permanently fixed in people's minds.

It also helps for a leader to be able to do something most of   5
us can't: FDR overcame polio; Mao swam the Yangtze River at the age of 72. We don't want our leaders to be "just like us." We want them to be like us but better, special, more so. Yet if they are *too* different, we reject them. Adlai Stevenson was too cerebral. Nelson Rockefeller, too rich.

Even television, which comes in for a lot of knocks as an   6
image-builder that magnifies form over substance, doesn't altogether obscure the qualities of leadership we recognize, or their absence. Television exposed Nixon's insecurity, Humphrey's fatal infatuation with his own voice.

A leader must know how to use power (that's what leadership   7
is about), but he also has to have a way of showing that he does. He has to be able to project firmness—no physical clumsiness (like Ford), no rapid eye movements (like Carter).

A Chinese philosopher once remarked that a leader must   8
have the grace of a good dancer, and there is a great deal of wisdom to this. A leader should know how to appear relaxed and confident. His walk should be firm and purposeful. He should be able, like Lincoln, FDR, Truman, Ike and JFK, to give a good, hearty, belly laugh, instead of the sickly grin that passes for good humor in Nixon or Carter. Ronald Reagan's training as an actor showed to good effect in the debate with Carter, when by his easy manner and apparent affability, he managed to convey the impression that in fact he was the President and Carter the challenger.

If we know what we're looking for, why is it so difficult to   9
find? The answer lies in a very simple truth about leadership. *People can only be led where they want to go.* The leader follows, though a step ahead. Americans *wanted* to climb out of the Depression and needed someone to tell them they could do it, and FDR did. The British believed that they could still win the war after the defeats of 1940, and Churchill told them they were right.

A leader rides the waves, moves with the tides, understands   10
the deepest yearnings of his people. He cannot make a nation that wants peace at any price go to war, or stop a nation determined to fight from doing so. His purpose must match the na-

tional mood. His task is to focus the people's energies and desires, to define them in simple terms, to inspire, to make what people already want seem attainable, important, within their grasp.

Above all, he must dignify our desires, convince us that we are taking part in the making of great history, give us a sense of glory about ourselves. Winston Churchill managed, by sheer rhetoric, to turn the British defeat and the evacuation of Dunkirk in 1940 into a major victory. FDR's words turned the sinking of the American fleet at Pearl Harbor into a national rallying cry instead of a humiliating national scandal. A leader must stir our blood, not appeal to our reason. . . .   11

A great leader must have a certain irrational quality, a stubborn refusal to face facts, infectious optimism, the ability to convince us that all is not lost even when we're afraid it is. Confucius suggested that, while the advisors of a great leader should be as cold as ice, the leader himself should have fire, a spark of divine madness.   12

He won't come until we're ready for him, for the leader is like a mirror, reflecting back to us our own sense of purpose, putting into words our own dreams and hopes, transforming our needs and fears into coherent policies and programs.   13

Our strength makes him strong; our determination makes him determined; our courage makes him a hero; he is, in the final analysis, the symbol of the best in us, shaped by our own spirit and will. And when these qualities are lacking in us, we can't produce him; and even with all our skill at image-building, we can't fake him. He is, after all, merely the sum of us.   14

Questions for Study and Discussion

1. What is Korda's thesis in this essay, and where is it stated? Why do you suppose he states his thesis where he does instead of elsewhere in the essay? (Glossary: *Thesis*)
2. What, for Korda, are the major characteristics of a leader?
3. Identify the topic sentence in paragraph 4. What would be gained or lost if the topic sentence were placed elsewhere in the paragraph?

4. Korda's knowledge of history and great leaders is reflected in the examples he uses to support his topic sentences. Using paragraphs 2, 4, 8, and 11 explain how
Korda's examples develop his topic sentences. (Glossary:
Example)

5. What does Korda gain by using a series of short examples
to support each point instead of a single extended example?

6. What does Korda mean when he says that "a great leader
must have a certain irrational quality" (12)?

7. What would be gained or lost if paragraphs 13 and 14
were combined?

8. At the beginning of paragraph 9 Korda asks a rhetorical
question, one that requires no answer and that is often
used for emphasis. What is the purpose of this question
in the context of his essay?

Vocabulary

Refer to your dictionary to define the following words as they
are used in this selection. Then use each word in a sentence of
your own.

ambivalent (1)	cerebral (5)
status quo (1)	affability (8)
eloquent (2)	infectious (12)

Suggested Writing Assignments

1. In his essay, Michael Korda presents his views on what
makes a great leader. Most people would agree, however,
that for a leader to lead there must be those who are willing to be led, to be good team players. Write an essay in
which you explain what it takes to be a willing and productive participant in a group effort, whether the group
be as small as a class or a basketball team or as large as
a major corporation. While writing be especially conscious of selecting examples that clearly illustrate your
thesis.

2. Select one of the following topics for a short essay:

What makes a good teacher?
What makes a good student?
What makes a good team captain?
What makes a good parent?

Make sure that your essay contains well-chosen examples.

RAMBOS OF THE ROAD

Martin Gottfried

*Martin Gottfried is a writer and drama critic
in New York City. His many books include* A
Theater Divided: The Postwar American Stage
(1968), Broadway Musicals *(1979), and* In Person:
The Great Entertainers *(1985). The antics of New
York City's drivers got Gottfried to thinking why
so many people have become uncivil, belligerent,
and a little crazy when behind the wheel. In the
following essay from the September 8, 1986 issue
of* Newsweek, *he describes the anti-social behavior of modern-day drivers and speculates that
they have no better way to vent their frustrations.*

The car pulled up and its driver glared at us with such   1
sudden intensity, such hatred, that I was truly afraid for
our lives. Except for the Mohawk haircut he didn't have, he
looked like Robert DeNiro in "Taxi Driver," the sort of young
man who, delirious for notoriety, might kill a president.

He was glaring because we had passed him and for that af-   2
front he pursued us to the next stoplight so as to express his in-
dignation and affirm his masculinity. I was with two women
and, believe it, was afraid for all three of us. It was nearly mid-
night and we were in a small, sleeping town with no other cars
on the road.

When the light turned green, I raced ahead, knowing it was   3
foolish and that I was not in a movie. He didn't merely follow,
he chased, and with his headlights turned off. No matter what
sudden turn I took, he followed. My passengers were silent. I
knew they were alarmed, and I prayed that I wouldn't be called
upon to protect them. In that cheerful frame of mind, I turned
off my own lights so I couldn't be followed. It was lunacy. I was
responding to a crazy *as* a crazy.

"I'll just drive to the police station," I finally said, and as if   4
those were the magic words, he disappeared.

230

It seems to me that there has recently been an epidemic of auto 5
macho—a competition perceived and expressed in driving. People fight it out over parking spaces. They bully into line at the gas pump. A toll booth becomes a signal for elbowing fenders. And beetle-eyed drivers hunch over their steering wheels, squeezing the rims, glowering, preparing the excuse of not having seen you as they muscle you off the road. Approaching a highway on an entrance ramp recently, I was strong-armed by a trailer truck so immense that its driver all but blew me away by blasting his horn. The behemoth was just inches from my hopelessly mismatched coupe when I fled for the safety of the shoulder.

And this is happening on city streets, too. A New York taxi 6
driver told me that "intimidation is the name of the game. Drive as if you're deaf and blind. You don't hear the other guy's horn and you sure as hell don't see him."

The odd thing is that long before I was even able to drive, it 7
seemed to me that people were at their finest and most civilized when in their cars. They seemed so orderly and considerate, so reasonable, staying in the right-hand lane unless passing, signaling all intentions. In those days you really eased into highway traffic, and the long, neat rows of cars seemed mobile testimony to the sanity of most people. Perhaps memory fails, perhaps there were always testy drivers, perhaps—but everyone didn't give you the finger.

A most amazing example of driver rage occurred recently at 8
the Manhattan end of the Lincoln Tunnel. We were four cars abreast, stopped at a traffic light. And there was no moving even when the light had changed. A bus had stopped in the cross traffic, blocking our paths: it was a normal-for-New-York-City gridlock. Perhaps impatient, perhaps late for important appointments, three of us nonetheless accepted what, after all, we could not alter. One, however, would not. He would not be helpless. He would go where he was going even if he couldn't get there. A Wall Street type in suit and tie, he got out of his car and strode toward the bus, rapping smartly on its doors. When they opened, he exchanged words with the driver. The doors folded shut. He then stepped in front of the bus, took hold of one of its large windshield wipers and broke it.

The bus doors reopened and the driver appeared, apparently 9
giving the fellow a good piece of his mind. If so, the lecture was

wasted, for the man started his car and proceeded to drive directly *into the bus*. He rammed it. Even though the point at which he struck the bus, the folding doors, was its most vulnerable point, ramming the side of a bus with your car has to rank very high on a futility index. My first thought was that it had to be a rented car.

To tell the truth, I could not believe my eyes. The bus driver opened his doors as much as they could be opened and he stepped directly onto the hood of the attacking car, jumping up and down with both his feet. He then retreated into the bus, closing the doors behind him. Obviously a man of action, the car driver backed up and rammed the bus again. How this exercise in absurdity would have been resolved none of us will ever know for at that point the traffic unclogged and the bus moved on. And the rest of us, we passives of the world, proceeded, our cars crossing a field of battle as if nothing untoward had happened.   10

It is tempting to blame such belligerent, uncivil and even neurotic behavior on the nuts of the world, but in our cars we all become a little crazy. How many of us speed up when a driver signals his intention of pulling in front of us? Are we resentful and anxious to pass him? How many of us try to squeeze in, or race along the shoulder at a lane merger? We may not jump on hoods, but driving the gauntlet, we seethe, cursing not so silently in the safety of our steel bodies on wheels—fortresses for cowards.   11

What is it within us that gives birth to such antisocial behavior and why, all of a sudden, have so many drivers gone around the bend? My friend Joel Katz, a Manhattan psychiatrist, calls it, "a Rambo pattern. People are running around thinking the American way is to take the law into your own hands when anyone does anything wrong. And what constitutes 'wrong?' Anything that cramps your style."   12

It seems to me that it is a new America we see on the road now. It has the mentality of a hoodlum and the backbone of a coward. The car is its weapon and hiding place, and it is still a symbol even in this. Road Rambos no longer bespeak a self-reliant, civil people tooling around in family cruisers. In fact, there aren't families in these machines that charge headlong with their brights on in broad daylight, demanding we get out   13 of their way. Bullies are loners, and they have perverted our liberty of the open road into drivers' license. They represent an America that derides the values of decency and good manners, then roam the highways riding shotgun and shrieking freedom. By allowing this to happen, the rest of us approve.

Questions for Study and Discussion

1. What image does Gottfried hope to evoke with his use of the word "Rambo" in his title? In what way does his choice of a title establish the tone of his essay?

2. Gottfried makes use of a single extended example as well as a series of related examples. Explain in what ways his examples contribute to the overall effectiveness of Gottfried's essay.

3. What are "elbowing fenders" and "lane mergers"? What is the difference between the two?

4. How does Gottfried describe his pursuer and the man who attacked the bus? Do these descriptions enhance or detract from Gottfried's image of the road "Rambo"?

5. What is Gottfried's attitude about "Rambos" of the road? (Glossary: *Attitude*) How do you know? Cite examples from the text to support your answer.

6. In paragraph 12 Gottfried asks why "have so many drivers gone around the bend?" What does he mean by this? Do you think that a significant number of today's drivers are guilty of the "antisocial behavior" Gottfried describes? Are you guilty of this behavior yourself on occasion? If so, in what situations.

Vocabulary

Refer to your dictionary to define the following words as they are used in this selection. Then use each word in a sentence of your own.

sullen (1)	affront (2)
notoriety (1)	indignation (2)

behemoth (5)   untoward (10)
futility (9)   gauntlet (11)

Suggested Writing Assignments

1. Write an essay in which you describe some different types of drivers on the road today—for example, out-of-towners, big-city, lead-foots, and defensive drivers. Be sure to include examples that illustrate each type clearly and precisely.

2. Write an essay using the following statement as your thesis: "Americans are too concerned with winning." Use examples from your own experiences and observations to illustrate your points.

11

NARRATION

To *narrate* is to tell a story or to tell what happened. Whenever you relate an incident or use an anecdote to make a point, you use narration. In its broadest sense, narration is any account of an event or series of events. Although most often associated with fiction, narration is effective and useful in all kinds of writing.

Good narration has four essential features: a clear context; well-chosen details; a logical, often chronological organization; and an appropriate and consistent point of view. Consider, for example, the following paragraph from Willie Morris's "On a Commuter Train":

> One afternoon in late August, as the summer's sun streamed into the [railroad] car and made little jumping shadows on the windows, I sat gazing out at the tenement-dwellers, who were themselves looking out of their windows from the gray crumbling buildings along the tracks of upper Manhattan. As we crossed into the Bronx, the train unexpectedly slowed down for a few miles. Suddenly from out of my window I saw a large crowd near the tracks, held back by two policemen. Then, on the other side from my window, I saw a sight I would never be able to forget: a little boy almost severed in halves, lying at an incredible angle near the track. The ground was covered with blood, and the boy's eyes were opened wide, strained and disbelieving in his sudden oblivion. A policeman stood next to him, his arms folded, staring straight ahead at the windows of our train. In the orange glow of late afternoon the policemen, the crowd, the corpse of the boy were for a brief moment immobile, motionless, a small tableau to violence and death in the city. Behind me, in the next row of seats, there was a game of bridge. I heard one of the four men say as he looked out at the sight, "God, that's horrible." Another said, in a whisper, "Terrible, terrible." There was a momentary silence, punctuated only by the clicking of the wheels

on the track. Then, after the pause, I heard the first man
say: "Two hearts."

Willie Morris

This paragraph contains all the elements of good narration.
At the beginning Morris establishes a clear context for his narrative, telling when, where, and to whom the action happened.
He has chosen details well, including enough detail so that we
know what is happening but not so much that we become overwhelmed, confused, or bored. Morris organizes his narration
logically, with a beginning that sets the scene, a middle that
paints the picture, and an end that makes his point, all arranged
chronologically. Finally, he tells the story from the first-person
point of view: We experience the event directly through the
writer's eyes and ears, as if we too had been on the scene of the
action.

Morris could have told his story from the third-person point
of view. In this point of view, the narrator is not a participant
in the action, and does not use the pronoun *I*. In the following example, William Allen White narrates his daughter's fatal
accident:

The last hour of her life was typical of its happiness. She
came home from a day's work at school, topped off by a
hard grind with the copy on the High School Annual, and
felt that a ride would refresh her. She climbed into her
khakis, chattering to her mother about the work she was
doing, and hurried to get her horse and be out on the dirt
roads for the country air and the radiant green fields of the
spring. As she rode through the town on an easy gallop she
kept waving at passers-by. She knew everyone in town. For
a decade the little figure with the long pig-tail and the red
hair ribbon has been familiar on the streets of Emporia,
and she got in the way of speaking to those who nodded at
her. She passed the Kerrs, walking the horse, in front of
the Normal Library, and waved at them; passed another
friend a few hundred feet further on, and waved at her. The
horse was walking and, as she turned into North Merchant
street she took off her cowboy hat, and the horse swung
into a lope. She passed the Tripletts and waved her cowboy
hat at them, still moving gaily north on Merchant street. A
Gazette carrier passed—a High School boy friend—and she
waved at him, but with her bridle hand: the horse veered

quickly, plunged into the parking area where the low-hanging limb faced her, and, while she still looked back waving the blow came. But she did not fall from the horse; she slipped off, dazed a bit, staggered and fell in a faint. She never quite recovered consciousness.

William Allen White

SHAME

Dick Gregory

Dick Gregory, the well-known comedian, has long been active in the civil rights movement. During the 1960s Gregory was also an outspoken critic of America's involvement in Vietnam. In the following episode from his autobiography Nigger *(1964), he narrates the story of a childhood experience that taught him the meaning of shame. Through his use of realistic dialogue and vivid details, he dramatically re-creates this experience for his readers.*

I never learned hate at home, or shame. I had to go to school for that. I was about seven years old when I got my first big lesson. I was in love with a little girl named Helene Tucker, a light-complexioned little girl with pigtails and nice manners. She was always clean and she was smart in school. I think I went to school then mostly to look at her. I brushed my hair and even got me a little old handkerchief. It was a lady's handkerchief, but I didn't want Helene to see me wipe my nose on my hand. The pipes were frozen again, there was no water in the house, but I washed my socks and shirt every night. I'd get a pot, and go over to Mister Ben's grocery store, and stick my pot down into his soda machine. Scoop out some chopped ice. By evening the ice melted to water for washing. I got sick a lot that winter because the fire would go out at night before the clothes were dry. In the morning I'd put them on, wet or dry, because they were the only clothes I had.

Everybody's got a Helene Tucker, a symbol of everything you want. I loved her for her goodness, her cleanness, her popularity. She'd walk down my street and my brothers and sisters would yell, "Here comes Helene," and I'd rub my tennis sneakers on the back of my pants and wish my hair wasn't so nappy and the white folks' shirt fit me better. I'd run out on the street. If I knew my place and didn't come too close, she'd wink at me and say hello. That was a good feeling. Sometimes I'd follow her all the way home, and shovel the snow off her walk and try to make friends with her Momma and her aunts. I'd drop money on her stoop late at night on my way back from shining shoes in the taverns. And she had a Daddy, and he had a good job. He was a paper hanger.

I guess I would have gotten over Helene by summertime, but something happened in that classroom that made her face hang in front of me for the next twenty-two years. When I played the drums in high school it was for Helene and when I broke track records in college it was for Helene and when I started standing behind microphones and heard applause I wished Helene could hear it, too. It wasn't until I was twenty-nine years old and married and making money that I finally got her out of my system. Helene was sitting in that classroom when I learned to be ashamed of myself. 3

It was on a Thursday. I was sitting in the back of the room, in a seat with a chalk circle drawn around it. The idiot's seat, the troublemaker's seat. 4

The teacher thought I was stupid. Couldn't spell, couldn't read, couldn't do arithmetic. Just stupid. Teachers were never interested in finding out that you couldn't concentrate because you were so hungry, because you hadn't had any breakfast. All you could think about was noontime, would it ever come? Maybe you could sneak into the cloakroom and steal a bite of some kid's lunch out of a coat pocket. A bite of something. Paste. You can't really make a meal of paste, or put it on bread for a sandwich, but sometimes I'd scoop a few spoonfuls out of the paste jar in the back of the room. Pregnant people get strange tastes. I was pregnant with poverty. Pregnant with dirt and pregnant with smells that made people turn away, pregnant with cold and pregnant with shoes that were never bought for me, pregnant with five other people in my bed and no Daddy in the next room, and pregnant with hunger. Paste doesn't taste too bad when you're hungry. 5

The teacher thought I was a troublemaker. All she saw from the front of the room was a little black boy who squirmed in his idiot's seat and made noises and poked the kids around him. I guess she couldn't see a kid who made noises because he wanted someone to know he was there. 6

It was on a Thursday, the day before the Negro payday. The 7
eagle always flew on Friday. The teacher was asking each student how much his father would give to the Community Chest.
On Friday night, each kid would get the money from his father,
and on Monday he would bring it to the school. I decided I was
going to buy me a Daddy right then. I had money in my pocket
from shining shoes and selling papers, and whatever Helene
Tucker pledged for her Daddy I was going to top it. And I'd hand
the money right in. I wasn't going to wait until Monday to buy
me a Daddy.

I was shaking, scared to death. The teacher opened her book 8
and started calling out names alphabetically.

"Helene Tucker?" 9

"My daddy said he'd give two dollars and fifty cents." 10

"That's very nice, Helene. Very, very nice indeed." 11

That made me feel pretty good. It wouldn't take too much to 12
top that. I had almost three dollars in dimes and quarters in my
pocket. I stuck my hand in my pocket and held onto the money,
waiting for her to call my name. But the teacher closed her
book after she called everybody else in the class.

I stood up and raised my hand. 13

"What is it now?" 14

"You forgot me." 15

She turned toward the blackboard. "I don't have time to be 16
playing with you, Richard."

"My Daddy said he'd . . ." 17

"Sit down, Richard, you're disturbing the class." 18

"My Daddy said he'd give . . . fifteen dollars." 19

She turned around and looked mad. "We are collecting this 20
money for you and your kind, Richard Gregory. If your Daddy
can give fifteen dollars you have no business being on relief."

"I got it right now, I got it right now, my Daddy gave it to me 21
to turn in today, my Daddy said . . ."

"And furthermore," she said, looking right at me, her nostrils 22
getting big and her lips getting thin and her eyes opening wide,
"we know you don't have a Daddy."

Helene Tucker turned around, her eyes full of tears. She felt 23
sorry for me. Then I couldn't see her too well because I was crying, too.

"Sit down, Richard." 24

And I always thought the teacher kind of liked me. She al- 25
ways picked me to wash the blackboard on Friday, after school.
That was a big thrill, it made me feel important. If I didn't wash
it, come Monday the school might not function right.

"Where are you going, Richard?" 26

I walked out of school that day, and for a long time I didn't go 27
back very often. There was shame there.

Now there was shame everywhere. It seemed like the whole 28
world had been inside that classroom, everyone had heard what
the teacher had said, everyone had turned around and <u>felt sorry</u>
for me. There was shame in going to the Worthy Boys Annual
Christmas Dinner for you and your kind, because everybody
knew what a worthy boy was. Why couldn't they just call it the
Boys Annual Dinner; why'd they have to give it a name? There
was shame in wearing the brown and orange and white plaid
mackinaw the welfare gave to three thousand boys. Why'd it
have to be the same for everybody so when you walked down
the street the people could see you were on relief? It was a nice
warm mackinaw and it had a hood, and my Momma beat me
and called me a little rat when she found out I stuffed it in the
bottom of a pail full of garbage way over on Cottage Street.
There was shame in running over to Mister Ben's at the end of
the day and asking for his rotten peaches, there was shame in
asking Mrs. Simmons for a spoonful of sugar, there was shame
in running out to meet the relief truck. I hated that truck, full
of food for you and your kind. I ran into the house and hid when
it came. And then I started to sneak through alleys, to take the
long way home so the people going into White's Eat Shop
wouldn't see me. Yeah, the whole world heard the teacher that
day, we all know you don't have a Daddy.

Questions for Study and Discussion

1. What does Gregory mean by "shame"? What precisely
was he ashamed of, and what in particular did he learn
from the incident?

2. How do the first three paragraphs of the essay help to establish a context for the narrative that follows?

3. Why do you think Gregory narrates this episode in the first-person point of view? What would be gained or lost if he instead wrote it in the third-person point of view?

4. What is the teacher's attitude toward Gregory? Consider her own words and actions as well as Gregory's opinion in arriving at your answer.

5. What role does money play in Gregory's narrative? How does money relate to his sense of shame?

6. Specific details can enhance the reader's understanding and appreciation of a narrative. Gregory's description of Helene Tucker's manners or the plaid of his mackinaw, for example, makes his account vivid and interesting. Cite several other specific details he gives, and consider how the narrative would be different without them.

7. Consider the diction of this essay. What effect does Gregory's repetition of the word *shame* have on you? Why do you think Gregory uses simple vocabulary to narrate this particular experience? (Glossary: *Diction*)

Vocabulary

Refer to your dictionary to define the following words as they are used in this selection. Then use each word in a sentence of your own.

nappy (2)   mackinaw (28)

Suggested Writing Assignments

1. Using Dick Gregory's essay as a model, write an essay narrating an experience that made you especially afraid, angry, surprised, embarrassed, or proud. Include sufficient detail so that your readers will know exactly what happened.

2. Most of us have had frustrating experiences with mechanical objects that seem to have perverse minds of their own. Write a brief narrative recounting one such experience with a vending machine, typewriter, television set, pay toilet, computer, pay telephone, or any other such machine. Be sure to establish a clear context for your narrative.

38 WHO SAW MURDER DIDN'T CALL POLICE

Martin Gansberg

Martin Gansberg was born in 1920 in Brooklyn, New York, and graduated from St. John's University. A long-time reporter, Gansberg wrote the following article for the New York Times *two weeks after the early morning events he so poignantly narrates. Once you've finished reading the essay, you will understand why it has been so often reprinted and why the name Kitty Genovese is still invoked whenever questions of public apathy arise.*

For more than half an hour 38 respectable, law-abiding citizens in Queens watched a killer stalk and stab a woman in three separate attacks in Kew Gardens.

Twice their chatter and the sudden glow of their bedroom lights interrupted him and frightened him off. Each time he returned, sought her out, and stabbed her again. Not one person telephoned the police during the assault; one witness called after the woman was dead.

That was two weeks ago today.

Still shocked is Assistant Chief Inspector Frederick M. Lussen, in charge of the borough's detectives and a veteran of 25 years of homicide investigations. He can give a matter-of-fact recitation on many murders. But the Kew Gardens slaying baffles him—not because it is a murder, but because the "good people" failed to call the police.

"As we have reconstructed the crime," he said, "the assailant had three chances to kill this woman during a 35-minute period. He returned twice to complete the job. If we had been called when he first attacked, the woman might not be dead now."

This is what the police say happened beginning at 3:20 A.M. in the staid, middle-class, tree-lined Austin Street area:

243

Twenty-eight-year-old Catherine Genovese, who was called 7
Kitty by almost everyone in the neighborhood, was returning
home from her job as manager of a bar in Hollis. She parked
her red Fiat in a lot adjacent to the Kew Gardens Long Island
Rail Road Station, facing Mowbray Place. Like many residents
of the neighborhood, she had parked there day after day since
her arrival from Connecticut a year ago, although the railroad
frowns on the practice.

She turned off the lights of her car, locked the door, and 8
started to walk the 100 feet to the entrance of her apartment at
82–70 Austin Street, which is in a Tudor building, with stores in
the first floor and apartments on the second.

The entrance to the apartment is in the rear of the building 9
because the front is rented to retail stores. At night the quiet
neighborhood is shrouded in the slumbering darkness that
marks most residential areas.

Miss Genovese noticed a man at the far end of the lot, near a 10
seven-story apartment house at 82–40 Austin Street. She halted.
Then, nervously, she headed up Austin Street toward Lefferts
Boulevard, where there is a call box to the 102nd Police Precinct
in nearby Richmond Hill.

She got as far as a street light in front of a bookstore before 11
the man grabbed her. She screamed. Lights went on in the 10-
story apartment house at 82–67 Austin Street, which faces the
bookstore. Windows slid open and voices punctuated the early-
morning stillness.

Miss Genovese screamed: "Oh, my God, he stabbed me! 12
Please help me! Please help me!"

From one of the upper windows in the apartment house, a 13
man called down: "Let that girl alone!"

The assailant looked up at him, shrugged, and walked down 14
Austin Street toward a white sedan parked a short distance
away. Miss Genovese struggled to her feet.

Lights went out. The killer returned to Miss Genovese, now 15
trying to make her way around the side of the building by the
parking lot to get to her apartment. The assailant stabbed her
again.

"I'm dying!" she shrieked. "I'm dying!" 16

Windows were opened again, and lights went on in many 17
apartments. The assailant got into his car and drove away. Miss

Genovese staggered to her feet. A city bus, O–10, the Lefferts Boulevard line to Kennedy International Airport, passed. It was 3:35 A.M.

The assailant returned. By then, Miss Genovese had crawled   18
to the back of the building, where the freshly painted brown doors to the apartment house held out hope for safety. The killer tried the first door; she wasn't there. At the second door, 82–62 Austin Street, he saw her slumped on the floor at the foot of the stairs. He stabbed her a third time—fatally.

It was 3:50 by the time the police received their first call,   19
from a man who was a neighbor of Miss Genovese. In two minutes they were at the scene. The neighbor, a 70-year-old woman, and another woman were the only persons on the street. Nobody else came forward.

The man explained that he had called the police after much   20
deliberation. He had phoned a friend in Nassau County for advice and then he had crossed the roof of the building to the apartment of the elderly woman to get her to make the call.

"I didn't want to get involved," he sheepishly told the police.   21

Six days later, the police arrested Winston Moseley, a 29-year-   22
old business-machine operator, and charged him with homicide. Moseley had no previous record. He is married, has two children and owns a home at 133–19 Sutter Avenue, South Ozone Park, Queens. On Wednesday, a court committed him to Kings County Hospital for psychiatric observation.

When questioned by the police, Moseley also said that he had   23
slain Mrs. Annie May Johnson, 24, of 146–12 133d Avenue, Jamaica, on Feb. 29 and Barbara Kralik, 15, of 174–17 140th Avenue, Springfield Gardens, last July. In the Kralik case, the police are holding Alvin L. Mitchell, who is said to have confessed that slaying.

The police stressed how simple it would have been to have   24
gotten in touch with them. "A phone call," said one of the detectives, "would have done it." The police may be reached by dialing "O" for operator or SPring 7–3100.

Today witnesses from the neighborhood, which is made up of   25
one-family homes in the $35,000 to $60,000 range with the exception of the two apartment houses near the railroad station, find it difficult to explain why they didn't call the police.

A housewife, knowingly if quite casually, said, "We thought   26 it was a lovers' quarrel." A husband and wife both said, "Frankly, we were afraid." They seemed aware of the fact that events might have been different. A distraught woman, wiping her hands in her apron, said, "I didn't want my husband to get involved."

One couple, now willing to talk about that night, said they heard the first screams. The husband looked thoughtfully at the bookstore where the killer first grabbed Miss Genovese. 27

"We went to the window to see what was happening," he said, "but the light from our bedroom made it difficult to see the street." The wife, still apprehensive, added: "I put out the light and we were able to see better." 28

Asked why they hadn't called the police, she shrugged and replied: "I don't know." 29

A man peeked out from a slight opening in the doorway to his apartment and rattled off an account of the killer's second attack. Why hadn't he called the police at the time? "I was tired," he said without emotion. "I went back to bed." 30

It was 4:25 A.M. when the ambulance arrived to take the body of Miss Genovese. It drove off. "Then," a solemn police detective said, "the people came out." 31

Questions for Study and Discussion

1. What is the author's purpose in this selection? What are the advantages or disadvantages in using narration to accomplish this purpose? Explain. (Glossary: *Purpose*)

2. Where does the narrative actually begin? What is the function of the material that precedes the beginning of the narrative proper?

3. What reasons did Kitty Genovese's neighbors give for not calling the police when they first heard her calls for help? What, in your opinion, do their reasons say about contemporary American society? Explain.

4. How would you describe Gansberg's tone? Is the tone appropriate for the story Gansberg narrates? Explain. (Glossary: *Tone*)

5. Gansberg uses dialogue throughout his essay. How many people does he quote? What does he accomplish by using dialogue? (Glossary: *Dialogue*)
6. What do you think Gansberg achieves by giving the addresses of the victims in paragraph 23?
7. Reflect on Gansberg's ending. What would be lost or gained by adding a paragraph that analyzed the meaning of the narrative for the reader? (Glossary: *Beginnings and Endings*)

Vocabulary

Refer to your dictionary to define the following words as they are used in this selection. Then use each word in a sentence of your own.

stalk (1)	shrouded (9)
recitation (4)	sheepishly (21)
assailant (5)	apprehensive (28)
staid (6)	

Suggested Writing Assignments

1. Gansberg's essay is about public apathy and fear. What is your own experience with the public? Modeling an essay after Gansberg's, narrate yet another event or series of events that you personally know about. Or, write a narration about public involvement, one that contradicts Gansberg's essay.
2. It is common when using narration to tell about firsthand experience and to tell the story in the first person. It is good practice, however, to try writing a narration about something you don't know about firsthand but must learn about, much the same as a newspaper reporter must do. For several days, be attentive to events occurring around you—in your neighborhood, school, community, region—events that would be an appropriate basis for a narrative essay. Interview the principal characters involved in your story, take detailed notes, and then write your narration.

THE DARE

Roger Hoffmann

Born in 1948, Roger Hoffmann is a free-lance writer and the author of The Complete Software Marketplace *(1984). Currently, he is at work on a novel about Vietnam. In "The Dare," first published in the* New York Times Magazine *in 1986, Hoffmann recounts how in his youth he accepted a friend's challenge to dive under a moving freight train and to roll out the other side. As an adult, Hoffmann appreciates the act for what it was—a crazy, dangerous childhood stunt. But he also remembers what the episode meant to him as a seventh grader trying to prove himself to his peers.*

The secret to diving under a moving freight train and rolling out the other side with all your parts attached lies in picking the right spot between the tracks to hit with your back. Ideally, you want soft dirt or pea gravel, clear of glass shards and railroad spikes that could cause you instinctively, and fatally, to sit up. Today, at thirty-eight, I couldn't be threatened or baited enough to attempt that dive. But as a seventh grader struggling to make the cut in a tough Atlanta grammar school, all it took was a dare. 1

I coasted through my first years of school as a fussed-over smart kid, the teacher's pet who finished his work first and then strutted around the room tutoring other students. By the seventh grade, I had more A's than friends. Even my old cronies, Dwayne and O.T., made it clear I'd never be one of the guys in junior high if I didn't dirty up my act. They challenged me to break the rules, and I did. The I-dare-you's escalated: shoplifting, sugaring teachers' gas tanks, dropping lighted matches into public mailboxes. Each guerrilla act won me the approval I never got for just being smart. 2

Walking home by the railroad tracks after school, we started 3

248

playing chicken with oncoming trains. O.T., who was failing that year, always won. One afternoon he charged a boxcar from the side, stopping just short of throwing himself between the wheels. I was stunned. After the train disappeared, we debated whether someone could dive under a moving car, stay put for a 10-count, then scramble out the other side. I thought it could be done and said so. O.T. immediately stepped in front of me and smiled. Not by me, I added quickly, I certainly didn't mean that I could do it. "A smart guy like you," he said, his smile evaporating, "you could figure it out easy." And then, squeezing each word for effect, "I . . . DARE . . . you." I'd just turned twelve. The monkey clawing my back was Teacher's Pet. And I'd been dared.

As an adult, I've been on both ends of life's implicit business and social I-dare-you's, although adults don't use those words. We provoke with body language, tone of voice, ambiguous phrases. I dare you to: argue with the boss, tell Fred what you think of him, send the wine back. Only rarely are the risks physical. How we respond to dares when we are young may have something to do with which of the truly hazardous male inner dares—attacking mountains, tempting bulls at Pamplona—we embrace or ignore as men.

For two weeks, I scouted trains and tracks. I studied moving boxcars close up, memorizing how they squatted on their axles, never getting used to the squeal or the way the air fell hot from the sides. I created an imaginary, friendly train and ran next to it. I mastered a shallow, head-first dive with a simple half-twist. I'd land on my back, count to ten, imagine wheels and, locking both hands on the rail to my left, heave myself over and out. Even under pure sky, though, I had to fight to keep my eyes open and my shoulders between the rails.

The next Saturday, O.T., Dwayne and three eighth graders met me below the hill that backed up to the lumberyard. The track followed a slow bend there and opened to a straight, slightly uphill climb for a solid third of a mile. My run started two hundred yards after the bend. The train would have its tongue hanging out.

The other boys huddled off to one side, a circle on another planet, and watched quietly as I double-knotted my shoelaces. My hands trembled. O.T. broke the circle and came over to me.

He kept his hands hidden in the pockets of his jacket. We looked at each other. BB's of sweat appeared beneath his nose. I stuffed my wallet in one of his pockets, rubbing it against his knuckles on the way in, and slid my house key, wired to a red-and-white fishing bobber, into the other. We backed away from each other, and he turned and ran to join the four already climbing up the hill.

I watched them all the way to the top. They clustered together 8 as if I were taking their picture. Their silhouette resembled a round-shouldered tombstone. They waved down to me, and I dropped them from my mind and sat down on the rail. Immediately, I jumped back. The steel was vibrating.

The train sounded like a cow going short of breath. I pulled 9 my shirttail out and looked down at my spot, then up the incline of track ahead of me. Suddenly the air went hot, and the engine was by me. I hadn't pictured it moving that fast. A man's bare head leaned out and stared at me. I waved to him with my left hand and turned into the train, burying my face in the incredible noise. When I looked up, the head was gone.

I started running alongside the boxcars. Quickly, I found 10 their pace, held it, and then eased off, concentrating on each thick wheel that cut past me. I slowed another notch. Over my shoulder, I picked my car as it came off the bend, locking in the image of the white mountain goat painted on its side. I waited, leaning forward like the anchor in a 440-relay, wishing the baton up the track behind me. Then the big goat fired by me, and I was flying and then tucking my shoulder as I dipped under the train.

A heavy blanket of red dust settled over me. I felt bolted to the 11 earth. Sheet-metal bellies thundered and shook above my face. Count to ten, a voice said, watch the axles and look to your left for daylight. But I couldn't count, and I couldn't find left if my life depended on it, which it did. The colors overhead went from brown to red to black to red again. Finally, I ripped my hands free, forced them to the rail, and, in one convulsive jerk, threw myself into the blue light.

I lay there face down until there was no more noise, and I 12 could feel the sun against the back of my neck. I sat up. The last ribbon of train was slipping away in the distance. Across the tracks, O.T. was leading a cavalry charge down the hill, five very

small, galloping boys, their fists whirling above them. I pulled
my knees to my chest. My corduroy pants puckered wet across
my thighs. I didn't care.

Questions for Study and Discussion

1. Why did Hoffmann accept O.T.'s dare when he was twelve
   years old? Would he accept the same dare today? Why or
   why not?
2. How does paragraph 4 function in the context of Hoffmann's narrative?
3. How has Hoffmann organized his essay? (Glossary: *Organization*) What period of time is covered in paragraphs
   2–5? In paragraphs 6–12? What conclusions about narrative time can you draw from what Hoffmann has done?
4. What were Hoffmann's feelings on the day of his dive under the moving freight train? Do you think he was afraid?
   How do you know?
5. Identify four figures of speech that Hoffmann uses in his
   essay. (Glossary: *Figures of Speech*) What does each figure
   add to his narrative?
6. Hoffmann tells his story in the first person: the narrator
   is the principal actor. What would have been gained or
   lost had Hoffmann used the third person, with O.T. or
   Dwayne telling the story? Explain.

Vocabulary

Refer to your dictionary to define the following words as they
are used in this selection. Then use each word in a sentence of
your own.

shards (1)	evaporating (3)
baited (1)	implicit (4)
cronies (2)	ambiguous (4)
escalated (2)	convulsive (11)
guerrilla (2)	

Suggested Writing Assignments

1. Can you remember any dares that you made or accepted while growing up? What were the consequences of these dares? Did you and your peers find dares a way to test or prove yourselves? Write a narrative essay about a dare that you made, accepted, or simply witnessed.

2. Each of us can tell of an experience that has been unusually significant for us. Think about your past, identify one experience that has been especially important for you, and write an essay about it. In preparing to write your narrative, you may find it helpful to ask such questions as: Why is the experience important for me? What details are necessary for me to re-create the experience in an interesting and engaging way? How can my narrative of the experience be most effectively organized? Over what period of time did the experience occur? What point of view will work best?

MOMMA, THE DENTIST, AND ME

Maya Angelou

Maya Angelou is perhaps best known as the author of I Know Why the Caged Bird Sings *(1970), the first of four books in the series which constitutes her autobiography. Starting with her beginnings in St. Louis in 1928, Angelou presents a life story of joyful triumph over hardships that tested her courage and threatened her spirit. Trained as a dancer, Angelou has also published three books of poetry, acted in the television series "Roots," and, at the request of Martin Luther King, Jr., served as a coordinator of the Southern Christian Leadership Conference. In the following excerpt from* I Know Why the Caged Bird Sings, *Angelou narrates what happened, and what might have happened, when her grandmother, the "Momma" of the story, takes her to the local dentist.*

The angel of the candy counter had found me out at last, and was exacting excruciating penance for all the stolen Milky Ways, Mounds, Mr. Goodbars and Hersheys with Almonds. I had two cavities that were rotten to the gums. The pain was beyond the bailiwick of crushed aspirins or oil of cloves. Only one thing could help me, so I prayed earnestly that I'd be allowed to sit under the house and have the building collapse on my left jaw. Since there was no Negro dentist in Stamps, nor doctor either, for that matter, Momma had dealt with previous toothaches by pulling them out (a string tied to the tooth with the other end looped over her fist), pain killers and prayer. In this particular instance the medicine had proved ineffective; there wasn't enough enamel left to hook a string on, and the prayers were being ignored because the Balancing Angel was blocking their passage.

I lived a few days and nights in blinding pain, not so much   2 toying with as seriously considering the idea of jumping in the well, and Momma decided I had to be taken to a dentist. The nearest Negro dentist was in Texarkana, twenty-five miles away, and I was certain that I'd be dead long before we reached half the distance. Momma said we'd go to Dr. Lincoln, right in Stamps, and he'd take care of me. She said he owed her a favor.

I knew there were a number of whitefolks in town that owed 3 her favors. Bailey and I had seen the books which showed how she had lent money to Blacks and whites alike during the Depression, and most still owed her. But I couldn't aptly remember seeing Dr. Lincoln's name, nor had I ever heard of a Negro's going to him as a patient. However, Momma said we were going, and put water on the stove for our baths. I had never been to a doctor, so she told me that after the bath (which would make my mouth feel better) I had to put on freshly starched and ironed underclothes from inside out. The ache failed to respond to the bath, and I knew then that the pain was more serious than that which anyone had ever suffered.

Before we left the Store, she ordered me to brush my teeth 4 and then wash my mouth with Listerine. The idea of even opening my clamped jaws increased the pain, but upon her explanation that when you go to a doctor you have to clean yourself all over, but most especially the part that's to be examined, I screwed up my courage and unlocked my teeth. The cool air in my mouth and the jarring of my molars dislodged what little remained of my reason. I had frozen to the pain, my family nearly had to tie me down to take the toothbrush away. It was no small effort to get me started on the road to the dentist. Momma spoke to all the passers-by, but didn't stop to chat. She explained over her shoulder that we were going to the doctor and she'd "pass the time of day" on our way home.

Until we reached the pond the pain was my world, an aura 5 that haloed me for three feet around. Crossing the bridge into whitefolks' county, pieces of sanity pushed themselves forward. I had to stop moaning and start walking straight. The white towel, which was drawn under my chin and tied over my head, had to be arranged. If one was dying, it had to be done in style if the dying took place in whitefolks' part of town.

On the other side of the bridge the ache seemed to lessen as 6 if a whitebreeze blew off the whitefolks and cushioned everything in their neighborhood—including my jaw. The gravel road was smoother, the stones smaller and the tree branches hung down around the path and nearly covered us. If the pain didn't diminish then, the familiar yet strange sights hypnotized me into believing that it had.

But my head continued to throb with the measured insistence   7 of a bass drum, and how could a toothache pass the calaboose, hear the songs of the prisoners, their blues and laughter, and not be changed? How could one or two or even a mouthful of angry tooth roots meet a wagonload of powhitetrash children, endure their idiotic snobbery and not feel less important?

Behind the building which housed the dentist's office ran a   8 small path used by servants and those tradespeople who catered to the butcher and Stamps' one restaurant. Momma and I followed that lane to the backstairs of Dentist Lincoln's office. The sun was bright and gave the day a hard reality as we climbed up the steps to the second floor.

Momma knocked on the back door and a young white girl   9 opened it to show surprise at seeing us there. Momma said she wanted to see Dentist Lincoln and to tell him Annie was there. The girl closed the door firmly. Now the humiliation of hearing Momma describe herself as if she had no last name to the young white girl was equal to the physical pain. It seemed terribly unfair to have a toothache and a headache and have to bear at the same time the heavy burden of Blackness.

It was always possible that the teeth would quiet down and   10 maybe drop out of their own accord. Momma said we would wait. We leaned in the harsh sunlight on the shaky railings of the dentist's back porch for over an hour.

He opened the door and looked at Momma. "Well, Annie,   11 what can I do for you?"

He didn't see the towel around my jaw or notice my swollen   12 face.

Momma said, "Dentist Lincoln. It's my grandbaby here. She   13 got two rotten teeth that's giving her a fit."

She waited for him to acknowledge the truth of her state-   14 ment. He made no comment, orally or facially.

"She had this toothache purt' near four days now, and today   15 I said, 'Young lady, you going to the Dentist.'"

"Annie?"   16

"Yes, sir, Dentist Lincoln." 17

He was choosing words the way people hunt for shells. 18
"Annie, you know I don't treat nigra, colored people."

"I know, Dentist Lincoln. But this here is just my little grand- 19
baby, and she ain't gone be no trouble to you . . ."

"Annie, everybody has a policy. In this world you have to have 20
a policy. Now, my policy is I don't treat colored people."

The sun had baked the oil out of Momma's skin and melted 21
the Vaseline in her hair. She shone greasily as she leaned out of
the dentist's shadow.

"Seem like to me, Dentist Lincoln, you might look after her, 22
she ain't nothing but a little mite. And seems like maybe you
owe me a favor or two."

He reddened slightly. "Favor or no favor. The money has all 23
been repaid to you and that's the end of it. Sorry, Annie." He
had his hand on the doorknob. "Sorry." His voice was a bit
kinder on the second "Sorry," as if he really was.

Momma said, "I wouldn't press on you like this for myself but 24
I can't take No. Not for my grandbaby. When you come to
borrow my money you didn't have to beg. You asked me, and I
lent it. Now, it wasn't my policy. I ain't no moneylender, but you
stood to lose this building and I tried to help you out."

"It's been paid, and raising your voice won't make me change 25
my mind. My policy . . ." He let go of the door and stepped
nearer Momma. The three of us were crowded on the small
landing. "Annie, my policy is I'd rather stick my hand in a dog's
mouth than in a nigger's."

He had never once looked at me. He turned his back and went 26
through the door into the cool beyond. Momma backed up inside herself for a few minutes. I forgot everything except her
face which was almost a new one to me. She leaned over and
took the doorknob, and in her everyday soft voice she said,
"Sister, go on downstairs. Wait for me. I'll be there directly."

Under the most common of circumstances I knew it did no 27
good to argue with Momma. So I walked down the steep stairs,
afraid to look back and afraid not to do so. I turned as the door
slammed, and she was gone.

Momma walked in that room as if she owned it. She shoved 28
that silly nurse aside with one hand and strode into the dentist's
office. He was sitting in his chair, sharpening his mean instru-

ments and putting extra sting into his medicines. Her eyes were blazing like live coals and her arms had doubled themselves in length. He looked up at her just before she caught him by the collar of his white jacket.

"Stand up when you see a lady, you contemptuous scoundrel." 29
Her tongue had thinned and the words rolled off well enunciated. Enunciated and sharp like little claps of thunder.

The dentist had no choice but to stand at R.O.T.C. attention. 30
His head dropped after a minute and his voice was humble. "Yes, ma'am, Mrs. Henderson."

"You knave, do you think you acted like a gentleman, speak- 31
ing to me like that in front of my granddaughter?" She didn't shake him, although she had the power. She simply held him upright.

"No, ma'am, Mrs. Henderson." 32

"No, ma'am, Mrs. Henderson, what?" Then she did give him 33
the tiniest of shakes, but because of her strength the action set his head and arms to shaking loose on the ends of his body. He stuttered much worse than Uncle Willie. "No, ma'am, Mrs. Henderson, I'm sorry."

With just an edge of her disgust showing, Momma slung him 34
back in his dentist's chair. "Sorry is as sorry does, and you're about the sorriest dentist I ever laid my eyes on." (She could afford to slip into the vernacular because she had such eloquent command of English.)

"I didn't ask you to apologize in front of Marguerite, because 35
I don't want her to know my power, but I order you, now and herewith. Leave Stamps by sundown."

"Mrs. Henderson, I can't get my equipment . . ." He was shak- 36
ing terribly now.

"Now, that brings me to my second order. You will never again 37
practice dentistry. Never! When you get settled in your next place, you will be a vegetarian caring for dogs with the mange, cats with the cholera and cows with the epizootic. Is that clear?"

The saliva ran down his chin and his eyes filled with tears. 38
"Yes, ma'am. Thank you for not killing me. Thank you, Mrs. Henderson."

Momma pulled herself back from being ten feet tall with 39
eight-foot arms and said, "You're welcome for nothing, you varlet, I wouldn't waste a killing on the likes of you."

On her way out she waved her handkerchief at the nurse and   40
turned her into a crocus sack of chicken feed.

Momma looked tired when she came down the stairs, but   41
who wouldn't be tired if they had gone through what she had.
She came close to me and adjusted the towel under my jaw (I
had forgotten the toothache; I only knew that she made her
hands gentle in order not to awaken the pain). She took my
hand. Her voice never changed. "Come on, Sister."

I reckoned we were going home where she would concoct a   42
brew to eliminate the pain and maybe give me new teeth too.
New teeth that would grow overnight out of my gums. She led
me toward the drugstore, which was in the opposite direction
from the Store. "I'm taking you to Dentist Baker in Texarkana."

I was glad after all that I had bathed and put on Mum and   43
Cashmere Bouquet talcum powder. It was a wonderful surprise. My toothache had quieted to solemn pain, Momma had
obliterated the evil white man, and we were going on a trip to
Texarkana, just the two of us.

On the Greyhound she took an inside seat in the back, and I   44
sat beside her. I was so proud of being her granddaughter and
sure that some of her magic must have come down to me. She
asked if I was scared. I only shook my head and leaned over on
her cool brown upper arm. There was no chance that a dentist,
especially a Negro dentist, would dare hurt me then. Not with
Momma there. The trip was uneventful, except that she put her
arm around me, which was very unusual for Momma to do.

The dentist showed me the medicine and the needle before he   45
deadened my gums, but if he hadn't I wouldn't have worried.
Momma stood right behind him. Her arms were folded and she
checked on everything he did. The teeth were extracted and she
bought me an ice cream cone from the side window of a drug
counter. The trip back to Stamps was quiet, except that I had to
spit into a very small empty snuff can which she had gotten for
me and it was difficult with the bus humping and jerking on
our country roads.

At home, I was given a warm salt solution, and when I washed   46
out my mouth I showed Bailey the empty holes, where the
clotted blood sat like filling in a pie crust. He said I was quite
brave, and that was my cue to reveal our confrontation with the
peckerwood dentist and Momma's incredible powers.

I had to admit that I didn't hear the conversation, but what   47

else could she have said than what I said she said? What else
done? He agreed with my analysis in a lukewarm way, and I
happily (after all, I'd been sick) flounced into the Store. Momma
was preparing our evening meal and Uncle Willie leaned on the
door sill. She gave her version.

"Dentist Lincoln got right uppity. Said he'd rather put his   48
hand in a dog's mouth. And when I reminded him of the favor,
he brushed it off like a piece of lint. Well, I sent Sister downstairs and went inside. I hadn't never been in his office before,
but I found the door to where he takes out teeth, and him and
the nurse was in there thick as thieves. I just stood there till he
caught sight of me." Crash bang the pots on the stove. "He
jumped just like he was sitting on a pin. He said, 'Annie, I done
tole you, I ain't gonna mess around in no niggah's mouth.' I
said, 'Somebody's got to do it then,' and he said, 'Take her to
Texarkana to the colored dentist' and that's when I said, 'If you
paid me my money I could afford to take her.' He said, 'It's all
been paid.' I tole him everything but the interest been paid. He
said ''Twasn't no interest.' I said, ''Tis now. I'll take ten dollars
as payment in full.' You know, Willie, it wasn't no right thing to
do, 'cause I lent that money without thinking about it.

"He tole that little snippety nurse of his'n to give me ten dol-   49
lars and make me sign a 'paid in full' receipt. She gave it to me
and I signed the papers. Even though by rights he was paid up
before, I figger, he gonna be that kind of nasty, he gonna have to
pay for it."

Momma and her son laughed and laughed over the white   50
man's evilness and her retributive sin.

I preferred, much preferred, my version.   51

Questions for Study and Discussion

1. What is Angelou's purpose in narrating the story she
   tells? (Glossary: *Purpose*)
2. Compare and contrast the content and style of the interac-
   tion between Momma and the dentist that is given in ital-
   ics with the one given at the end of the narrative.
   (Glossary: *Comparison and Contrast*)

3. Angelou tells her story chronologically and in the first person. What are the advantages of the first-person narrative?

4. Identify three similes that Angelou uses in her narrative. Explain how each simile serves her purposes. (Glossary: *Figures of Speech*)

5. Why do you suppose Angelou says she prefers her own version of the episode to that of her grandmother?

6. This story is a story of pain and not just the pain of a toothache. How does Angelou describe the pain of the toothache? What other pain does Angelou tell of in this autobiographical narrative?

Vocabulary

Refer to your dictionary to define the following words as they are used in this selection. Then use each word in a sentence of your own.

bailiwick (1)	varlet (39)
calaboose (7)	concoct (42)
mite (22)	snippety (49)
vernacular (34)	retributive (50)

Suggested Writing Assignments

1. One of Angelou's themes in "Momma, the Dentist, and Me" is that cruelty, whether racial, social, professional, or personal, is very difficult to endure and leaves a lasting impression on a person. Think of a situation where an unthinking or insensitive person made you feel inferior for reasons beyond your control. List the sequence of events in your narrative before you draft it. You may find it helpful to reread the introduction to this section before you begin working.

2. Write a narrative in which, like Angelou, you give two versions of an actual event—one the way you thought or wished it happened and the other the way events actually took place.

12

DESCRIPTION

To describe is to create a verbal picture. A person, a place, a thing—even an idea or a state of mind—can be made vividly concrete through description. Here, for example, is Thomas Mann's brief description of a delicatessen:

> It was a narrow room, with a rather high ceiling, and crowded from floor to ceiling with goodies. There were rows and rows of hams and sausages of all shapes and colors—white, yellow, red, and black; fat and lean and round and long—rows of canned preserves, cocoa and tea, bright translucent glass bottles of honey, marmalade, and jam; round bottles and slender bottles, filled with liqueurs and punch—all these things crowded every inch of the shelves from top to bottom.

Writing any description requires, first of all, that the writer gather many details about a subject, relying not only on what the eyes see but on the other sense impressions—touch, taste, smell, hearing—as well. From this catalogue of details the writer selects those that will most effectively create a *dominant impression*—the single quality, mood, or atmosphere that the writer wishes to emphasize. Consider, for example, the details that Mary McCarthy uses to evoke the dominant impression in the following passage from *Memories of a Catholic Girlhood:*

> Whenever we children came to stay at my grandmother's house, we were put to sleep in the sewing room, a bleak, shabby, utilitarian rectangle, more office than bedroom, more attic than office, that played to the hierarchy of chambers the role of poor relation. It was a room without pride: the old sewing machine, some cast-off chairs, a shadeless lamp, rolls of wrapping paper, piles of cardboard boxes that might someday come in handy, papers of pins, and remnants of a material united with the iron folding cots put out for our use and the bare floor boards to give an impression of intense and ruthless temporality. Thin white

261

spreads, of the kind used in hospitals and charity institutions, and naked blinds at the windows reminded us of our orphaned condition and of the ephemeral character of our visit; there was nothing here to encourage us to consider this our home.

The dominant impression that McCarthy creates is one of clutter, bleakness, and shabbiness. There is nothing in the sewing room that suggests permanence or warmth.

Writers must also carefully plan the order in which to present their descriptive details. The pattern of organization must fit the subject of the description logically and naturally, and must also be easy to follow. For example, visual details can be arranged spatially—from left to right, top to bottom, near to far, or in any other logical order. Other patterns include smallest to largest, softest to loudest, least significant to most significant, most unusual to least unusual. McCarthy suggests a jumble of junk not only by her choice of details but by the apparently random order in which she presents them.

How much detail is enough? There is no fixed answer. A good description includes enough vivid details to create a dominant impression and to bring a scene to life, but not so many that readers are distracted, confused, or bored. In an essay that is purely descriptive, there is room for much detail. Usually, however, writers use description to create the setting for a story, to illustrate ideas, to help clarify a definition or a comparison, or to make the complexities of a process more understandable. Such descriptions should be kept short, and should include just enough detail to make them clear and helpful.

SUBWAY STATION

Gilbert Highet

Gilbert Highet (1906–1978) was born in Scotland and became a naturalized United States citizen in 1951. A prolific writer and translator, Highet was for many years a professor of classics at Columbia University. The following selection is taken from his book Talents and Geniuses *(1957). Notice the author's keen eye for detail as he describes the unseemly world of a subway station.*

Standing in a subway station, I began to appreciate the place—almost to enjoy it. First of all, I looked at the lighting: a row of meager electric bulbs, unscreened, yellow, and coated with filth, stretched toward the black mouth of the tunnel, as though it were a bolt hole in an abandoned coal mine. Then I lingered, with zest, on the walls and ceiling: lavatory tiles which had been white about fifty years ago, and were now encrusted with soot, coated with the remains of a dirty liquid which might be either atmospheric humidity mingled with smog or the result of a perfunctory attempt to clean them with cold water; and, above them, gloomy vaulting from which dingy paint was peeling off like scabs from an old wound, sick black paint leaving a leprous white undersurface. Beneath my feet, the floor was a nauseating dark brown with black stains upon it which might be stale oil or dry chewing gum or some worse defilement; it looked like the hallway of a condemned slum building. Then my eye traveled to the tracks, where two lines of glittering steel—the only positively clean objects in the whole place—ran out of darkness into darkness above an unspeakable mass of congealed oil, puddles of dubious liquid, and a mishmash of old cigarette packets, mutilated and filthy newspapers, and the débris that filtered down from the street above through a barred grating in the roof. As I looked up toward the sunlight, I could see more débris sifting slowly downward, and making an abominable pattern in the slanting beam of dirt-laden sunlight. I was going on to relish more features of this unique scene: such as the advertisement posters on the walls—here a text from the Bible, there a half-naked girl, here a woman wearing a hat consisting of a hen sitting on a nest full of eggs, and there a pair of girl's legs walking up the keys of a cash register—all scribbled over with unknown names and well-known obscenities in black crayon and red lipstick; but then my train came in at last, I boarded it, and began to read. The experience was over for the time.

Questions for Study and Discussion

1. What dominant impression of the subway station does Highet create in his description? (Glossary: *Dominant Impression*)
2. To present a clearly focused dominant impression, a writer must be selective in the use of details. Make a list of those details that help create Highet's dominant impression.
3. Highet uses a spatial organization in his essay. Trace the order in which he describes the various elements of the subway station. (Glossary: *Organization*)
4. What similes and metaphors can you find in Highet's description? How do they help to make the description vivid? (Glossary: *Figures of Speech*)
5. Is this a first-time experience for Highet, or do you think he is a regular subway traveler? What in the essay leads you to your conclusion?

Vocabulary

Refer to your dictionary to define the following words as they are used in this selection. Then use each word in a sentence of your own.

meager	congealed
zest	dubious
defilement	unique

Suggested Writing Assignments

1. If you are familiar with a subway station, write a lengthy one-paragraph description of it just as Highet has done. Once you have completed your description, compare and contrast your description with Highet's. How does the dominant impression you have created differ from the one Highet has created?

2. Write a short essay in which you describe one of the following places, or another place of your choice. Arrange the details of your description from top to bottom, left to right, near to far, or according to some other spatial organization.

   an airport terminal
   a pizza parlor
   a locker room
   a barbershop or beauty salon
   a bookstore
   a campus dining hall

THE SOUNDS OF THE CITY

James Tuite

James Tuite has had a long career at The New York Times, *where he once served as sports editor. As a free-lance writer he has contributed to all of the major sports magazines and has written* Snowmobiles and Snowmobiling *(1973) and* How to Enjoy Sports on TV *(1976). The following selection is a model of how a place can be described by using a sense other than sight. Tuite describes New York City by its sounds, which for him comprise the very life of the city.*

New York is a city of sounds: muted sounds and shrill sounds; shattering sounds and soothing sounds; urgent sounds and aimless sounds. The cliff dwellers of Manhattan—who would be racked by the silence of the lonely woods—do not hear these sounds because they are constant and eternally urban.

The visitor to the city can hear them, though, just as some animals can hear a high-pitched whistle inaudible to humans. To the casual caller to Manhattan, lying restive and sleepless in a hotel twenty or thirty floors above the street, they tell a story as fascinating as life itself. And back of the sounds broods the silence.

Night in midtown is the noise of tinseled honky-tonk and violence. Thin strains of music, usually the firm beat of rock 'n' roll or the frenzied outbursts of the discotheque, rise from ground level. This is the cacophony, the discordance of youth, and it comes on strongest when nights are hot and young blood restless.

Somewhere in the canyons below there is shrill laughter or raucous shouting. A bottle shatters against concrete. The whine of a police siren slices through the night, moving ever closer, until an eerie Doppler effect* brings it to a guttural halt.

There are few sounds so exciting in Manhattan as those of fire apparatus dashing through the night. At the outset there is the tentative hint of the first-due company bullying his way through midtown traffic. Now a fire whistle from the opposite direction affirms that trouble is, indeed, afoot. In seconds, other sirens converging from other streets help the skytop listener focus on the scene of excitement.

But he can only hear and not see, and imagination takes flight. Are the flames and smoke gushing from windows not far away? Are victims trapped there, crying out for help? Is it a conflagration, or only a trash-basket fire? Or, perhaps, it is merely a false alarm.

The questions go unanswered and the urgency of the moment dissolves. Now the mind and the ear detect the snarling, arrogant bickering of automobile horns. People in a hurry. Taxicabs blaring, insisting on their checkered priority.

Even the taxi horns dwindle down to a precocious few in the gray and pink moments of dawn. Suddenly there is another sound, a morning sound that taunts the memory for recognition. The growl of a predatory monster? No, just garbage trucks that have begun a day of scavenging.

Trash cans rattle outside restaurants. Metallic jaws on sanitation trucks gulp and masticate the residue of daily living, then digest it with a satisfied groan of gears. The sounds of the new day are businesslike. The growl of buses, so scattered and distant at night, becomes a demanding part of the traffic bedlam. An occasional jet or helicopter injects an exclamation point from an unexpected quarter. When the wind is right, the vibrant bellow of an ocean liner can be heard.

The sounds of the day are as jarring as the glare of a sun that outlines the canyons of midtown in drab relief. A pneumatic drill frays countless nerves with its rat-a-tat-tat, for dig they must to perpetuate the city's dizzy motion. After each screech

---

*The drop in pitch that occurs as a source of sound quickly passes by a listener.

of brakes there is a moment of suspension, of waiting for the
thud or crash that never seems to follow.

The whistles of traffic policemen and hotel doormen chirp   11
from all sides, like birds calling for their mates across a frenzied aviary. And all of these sounds are adult sounds, for childish laughter has no place in these canyons.

Night falls again, the cycle is complete, but there is no sur-   12
cease from sound. For the beautiful dreamers, perhaps, the
"sounds of the rude world heard in the day, lulled by the moon-
light have all passed away," but this is not so in the city.

Too many New Yorkers accept the sounds about them as   13
bland parts of everyday existence. They seldom stop to listen to
the sounds, to think about them, to be appalled or enchanted by
them. In the big city, sounds are life.

Questions for Study and Discussion

1. What is Tuite's purpose in describing the sounds of New
   York City? (Glossary: *Purpose*)
2. How does Tuite organize his essay? Do you think that the
   organization is effective? (Glossary: *Organization*)
3. Tuite describes "raucous shouting" and the "screech of
   brakes." Make a list of the various other sounds that he
   describes in his essay. How do the varied adjectives and
   verbs Tuite uses to capture the essence of each sound enhance his description? (Glossary: *Diction*)
4. According to Tuite, why are visitors to New York City
   more sensitive to or aware of the multitude of sounds
   than the "cliff dwellers of Manhattan" (1)? What does he
   believe New Yorkers have missed when they fail to take
   notice of these sounds?
5. Locate several metaphors and similes in the essay. What
   picture of the city does each one give you? (Glossary: *Figures of Speech*)
6. What dominant impression of New York City does Tuite
   create in this essay? (Glossary: *Dominant Impression*)

Vocabulary

Refer to your dictionary to define the following words as they are used in this selection. Then use each word in a sentence of your own.

muted (1)   precocious (8)
inaudible (2)   taunts (8)
restive (2)   vibrant (9)
raucous (4)   perpetuate (10)
tentative (5)

Suggested Writing Assignments

1. In a short composition describe a city or another place that you know well. Try to capture as many sights, sounds, and smells as you can to depict the place you describe. Your goal should be to create a single dominant impression of the place, as Tuite does in his essay.

2. Describe an inanimate object familiar to you so as to bring out its character and make it interesting to a reader. First determine your purpose for describing the object. For example, suppose your family has had a dining table ever since you can remember. Think of what that table has been a part of over the years—the birthday parties, the fights, the holiday meals, the sad times, the intimate times, the long hours of studying and doing homework. Probably such a table would be worth describing for the way it has figured prominently in the history of your family. Next make an exhaustive list of the object's physical features; then write your descriptive essay.

UNFORGETTABLE MISS BESSIE

Carl T. Rowan

Carl T. Rowan is a former ambassador to Finland and was director of the United States Information Agency. Born in 1925 in Ravenscroft, Tennessee, he received degrees from Oberlin College and the University of Minnesota. Once a columnist for the Minneapolis Tribune *and the* Chicago Sun-Times, *Rowan is now a syndicated columnist and a* Reader's Digest *roving editor. In the following essay, Rowan describes his former high-school teacher whose lessons went far beyond the subjects she taught.*

She was only about five feet fall and probably never 1 weighed more than 110 pounds, but Miss Bessie was a towering presence in the classroom. She was the only woman tough enough to make me read *Beowulf* and think for a few foolish days that I liked it. From 1938 to 1942, when I attended Bernard High School in McMinnville, Tenn., she taught me English, history, civics—and a lot more than I realized.

I shall never forget the day she scolded me into reading 2 *Beowulf.*

"But Miss Bessie," I complained, "I ain't much interested in 3 it."

Her large brown eyes became daggerish slits. "Boy," she said, 4 "how dare you say 'ain't' to me! I've taught you better than that."

"Miss Bessie," I pleaded, "I'm trying to make first-string end 5 on the football team, and if I go around saying 'it isn't' and 'they aren't,' the guys are gonna laugh me off the squad."

"Boy," she responded, "you'll play football because you have 6 guts. But do you know what *really* takes guts? Refusing to lower your standards to those of the crowd. It takes guts to say you've got to live and be somebody fifty years after all the football games are over."

I started saying "it isn't" and "they aren't," and I still made 7
first-string end—and class valedictorian—without losing my
buddies' respect.

During her remarkable 44-year career, Mrs. Bessie Taylor 8
Gwynn taught hundreds of economically deprived black youngsters—including my mother, my brother, my sisters and me. I
remember her now with gratitude and affection—especially in
this era when Americans are so wrought-up about a "rising tide
of mediocrity" in public education and the problems of finding
competent, caring teachers. Miss Bessie was an example of an
informed, dedicated teacher, a blessing to children and an asset
to the nation.

Born in 1895, in poverty, she grew up in Athens, Ala., where 9
there was no public school for blacks. She attended Trinity
School, a private institution for blacks run by the American
Missionary Association, and in 1911 graduated from the Normal School (a "super" high school) at Fisk University in Nashville. Mrs. Gwynn, the essence of pride and privacy, never
talked about her years in Athens; only in the months before her
death did she reveal that she had never attended Fisk University
itself because she could not afford the four-year course.

At Normal School she learned a lot about Shakespeare, but 10
most of all about the profound importance of education—
especially, for a people trying to move up from slavery. "What
you put in your head, boy," she once said, "can never be pulled
out by the Ku Klux Klan, the Congress or anybody."

Miss Bessie's bearing of dignity told anyone who met her that 11
she was "educated" in the best sense of the word. There was
never a discipline problem in her classes. We didn't dare mess
with a woman who knew about the Battle of Hastings, the Magna
Carta and the Bill of Rights—and who could also play the piano.

This frail-looking woman could make sense of Shakespeare, 12
Milton, Voltaire, and bring to life Booker T. Washington and
W. E. B. DuBois. Believing that it was important to know who
the officials were that spent taxpayers' money and made public
policy, she made us memorize the names of everyone on the
Supreme Court and in the President's Cabinet. It could be embarrassing to be unprepared when Miss Bessie said, "Get up
and tell the class who Frances Perkins is and what you think
about her."

Miss Bessie knew that my family, like so many others during   13
the Depression, couldn't afford to subscribe to a newspaper.
She knew we didn't even own a radio. Still, she prodded me to
"look out for your future and find some way to keep up with
what's going on in the world." So I became a delivery boy for
the Chattanooga *Times*. I rarely made a dollar a week, but I got
to read a newspaper every day.

Miss Bessie noticed things that had nothing to do with   14
schoolwork, but were vital to a youngster's development. Once
a few classmates made fun of my frayed, hand-me-down overcoat, calling me "Strings." As I was leaving school, Miss Bessie
patted me on the back of that old overcoat and said, "Carl,
never fret about what you *don't* have. Just make the most of
what you *do* have—a brain."

Among the things that I did not have was electricity in the lit-   15
tle frame house that my father had built for $400 with his
World War I bonus. But because of her inspiration, I spent
many hours squinting beside a kerosene lamp reading Shakespeare and Thoreau, Samuel Pepys and William Cullen Bryant.

No one in my family had ever graduated from high school, so   16
there was no tradition of commitment to learning for me to lean
on. Like millions of youngsters in today's ghettos and barrios, I
needed the push and stimulation of a teacher who truly cared.
Miss Bessie gave plenty of both, as she immersed me in a wonderful world of similes, metaphors and even onomatopoeia. She
led me to believe that I could write sonnets as well as Shakespeare, or iambic-pentameter verse to put Alexander Pope to
shame.

In those days the McMinnville school system was rigidly "Jim   17
Crow," and poor black children had to struggle to put anything
in their heads. Our high school was only slightly larger than the
once-typical little red schoolhouse, and its library was outra-
geously inadequate—so small, I like to say, that if two students
were in it and one wanted to turn a page, the other one had to
step outside.

Negroes, as we were called then, were not allowed in the town   18
library, except to mop floors or dust tables. But through one of
those secret Old South arrangements between whites of conscience and blacks of stature, Miss Bessie kept getting books
smuggled out of the white library. That is how she introduced

me to the Brontës, Byron, Coleridge, Keats and Tennyson. "If you don't read, you can't write, and if you can't write, you might as well stop dreaming," Miss Bessie once told me.

So I read whatever Miss Bessie told me to, and tried to re- 19 member the things she insisted that I store away. Forty-five years later, I can still recite her "truths to live by," such as Henry Wadsworth Longfellow's lines from "The Ladder of St. Augustine":

> The heights by great men reached and kept
> Were not attained by sudden flight.
> But they, while their companions slept,
> Were toiling upward in the night.

Years later, her inspiration, prodding, anger, cajoling and al- 20 most osmotic infusion of learning finally led to that lovely day when Miss Bessie dropped me a note saying, "I'm so proud to read your column in the Nashville *Tennessean*."

Miss Bessie was a spry 80 when I went back to McMinnville 21 and visited her in a senior citizens' apartment building. Pointing out proudly that her building was racially integrated, she reached for two glasses and a pint of bourbon. I was momentarily shocked, because it would have been scandalous in the 1930s and '40s for word to get out that a teacher drank, and nobody had ever raised a rumor that Miss Bessie did.

I felt a new sense of equality as she lifted her glass to mine. 22 Then she revealed a softness and compassion that I had never known as a student.

"I've never forgotten that examination day," she said, "when 23 Buster Martin held up seven fingers, obviously asking you for help with question number seven, 'Name a common carrier.' I can still picture you looking at your exam paper and humming a few bars of 'Chattanooga Choo Choo.' I was so tickled, I couldn't punish either of you."

Miss Bessie was telling me, with bourbon-laced grace, that I 24 never fooled her for a moment.

When Miss Bessie died in 1980, at age 85, hundreds of her 25 former students mourned. They knew the measure of a great teacher: love and motivation. Her wisdom and influence had rippled out across generations.

Some of her students who might normally have been doomed 26

to poverty when on to become doctors, dentists and college professors. Many, guided by Miss Bessie's example, became public-
school teachers.

"The memory of Miss Bessie and how she conducted her   27
classroom did more for me than anything I learned in college,"
recalls Gladys Wood of Knoxville, Tenn., a highly respected English teacher who spent 43 years in the state's school system.
"So many times, when I faced a difficult classroom problem, I
asked myself, *How would Miss Bessie deal with this?* And I'd
remember that she would handle it with laughter and love."

No child can get all the necessary support at home, and mil-   28
lions of poor children get *no* support at all. This is what makes
a wise, educated, warm-hearted teacher like Miss Bessie so vital to the minds, hearts and souls of this country's children.

Questions for Study and Discussion

1. Throughout the essay Rowan offers details of Miss
   Bessie's physical appearance. What specific details does
   he give, and in what context does he give them? Did Miss
   Bessie's physical characteristics match the quality of her
   character? Explain.

2. How would you sum up the character of Miss Bessie?
   Make a list of the key words that Rowan uses that you feel
   best describe her.

3. At what point in the essay does Rowan give us the details
   of Miss Bessie's background? Why do you suppose he de-
   lays giving us this important information? (Glossary: *Beginnings and Endings*)

4. How does dialogue serve Rowan's purposes? (Glossary:
   Dialogue)

5. Does Miss Bessie's drinking influence your opinion of
   her? Explain. Why do you think Rowan included this part
   of her behavior in his essay?

6. In his opening paragraph Rowan states that Miss Bessie
   "taught me English, history, civics—and a lot more than I

realized." What did she teach her students beyond the traditional public school curriculum?

Vocabulary

Refer to your dictionary to define the following words as they are used in this selection. Then use each word in a sentence of your own.

civics (1)	cajoling (20)
barrios (16)	osmotic (20)
conscience (18)	measure (25)

Suggested Writing Assignments

1. Think of all the teachers you have had, and write a description of the one that has had the greatest influence on you. Remember to give some consideration to the balance you want to achieve between physical attributes and personality traits.

2. In paragraph 18 Rowan writes the following: "'If you don't read, you can't write, and if you can't write, you might as well stop dreaming,' Miss Bessie once told me." Write an essay in which you explore this theme that, in essence, is also the theme of *Models for Writers*.

MY FRIEND, ALBERT EINSTEIN

Banesh Hoffmann

A mathematician, Banesh Hoffmann has served on the faculties of the University of Rochester, the Institute for Advanced Study at Princeton University, and Queens College. Hoffmann is the author of The Strange Story of the Quantum *(1959) and* The Tyranny of Testing *(1964) and co-author with Albert Einstein of an article on the theory of relativity. Hoffmann has also collaborated with Helen Dukas, Einstein's personal secretary, on two biographical studies:* Albert Einstein: Creator and Rebel *(1973) and* Albert Einstein: The Human Side *(1979). In the following selection, Hoffmann describes the kind of man he found Einstein to be.*

H e was one of the greatest scientists the world has ever   1
known, yet if I had to convey the essence of Albert Einstein in a single word, I would choose *simplicity.* Perhaps an anecdote will help. Once, caught in a downpour, he took off his hat and held it under his coat. Asked why, he explained, with admirable logic, that the rain would damage the hat, but his hair would be none the worse for its wetting. This knack for going instinctively to the heart of a matter was the secret of his major scientific discoveries—this and his extraordinary feeling for beauty.

I first met Albert Einstein in 1935, at the famous Institute for   2
Advanced Study in Princeton, N.J. He had been among the first to be invited to the Institute, and was offered *carte blanche* as to salary. To the director's dismay, Einstein asked for an impossible sum: it was far too *small.* The director had to plead with him to accept a larger salary.

I was in awe of Einstein, and hesitated before approaching   3
him about some ideas I had been working on. When I finally knocked on his door, a gentle voice said, "Come"—with a rising

inflection that made the single word both a welcome and a question. I entered his office and found him seated at a table, calculating and smoking his pipe. Dressed in ill-fitting clothes, his hair characteristically awry, he smiled a warm welcome. His utter naturalness at once set me at ease.

As I began to explain my ideas, he asked me to write the equations on the blackboard so he could see how they developed. Then came the staggering—and altogether endearing—request: "Please go slowly. I do not understand things quickly." This from Einstein! He said it gently, and I laughed. From then on, all vestiges of fear were gone.   4

Einstein was born in 1879 in the German city of Ulm. He had been no infant prodigy; indeed, he was so late in learning to speak that his parents feared he was a dullard. In school, though his teachers saw no special talent in him, the signs were already there. He taught himself calculus, for example, and his teachers seemed a little afraid of him because he asked questions they could not answer. At the age of 16, he asked himself whether a light wave would seem stationary if one ran abreast of it. From that innocent question would arise, ten years later, his theory of relativity.   5

Einstein failed his entrance examinations at the Swiss Federal Polytechnic School, in Zurich, but was admitted a year later. There he went beyond his regular work to study the masterworks of physics on his own. Rejected when he applied for academic positions, he ultimately found work, in 1902, as a patent examiner in Berne, and there in 1905 his genius burst into fabulous flower.   6

Among the extraordinary things he produced in that memorable year were his theory of relativity, with its famous offshoot, $E = mc^2$ (energy equals mass times the speed of light squared), and his quantum theory of light. These two theories were not only revolutionary, but seemingly contradictory: the former was intimately linked to the theory that light consists of waves, while the latter said it consists somehow of particles. Yet this unknown young man boldly proposed both at once— and he was right in both cases, though how he could have been is far too complex a story to tell here.   7

Collaborating with Einstein was an unforgettable experience. In 1937, the Polish physicist Leopold Infeld and I asked if we   8 could work with him. He was pleased with the proposal, since he had an idea about gravitation waiting to be worked out in detail. Thus we got to know not merely the man and the friend, but also the professional.

The intensity and depth of his concentration were fantastic.   9
When battling a recalcitrant problem, he worried it as an animal worries its prey. Often, when we found ourselves up against a seemingly insuperable difficulty, he would stand up, put his pipe on the table, and say in his quaint English, "I will a little tink" (he could not pronounce "th"). Then he would pace up and down, twirling a lock of his long, graying hair around his forefinger.

A dreamy, faraway and yet inward look would come over his   10
face. There was no appearance of concentration, no furrowing of the brow—only a placid inner communion. The minutes would pass, and then suddenly Einstein would stop pacing as his face relaxed into a gentle smile. He had found the solution to the problem. Sometimes it was so simple that Infeld and I could have kicked ourselves for not having thought of it. But the magic had been performed invisibly in the depths of Einstein's mind, by a process we could not fathom.

Although Einstein felt no need for religious ritual and be-   11
longed to no formal religious group, he was the most deeply religious man I have known. He once said to me, "Ideas come from God," and one could hear the capital "G" in the reverence with which he pronounced the word. On the marble fireplace in the mathematics building at Princeton University is carved, in the original German, what one might call his scientific credo: "God is subtle, but he is not malicious." By this Einstein meant that scientists could expect to find their task difficult, but not hopeless: the Universe was a Universe of law, and God was not confusing us with deliberate paradoxes and contradictions.

Einstein was an accomplished amateur musician. We used to   12
play duets, he on the violin, I at the piano. One day he surprised me by saying Mozart was the greatest composer of all. Beethoven "created" his music, but the music of Mozart was of such purity and beauty one felt he had merely "found" it—that it had always existed as part of the inner beauty of the Universe, waiting to be revealed.

It was this very Mozartean simplicity that most characterized   13

Einstein's methods. His 1905 theory of relativity, for example, was built on just two simple assumptions. One is the so-called principle of relativity, which means, roughly speaking, that we cannot tell whether we are at rest or moving smoothly. The other assumption is that the speed of light is the same no matter what the speed of the object that produces it. You can see how reasonable this is if you think of agitating a stick in a lake to create waves. Whether you wiggle the stick from a stationary pier, or from a rushing speedboat, the waves, once generated, are on their own, and their speed has nothing to do with that of the stick.

Each of these assumptions, by itself, was so plausible as to 14 seem primitively obvious. But together they were in such violent conflict that a lesser man would have dropped one or the other and fled in panic. Einstein daringly kept both—and by so doing he revolutionized physics. For he demonstrated they could, after all, exist peacefully side by side, provided we gave up cherished beliefs about the nature of time.

Science is like a house of cards, with concepts like time and 15 space at the lowest level. Tampering with time brought most of the house tumbling down, and it was this that made Einstein's work so important—and controversial. At a conference in Princeton in honor of his 70th birthday, one of the speakers, a Nobel Prize-winner, tried to convey the magical quality of Einstein's achievement. Words failed him, and with a shrug of helplessness he pointed to his wristwatch, and said in tones of awed amazement, "It all came from this." His very ineloquence made this the most eloquent tribute I have heard to Einstein's genius.

We think of Einstein as one concerned only with the deepest 16 aspects of science. But he saw scientific principles in everyday things to which most of us would give barely a second thought. He once asked me if I had ever wondered why a man's feet will sink into either dry or completely submerged sand, while sand that is merely damp provides a firm surface. When I could not answer, he offered a simple explanation.

It depends, he pointed out, on *surface tension*, the elastic-skin 17 effect of a liquid surface. This is what holds a drop together, or causes two small raindrops on a windowpane to pull into one big drop the moment their surfaces touch.

When sand is damp, Einstein explained, there are tiny   18
amounts of water between grains. The surface tensions of these
tiny amounts of water pull all the grains together, and friction
then makes them hard to budge. When the sand is dry, there is
obviously no water between grains. If the sand is fully immersed, there is water between grains, but no water *surface* to
pull them together.

This is not as important as relativity; yet there is no telling   19
what seeming trifle will lead an Einstein to a major discovery.
And the puzzle of the sand does give us an inkling of the power
and elegance of his mind.

Einstein's work, performed quietly with pencil and paper,   20
seemed remote from the turmoil of everyday life. But his ideas
were so revolutionary they caused violent controversy and irrational anger. Indeed, in order to be able to award him a belated
Nobel Prize, the selection committee had to avoid mentioning
relativity, and pretend the prize was awarded primarily for his
work on the quantum theory.

Political events upset the serenity of his life even more. When   21
the Nazis came to power in Germany, his theories were officially declared false because they had been formulated by a
Jew. His property was confiscated, and it is said a price was put
on his head.

When scientists in the United States, fearful that the Nazis   22
might develop an atomic bomb, sought to alert American authorities to the danger, they were scarcely heeded. In desperation, they drafted a letter which Einstein signed and sent directly to President Roosevelt. It was this act that led to the
fateful decision to go all-out on the production of an atomic
bomb—an endeavor in which Einstein took no active part.
When he heard of the agony and destruction that his $E = mc^2$
had wrought, he was dismayed beyond measure, and from then
on there was a look of ineffable sadness in his eyes.

There was something elusively whimsical about Einstein. It   23
is illustrated by my favorite anecdote about him. In his first
year in Princeton, on Christmas Eve, so the story goes, some
children sang carols outside his house. Having finished, they
knocked on his door and explained they were collecting money
to buy Christmas presents. Einstein listened, then said, "Wait a
moment." He put on his scarf and overcoat, and took his violin

from its case. Then, joining the children as they went from door to door, he accompanied their singing of "Silent Night" on his violin.

How shall I sum up what it meant to have known Einstein   24 and his works? Like the Nobel Prize-winner who pointed helplessly at his watch, I can find no adequate words. It was akin to the revelation of great art that lets one see what was formerly hidden. And when, for example, I walk on the sand of a lonely beach, I am reminded of his ceaseless search for cosmic simplicity—and the scene takes on a deeper, sadder beauty.

Questions for Study and Discussion

1. Hoffmann feels that the word *simplicity* captures the essence of Albert Einstein. What character traits does Hoffmann describe in order to substantiate this impression of the man?

2. Make a list of the details of Einstein's physical features. From these details, can you tell what Einstein looked like?

3. Hoffmann uses a number of anecdotes to develop his description of Einstein. In what ways are such anecdotes preferable to mere statements regarding Einstein's character? Refer to several examples to illustrate your opinion.

4. Why do you suppose Hoffmann begins his essay where he does instead of the sentence "Einstein was born in 1879 in the German city of Ulm" (5)? (Glossary: *Beginnings and Endings*)

5. What, for Hoffmann, was the secret of Einstein's major scientific discoveries? Explain.

6. In 1905 Einstein produced his theory of relativity and his quantum theory of light. Although both theories are revolutionary, what is remarkable about the fact that they were both advanced by the same man?

7. What are the two assumptions on which Einstein built his theory of relativity? What analogy does Hoffmann use to explain the reasonableness of these assumptions? (Glossary: *Analogy*)

Vocabulary

Refer to your dictionary to define the following words as they are used in this selection. Then use each word in a sentence of your own.

anecdote (1)	fathom (10)
awry (3)	credo (11)
vestiges (4)	trifle (19)
prodigy (5)	ineffable (22)
recalcitrant (9)	

Suggested Writing Assignments

1. Write a descriptive essay on a person you know well, perhaps a friend or a relative. Before writing, be sure that you establish a purpose for your description. Remember that your reader will not know that person; therefore, try to show what makes your subject different from other people.
2. In his essay Hoffmann reveals something of himself—his beliefs, his tastes, his intelligence, his values. Write an essay in which you argue that every writer, to a lesser or greater degree, reveals something of himself or herself in writing about any subject. Choose whatever examples you wish to make your point. You might, however, decide to use Carl Rowan and his essay on Miss Bessie as your primary example. Finally, you might wish to emphasize the significance of the self-revealing qualities of writing.

13

PROCESS ANALYSIS

When you give directions for getting to your house, tell how to make ice cream, or explain how a president is elected, you are using *process analysis*.

Process analysis usually arranges a series of events in order and relates them to one another, as narration and cause and effect do, but it has different emphases. Whereas narration tells mainly *what* happens and cause and effect focuses on *why* it happens, process analysis tries to explain—in detail—*how* it happens.

There are two types of process analysis: directional and informational. The *directional* type provides instructions on how to do something. These instructions can be as brief as the directions printed on a label for making instant coffee or as complex as the directions in a manual for building a home computer. The purpose of directional process analysis is simple: to give the reader directions to follow that lead to the desired results.

Consider the directions for constructing an Astro Tube, a cylindrical airfoil made out of a sheet of heavy writing paper, on p. 284.

The *informational* type of process analysis, on the other hand, tells how something works, how something is made, or how something occurred. You would use informational process analysis if you wanted to explain how the human heart functions, how an atomic bomb works, how hailstones are formed, how you selected the college you are attending, or how the polio vaccine was developed. Rather than giving specific directions, informational process analysis explains and informs.

Clarity is crucial for successful process analysis. The most effective way to explain a process is to divide it into steps and to present those steps in a clear (usually chronological) sequence. Transitional words and phrases such as *first, next, after* and *before* help to connect steps to one another. Naturally, you must be sure that no step is omitted or out of order. Also, you

283

may sometimes have to explain *why* a certain step is necessary, especially if it is not obvious. With intricate, abstract, or particularly difficult steps, you might use analogy or comparison to clarify the steps for your reader.

Start with an 8.5-inch by 11-inch sheet of heavy writing paper. (Never use newspaper in making paper models because it isn't strongly bonded and can't hold a crease.) Follow these numbered steps, corresponding to the illustrations.

1. With the long side of the sheet toward you, fold up one third of the paper.
2. Fold the doubled section in half.
3. Fold the section in half once more and crease well.
4. Unfold preceding crease.
5. Curve the ends together to form a tube, as shown in the illustration.

6. Insert the right end inside the left end between the single outer layer and the doubled layers. Overlap the ends about an inch and a half. (This makes a tube for right-handers, to be used with an underhand throw. For an overhand tube, or an underhand version to be thrown by a lefty, reverse the directions, and insert the left end inside the right end at this step.)
7. Hold the tube at the seam with one hand, where shown by the dot in the illustration, and turn the rim made in step 3. Start turning in at the seam and roll the rim under, moving around the circumference in a circular manner. Then

round out the rim.
8. Fold the fin to the left, as shown, then raise it so that it's perpendicular to the tube. Be careful not to tear the paper at the front.
9. Hold the tube from above, near the rim. Hold it between the thumb and fingers. The rim end should be forward, with the fin on the bottom. Throw the tube underhanded, with a motion like throwing a bowling ball, letting it spin off the fingers as it is released. The tube will float through the air, spinning as it goes. Indoor flights of 30 feet or more are easy. With practice you can achieve remarkable accuracy.

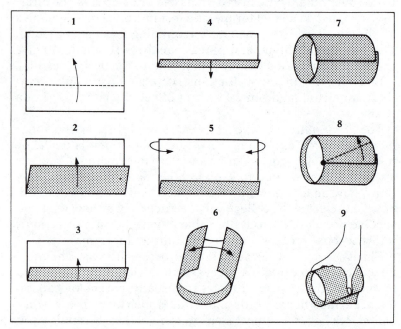

HOW TO CRAM

Jill Young Miller

Cramming for exams is an accepted part of college life. Our parents did it, we do it, and our children will probably do the same. In this essay, taken from the Fall 1987 issue of Campus Voice, *Jill Young Miller hopes to dispel the notion that cramming is an effective way to study. But, just in case "you're forced into a late-night, last-minute study session," Miller has some helpful advice for the anxious exam-taker.*

Frances Avila learned the hard way not to expect miracles overnight. A chronic crammer, the New York University senior did the usual for her midterm in "Major British Writers" last fall: she pulled an all-nighter. Fighting off fatigue and anxiety, Avila forced herself to concentrate on the novels and her notes through dawn, breaking only to splash cold water on her face. Near noon, she closed her books to head for the test.

The first question—"Expand on the gap between her front teeth"—was a lulu. Avila didn't recognize the allusion to Chaucer's Wife of Bath, even though she'd read the section only hours before. "Not only did I blank out, but I was also frightened," she recalls. "I didn't expect the test to be that elaborate." The bad situation only got worse. She fumbled through 14 more stray lines before plunging into part two, which wasn't any easier. Avila had studied innumerable facts for hours, but she knew only one thing for sure: she was in trouble.

"I failed the exam," she explains, "because I had to compare and contrast two poets from different time periods. In order to do that, I had to elaborate on all the details within the poetry. But I'd absorbed just enough information the night before to understand what I was reading and not enough to catch all the details."

Sound familiar? Almost all of us have stood (and sleep-walked) in Avila's shoes at one time or another. Sometimes push comes to shove, crunch comes to cram, and before you know it, you have to read 450 pages in six hours. Pour on the caffeine, you mumble.

About 90 percent of all students cram, estimates Don   5
Dansereau, a psychology professor at Texas Christian University, who define cramming as "intense studying the night before or the day of a test." Quips Ric Schank, a University of Florida senior, "Down here, it's the rule rather than the exception."

Despite its popularity, cramming gets low marks from edu-   6
cators and memory experts, who claim that the last-minute nature of the act kills your chances for payoff at test time.

A quick stroll down memory lane explains why. Most experts   7
identify three types of memory: immediate, short-term, and long-term. You use your immediate memory as you read this, remembering each word just long enough to make the transition to the next.

Short-term memory is limited, too. For example, you use it   8
when you look up a phone number, close the book, and dial. Short-term memory can supposedly hold a maximum of seven items for only a few seconds.

Long-term memory is the big daddy, the one that holds   9
everything you know about the world. It's the memory that last-minute learners need to respect.

How well you organize information on its way into your   10
long-term memory determines how quickly you can retrieve it later, or whether you retrieve it at all. Think of a backpack you'd take on a hike, says Laird Cermak, a research psychologist at the Boston Veterans Administration Hospital and the author of *Improving Your Memory* (McGraw-Hill, 1975). "If your backpack is organized and you get bit by a snake, you can go right for the snakebite kit," he explains.

The magic lies in spacing your study over days, weeks, or   11
even months. That gives you time to mull over the new stuff, relate it to what you already know, and organize it for exam-time recall. "The reason you forget the information is not because it was learned the night before," Cermak explains. "It's because when you crammed you didn't give yourself good ways to remember it in the future." In other words, last-minute studying limits the number of mental retrieval routes you can create.

But it doesn't take a psychologist to explain why cramming 12 often fails. "You throw things into your mind, knowing that you're going to spit them out in a couple of hours and forget them. It's not a good way to learn at all," says NYU journalism senior David Reilly.

No quick-and-dirty detours to long-term retention and instant 13 recall exist. But if you're forced into a late-night, last-minute study session, the results don't have to be disastrous. Here's some advice to help make the morning after less anxious than the night before:

Find out what kind of test you're in for. If you cram, you're 14 likely to fare better on multiple-choice and fill-in-the-blank tests because they jog your memory with cues, Cermak says.

Find a quiet place to study. When Avila crams, she seeks out 15 a small room at the library that's devoid of distractions. "I'm cornered," she says. "I have no choice but to look at the print."

If you like to study with music in the background, go for 16 something without lyrics and keep the volume down low. Classical music such as Bach can have a soothing effect if your nerves are impeding your studies, says Danielle Lapp, a memory researcher at Stanford University and the author of *Don't Forget! Easy Exercises for a Better Memory at Any Age* (McGraw-Hill, 1987).

Compose a scene that you can recreate during the exam. If 17 you can, study at the desk or in the room where you'll take the test, or do something while you study that you can do again when you take the test. For example, Dansereau suggests that you chew grape gum. "The flavor acts as a cueing device," he explains.

Build your concentration. Spend 10 minutes warming up 18 with a novel or magazine before you tackle a tough chapter. Says Cermak, "It helps you block out whatever else is going on."

Watch what you eat and drink. Avoid heavy meals and 19 alcohol. Both could make you drowsy, cautions Lapp. If you need a cup of coffee to perk up, fine. But putting too much caffeine in your system can make you jittery and break your concentration.

Mark your book. Even if you only have time to read the 20 chapter once, it helps to highlight important terms and sections. Identifying the key words and passages requires you to be mentally alert and forces you to be an active rather than a passive reader.

Spend time repeating or discussing facts out loud. Recitation 21 promotes faster learning because it's more active than reading or listening. (Try it out when you study for your next foreign-language vocabulary quiz.) Discussion groups are helpful for this reason.

Take short breaks at least every few hours. They'll help you 22 beat fatigue, which takes a heavy toll on learning. Two hour-long sittings separated by a 15-minute break are more productive than one two-hour session in which your mind wanders throughout the second half. It doesn't matter what you do during those breaks; just take them.

Experiment with memory techniques. They impose structure 23 on new information, making it easier to remember at test time. The "house" method is one of the oldest. Let's say you want to remember a list of sequential events for a history exam. Try to imagine the events taking place in separate but connected rooms of your house. When the test asks you to recall the events, take a mental amble through the rooms.

Another simple technique involves acronyms. You may have 24 learned the names of the Great Lakes (Huron, Ontario, Michigan, Erie, and Superior) with this one: **HOMES.**

Try some proven learning strategies. Richard Yates, a coun- 25 selor and time-management expert at Cleveland State University, recommends the SQ3R method: survey, question, read, recite, review. Survey the material to formulate a general impression; rephrase titles and headings into questions; read through the material quickly to find the main points and the answers to your questions; recite those main ideas, taking brief notes; and review. Even when you're pressed for time, the strategy can help. "It may take a little longer," says Yates, "but it's worth the effort."

Get some sleep. UF's Schank quit all-nighters after his fresh- 26 man year. "I'd go into a final and be so wired from staying up all night that I'd lose my concentration," he says. "I'd miss questions that I knew I wouldn't miss if I were in a good frame of mind." Now he crams until about 3 a.m., sleeps for about four hours, and hits the books again at 8 a.m.

Psychologists and memory researchers can't specify how much sleep you need—everyone has his or her own threshold—but they do stress its importance. Says Lapp, "You're better off getting some sleep so that your mind is rested for the exam than you are cramming the whole night." Just don't forget to set that alarm clock before you go to bed. 27

For an early-morning exam, it's best to do heavy-duty studying right before you go to sleep. In other words, unless you've got back-to-back exams, don't cram and then do something else for a few hours before a test. Freshly learned material is remembered much better after a period of sleep than after an equal period of daytime activity. 28

Relax. It may sound simplistic, but it's key to good test performance. "Anxiety is enemy number one of memory," Lapp explains. She compares a student taking a test to a singer performing onstage. "There's no way a completely anxious singer can utter a sound," she says. 29

Cramming is like going to the dentist; if you have to do it, you want it to be as painless and as productive as it can be. After all, no one goes to college to take a semester-long class and promptly forget all the new information that's been taught. At least Frances Avila didn't. After her disastrous midterm, she didn't dare risk cramming for her "Major British Writers" final exam. This time, she spaced her studying over a period of weeks, earned an A, and salvaged her grade for the semester. 30

That doesn't mean she's quit cramming for good—in fact, she hasn't even tried to. Instead she's perfected her technique. Ditto for Reilly, who's tried unsuccessfully to break the habit. "Every semester I kick myself a million times and scream that I'm not going to cram next semester," he laments. "But it never seems to work." 31

Questions for Study and Discussion

1. Recall a time during an exam when you "blanked out" or became "frightened." (2) Explain the feeling. What was going through your mind? How did it affect your concentration?

2. In your own words, explain the difference among immediate, short-term, and long-term memory.
3. According to Miller why doesn't cramming work? Where in the essay does she best explain this?
4. Is the process Miller explains in her essay informational or directional?
5. What thread of advice runs through all of Miller's suggestions and ideas? In other words, what is the key to studying?
6. Whom does Miller intend for her audience? (Glossary: *Audience*) How do you know? Cite examples of her diction and explain the way in which particular word choices led you to your conclusion. (Glossary: *Diction*)
7. Who are Miller's sources? In what way, if any, do they add to the credibility of her essay?

Vocabulary

Refer to your dictionary to define the following words as they are used in this selection. Then use each word in a sentence of your own.

allusion (2)   impeding (16)
innumerable (2)   acronyms (24)
quips (5)

Suggested Writing Assignments

1. Most do-it-yourself jobs require that you follow a set process in order to achieve the best results. Write a process essay in which you provide direction for doing one of the following household activities:

    paint a room
    clean windows
    repot a plant
    prune shrubbery
    apply driveway sealer
    do laundry

care for a lawn
wash a car
bake bread or chocolate chip cookies
change a flat tire
give a home permanent

2. Write an essay in which you give directions or advice for finding a summer job or part-time employment during the school year. In what ways is looking for such jobs different from looking for permanent positions?

HOW TO SURVIVE A HOTEL FIRE

R. H. Kauffman

R. H. Kauffman, born in Portland, Oregon, in 1941, is a captain in the Los Angeles Fire Department. He is best known, however, as the author of a booklet entitled Caution: Hotels Could Be Hazardous to Your Health *(1981), which has over 44 million copies in print. As you read the following selection, an excerpt from his booklet, notice how clearly Kauffman has presented the steps you should follow and those you should avoid if you are caught in a hotel fire.*

A s a firefighter, I have seen many people die in hotel fires. Most could have saved themselves had they been prepared. There are *over 10,000 hotel fires per year* in the United States. In 1979, the latest year for which figures are available, there were 11,500 such fires, resulting in 140 deaths and 1225 injuries. 1

Contrary to what you have seen in the movies, fire is not likely to chase you down and burn you to death. It's the by-products of fire—smoke and panic—that are almost always the causes of death. 2

For example, a man wakes up at 2:30 A.M. to the smell of smoke. He pulls on his pants and runs into the hallway—to be greeted by heavy smoke. He has no idea where the exit is, so he runs first to the right. No exit. Where is it? Panic sets in. He's coughing and gagging now; his eyes hurt. He can't see his way back to his room. His chest hurts; he needs oxygen desperately. He runs in the other direction, completely disoriented. At 2:50 A.M. we find him . . . dead of smoke inhalation. 3

Remember, the presence of smoke doesn't necessarily mean that the hotel will burn down. Air-conditioning and air-exchange systems will sometimes pick up smoke from one room and carry it to other rooms or floors. 4

Smoke, because it is warmer than air, will start accumulating 5

292

at the ceiling and work its way down. The fresh air you should breathe is near the floor. What's more, smoke is extremely irritating to the eyes. Your eyes will take only so much irritation, then they will close and you won't be able to open them.

Your other enemy, panic—a contagious, overpowering terror—can make you do things that could kill you. The man in the foregoing example would not have died if he had known what to do. Had he found out beforehand where the exit was—four doors down on the left—he could have gotten down on his hands and knees close to the floor, where the air is fresher. Then, even if he couldn't keep his eyes open, he could have felt the wall as he crawled, counting doors.

Here are my rules for surviving hotel fires:

Know where the exits are. As soon as you drop your luggage in your room, turn around and go back into the hallway to check for an exit. If two share a room, both should locate the exit. Open the exit door. Are there stairs or another door beyond? As you return to your room, count the doors you pass. Is there anything in the hallway that would be in your way—an ice machine, maybe? This procedure takes very little time and, to be effective, it must become a habit.

Become familiar with your room. See if your bathroom has an exhaust fan. In an emergency you can turn it on to help remove smoke. Check the window. If it opens, look outside. Do you see any ledges? How high up are you?

Leave the hotel at the first sign of smoke. If something awakens you during the night, investigate it before you go back to sleep. In a hotel fire near Los Angeles airport, one of the guests was awakened by people yelling but went back to bed thinking it was a party. He nearly died in bed.

Always take your key. Don't lock yourself out of your room. You may find conditions elsewhere unbearable. Get in the habit of putting the key in the same place. The night stand, close to the bed, is an excellent spot.

Stay on your hands and knees. If you do wake up to smoke, grab your key from the night stand, roll off the bed and crawl toward the door. Even if you could tolerate the smoke when standing, don't. Save your eyes and lungs for as long as possible. Five feet up, the air may already be full of carbon monoxide. If the door isn't hot, open it slowly and check the hallway.

Should you decide to leave, close the door behind you. Most [13] doors take hours to burn. They are excellent fire shields, so close every one you go through.

Make your way to the exit. Stay against the wall closest to the [14] exit, counting doors as you pass.

Don't use the elevator. Elevator shafts extend through all [15] floors of a building, and easily fill with smoke and carbon monoxide. Smoke, heat, and fire do odd things to elevator controls. Several years ago a group of firemen used an elevator in responding to a fire on a 20th floor. They pushed No. 18, but the elevator shot past the 18th floor and opened on the 20th—to an inferno that killed the firemen.

If you can't go down, go up. When you reach the exit stairwell [16] and begin to descend, hang on to the handrail as you go. People may be running and they could knock you down.

Sometimes smoke gets into the stairwell. If it's a tall build- [17] ing, the smoke may not rise very high before it cools and becomes heavy, or "stacked." You could enter the stairwell on the 23rd floor and find it clear, then as you descend, encounter smoke. Do not try to run through it; people die that way. Turn around and walk up.

When you reach the roof, prop open the door. (This is the *only* [18] time to leave a door open.) Any smoke in the stairwell can now vent itself. Find the windward side of the building (the side that the wind is blowing *from*) and wait until the firefighters reach you. Don't panic if you can't get out onto the roof because the door is locked. Many people have survived by staying put in the stairwell until the firefighters arrived. Again, don't try to run through the smoke.

Look before you leap. If you're on the ground floor, of course, [19] just open the window and climb out. From the next floor you might make it with only a sprained ankle, but you must jump out far enough to clear the building. Many people hit windowsills and ledges on the way down, and cartwheel to the ground. If you're any higher than the third floor, chances are that you won't survive the fall. You would probably be better off staying inside, and fighting the fire.

If you can't leave your room, fight the fire. If your door is too [20] hot to open or the hallway is completely filled with smoke, don't panic. First, open the window to help vent any smoke in your room. (Don't break the window; if there is smoke outside, you may need to close it.)

If your phone is still working, call the fire department. (Do   21
not assume it has been notified. Incredibly enough, some hotels will not call the fire department until they verify whether there is really a fire and try to put it out themselves.)

Flip on the bathroom fan. Fill the tub with water. Wet some   22
sheets or towels, and stuff them into the cracks around your door to keep out smoke. Fill your ice bucket or wastebasket with water from the bathtub and douse the door and walls to keep them cool. If possible, put your mattress up against the door and secure it with the dresser. Keep everything wet. A wet towel tied around your nose and mouth can be an effective filter of smoke particles. Swing a wet towel around the room; it will help clear the smoke. If there is fire outside the window, remove the drapes, move away as much combustible material as you can, and throw water around the window. Use your common sense, and keep fighting until help arrives.

Questions for Study and Discussion

1. What are the two by-products of fire that Kauffman says are most often the cause of death?
2. What advice does Kauffman offer to handle heavy smoke?
3. What do we learn from Kauffman's opening paragraph? In what ways is such information both appropriate and effective as an introduction to Kauffman's essay? (Glossary: *Beginnings and Endings*)
4. What is the relationship between paragraph 2 and paragraph 3?
5. At what point in the essay does Kauffman begin to give directions or use directional process? Can any steps in this process be reordered? What would be the effect of any suggested changes?
6. What is Kauffman's tone in this essay? How, specifically, has he established his tone? Is the tone appropriate for his material? Explain. (Glossary: *Tone*)

Vocabulary

Refer to your dictionary to define the following words as they are used in this selection. Then use each word in a sentence of your own.

disoriented (3)   inferno (3)
unbearable (11)   incredibly (21)
carbon monoxide (12)

Suggested Writing Assignments

1. Knowing what to do and what not to do in a potentially dangerous situation can be lifesaving information. Frequently such information is process oriented. Write an essay in which you explain the process to follow if you observe one of the following situations:

   a heart attack
   a drowning
   an automobile accident
   a house fire
   a choking episode
   a farm machinery accident
   a mugging
   an accidental poisoning

2. In order to give another person directions about how to do something, you yourself need a thorough understanding of the process. Analyze one of the following activities by listing materials you would need and the steps you would follow in completing it:

   studying for an exam
   determining miles per gallon for an automobile
   getting from where your writing class meets to where
     you normally have lunch
   preparing for a week-long camping trip
   writing an essay

buying a used car

beginning an exercise program

Now write an essay in which you give directions for successfully performing the task.

WHY LEAVES TURN COLOR
IN THE FALL

Diane Ackerman

Born in Waukegan, Illinois, in 1948, Diane Ack-
erman received degrees from Pennsylvania State
University and Cornell University. She has writ-
ten several books of poetry, a prose memoir, and
a play, and has directed The Writers' Program at
Washington University in St. Louis. Her most
recent book is A Natural History of the Senses
(1990), from which the following selection has
been taken. Every October nature surprises us
all with a spectacular color show that leaves us
wondering "Where do the colors come from"?
We know when to expect the beautiful leaves,
but we don't know how *the color change hap-*
pens. In this selection Ackerman lets us in on
one of nature's secrets. Notice the way in which
she shares her enthusiasm for the natural world
as she explains the process by which autumn
leaves assume their brilliant color. Ackerman is
currently a staff writer at The New Yorker, *and*
lives in upstate New York.

The stealth of autumn catches one unaware. Was that a   1
goldfinch perching in the early September woods, or just
the first turning leaf? A red-winged blackbird or a sugar maple
closing up shop for the winter? Keen-eyed as leopards, we stand
still and squint hard, looking for signs of movement. Early-
morning frost sits heavily on the grass, and turns barbed wire
into a string of stars. On a distant hill, a small square of yellow
appears to be a lighted stage. At last the truth dawns on us: Fall
is staggering in, right on schedule, with its baggage of chilly
nights, macabre holidays, and spectacular, heart-stoppingly
beautiful leaves. Soon the leaves will start cringing on the trees,
and roll up in clenched fists before they actually fall off. Dry

seedpods will rattle like tiny gourds. But first there will be weeks of gushing color so bright, so pastel, so confettilike, that people will travel up and down the East Coast just to stare at it—a whole season of leaves.

Where do the colors come from? Sunlight rules most living things with its golden edicts. When the days begin to shorten, soon after the summer solstice on June 21, a tree reconsiders its leaves. All summer it feeds them so they can process sunlight, but in the dog days of summer the tree begins pulling nutrients back into its trunk and roots, pares down, and gradually chokes off its leaves. A corky layer of cells forms at the leaves' slender petioles, then scars over. Undernourished, the leaves stop producing the pigment chlorophyll, and photosynthesis ceases. Animals can migrate, hibernate, or store food to prepare for winter. But where can a tree go? It survives by dropping its leaves, and by the end of autumn only a few fragile threads of fluid-carrying xylem hold leaves to their stems.

A turning leaf stays partly green at first, then reveals splotches of yellow and red as the chlorophyll gradually breaks down. Dark green seems to stay longest in the veins, outlining and defining them. During the summer, chlorophyll dissolves in the heat and light, but it is also being steadily replaced. In the fall, on the other hand, no new pigment is produced, and so we notice the other colors that were always there, right in the leaf, although chlorophyll's shocking green hid them from view. With their camouflage gone, we see these colors for the first time all year, and marvel, but they were always there, hidden like a vivid secret beneath the hot glowing greens of summer.

The most spectacular range of fall foliage occurs in the northeastern United States and in eastern China, where the leaves are robustly colored, thanks in part to a rich climate. European maples don't achieve the same flaming reds as their American relatives, which thrive on cold nights and sunny days. In Europe, the warm, humid weather turns the leaves brown or mildly yellow. Anthocyanin, the pigment that gives apples their red and turns leaves red or red-violet, is produced by sugars that remain in the leaf after the supply of nutrients dwindles. Unlike the carotenoids, which color carrots, squash, and corn, and turn leaves orange and yellow, anthocyanin varies from year to year, depending on the temperature and amount of sunlight.

The fiercest colors occur in years when the fall sunlight is strongest and the nights are cool and dry. This is also why leaves appear dizzyingly bright and clear on a sunny fall day: The anthocyanin flashes like a marquee. Not all leaves turn the same colors. Elms, weeping willows, 5 and the ancient ginkgo all grow radiant yellow, along with hickories, aspens, bottlebrush buckeyes, cottonweeds, and tall, keening poplars. Basswood turns bronze, birches bright gold. Water-loving maples put on a symphonic display of scarlets. Sumacs turn red, too, as do flowering dogwoods, black gums, and sweet gums. Though some oaks yellow, most turn a pinkish brown. The farmlands also change color, as tepees of cornstalks and bales of shredded-wheat-textured hay stand drying in the fields. In some spots, one slope of a hill may be green and the other already in bright color, because the hillside facing south gets more sun and heat than the northern one.

An odd feature of the colors is that they don't seem to have 6 any special purpose. We are predisposed to respond to their beauty, of course. They shimmer with the colors of sunset, spring flowers, the tawny buff of a colt's pretty rump, the shuddering pink of a blush. Animals and flowers color for a reason—adaptation to their environment—but there is no adaptive reason for leaves to color so beautifully in the fall any more than there is for the sky or ocean to be blue. It's just one of the haphazard marvels the planet bestows every year. We find the sizzling colors thrilling, and in a sense they dupe us. Colored like living things, they signal death and disintegration. In time, they will become fragile and, like the body, return to dust. They are as we hope our own fate will be when we die: Not to vanish, just to sublime from one beautiful state into another. Though leaves lose their green life, they bloom with urgent colors, as the woods grow mummified day by day, and Nature becomes more carnal, mute, and radiant. . . .

But how do the colored leaves fall? As a leaf ages, the growth 7 hormone, auxin, fades, and cells at the base of the petiole divide. Two or three rows of small cells, lying at right angles to the axis of the petiole, react with water, then come apart, leaving the petioles hanging on by only a few threads of xylem. A light breeze, and the leaves are airborne. They glide and swoop, rocking in invisible cradles. They are all wing and may flutter from yard to yard on small whirlwinds or updrafts, swiveling as they go. Firmly tethered to earth, we love to see things rise up and fly—soap bubbles, balloons, birds, fall leaves. They remind us that the end of a season is capricious, as is the end of life. We especially like the way leaves rock, careen, and swoop as they fall. Everyone knows the motion. . . .

At last the leaves leave. But first they turn color and thrill us for weeks on end. Then they crunch and crackle underfoot. They *shush*, as children drag their small feet through leaves heaped along the curb. Dark, slimy mats of leaves cling to one's heels after a rain. A damp, stuccolike mortar of semidecayed leaves protects the tender shoots with a roof until spring, and makes a rich humus. An occasional bulge or ripple in the leafy mounds signals a shrew or a field mouse tunneling out of sight. Sometimes one finds in fossil stones the imprint of a leaf, long since disintegrated, whose outlines remind us how detailed, vibrant, and alive are the things of this earth that perish.

8

Questions for Study and Discussion

1. Exactly what causes leaves to change color? What particular conditions cause the brightest colors in autumn leaves?

2. Explain how Ackerman personifies autumn in paragraph 1. (Glossary: *Figurative Language*)

3. Briefly summarize the steps of the process by which leaves change color in autumn.

4. Not only does Ackerman describe the process by which leaves change color, she includes other information as well. Identify this information. Did you find it useful? What, if anything, did it add to your appreciation of her analysis?

5. What is Ackerman's attitude toward her subject? (Glossary: *Attitude*) Cite examples of her diction to support your answer. (Glossary: *Diction*)

6. Reread Ackerman's concluding sentence. What does she mean? Why do you suppose she has chosen to end her es-

say in this way? In what ways, if any, is it a particularly appropriate ending for her essay? (Glossary: *Beginnings and Endings*)

Vocabulary

Refer to your dictionary to define the following words as they are used in this selection. Then use each word in a sentence of your own.

stealth (1)	camouflage (3)
clenched (1)	tawny (6)
gushing (1)	vibrant (8)

Suggested Writing Assignments

1. Our world is filled with hundreds of natural processes—for example, the cycle of the moon, the "rising" and "setting" of the sun, the germination of a seed, the movement of the tides, the formation of a tornado, and the flowering of a tree. Write an informational process analysis explaining one such natural process.

2. Use a directional process analyses for a "simple" task which could prove disastrous if not explained correctly. For example, changing a tire, driving a standard shift, packing for a weekend in the woods, or loading a camera.

Symbols of Humankind

Don Lago

*Freelance writer Don Lago was born in 1957. His
articles have appeared in* Science Digest *and the*
Bulletin of the Atomic Scientists. *In 1980 he won*
Cosmic Search *magazine's award for young writers. As a writer, Lago knows full well the importance and power of written language to preserve
thought. In the following essay, which first appeared in* Science Digest *in March 1981, Lago
describes how written language has developed
through history, and speculates about its future
as we attempt to contact other intelligence in the
universe.*

Many thousands of years ago, a man quietly resting on a   1
log reached down and picked up a stick and with it
began scratching upon the sand at his feet. He moved the stick
slowly back and forth and up and down, carefully guiding it
through curves and straight lines. He gazed upon what he had
made, and a gentle satisfaction lighted his face.

Other people noticed this man drawing on the sand. They   2
gazed upon the figures he had made, and though they at once
recognized the shapes of familiar things such as fish or birds or
humans, they took a bit longer to realize what the man had
meant to say by arranging these familiar shapes in this particular way. Understanding what he had done, they nodded or
smiled in recognition.

This small band of humans didn't realize what they were   3
beginning. The images these people left in the sand would soon
be swept away by the wind, but their new idea would slowly
grow until it had remade the human species. These people had
discovered writing.

Writing, early people would learn, could contain much more   4
information than human memory could and contain it more
accurately. It could carry thoughts much farther than mere

sounds could—farther in distance and in time. Profound thoughts born in a single mind could spread and endure.

The first written messages were simply pictures relating 5 familiar objects in some meaningful way—pictographs. Yet there were no images for much that was important in human life. What, for instance, was the image for sorrow or bravery? So from pictographs humans developed ideograms to represent more abstract ideas. An eye flowing with tears could represent sorrow, and a man with the head of a lion might be bravery.

The next leap occurred when the figures became independent 6 of things or ideas and came to stand for spoken sounds. Written figures were free to lose all resemblance to actual objects. Some societies developed syllabic systems of writing in which several hundred signs corresponded to several hundred spoken sounds. Others discovered the much simpler alphabetic system, in which a handful of signs represented the basic sounds the human voice can make.

At first, ideas flowed only slightly faster when written than 7 they had through speech. But as technologies evolved, humans embodied their thoughts in new ways: through the printing press, in Morse code, in electromagnetic waves bouncing through the atmosphere and in the binary language of computers.

Today, when the Earth is covered with a swarming inter- 8 change of ideas, we are even trying to send our thoughts beyond our planet to other minds in the Universe. Our first efforts at sending our thoughts beyond Earth have taken a very ancient form: pictographs. The first message, on plaques aboard Pioneer spacecraft launched in 1972 and 1973, featured a simple line drawing of two humans, one male and one female, the male holding up his hand in greeting. Behind them was an outline of the Pioneer spacecraft, from which the size of the humans could be judged. The plaque also included the "address" of the two human figures: a picture of the solar system, with a spacecraft emerging from the third planet. Most exobiologists believe that when other civilizations attempt to communicate with us they too will use pictures.

All the accomplishments since humans first scribbled in the 9 sand have led us back to where we began. Written language only works when two individuals know what the symbols mean.

We can only return to the simplest form of symbol available and work from there. In interstellar communication, we are at the same stage our ancestors were when they used sticks to trace a few simple images in the sand.

We still hold their sticks in our hands and draw pictures with   10
them. But the stick is no longer made of wood; over the ages that piece of wood has been transformed into a massive radio telescope. And we no longer scratch on sand; now we write our thoughts onto the emptiness of space itself.

Questions for Study and Discussion

1. What is Lago's thesis? Where is it best stated? (Glossary: *Thesis*)
2. Lago uses process analysis to describe the evolution of written language. Are the steps in the process stated clearly? Why do you suppose Lago chose not to include a final step? Explain.
3. Why was the introduction of writing so important, according to Lago?
4. What special significance does Lago attach to the message on the Pioneer spacecraft, and how does it relate to the rest of Lago's essay?
5. In Lago's last paragraph he says, "And we no longer scratch on sand; now we write our thoughts onto the emptiness of space itself." What is implied by this statement?

Vocabulary

Refer to your dictionary to define the following words as they are used in this selection. Then use each word in a sentence of your own.

pictographs (5)   embodied (7)
ideograms (5)   exobiologists (8)
resemblance (6)

Suggested Writing Assignments

1. Write an informational process analysis explaining how one of the following works:

   a checking account
   cell division
   an automobile engine
   the human eye
   economic supply and demand
   a microwave oven

2. Describe the evolution of a particular aspect of our American culture such as farming, transportation, manufacturing, the media or marriage. Be sure to distinguish the steps in the evolution clearly. If the evolution is ongoing offer a prediction of what future steps might be like.

14

DEFINITION

To communicate precisely what you want to say, you will frequently need to *define* key words. Your reader needs to know just what you mean when you use unfamiliar words, such as *accouterment*, or words that are open to various interpretations, such as *liberal*, or words that, while generally familiar, are used in a particular sense. Failure to define important terms, or to define them accurately, confuses readers and hampers communication.

There are three basic ways to define a word; each is useful in its own way. The first method is to give a *synonym*, a word that has nearly the same meaning as the word you wish to define: *face* for *countenance, nervousness* for *anxiety*. No two words ever have *exactly* the same meaning, but you can, nevertheless, pair an unfamiliar word with a familiar one and thereby clarify your meaning.

Another way to define a word quickly, often within a single sentence, is to give a *formal definition;* that is, to place the term to be defined in a general class and then to distinguish it from other members of that class by describing its particular characteristics. For example:

WORD	CLASS	CHARACTERISTICS
A *watch*	is a *mechanical device*	*for telling time* and is usually *carried* or *worn*.
Semantics	is an *area of linguistics*	*concerned with the study of the meaning of words*.

The third method is known as *extended definition*. While some extended definitions require only a single paragraph, more often than not you will need several paragraphs or even an entire essay to define a new or difficult term or to rescue a controversial word from misconceptions and associations that may obscure its meaning.

One controversial term that illustrates the need for extended definition is *obscene.* What is obscene? Books that are banned in one school system are considered perfectly acceptable in another. Movies that are shown in one town cannot be shown in a neighboring town. Clearly, the meaning of *obscene* has been clouded by contrasting personal opinions as well as by conflicting social norms. Therefore, if you use the term *obscene* (and especially if you tackle the issue of obscenity itself), you must be careful to define clearly and thoroughly what you mean by that term—that is, you have to give an extended definition. There are a number of methods you might use to develop such a definition. You could define *obscene* by explaining what it does not mean. You could also make your meaning clear by narrating an experience, by comparing and contrasting it to related terms such as *pornographic* or *exotic,* by citing specific examples, or by classifying the various types of obscenity.

A JERK

Sydney J. Harris

For over forty years Sydney J. Harris wrote a syndicated column for the Chicago Daily News *entitled "Strictly Personal," in which he considered virtually every aspect of contemporary American life. In the following essay from his book* Last Things First *(1961), Harris defines the term* jerk *by differentiating it from other similar slang terms.*

I don't know whether history repeats itself, but biography certainly does. The other day, Michael came in and asked me what a "jerk" was—the same question Carolyn put to me a dozen years ago. 1

At that time, I fluffed her off with some inane answer, such as "A jerk isn't a very nice person," but both of us knew it was an unsatisfactory reply. When she went to bed, I began trying to work up a suitable definition. 2

It is a marvelously apt word, of course. Until it was coined, not more than 25 years ago, there was really no single word in English to describe the kind of person who is a jerk—"boob" and "simp" were too old hat, and besides they really didn't fit, for they could be lovable, and a jerk never is. 3

Thinking it over, I decided that a jerk is basically a person without insight. He is not necessarily a fool or a dope, because some extremely clever persons can be jerks. In fact, it has little to do with intelligence as we commonly think of it; it is, rather, a kind of subtle but persuasive aroma emanating from the inner part of the personality. 4

I know a college president who can be described only as a jerk. He is not an unintelligent man, nor unlearned, nor even unschooled in the social amenities. Yet he is a jerk *cum laude,* because of a fatal flaw in his nature—he is totally incapable of looking into the mirror of his soul and shuddering at what he sees there. 5

A jerk, then, is a man (or woman) who is utterly unable to see   6
himself as he appears to others. He has no grace, he is tactless
without meaning to be, he is a bore even to his best friends, he
is an egotist without charm. All of us are egotists to some extent, but most of us—unlike the jerk—are perfectly and horribly aware of it when we make asses of ourselves. The jerk never
knows.

Questions for Study and Discussion

1. What, according to Harris, is a jerk?
2. Jerks, boobs, simps, fools, and dopes are all in the same
   class. How does Harris differentiate a jerk from a boob or a
   simp on the one hand, and a fool or a dope on the other?
3. What does Harris see as the relationship between intelligence and/or cleverness and the idea of a jerk?
4. In paragraph 5 Harris presents the example of the college
   president. How does this example support his definition?
5. In the first two paragraphs Harris tells how both his son
   and daughter asked him what *jerk* was. How does this
   brief anecdote serve to introduce Harris's essay? (Glossary: *Beginnings and Endings*) Do you think it works well?
   Explain.

Vocabulary

Refer to your dictionary to define the following words as they
are used in this selection. Then use each word in a sentence of
your own.

inane (2)	emanating (4)
apt (3)	amenities (5)
coined (3)	tactless (6)

Suggested Writing Assignments

1. Write one or two paragraphs in which you give your own
   definition of *jerk* or another slang term of your choice.

2. Every generation develops its own slang, which generally enlivens the speech and writing of those who use it. Ironically, however, no generation can arrive at a consensus definition of even its most popular slang terms—for example, *nimrod, air-head, flag*. Select a slang term that you use frequently, and write an essay in which you define the term. Read your definition aloud in class. Do the other members of your class agree with your definition?

AMBITION

Perri Klass

Perri Klass is a pediatrician, author of four books, and mother of two. She knows from experience the power of ambition and candidly confesses that "I've had to scale down my ambitions and make them more specific." In the following essay from the June 1990 issue of Self, *Klass shows us that ambition is the necessary impetus to our dreams and our success. Nevertheless, she asks us to consider what exactly ambition is, and just "how much is too much?"*

I n college, my friend Beth was very ambitious, not only for herself but for her friends. She was interested in foreign relations, in travel, in going to law school. "I plan to be secretary of state someday," she would say matter-of-factly. One mutual friend was studying literature, planning to go to graduate school; he would be the chairman of the Yale English department. Another friend was interested in political journalism and would someday edit *Time* magazine. I was a biology major, which was a problem: Beth's best friend from childhood was also studying biology, and Beth had already decided *she* would win the Nobel Prize. This was resolved by my interest in writing fiction. I would win *that* Nobel, while her other friend would win for science.

It was a joke; we were all smart-ass college freshmen, pretending the world was ours for the asking. But it was not entirely a joke. We were *smart* college freshmen, and why should we limit our ambitions?

I've always liked ambitious people, and many of my closest friends have had grandiose dreams. I like such people, not because I am desperate to be buddies with a future secretary of state but because I find ambitious people entertaining, interesting to talk to, fun to watch. And, of course, I like such people because I am ambitious myself, and I would rather not feel apologetic about it.

Ambition has gotten bad press. Back in the seventeenth cen- 4 tury, Spinoza thought ambition and lust were "nothing but species of madness, although they are not enumerated among diseases." Especially in women, ambition has often been seen as a profoundly dislikable quality; the word "ambitious" linked to a "career woman" suggested that she was ruthless, hard as nails, clawing her way to success on top of the bleeding bodies of her friends.

Then, in the late Seventies and the Eighties, ambition became 5 desirable, as books with titles like *How to Stomp Your Way to Success* became bestsellers. It was still a nasty sort of attribute, but nasty attributes were good because they helped you look out for number one.

But what I mean by ambition is dreaming big dreams, putting 6 no limits on your expectations and your hopes. I don't really like very specific, attainable ambitions, the kind you learn to set in the career-strategy course taught by the author of *How to Stomp Your Way to Success*. I like big ambitions that suggest that the world could open up at any time, with work and luck and determination. The next book could hit it big. The next research project could lead to something fantastic. The next bright idea could change history.

Of course, eventually you have to stop being a freshman in 7 college. You limit your ambitions and become more realistic, wiser about your potential, your abilities, the number of things your life can hold. Sometimes you get close to something you wanted to do, only to find it looks better from far away. Back when I was a freshman, to tell the truth, I wanted to be Jane Goodall, go into the jungle to study monkeys and learn things no one had ever dreamed of. This ambition was based on an interest in biology and several *National Geographic* television specials; it turned out that wasn't enough of a basis for a life. There were a number of other early ambitions that didn't pan out either. I was not fated to live a wild, adventurous life, to travel alone to all the most exotic parts of the world, to leave behind a string of broken hearts. Oh well, you have to grow up, at least a little.

One of the worst things ambition can do is tell you you're a   8
failure. The world is full of measuring tapes, books and articles
to tell you where you should be at your age, after so-and-so
many years of doing what you do.

Almost all of us have to deal with the tremendous success of   9
friends (or enemies), with those who somehow started out
where we did but are now way in front. My college-alumni
magazine arrives every two months without fail, so I can find
out who graduated two years *after* I did but is now running a
groundbreaking clinic at a major university hospital (and I'm
only just finishing my residency!). Who is restoring a fabulous
mansion in a highly desirable town by the sea. Who got
promoted yet again, due to natural brilliance and industry.

I read an article recently about how one's twenties are the   10
decade for deciding on a career and finishing your training, and
the thirties are for consolidating your success and rising within
your chosen job (and here I am in my thirties, not even sure
what I want to do yet!). With all these external yardsticks, the
last thing anyone needs is an internal voice as well, whispering
irritably that you were supposed to do it better, get further and
that all you've actually accomplished is mush, since you haven't
met your own goals.

The world is full of disappointed people. Some of them   11
probably never had much ambition to start with; they sat back
and waited for something good and feel cheated because it
never happened. Some of them had very set, specific ambitions
and, for one reason or another, never got what they wanted.
Others got what they wanted but found it wasn't exactly what
they'd expected it to be. Disappointed ambition provides fodder
for both drama and melodrama: aspiring athletes (who coulda
been contenders), aspiring dancers (all they ever needed was
the music and the mirror).

The world is also full of people so ambitious, so consumed by   12
drive and overdrive that nothing they pass on the way to success has any value at all. Life becomes one long exercise in delayed gratification; everything you do, you're doing only because it will one day get you where you want to be. Medical
training is an excellent example of delayed gratification. You
spend years in medical school doing things with no obvious re-

lationship to your future as a doctor, and then you spend years in residency, living life on a miserable schedule, staying up all night and slogging through the day, telling yourself that one day all this will be over. It's what you have to do to become a doctor, but it's a lousy model for life in general. There's nothing wrong with a little delayed gratification every now and then, but a job you do only because of where it will get you—and not because you like it—means a life of muttering to yourself, "Someday this will be over." This is bad for the disposition.

As you grow up, your ambitions may come into conflict. Most 13
prominently nowadays, we have to hear about Women Torn Between Family and Career, about women who make it to the top only to realize they left their ovaries behind. Part of growing up, of course, is realizing that there is only so much room in one life, whether you are male or female. You can do one thing wholeheartedly and single-mindedly and give up some other things. Or you can be greedy and grab for something new without wanting to give up what you already have. This leads to a chaotic and crowded life in which you are always late, always overdue, always behind, but rarely bored. Even so, you have to come to terms with limitations; you cannot crowd your life with occupations and then expect to do each one as well as you might if it were all you had to do. I realize this when I race out of the hospital, offending a senior doctor who had offered to explain something to me, only to arrive late at the day-care center, annoying the people who have been taking care of my daughter.

People consumed by ambition, living with ambition, get to be 14
a little humorless, a little one-sided. On the other hand, people who completely abrogate their ambition aren't all fun and games either. I've met a certain number of women whose ambitions are no longer for themselves at all; their lives are now dedicated to their offspring. I hope my children grow up to be nice people, smart people, people who use good grammar; and I hope they grow up to find things they love to do, and do well. But my ambitions are still for *me*.

Of course, I try to be mature about it all. I don't assign my 15
friends Nobel Prizes or top government posts. I don't pretend that there is room in my life for any and every kind of ambition

I can imagine. Instead, I say piously that all I want are three things: I want to write as well as I can, I want to have a family and I want to be a good pediatrician. And then, of course, a voice inside whispers . . . to write a bestseller, to have ten children, to do stunning medical research. Fame and fortune, it whispers, fame and fortune. Even though I'm not a college freshman anymore, I'm glad to find that little voice still there, whispering sweet nothings in my ear.

Questions for Study and Discussion

1. What is Klass's thesis? Is it stated or implied? (Glossary: *Thesis*)
2. Klass defines three kinds of ambition. What are they? Which type does she prefer? Why?
3. What factors, according to Klass, limit ambition?
4. Klass relies heavily on her own opinions to support her thesis. Is she convincing? Why or why not?
5. Why does Klass prefer ambitious people to non-ambitious people? Do you agree with her reasoning?
6. What is "delayed gratification"? What are its pluses and minuses? In what way is medical training a breeding-ground for delayed gratification?
7. In her concluding paragraph, Klass admits to being "glad" for the vestige of outrageous ambition that still plagues her. Isn't this a contradiction? Has she resolved the "conflict" she refers to in paragraph 13? Explain.

Vocabulary

Refer to your dictionary to define the following words as they are used in this selection. Then use each word in a sentence of your own.

grandiose (3)   consumed (12)
ruthless (4)   abrogate (14)

Suggested Writing Assignments

1. Klass believes it is necessary to limit ambition. In an essay of your own, discuss whether you agree or disagree with her position. Use examples from your experience or reading to support your opinion.

2. Write a short essay in which you define one of the following abstract terms. You may find it useful to begin your essay with a concrete example that illustrates your point.

   friendship
   freedom
   trust
   commitment
   love
   hatred
   patriotism
   choice
   charm
   peace

THE MEANINGS OF A WORD

Gloria Naylor

*American novelist and essayist Gloria Naylor
was born in 1950 in New York City. She worked
first as a missionary for the Jehovah's Witnesses
from 1967 to 1975, then as a telephone operator
until 1981. That year she graduated from Brooklyn College of the City of New York and began
graduate work in African-American studies at
Yale University. She has published three novels
on the "black experience":* The Women of Brew-
ster Place *(1982),* Linden Hills *(1985), and* Mama
Day *(1988). The following essay first appeared in
the* New York Times *in 1986. In it Naylor examines the ways in which words can take on meaning depending on who uses them and to what
purpose.*

Language is the subject. It is the written form with which 1
I've managed to keep the wolf away from the door and, in
diaries, to keep my sanity. In spite of this, I consider the written
word inferior to the spoken, and much of the frustration
experienced by novelists is the awareness that whatever we
manage to capture in even the most transcendent passages falls
far short of the richness of life. Dialogue achieves its power in
the dynamics of a fleeting moment of sight, sound, smell, and
touch.

I'm not going to enter the debate here about whether it is lan- 2
guage that shapes reality or vice versa. That battle is doomed to
be waged whenever we seek intermittent reprieve from the
chicken and egg dispute. I will simply take the position that the
spoken word, like the written word, amounts to a nonsensical
arrangement of sounds or letters without a consensus that
assigns "meaning." And building from the meanings of what we
hear, we order reality. Words themselves are innocuous; it is the
consensus that gives them true power.

I remember the first time I heard the word *nigger*. In my 3
third-grade class, our math tests were being passed down the
rows, and as I handed the papers to a little boy in back of me,
I remarked that once again he had received a much lower mark
than I did. He snatched his test from me and spit out that word.
Had he called me a nymphomaniac or a necrophiliac, I couldn't
have been more puzzled. I didn't know what a nigger was, but I
knew that whatever it meant, it was something he shouldn't
have called me. This was verified when I raised my hand, and in
a loud voice repeated what he had said and watched the teacher
scold him for using a "bad" word. I was later to go home and
ask the inevitable question that every black parent must face—
"Mommy, what does *nigger* mean?"

And what exactly did it mean? Thinking back, I realize that 4
this could not have been the first time the word was used in my
presence. I was part of a large extended family that had mi-
grated from the rural South after World War II and formed a
close-knit network that gravitated around my maternal grandparents. Their ground-floor apartment in one of the buildings
they owned in Harlem was a weekend mecca for my immediate
family, along with countless aunts, uncles, and cousins who
brought along assorted friends. It was a bustling and open
house with assorted neighbors and tenants popping in and out
to exchange bits of gossip, pick up an old quarrel, or referee the
ongoing checkers game in which my grandmother cheated
shamelessly. They were all there to let down their hair and put
up their feet after a week of labor in the factories, laundries,
and shipyards of New York.

Amid the clamor, which could reach deafening proportions— 5
two or three conversations going on simultaneously, punctuated by the sound of a baby's crying somewhere in the back
rooms or out on the street—there was still a rigid set of rules
about what was said and how. Older children were sent out of
the living room when it was time to get into the juicy details
about "you-know-who" up on the third floor who had gone and
gotten herself "p-r-e-g-n-a-n-t!" But my parents, knowing that I
could spell well beyond my years, always demanded that I
follow the others out to play. Beyond sexual misconduct and
death, everything else was considered harmless for our young
ears. And so among the anecdotes of the triumphs and disap-

pointments in the various workings of their lives, the word
nigger was used in my presence, but it was set within contexts
and inflections that caused it to register in my mind as something else.

In the singular, the word was always applied to a man who   6
had distinguished himself in some situation that brought their
approval for his strength, intelligence, or drive:

"Did Johnny *really* do that?"   7

"I'm telling you, that nigger pulled in $6,000 of overtime last   8
year. Said he got enough for a down payment on a house."

When used with a possessive adjective by a woman—"my   9
nigger"—it became a term of endearment for her husband or
boyfriend. But it could be more than just a term applied to a
man. In their mouths it became the pure essence of manhood—a disembodied force that channeled their past history of
struggle and present survival against the odds into a victorious
statement of being: "Yeah, that old foreman found out quick
enough—you don't mess with a nigger."

In the plural, it became a description of some group within   10
the community that had overstepped the bounds of decency as
my family defined it. Parents who neglected their children, a
drunken couple who fought in public, people who simply refused to look for work, those with excessively dirty mouths or
unkempt households were all "trifling niggers." This particular
circle could forgive hard times, unemployment, the occasional
bout of depression—they had gone through all of that themselves—but the unforgivable sin was a lack of self-respect.

A woman could never be a "nigger" in the singular, with its   11
connotation of confirming worth. The noun *girl* was its closest
equivalent in that sense, but only when used in direct address
and regardless of the gender doing the addressing. *Girl* was a
token of respect for a woman. The one-syllable word was drawn
out to sound like three in recognition of the extra ounce of wit,
nerve, or daring that the woman had shown in the situation
under discussion.

"G-i-r-l, stop. You mean you said that to his face?"   12

But if the word was used in a third-person reference or   13
shortened so that it almost snapped out of the mouth, it always
involved some element of communal disapproval. And age became an important factor in these exchanges. It was only be-

tween individuals of the same generation, or from any older person to a younger (but never the other way around), that *girl* would be considered a compliment.

I don't agree with the argument that use of the word *nigger* at this social stratum of the black community was an internalization of racism. The dynamics were the exact opposite: the people in my grandmother's living room took a word that whites used to signify worthlessness or degradation and rendered it impotent. Gathering there together, they transformed *nigger* to signify the varied and complex human beings they knew themselves to be. If the word was to disappear totally from the mouths of even the most liberal of white society, no one in that room was naive enough to believe it would disappear from white minds. Meeting the word head-on, they proved it had absolutely nothing to do with the way they were determined to live their lives.

So there must have been dozens of times that *nigger* was spoken in front of me before I reached the third grade. But I didn't "hear" it until it was said by a small pair of lips that had already learned it could be a way to humiliate me. That was the word I went home and asked my mother about. And since she knew that I had to grow up in America, she took me in her lap and explained.

Questions for Study and Discussion

1. How does Naylor explain her preference for the spoken word over the written word? What does she mean by "context"?

2. What are the two meanings of the word "nigger" as Naylor uses it in her essay? Where in the essay is the clearest definition of each use of the word presented?

3. Naylor said she must have heard the word "nigger" many times while she was growing up; yet she "heard" it for the first time when she was in the third grade. How does she explain this seeming contradiction?

4. Naylor gives a detailed narration of her family and its lifestyle in paragraphs 4 and 5. What kinds of detail does she

include in her brief story? How does this narration contribute to your understanding of the word "nigger" as
used by her family? Why do you suppose she offers so little in the way of a definition of the other use of the word
"nigger"? What is the effect on you as a reader? Explain.

5. Would you characterize Naylor's tone as angry, objective,
cynical, or something else? (Glossary: *Tone*) Cite examples
of her diction to support your answer. (Glossary: *Diction*)

6. What is the meaning of Naylor's last sentence? How well
does it work as an ending for her essay? (Glossary: *Endings*)

Vocabulary

Refer to your dictionary to define the following words as they
are used in this selection. Then use each word in a sentence of
your own.

transcendent (1)   anecdotes (5)
consensus (2)   inflections (5)
innocuous (2)   unkempt (10)
nymphomaniac (3)   trifling (10)
necrophiliac (3)   internalization (14)
mecca (4)   impotent (14)
clamor (5)

Suggested Writing Assignments

1. Write a short essay in which you define a word that has
more than one meaning, depending on one's point of view.
For example, wife, macho, liberal, success, and marriage.

2. Naylor disagrees with the notion that use of the word
"nigger" in the African-American community can be taken
as an "internalization of racism." Re-examine her essay
and discuss in what ways her definition of the word "nigger" affirms or denies her position. Draw on your own
experiences, observations, and reading to add support to
your answer.

15

DIVISION AND CLASSIFICATION

To divide is to separate a class of things or ideas into categories, whereas to classify is to group separate things or ideas into those categories. The two processes can operate separately but often go together. Division and classification can be a useful organizational strategy in writing. Here, for example, is a passage about levers in which the writer first discusses generally how levers work and then, in the second paragraph, uses division to establish three categories of levers and classification to group individual levers into those categories:

> Every lever has one fixed point called the "fulcrum" and is acted upon by two forces—the "effort" (exertion of hand muscles) and the "weight" (object's resistance). Levers work according to a simple formula: the effort (how hard you push or pull) multiplied by its distance from the fulcrum (effort arm) equals the weight multiplied by its distance from the fulcrum (weight arm). Thus two pounds of effort exerted at a distance of four feet from the fulcrum will raise eight pounds located one foot from the fulcrum.
> There are three types of levers, conventionally called "first kind," "second kind," and "third kind." Levers of the first kind have the fulcrum located between the effort and the weight. Examples are a pump handle, an oar, a crowbar, a weighing balance, a pair of scissors, and a pair of pliers. Levers of the second kind have the weight in the middle and magnify the effort. Examples are the handcar crank and doors. Levers of the third kind, such as a power shovel or a baseball batter's forearm, have the effort in the middle and always magnify the distance.

In writing, division and classification are affected directly by the writer's practical purpose. That purpose—what the writer wants to explain or prove—determines the class of things or ideas being divided and classified. For instance, a writer might divide television programs according to their audiences—adults, families, or children—and then classify individual programs into each of these categories in order to show how much emphasis the television stations place on reaching each audience. A different purpose would require different categories. A writer concerned about the prevalence of violence in television programming would first divide television programs into those which include fights and murders, and those which do not, and would then classify a large sample of programs into those categories. Other writers with different purposes might divide television programs differently—by the day and time of broadcast, for example, or by the number of women featured in prominent roles—and then classify individual programs accordingly.

The following guidelines can help you in using division and classification in your writing:

1. *Identify a clear purpose, and be sure that your principle of division is appropriate to that purpose.* To determine the makeup of a student body, for example, you might consider the following principles of division: college or program, major, class level, sex. It would not be helpful to divide students on the basis of their toothpaste unless you had a purpose and thus a reason for doing so.

2. *Divide your subject into categories that are mutually exclusive.* An item can belong to only one category. For example, it would be unsatisfactory to divide students as men, women, and athletes.

3. *Make your division and classification complete.* Your categories should account for all items in a subject class. In dividing students on the basis of geographic origin, for example, it would be inappropriate to consider only home states, for such a division would not account for foreign students. Then, for your classification to be complete, every student must be placed in one of the established categories.

4. *Be sure to state clearly the conclusion that your division and classification lead you to draw.* For example, a study of the student body might lead to the conclusion that 45 percent of the male athletes with athletic scholarships come from west of the Mississippi.

CHILDREN'S INSULTS

Peter Farb

*Beginning with his undergraduate years at Van-
derbilt University, Peter Farb (1929–1980) developed an intense interest in language and its role
in human behavior. Farb was a consultant to the
Smithsonian Institution, a curator of the River-
side Museum in New York City, and a visiting
lecturer in English at Yale. In this essay, taken
from* Word Play: What Happens When People
Talk *(1973), Farb classifies the names children
use to insult one another.*

The insults spoken by adults are usually more subtle than   1
the simple name-calling used by children, but children's
insults make obvious some of the verbal strategies people carry
into adult life. Most parents engage in wishful thinking when
they regard name-calling as good-natured fun which their children will soon grow out of. Name-calling is not good-natured
and children do not grow out of it; as adults they merely become more expert in its use. Nor is it true that "sticks and
stones may break my bones, but names will never hurt me."
Names can hurt very much because children seek out the victim's true weakness, then jab exactly where the skin is thin-
nest. Name-calling can have major impact on a child's feelings
about his identity, and it can sometimes be devastating to his
psychological development.

Almost all examples of name-calling by children fall into four   2
categories:

1. Names based on physical peculiarities, such as deformities, use of eyeglasses, racial characteristics, and so forth.
   A child may be called *Flattop* because he was born with a
   misshapen skull—or, for obvious reasons, *Fat Lips, Gimpy,
   Four Eyes, Peanuts, Fatso, Kinky,* and so on.
2. Names based on a pun or parody of the child's own name.

Children with last names like Fitts, McClure, and Farb usually find them converted to *Shits, Manure,* and *Fart.*

3. Names based on social relationships. Examples are *Baby* used by a sibling rival or *Chicken Shit* for someone whose courage is questioned by his social group.

4. Names based on mental traits—such as *Clunkhead, Dummy, Jerk,* and *Smartass.*

These four categories were listed in order of decreasing offen- ₃
siveness to the victims. Children regard names based on physical peculiarities as the most cutting, whereas names based on
mental traits are, surprisingly, not usually regarded as very offensive. Most children are very vulnerable to names that play
upon the child's rightful name—no doubt because one's name
is a precious possession, the mark of a unique identity and
one's masculinity or femininity. Those American Indian tribes
that had the custom of never revealing true names undoubtedly
avoided considerable psychological damage.

Questions for Study and Discussion

1. What is Farb's contention in this selection? Where is it revealed? (Glossary: *Thesis*)

2. For what reason does Farb divide and classify children's insults?

3. Why does Farb feel that name-calling should not be dismissed lightly?

4. Farb states that children "regard names based on physical peculiarities as the most cutting" (2) Why do you suppose this might be true?

5. What principle of division does Farb use to establish his four categories of children's insults? What are the categories, and how does he order them? Be prepared to cite examples from the text.

6. List some insults that you remember from your own childhood or adolescence. Classify the insults according to Farb's system. Do any items on your list not fit into one of his categories? What new categories can you establish?

Vocabulary

Refer to your dictionary to define the following words as they are used in this selection. Then use each word in a sentence of your own.

subtle (1)
peculiarities (2)
deformities (2)

sibling (2)
vulnerable (2)
unique (2)

Suggested Writing Assignments

1. Using the following sentence as your thesis, write an essay that divides and classifies the students at your college or university:

   There are (number) types of students at (institution).

   Be sure to follow the guidelines for division and classification that appear on page 324.

2. Consider the following classes of items and determine at least two principles of division that can be used for each class. Then write a paragraph or two in which you classify one of the groups of items according to a single principle of division. For example, in discussing crime one could use the seriousness of the crime or the type of crime as principles of division. If the seriousness of the crime were used, this might yield two categories: felonies, or major crimes; and misdemeanors, or minor crimes. If the type of crime were used, this would yield categories such as burglary, murder, assault, larceny, and embezzlement.

   professional sports
   social sciences
   movies
   roommates
   cars
   slang used by college students

WHAT'S IN YOUR TOOTHPASTE?

Paul Bodanis

The average American's morning bathroom ritual would be incomplete without a thorough brushing of the teeth. But how many of us have stopped to think what is in the toothpaste we use each morning? Well, Paul Bodanis has. In the following selection from his book The Secret House *(1986), he carefully analyzes and describes the various unexpected and unappetizing ingredients that can be found in a simple tube of toothpaste.*

I nto the bathroom goes our male resident, and after the most   1
pressing need is satisfied it's time to brush the teeth. The tube of toothpaste is squeezed, its pinched metal seams are splayed, pressure waves are generated inside, and the paste begins to flow. But what's in this toothpaste, so carefully being extruded out?

Water mostly, 30 to 45 percent in most brands: ordinary, ev-   2
eryday simple tap water. It's there because people like to have a big gob of toothpaste to spread on the brush, and water is the cheapest stuff there is when it comes to making big gobs. Dripping a bit from the tap onto your brush would cost virtually nothing; whipped in with the rest of the toothpaste the manufacturers can sell it at a neat and accountant-pleasing $2 per pound equivalent. Toothpaste manufacture is a very lucrative occupation.

Second to water in quantity is chalk: exactly the same   3
material that schoolteachers use to write on blackboards. It is collected from the crushed remains of long-dead ocean creatures. In the Cretaceous seas chalk particles served as part of the wickedly sharp outer skeleton that these creatures had to wrap around themselves to keep from getting chomped by all the slightly larger other ocean creatures they met. Their massed graves are our present chalk deposits.

The individual chalk particles—the size of the smallest mud 4
particles in your garden—have kept their toughness over the
aeons, and now on the toothbrush they'll need it. The enamel
outer coating of the tooth they'll have to face is the hardest substance in the body—tougher than skull, or bone, or nail. Only
the chalk particles in toothpaste can successfully grind into the
teeth during brushing, ripping off the surface layers like an
abrading wheel grinding down a boulder in a quarry.

The craters, slashes, and channels that the chalk tears into 5
the teeth will also remove a certain amount of build-up yellow
in the carnage, and it is for that polishing function that it's
there. A certain amount of unduly enlarged extra-abrasive
chalk fragments tear such cavernous pits into the teeth that future decay bacteria will be able to bunker down there and
thrive; the quality control people find it almost impossible to
screen out these errant super-chalk pieces, and government
regulations allow them to stay in.

In case even the gouging doesn't get all the yellow off, 6
another substance is worked into the toothpaste cream. This is
titanium dioxide. It comes in tiny spheres, and it's the stuff
bobbing around in white wall paint to make it come out white.
Splashed around onto your teeth during the brushing it coats
much of the yellow that remains. Being water soluble it leaks
off in the next few hours and is swallowed, but at least for the
quick glance up in the mirror after finishing it will make the
user think his teeth are truly white. Some manufacturers add
optical whitening dyes—the stuff more commonly found in
washing machine bleach—to make extra sure that that glance
in the mirror shows reassuring white.

These ingredients alone would not make a very attractive con- 7
coction. They would stick in the tube like a sloppy white plastic
lump, hard to squeeze out as well as revolting to the touch. Few
consumers would savor rubbing in a mixture of water, ground-
up blackboard chalk, and the whitener from latex paint first
thing in the morning. To get around that finicky distaste the
manufacturers have mixed in a host of other goodies.

To keep the glop from drying out, a mixture including glyc- 8
erine glycol—related to the most common car antifreeze ingredient—is whipped in with the chalk and water, and to give *that*
concoction a bit of substance (all we really have so far is wet

colored chalk) a large helping is added of gummy molecules from the seaweed *Chondrus Crispus.* This seaweed ooze spreads in among the chalk, paint, and antifreeze, then stretches itself in all directions to hold the whole mass together. A bit of paraffin oil (the fuel that flickers in camping lamps) is pumped in with it to help the moss ooze keep the whole substance smooth.

With the glycol, ooze, and paraffin we're almost there. Only two major chemicals are left to make the refreshing, cleansing substance we know as toothpaste. The ingredients so far are fine for cleaning, but they wouldn't make much of the satisfying foam we have come to expect in the morning brushing. 9

To remedy that every toothpaste on the market has a big dollop of detergent added too. You've seen the suds detergent will make in a washing machine. The same substance added here will duplicate that inside the mouth. It's not particularly necessary, but it sells. 10

The only problem is that by itself this ingredient tastes, well, too like detergent. It's horribly bitter and harsh. The chalk put in toothpaste is pretty foul-tasting too for that matter. It's to get around that gustatory discomfort that the manufacturers put in the ingredient they tout perhaps the most of all. This is the flavoring, and it has to be strong. Double rectified peppermint oil is used—a flavorer so powerful that chemists know better than to sniff it in the raw state in the laboratory. Menthol crystals and saccharin or other sugar simulators are added to complete the camouflage operation. 11

Is that it? Chalk, water, paint, seaweed, antifreeze, paraffin oil, detergent, and peppermint? Not quite. A mix like that would be irresistible to the hundreds of thousands of individual bacteria lying on the surface of even an immaculately cleaned bathroom sink. They would get in, float in the water bubbles, ingest the ooze and paraffin, maybe even spray out enzymes to break down the chalk. The result would be an uninviting mess. The way manufacturers avoid that final obstacle is by putting something in to kill the bacteria. Something good and strong is needed, something that will zap any accidentally intrudant bacteria into oblivion. And that something is formaldehyde— the disinfectant used in anatomy labs. 12

So it's chalk, water, paint, seaweed, antifreeze, paraffin oil, detergent, peppermint, formaldehyde, and fluoride (which can go some way towards preserving children's teeth)—that's the 13 usual mixture raised to the mouth on the toothbrush for a fresh morning's clean. If it sounds too unfortunate, take heart. Studies show that a thorough brushing with just plain water will often do as good a job.

Questions for Study and Discussion

1. What is Bodanis's thesis? Is it stated or implied? (Glossary: *Thesis*)
2. Into what categories does Bodanis divide toothpaste ingredients? Does he clearly establish the principle of division he used to establish these categories? Were his categories distinct? Explain.
3. Does Bodanis offer any explanation for the kinds of ingredients found in toothpaste?
4. In what ways, if any, has your attitude toward toothpaste changed since reading Bodanis's essay?
5. What is Bodanis's purpose in writing this essay? Is he trying to persuade people to avoid toothpaste, or is he merely trying to explain the different kinds of ingredients that go into toothpaste? What in his essay led you to your conclusion?

Vocabulary

Refer to your dictionary to define the following words as they are used in this selection. Then use each word in a sentence of your own.

splayed (1)   abrading (4)
extruded (1)   gustatory (11)
Cretaceous (3)

Suggested Writing Assignments

1. Using Bodanis's essay as a model, write a brief essay in which you classify people who are or have been included in one of the following groups:

television addicts
drivers
dieters
athletes
teachers
fashionable dressers
sports fans

2. College is a time of stress for many students. In an essay, discuss the different kinds of pressure students experience at your school.

THE WAYS OF MEETING OPPRESSION

Martin Luther King, Jr.

Martin Luther King, Jr. (1929–1968) was the lead-
ing spokesman for the rights of African-Amer-
icans during the 1950s and 1960s before he was
assassinated in 1968. He established the South-
ern Christian Leadership Conference, organized
many civil rights demonstrations, and opposed
the Vietnam War and the draft. In 1964 he was
awarded the Nobel Prize for Peace. In the follow-
ing essay, taken from his book Stride Toward
Freedom *(1958), King classifies the three ways*
oppressed people throughout history have re-
acted to their oppressors.

Oppressed people deal with their oppression in three char-   1
acteristic ways. One way is acquiescence: the oppressed
resign themselves to their doom. They tacitly adjust themselves
to oppression, and thereby become conditioned to it. In every
movement toward freedom some of the oppressed prefer to remain oppressed. Almost 2800 years ago Moses set out to lead
the children of Israel from the slavery of Egypt to the freedom
of the promised land. He soon discovered that slaves do not always welcome their deliverers. They become accustomed to
being slaves. They would rather bear those ills they have, as
Shakespeare pointed out, than flee to others that they know not
of. They prefer the "fleshpots of Egypt" to the ordeals of eman-
cipation.

There is such a thing as the freedom of exhaustion. Some   2
people are so worn down by the yoke of oppression that they
give up. A few years ago in the slum areas of Atlanta, a Negro
guitarist used to sing almost daily: "Been down so long that
down don't bother me." This is the type of negative freedom
and resignation that often engulfs the life of the oppressed.

But this is not the way out. To accept passively an unjust sys-   3
tem is to cooperate with that system; thereby the oppressed be-

come as evil as the oppressor. Noncooperation with evil is as much a moral obligation as is cooperation with good. The oppressed must never allow the conscience of the oppressor to slumber. Religion reminds every man that he is his brother's keeper. To accept injustice or segregation passively is to say to the oppressor that his actions are morally right. It is a way of allowing his conscience to fall asleep. At this moment the oppressed fails to be his brother's keeper. So acquiescence—while often the easier way—is not the moral way. It is the way of the coward. The Negro cannot win the respect of his oppressor by acquiescing; he merely increases the oppressor's arrogance and contempt. Acquiescence is interpreted as proof of the Negro's inferiority. The Negro cannot win the respect of the white people of the South or the peoples of the world if he is willing to sell the future of his children for his personal and immediate comfort and safety.

A second way that oppressed people sometimes deal with op- 4 pression is to resort to physical violence and corroding hatred. Violence often brings about momentary results. Nations have frequently won their independence in battle. But in spite of temporary victories, violence never brings permanent peace. It solves no social problem; it merely creates new and more complicated ones.

Violence as a way of achieving racial justice is both imprac- 5 tical and immoral. It is impractical because it is a descending spiral ending in destruction for all. The old law of an eye for an eye leaves everybody blind. It is immoral because it seeks to humiliate the opponent rather than win his understanding; it seeks to annihilate rather than to convert. Violence is immoral because it thrives on hatred rather than love. It destroys community and makes brotherhood impossible. It leaves society in monologue rather than dialogue. Violence ends by defeating itself. It creates bitterness in the survivors and brutality in the destroyers. A voice echoes through time saying to every potential Peter, "Put up your sword."* History is cluttered with the wreckage of nations that failed to follow this command.

If the American Negro and other victims of oppression suc- 6

---

*The apostle Peter had drawn his sword to defend Christ from arrest. The voice was Christ's, who surrendered himself for trial and crucifixion (John 18:11).

cumb to the temptation of using violence in the struggle for freedom, future generations will be the recipients of a desolate night of bitterness, and our chief legacy to them will be an endless reign of meaningless chaos. Violence is not the way.

The third way open to oppressed people in their quest for freedom is the way of nonviolent resistance. Like the synthesis in Hegelian philosophy, the principle of nonviolent resistance seeks to reconcile the truths of two opposites—the acquiescence and violence—while avoiding the extremes and immoralities of both. The nonviolent resister agrees with the person who acquiesces that one should not be physically aggressive toward his opponent; but he balances the equation by agreeing with the person of violence that evil must be resisted. He avoids the nonresistance of the former and the violent resistance of the latter. With nonviolent resistance, no individual or group need submit to any wrong, nor need anyone resort to violence in order to right a wrong.   7

It seems to me that this is the method that must guide the actions of the Negro in the present crisis in race relations. Through nonviolent resistance the Negro will be able to rise to the noble height of opposing the unjust system while loving the perpetrators of the system. The Negro must work passionately and unrelentingly for full stature as a citizen, but he must not use inferior methods to gain it. He must never come to terms with falsehood, malice, hate, or destruction.   8

Nonviolent resistance makes it possible for the Negro to remain in the South and struggle for his rights. The Negro's problem will not be solved by running away. He cannot listen to the glib suggestion of those who would urge him to migrate en masse to other sections of the country. By grasping his great opportunity in the South he can make a lasting contribution to the moral strength of the nation and set a sublime example of courage for generations yet unborn.   9

By nonviolent resistance, the Negro can also enlist all men of good will in his struggle for equality. The problem is not a purely racial one, with Negroes set against whites. In the end, it is not a struggle between people at all, but a tension between justice and injustice. Nonviolent resistance is not aimed against oppressors but against oppression. Under its banner consciences, not racial groups, are enlisted.   10

Questions for Study and Discussion

1. What are the disadvantages that King sees in meeting oppression with acquiescence or with violence?
2. Why, according to King, do slaves not always welcome their deliverers?
3. What does King mean by the "freedom of exhaustion" (2)?
4. What is King's purpose in writing this essay? How does classifying the three types of resistance to oppression serve this purpose? (Glossary: *Purpose*)
5. What principle of division does King use in this essay?
6. Why do you suppose that King discusses acquiescence, violence, and nonviolent resistance in that order? (Glossary: *Organization*)
7. King states that he favors nonviolent resistance over the other two ways of meeting oppression. Look closely at the words he uses to describe nonviolent resistance and those he uses to describe acquiescence and violence. How does his choice of words contribute to his argument? Show examples. (Glossary: *Connotation/Denotation*)

Vocabulary

Refer to your dictionary to define the following words as they are used in this selection. Then use each word in a sentence of your own.

acquiescence (1)	desolate (6)
tacitly (1)	synthesis (7)
corroding (4)	sublime (9)
annihilate (5)	

Suggested Writing Assignments

1. Write an essay about a problem of some sort in which you use division and classification to discuss various possible solutions. You might discuss something personal such as the problems of giving up smoking or something that concerns everyone such as the difficulties of coping with the

homeless. Whatever your topic, use an appropriate principle of division to establish categories that suit the purpose of your discussion.

2. Consider any one of the following topics for an essay of classification:

   movies
   college courses
   spectators
   life styles
   country music
   newspapers
   pets
   grandparents

FRIENDS, GOOD FRIENDS
—AND SUCH GOOD FRIENDS

Judith Viorst

Judith Viorst has written several volumes of light verse as well as many articles that have appeared in popular magazines. The following essay appeared in her regular column in Redbook. *In it she analyzes and classifies the various types of friends that a person can have. As you read the essay, assess its validity by trying to place your friends in Viorst's categories.*

W omen are friends, I once would have said, when they totally love and support and trust each other, and bare to each other the secrets of their souls, and run—no questions asked—to help each other, and tell harsh truths to each other (no, you can't wear that dress unless you lose ten pounds first) when harsh truths must be told. 1

Women are friends, I once would have said, when they share the same affection for Ingmar Bergman, plus train rides, cats, warm rain, charades, Camus, and hate with equal ardor Newark and Brussels sprouts and Lawrence Welk and camping. 2

In other words, I once would have said that a friend is a friend all the way, but now I believe that's a narrow point of view. For the friendships I have and the friendships I see are conducted at many levels of intensity, serve many different functions, meet different needs and range from those as all-the-way as the friendship of the soul sisters mentioned above to that of the most nonchalant and casual playmates. 3

Consider these varieties of friendship: 4

1. Convenience friends. These are women with whom, if our paths weren't crossing all the time, we'd have no particular reason to be friends: a next-door neighbor, a woman in our car pool, the mother of one of our children's closest friends or maybe some mommy with whom we serve juice and cookies each week at the Glenwood Co-op Nursery. 5

Convenience friends are convenient indeed. They'll lend us   6
their cups and silverware for a party. They'll drive our kids to
soccer when we're sick. They'll take us to pick up our car when
we need a lift to the garage. They'll even take our cats when we
go on vacation. As we will for them.

But we don't, with convenience friends, ever come too close   7
or tell too much; we maintain our public face and emotional
distance. "Which means," says Elaine, "that I'll talk about being overweight but not about being depressed. Which means I'll
admit being mad but not blind with rage. Which means that I
might say that we're pinched this month but never that I'm
worried sick over money."

But which doesn't mean that there isn't sufficient value to be   8
found in these friendships of mutual aid, in convenience
friends.

2. Special-interest friends. These friendships aren't intimate,   9
and they needn't involve kids or silverware or cats. Their value
lies in some interest jointly shared. And so we may have an
office friend or a yoga friend or a tennis friend or a friend from
the Women's Democratic Club.

"I've got one woman friend," says Joyce, "who likes, as I do,   10
to take psychology courses. Which makes it nice for me—and
nice for her. It's fun to go with someone you know and it's fun
to discuss what you've learned, driving back from the classes."
And for the most part, she says, that's all they discuss.

"I'd say that what we're doing is *doing* together, not being to-   11
gether," Suzanne says of her Tuesday-doubles friends. "It's
mainly a tennis relationship, but we play together well. And I
guess we all need to have a couple of playmates."

I agree.   12

My playmate is a shopping friend, a woman of marvelous   13
taste, a woman who knows exactly *where* to buy *what*, and furthermore is a woman who always knows beyond a doubt what
one ought to be buying. I don't have the time to keep up with
what's new in eyeshadow, hemlines and shoes and whether the
smock look is in or finished already. But since (oh, shame!) I
care a lot about eyeshadow, hemlines and shoes, and since I
don't *want* to wear smocks if the smock look is finished, I'm
very glad to have a shopping friend.

3. Historical friends. We all have a friend who knew us   14

when . . . maybe way back in Miss Meltzer's second grade, when our family lived in that three-room flat in Brooklyn, when our dad was out of work for seven months, when our brother Allie got in that fight where they had to call the police, when our sister married the endodontist from Yonkers and when, the morning after we lost our virginity, she was the first, the only, friend we told.

The years have gone by and we've gone separate ways and   15
we've little in common now, but we're still an intimate part of each other's past. And so whenever we go to Detroit we always go to visit this friend of our girlhood. Who knows how we looked before our teeth were straightened. Who knows how we talked before our voice got un-Brooklyned. Who knows what we ate before we learned about artichokes. And who, by her presence, puts us in touch with an earlier part of ourself, a part of ourself it's important never to lose.

"What this friend means to me and what I mean to her," says   16
Grace, "is having a sister without sibling rivalry. We know the texture of each other's lives. She remembers my grandmother's cabbage soup. I remember the way her uncle played the piano. There's simply no other friend who remembers those things."

4. Crossroads friends. Like historical friends, our crossroads   17
friends are important for *what was*—for the friendship we shared at a crucial, now past, time of life. A time, perhaps, when we roomed in college together; or worked as eager young singles in the Big City together; or went together, as my friend Elizabeth and I did, through pregnancy, birth and that scary first year of new motherhood.

Crossroads friends forge powerful links, links strong enough   18
to endure with not much more contact than once-a-year letters at Christmas. And out of respect for those crossroad years, for those dramas and dreams we once shared, we will always be friends.

5. Cross-generational friends. Historical friends and cross-   19
roads friends seem to maintain a special kind of intimacy—dormant but always ready to be revived—and though we may rarely meet, whenever we do connect, it's personal and intense. Another kind of intimacy exists in the friendships that form across generations in what one woman calls her daughter-mother and her mother-daughter relationships.

Evelyn's friend is her mother's age—"but I share so much   20
more than I ever could with my mother"—a woman she talks to
of music, of books and of life. "What I get from her is the benefit of her experience. What she gets—and enjoys—from me is a
youthful perspective. It's a pleasure for both of us."

I have in my own life a precious friend, a woman of 65 who   21
has lived very hard, who is wise, who listens well; who has been
where I am and can help me understand it; and who represents
not only an ultimate ideal mother to me but also the person I'd
like to be when I grow up.

In our daughter role we tend to do more than our share of   22
self-revelation; in our mother role we tend to receive what's
revealed. It's another kind of pleasure—playing wise mother to
a questing younger person. It's another very lovely kind of
friendship.

6. Part-of-a-couple friends. Some of the women we call our   23
friends we never see alone—we see them as part of a couple at
couples' parties. And though we share interests in many things
and respect each other's views, we aren't moved to deepen the
relationship. Whatever the reason, a lack of time or—and this is
more likely—a lack of chemistry, our friendship remains in the
context of a group. But the fact that our feeling on seeing each
other is always, "I'm *so* glad she's here" and the fact that we
spend half the evening talking together says that this too, in its
own way, counts as a friendship.

(Other part-of-a-couple friends are the friends that came with   24
the marriage, and some of these are friends we could live without. But sometimes, alas, she married our husband's best
friend; and sometimes, alas, she *is* our husband's best friend.
And so we find ourself dealing with her, somewhat against our
will, in a spirit of what I'll call *reluctant* friendship.)

7. Men who are friends. I wanted to write just of women   25
friends, but the women I've talked to won't let me—they say I
must mention man-woman friendships too. For these friendships can be just as close and as dear as those that we form
with women. Listen to Lucy's description of one such friendship:

"We've found we have things to talk about that are different   26
from what he talks about with my husband and different from
what I talk about with his wife. So sometimes we call on the

phone or meet for lunch. There are similar intellectual interests—we always pass on to each other the books that we love—
but there's also something tender and caring too."

In a couple of crises, Lucy says, "he offered himself for talk-   27
ing and for helping. And when someone died in his family he
wanted me there. The sexual, flirty part of our friendship is
very small, but *some*—just enough to make it fun and different." She thinks—and I agree—that the sexual part, though
small, is always *some*, is always there when a man and a woman
are friends.

It's only in the past few years that I've made friends with   28
men, in the sense of a friendship that's *mine*, not just part of
two couples. And achieving with them the ease and the trust
I've found with women friends has value indeed. Under the
dryer at home last week, putting on mascara and rouge, I comfortably sat and talked with a fellow named Peter. Peter, I
finally decided, could handle the shock of me minus mascara
under the dryer. Because we care for each other. Because we're
friends.

8. There are medium friends, and pretty good friends, and   29
very good friends indeed, and these friendships are defined by
their level of intimacy. And what we'll reveal at each of these
levels of intimacy is calibrated with care. We might tell a medium friend, for example, that yesterday we had a fight with
our husband. And we might tell a pretty good friend that this
fight with our husband made us so mad that we slept on the
couch. And we might tell a very good friend that the reason we
got so mad in that fight that we slept on the couch had
something to do with that girl that works in his office. But it's
only to our very best friends that we're willing to tell all, to tell
what's going on with that girl in his office.

The best of friends, I still believe, totally love and support   30
and trust each other, and bare to each other the secrets of their
souls, and run—no questions asked—to help each other, and
tell harsh truths to each other when they must be told.

But we needn't agree about everything (only 12-year-old girl   31
friends agree about *everything*) to tolerate each other's point of
view. To accept without judgment. To give and to take without
ever keeping score. And to *be* there, as I am for them and as they
are for me, to comfort our sorrows, to celebrate our joys.

Questions for Study and Discussion

1. In her opening paragraph Viorst explains how she once would have defined friendship. Why does she now think differently?
2. What is Viorst's purpose in this essay? Why is division and classification an appropriate strategy for her to use? (Glossary: *Purpose*)
3. Into what categories does Viorst divide her friends?
4. What principles of division does Viorst use to establish her categories of friends? Where does she state these principles?
5. Discuss the ways in which Viorst makes her categories distinct and memorable.
6. Viorst wrote this essay for *Redbook,* and so her audience was women between the ages of twenty-five and thirty-five. If she had been writing on the same topic for an audience of men of the same age, how might her categories have been different? How might her examples have been different? (Glossary: *Audience*)

Vocabulary

Refer to your dictionary to define the following words as they are used in this selection. Then use each word in a sentence of your own.

ardor (2)   forge (18)
nonchalant (3)   dormant (19)
sibling (16)   perspective (20)

Suggested Writing Assignments

1. If for any reason you dislike or disagree with Viorst's classification of friends, write a classification essay of your own on the same topic. In preparation for writing, you may wish to interview your classmates and dorm members for their ideas on the various types of friends a person can have.

2. The following (p. 345) is a basic exercise in classification. By determining the features that the figures have in common, establish the general class to which they all belong. Next, establish subclasses by determining the distinctive features that distinguish one subclass from another. Finally, place each figure in an appropriate subclass within your classification system. You may wish to compare your classification system with those developed by other members of your class and to discuss any differences that exist.

16

COMPARISON AND CONTRAST

A *comparison* points out the ways that two or more persons, places, or things are alike. A *contrast* points out how they differ. The subjects of a comparison or contrast should be in the same class or general category; if they have nothing in common, there is no good reason for setting them side by side.

The function of any comparison or contrast is to clarify and explain. The writer's purpose may be simply to inform, or to make readers aware of similarities or differences that are interesting and significant in themselves. Or, the writer may explain something unfamiliar by comparing it with something very familiar, perhaps explaining squash by comparing it with tennis. Finally, the writer can point out the superiority of one thing by contrasting it with another—for example, showing that one product is the best by contrasting it with all its competitors.

As a writer, you have two main options for organizing a comparison or contrast: the subject-by-subject pattern or the point-by-point pattern. For a short essay comparing and contrasting the Atlanta Braves and the Los Angeles Dodgers, you would probably follow the *subject-by-subject* pattern of organization. By this pattern you first discuss the points you wish to make about one team, and then go on to discuss the corresponding points for the other team. An outline of your essay might look like this:

    I. Atlanta Braves
      A. Pitching
      B. Fielding
      C. Hitting
   II. Los Angeles Dodgers
      A. Pitching
      B. Fielding
      C. Hitting

The subject-by-subject pattern presents a unified discussion of each team by placing the emphasis on the teams and not on the three points of comparison. Since these points are relatively few, readers should easily remember what was said about the Braves' pitching when you later discuss the Dodgers' pitching and should be able to make the appropriate connections between them.

For a somewhat longer essay comparing and contrasting solar energy and wind energy, however, you should consider the *point-by-point* pattern of organization. With this pattern, your essay is organized according to the various points of comparison. Discussion alternates between solar and wind energy for each point of comparison. An outline of your essay might look like this:

I. Installation Expenses	IV. Convenience
A. Solar	A. Solar
B. Wind	B. Wind
II. Efficiency	V. Maintenance
A. Solar	A. Solar
B. Wind	B. Wind
III. Operating Costs	VI. Safety
A. Solar	A. Solar
B. Wind	B. Wind

The point-by-point pattern allows the writer to make immediate comparisons between solar and wind energy, thus enabling readers to consider each of the similarities and differences separately.

Each organizational pattern has its advantages. In general, the subject-by-subject pattern is useful in short essays where there are few points to be considered, whereas the point-by-point pattern is preferable in long essays where there are numerous points under consideration.

A good essay of comparison and contrast tells readers something significant that they do not already know. That is, it must do more than merely point out the obvious. As a rule, therefore, writers tend to draw contrasts between things that are usually perceived as being similar or comparisons between things usually perceived as different. In fact, comparison and contrast often go together. For example, an essay about Minneapolis and St. Paul might begin by showing how much they are alike, but end with a series of contrasts revealing how much they differ. Or, a consumer magazine might report the contrasting claims made by six car manufacturers, and then go on to demonstrate that the cars all actually do much the same thing in the same way.

Analogy is a special form of comparison. When a subject is unobservable, complex, or abstract—when it is so generally unfamiliar that readers may have trouble understanding it—*analogy* can be most effective. By pointing out the certain similarities between a difficult subject and a more familiar or concrete subject, writers can help their readers achieve a firmer grasp of the difficult subject. Unlike a true comparison, though, which analyzes items that belong to the same class—breeds of dogs or types of engines—analogy pairs things from different classes, things that have nothing in common except through the imagination of the writer. In addition, whereas comparison seeks to illuminate specific features of both subjects, the primary purpose of analogy is to clarify the one subject that is complex or unfamiliar. For example, an exploration of the similarities (and differences) between short stories and novels—two forms of fiction—would constitute a logical comparison; short stories and novels belong to the same class (fiction), and your purpose is to reveal something about both. If, however, your purpose is to explain the craft of fiction writing, you might note its similarities to the craft of carpentry. Then, you would be drawing an analogy, because the two subjects clearly belong to different classes. Carpentry is the more concrete subject and the one more people will have direct experience with. If you use your imagination, you will easily see many ways the tangible work of the carpenter can be used to help readers understand the more abstract work of the novelist. Depending on its purpose, an analogy can be made in several paragraphs to clarify a particular aspect of the larger topic being discussed, as in the example below, or it can provide the organizational strategy for an entire essay.

It has long struck me that the familiar metaphor of "climbing the ladder" for describing the ascent to success or fulfillment in any field is inappropriate and misleading. There are no ladders that lead to success, although there may be some escalators for those lucky enough to follow in a family's fortunes.

A ladder proceeds vertically, rung by rung, with each rung evenly spaced, and with the whole apparatus leaning against a relatively flat and even surface. A child can climb a ladder as easily as an adult, and perhaps with a surer footing.

Making the ascent in one's vocation or profession is far less like ladder climbing than mountain climbing, and here the analogy is a very real one. Going up a mountain requires a variety of skills, and includes a diversity of dangers, that are in no way involved in mounting a ladder.

Young people starting out should be told this, both to dampen their expectations and to allay their disappointments. A mountain is rough and precipitous, with uncertain footing and a predictable number of falls and scrapes, and sometimes one has to take the long way around to reach the shortest distance.

Sydney J. Harris

THAT LEAN AND HUNGRY LOOK

Suzanne Britt

Suzanne Britt makes her home in Raleigh, North Carolina, where she is a free-lance writer. In 1983 she published Show & Tell, *a collection of her characteristically informal essays. The following essay first appeared in* Newsweek *and became the basis for her book,* Skinny People Are Dull and Crunchy Like Carrots *(1982), titled after a line in the essay. As you read her essay, notice the way that Britt has organized the points of her contrast of fat and thin people.*

Caesar was right. Thin people need watching. I've been watching them for most of my adult life, and I don't like what I see. When these narrow fellows spring at me, I quiver to my toes. Thin people come in all personalities, most of them menacing. You've got your "together" thin person, your mechanical thin person, your condescending thin person, your tsk-tsk thin person, your efficiency-expert thin person. All of them are dangerous. 1

In the first place, thin people aren't fun. They don't know how to goof off, at least in the best, fat sense of the word. They've always got to be a doing. Give them a coffee break, and they'll jog around the block. Supply them with a quiet evening at home, and they'll fix the screen door and lick S&H green stamps. They say things like "there aren't enough hours in the day." Fat people never say that. Fat people think the day is too damn long already. 2

Thin people make me tired. They've got speedy little metabolisms that cause them to bustle briskly. They're forever rubbing their bony hands together and eyeing new problems to "tackle." I like to surround myself with sluggish, inert, easygoing fat people, the kind who believe that if you clean it up today, it'll just get dirty again tomorrow. 3

Some people say the business about the jolly fat person is a myth, that all of us chubbies are neurotic, sick, sad people. I 4 disagree. Fat people may not be chortling all day long, but they're a hell of a lot *nicer* than the wizened and shriveled. Thin people turn surly, mean, and hard at a young age because they never learn the value of a hot-fudge sundae for easing tension. Thin people don't like gooey soft things because they themselves are neither gooey nor soft. They are crunchy and dull, like carrots. They go straight to the heart of the matter while fat people let things stay all blurry and hazy and vague, the way things actually are. Thin people want to face the truth. Fat people know there is no truth. One of my thin friends is always staring at complex, unsolvable problems and saying, "The key thing is . . ." Fat people never say that. They know there isn't any such thing as the key thing about anything.

Thin people believe in logic. Fat people see all sides. The sides   5
fat people see are rounded blobs, usually gray, always nebulous and truly not worth worrying about. But the thin person persists. "If you consume more calories than you burn," says one of my thin friends, "you will gain weight. It's that simple." Fat people always grin when they hear statements like that. They know better.

Fat people realize that life is illogical and unfair. They know   6
very well that God is not in his heaven and all is not right with the world. If God was up there, fat people could have two doughnuts and a big orange drink anytime they wanted it.

Thin people have a long list of logical things they are always   7
spouting off to me. They hold up one finger at a time as they reel off these things, so I won't lose track. They speak slowly as if to a young child. The list is long and full of holes. It contains tidbits like "get a grip on yourself," "cigarettes kill," "cholesterol clogs," "fit as a fiddle," "ducks in a row," "organize," and "sound fiscal management." Phrases like that.

They think these 2,000-point plans lead to happiness. Fat peo-   8
ple know happiness is elusive at best and even if they could get the kind thin people talk about, they wouldn't want it. Wisely, fat people see that such programs are too dull, too hard, too off the mark. They are never better than a whole cheesecake.

Fat people know all about the mystery of life. They are the   9
ones acquainted with the night, with luck, with fate, with playing it by ear. One thin person I know once suggested that we arrange all the parts of a jigsaw puzzle into groups according to

size, shape, and color. He figured this would cut the time needed to complete the puzzle by at least 50 percent. I said I wouldn't do it. One, I like to muddle through. Two, what good would it do to finish early? Three, the jigsaw puzzle isn't the important thing. The important thing is the fun of four people (one thin person included) sitting around a card table, working a jigsaw puzzle. My thin friend had no use for my list. Instead of joining us, he went outside and mulched the boxwoods. The three remaining fat people finished the puzzle and made chocolate, double-fudged brownies to celebrate.

The main problem with thin people is they oppress. Their good intentions, bony torsos, tight ships, neat corners, cerebral machinations, and pat solutions loom like dark clouds over the loose, comfortable, spread-out, soft world of the fat. Long after fat people have removed their coats and shoes and put their feet up on the coffee table, thin people are still sitting on the edge of the sofa, looking neat as a pin, discussing rutabagas. Fat people are heavily into fits of laughter, slapping their thighs and whopping it up, while thin people are still politely waiting for the punch line.

Thin people are downers. They like math and morality and reasoned evaluation of the limitations of human beings. They have their skinny little acts together. They expound, prognose, probe, and prick.

Fat people are convivial. They will like you even if you're irregular and have acne. They will come up with a good reason why you never wrote the great American novel. They will cry in your beer with you. They will put your name in the pot. They will let you off the hook. Fat people will gab, giggle, guffaw, gallumph, gyrate, and gossip. They are generous, giving, and gallant. They are gluttonous and goodly and great. What you want when you're down is soft and jiggly, not muscled and stable. Fat people know this. Fat people have plenty of room. Fat people will take you in.

Questions for Study and Discussion

1. Does Britt use a subject-by-subject or a point-by-point pattern of organization to contrast fat and thin people? Explain. What points of contrast does Britt discuss?

2. How does Britt characterize thin people? Fat people?

3. What does Britt seem to have against thin people? Why does she consider thin "dangerous"? What do you think Britt looks like? How do you know?

4. What is Britt's purpose in this essay? (Glossary: *Purpose*) Is she serious, partially serious, mostly humorous? Are fat and thin people really her subject?

5. Britt makes effective use of the short sentence. Identify examples of sentences with three or fewer words and explain what function they serve.

6. Britt uses many clichés in her essay. Identify at least a dozen examples. What do you suppose is her purpose in using them? (Glossary: *Cliché*)

7. It is somewhat unusual for an essayist to use alliteration (the repetition of initial consonant sounds), a technique more commonly found in poetry. Where has Britt used alliteration and why do you suppose she has used this particular technique?

Vocabulary

Refer to your dictionary to define the following words as they are used in this selection. Then use each word in a sentence of your own.

menacing (1)	nebulous (5)
adoing (2)	rutabagas (10)
metabolism (3)	prognose (11)
inert (3)	convivial (12)
chortling (4)	gallant (12)

Suggested Writing Assignments

1. Write a counter-argument in favor of thin people, using comparison and contrast and modeled on Britt's "That Lean and Hungry Look."

2. Reread paragraphs 3–6, and notice how these paragraphs are developed by contrasting the features of thin and fat people. Select two items from the following categories—

people, products, events, institutions, places—and make a list of their contrasting features. Then write an essay modeled on Britt's, using the entries on your list.

GRANT AND LEE: A STUDY IN CONTRASTS

Bruce Catton

Bruce Catton (1899–1978) was born in Petoskey, Michigan, and attended Oberlin College. Early in his career, Catton worked as a reporter for various newspapers, among them the Cleveland Plain Dealer. *Having an interest in history, Catton became a leading authority on the Civil War and published a number of books on this subject. These include* Mr. Lincoln's Army *(1951),* Glory Road *(1952), a* Stillness at Appomattox *(1953),* The Hallowed Ground *(1956),* The Coming Fury *(1961),* Never Call Retreat *(1966), and* Gettysburg: The Final Fury *(1974). Catton was awarded both the Pulitzer Prize and the National Book Award in 1954.*

The following selection was included in The American Story, *a collection of historical essays edited by Earl Schenk Miers. In it Catton considers "two great Americans, Grant and Lee— very different, yet under everything very much alike."*

When Ulysses S. Grant and Robert E. Lee met in the parlor of a modest house at Appomattox Court House, Virginia, on April 9, 1865, to work out the terms for the surrender of Lee's Army of Northern Virginia, a great chapter in American life came to a close, and a great new chapter began.

These men were bringing the Civil War to its virtual finish. To be sure, other armies had yet to surrender, and for a few days the fugitive Confederate government would struggle desperately and vainly, trying to find some way to go on living now that its chief support was gone. But in effect it was all over when Grant and Lee signed the papers. And the little room where they wrote out the terms was the scene of one of the poignant, dramatic contrasts in American history.

They were two strong men, these oddly different generals, 3 and they represented the strengths of two conflicing currents that, through them, had come into final collision.

Back of Robert E. Lee was the notion that the old aristocratic 4 concept might somehow survive and be dominant in American life.

Lee was tidewater Virginia, and in his background were fam- 5 ily, culture, and tradition . . . the age of chivalry transplanted to a New World which was making its own legends and its own myths. He embodied a way of life that had come down through the age of knighthood and the English country squire. America was a land that was beginning all over again, dedicated to nothing much more complicated than the rather hazy belief that all men had equal rights and should have an equal chance in the world. In such a land Lee stood for the feeling that it was somehow of advantage to human society to have a pronounced inequality in the social structure. There should be a leisure class, backed by ownerhsip of land; in turn, society itself should be keyed to the land as the chief source of wealth and influence. It would bring forth (according to this ideal) a class of men with a strong sense of obligation to the community; men who lived not to gain advantage for themselves, but to meet the solemn obligations which had been laid on them by the very fact that they were privileged. From them the country would get its leadership; to them it could look for the higher values—of thought, of conduct, of personal deportment—to give it strength and virtue.

Lee embodied the noblest elements of this aristocratic ideal. 6 Through him, the landed nobility justified itself. For four years, the Southern states had fought a desperate war to uphold the ideals for which Lee stood. In the end, it almost seemed as if the Confederacy fought for Lee; as if he himself was the Confederacy . . . the best thing that the way of life for which the Confederacy stood could ever have to offer. He had passed into legend before Appomattox. Thousands of tired, underfed, poorly clothed Confederate soldiers, long since past the simple enthusiasm of the early days of the struggle, somehow considered Lee the symbol of everything for which they had been willing to die. But they could not quite put this feeling into words. If the Lost Cause, sanctified by so much heroism and so many deaths, had a living justification, its justification was General Lee.

Grant, the son of a tanner on the Western frontier, was every- 7 thing Lee was not. He had come up the hard way and embodied nothing in particular except the eternal toughness and sinewy fiber of the men who grew up beyond the mountains. He was one of a body of men who owed reverence and obeisance to no one, who were self-reliant to a fault, who cared hardly anything for the past but who had a sharp eye for the future.

These frontier men were the precise opposite of the tidewater 8 aristocrats. Back of them, in the great surge that had taken people over the Alleghenies and into the opening Western country, there was a deep, implicit dissatisfaction with a past that had settled into grooves. They stood for democracy, not from any reasoned conclusion about the proper ordering of human society, but simply because they had grown up in the middle of democracy and knew how it worked. Their society might have privileges, but they would be privileges each man had won for himself. Forms and patterns meant nothing. No man was born to anything, except perhaps to a chance to show how far he could rise. Life was competition.

Yet along with this feeling had come a deep sense of belong- 9 ing to a national community. The Westerner who developed a farm, opened a shop, or set up in business as a trader, could hope to prosper only as his own community prospered—and his community ran from the Atlantic to the Pacific and from Canada down to Mexico. If the land was settled, with towns and highways and accessible markets, he could better himself. He saw his fate in terms of the nation's own destiny. As its horizons expanded, so did his. He had, in other words, an acute dollars-and-cents stake in the continued growth and development of his country.

And that, perhaps, is where the contrast between Grant and 10 Lee becomes most striking. The Virginia aristocrat, inevitably, saw himself in relation to his own region. He lived in a static society which could endure almost anything except change. Instinctively, his first loyalty would go to the locality in which that society existed. He would fight to the limit of endurance to defend it, because in defending it he was defending everything that gave his own life its deepest meaning.

The Westerner, on the other hand, would fight with an equal   11
tenacity for the broader concept of society. He fought so because everything he lived by was tied to growth, expansion, and a constantly widening horizon. What he lived by would survive or fall with the nation itself. He could not possibly stand by unmoved in the face of an attempt to destroy the Union. He would combat it with everything he had, because he could only see it as an effort to cut the ground out from under his feet.

So Grant and Lee were in complete contrast, representing two   12
diametrically opposed elements in American life. Grant was the modern man emerging; beyond him, ready to come on the stage, was the great age of steel and machinery, of crowded cities and a restless burgeoning vitality. Lee might have ridden down from the old age of chivalry, lance in hand, silken banner fluttering over his head. Each man was the perfect champion of his cause, drawing both his strengths and his weaknesses from the people he led.

Yet is was not all contrast, after all. Different as they were—in   13
background, in personality, in underlying aspiration—these two great soldiers had much in common. Under everything else, they were marvelous fighters. Furthermore, their fighting qualities were really very much alike.

Each man had, to begin with, the great virtue of utter tenacity   14
and fidelity. Grant fought his way down the Mississippi Valley in spite of acute personal discouragement and profound military handicaps. Lee hung on in the trenches at Petersburg after hope itself had died. In each man there was an indomitable quality . . . the born fighter's refusal to give up as long as he can still remain on his feet and lift his two fists.

Daring and resourcefulness they had, too; the ability to think   15
faster and move faster than the enemy. These were the qualities which gave Lee the dazzling campaigns of Second Manassas and Chancellorsville and won Vicksburg for Grant.

Lastly, and perhaps greatest of all, there was the ability, at   16
the end, to turn quickly from war to peace once the fighting was over. Out of the way these two men behaved at Appomattox

came the possibility of a peace of reconciliation. It was a possibility not wholly realized, in the years to come, but which did, in the end, help the two sections to become one nation again . . . after a war whose bitterness might have seemed to make such a reunion wholly impossible. No part of either man's life became him more than the part he played in their brief meeting in the McLean house at Appomattox. Their behavior there put all succeeding generations of Americans in their debt. Two great Americans, Grant and Lee—very different, yet under everything very much alike. Their encounter at Appomattox was one of the great moments of American history.

Questions for Study and Discussion

1. In paragraphs 10–12 Catton discusses what he considers to be the most striking contrast between Grant and Lee. What is that difference?
2. List the similarities that Catton sees between Grant and Lee. Which similarity does Catton believe is most important? Why?
3. What would have been lost had Catton compared Grant and Lee before contrasting them? Would anything have been gained?
4. How does Catton organize the body of his essay (3–16)? You may find it helpful in answering this question to summarize the point of comparison in each paragraph and label it as being concerned with Lee, Grant, or both.
5. What attitudes and ideas does Catton describe to support the view that tidewater Virginia was a throwback to the "age of chivalry" (5)?
6. Catton says that Grant was "the modern man emerging" (12). How does he support that statement? Do you agree?
7. Catton has carefully made clear transitions between paragraphs. For each paragraph identify the transitional devices he uses. How do they help your reading? (Glossary: *Transitions*)

Vocabulary

Refer to your dictionary to define the following words as they are used in this selection. Then use each word in a sentence of your own.

poignant (2)   obeisance (7)
chivalry (5)   tidewater (8)
sanctified (6)   tenacity (11)
sinewy (7)   aspiration (13)

Suggested Writing Assignments

1. Compare and contrast any two world leaders (or popular singers or singing groups). In selecting a topic, you should consider (1) what your purpose will be, (2) whether you will emphasize similarities or differences, (3) what specific points you will discuss, and (4) what organizational pattern will best suit your purpose.

2. Select one of the following topics for an essay of comparison and contrast:

   two cities
   two friends
   two ways to heat a home
   two restaurants
   two actors or actresses
   two mountains
   two books by the same author
   two sports heroes
   two cars
   two teachers
   two brands of pizza

WHAT CHILDREN DO
FOR THEIR PARENTS

Barney Cohen

Few people stop to think of the beneficial influence that children have over their parents, how they expand them, sharpen them, polish them—making their parents better people. In the following essay, first published in the June/July (1990) issue of Parenting, *Barney Cohen reflects on his relationship with his son Ivan. Cohen uses a central analogy to both explain and describe the steady, unseen, and beneficial influence that Ivan had not only on his tennis game but also on his life.*

T here was once this guy, this mythological guy, who was the strongest guy there ever was—for his time. When he was a little kid, his father gave him a baby calf and told him to take care of it. The little fellow was instructed to feed and clean the calf every day, and then to lift it up, once, over his head.

Well, you can figure out what happened. As the kid grew, so did the calf. Every day, when the boy lifted the calf up over his head, he was lifting another pound or so. And by the time the guy was 15 he was able to lift a kicking, bucking, full-grown bull over his head.

But who was this guy? My friend Dennis, a movie director, says it was Beowulf, but I suspect he just says that because he worked on a film about that antique English hero and thinks he knows his stuff. I looked for the reference in the Beowulf poem and I couldn't find it. My Aunt Harriet, who graduated from a prestigious Eastern college, thinks it comes from the myth of Hercules. But I haven't found it there either.

If you know the name of this guy, and of his fabulously epistemological father, please drop me a line. If not, don't worry; just hold the thought for a minute because, as I relate this story about my own son, Ivan, we'll be coming back to it.

You know me. I take my kids' athletic training fairly seri- 5
ously. I'm no martinet with a whistle and a "personal best" chart, but I believe that stuff about a sound mind and a sound body, and I encourage the kids every chance I get. This includes, of course, playing sports with them whenever I can.

Now here's where I'd love to tell you that I, myself, figured 6
out something akin to our obscure mythological hero's calf and that now my kids are superathletes. But I didn't. No, this is a story about something my kids did for me and that your kids are probably doing for you, whether you know it or not.

In my case, it begins on a municipal tennis court in Seattle. I 7
am playing a couple of sets with my son. He's ten at the time, but I have been doing this with him since he was three. In fact, Ivan has been, since the age of five, my only tennis partner.

Anyway, there's this local tennis team, a bunch of kids, 8
playing on the next court. The grown-up, probably the coach, comes over to me as I'm picking up some stray balls and says, "Your son really carries a gun."

Realizing immediately that Ivan not only is being compli- 9
mented, but also being recruited, I let the guy down easy. "We're from New York City," I say.

"Shame," he says. 10

I'm flattered for Ivan, and happy for him. I tell him about the 11
coach's comments on the drive back to his aunt and uncle's house. But I'm also curious about what, exactly, the guy saw in Ivan's game.

For the last few years, Ivan has been telling me about his 12
rapid progress in school tennis. He's been telling me that he's moved ahead of this guy or that guy. That he beat some kid who's a country-club champ. And I sort of let all this go in one ear and out the other because, to tell you the truth, I really haven't seen much improvement.

Oh, he's grown more proficient at certain things. He's making 13
far fewer unforced errors. He's certainly able to hit the ball harder than he used to. He's able to hit the ball harder than me! Still, I wonder, how could Ivan be getting so darn much better if he keeps getting his ears pinned by his old man?

One thing you need to know about me before we go any 14

further: I've always believed that it's the ultimate insult to any human being to compete against him at anything less than your best. I mean, when Ivan was five, I didn't smash the ball at his feet, but I didn't throw games to him either. He had to measure himself against me by how well he played, not by whether he won or lost. The fact is, he always lost.

At the time of our Seattle match, Ivan had never beaten me in   15
tennis. He had not even won a set. And we'd played a thousand games. Then, after we returned to New York, a strange thing happened. An old friend came into town and was staying at a hotel that had court rights at a local tennis bubble. He invited me for a game. Now this guy used to beat me regularly. And when I asked if he'd kept up his game, he smiled at me his sparkly California grin and said, "Every day of the year."

I threw up my first serve with enormous foreboding. It sliced   16
past him and hit the green retainer. I won't bore you with the details of my spectacular demolition of this dude. Suffice it to say, it surprised us both.

Then, in the taxi home, I figured it out. It was Ivan! It had to   17
be. He was my only tennis partner. Remember the guy with the calf? Ivan was my calf! As Ivan's tennis had improved, so had my own. In my desire to always be out front as an example, to always give him a good match, I had lifted my game without knowing it. Each time Ivan improved, he forced a consequent gain in my own game. Like the calf that got heavier every morning, Ivan got better each time out. And like the guy who lifted the calf, I lifted my own increasing burden. As I urged and taught and challenged, Ivan was giving me something back. He was forcing me to push the envelope of my own abilities. To discover new strength and new resolve. He was teaching me that I could work harder, stretch farther, go longer than I ever thought I could. And he was doing it in increments so small, I never realized that I was growing.

You know, I think all kids must be doing this. In a thousand   18
ways that you never even thought about, they're making you pick yourself up a notch. They work on the quality of your caring and the coolness of your panic response. They teach you when to surrender and when to hold firm.

I saw it in sport. But it must be happening, unseen, in every   19
phase of your life. It's weird when you think about kids that

way. While you're training them, teaching them, growing them up, they're expanding you, sharpening you, polishing you, making you not just better parents, but better tennis players. In fact, better people all around.

Questions for Study and Discussion

1. Cohen opens his essay with the story of the small boy and the baby calf. How does this story function in the context of his essay? (Glossary: *Analogy*) Is the analogy of the boy and the calf an effective one for the point Cohen wishes to make? Explain.

2. Cohen failed to see his son's improvement. How does he explain his failure? What caused him to recognize his mistake?

3. In paragraph 14, Cohen says he never let his son win. Why not? Do you agree with his reasoning? Explain.

4. Cohen explains the way in which his son helped his tennis game and then goes on to make a larger point. What is it?

5. Cite examples of Cohen's use of slang, and describe the tone it sets for his essay. (Glossary: *Tone*) What does Cohen's choice of language suggest to you about his relationship with his son?

Vocabulary

Refer to your dictionary to define the following words as they are used in this selection. Then use each word in a sentence of your own.

mythological (1)	demolition (16)
epistemological (4)	suffice (16)
martinet (5)	resolve (17)
recruited (9)	notch (18)
proficient (13)	surrender (18)
throw (14)	

Suggested Writing Assignments

1. In an essay use comparison and contrast to explain the different ways a child and a parent might approach the same activity. For example, handling money, driving a car, conducting a relationship, relaxing, or performing household tasks.
2. Use an analogy to explain your relationship with one of your parents or another adult you are close to.

FABLE FOR TOMORROW

Rachel Carson

Naturalist Rachel Carson (1907–1964) wrote The Sea Around Us *(1951),* Under the Sea Wind *(1952), and* The Edge of the Sea *(1955), sensitive investigations of marine life. But it was* Silent Spring *(1962), her study of herbicides and insecticides, that made Carson a controversial figure. Once denounced as an alarmist, she is now regarded as an early prophet of the ecology movement. In the following fable taken from* Silent Spring, *Carson uses contrast to show her readers the devastating effects of indiscriminate use of pesticides.*

There was once a town in the heart of America where all life seemed to live in harmony with its surroundings. The town lay in the midst of a checkerboard of prosperous farms, with fields of grain and hillsides of orchards where, in spring, white clouds of bloom drifted above the green fields. In autumn, oak and maple and birch set up a blaze of color that flamed and flickered across a backdrop of pines. Then foxes barked in the hills and deer silently crossed the fields, half hidden in the mists of the fall mornings.

Along the roads, laurel, viburnum and alder, great ferns and wildflowers delighted the traveler's eye through much of the year. Even in winter the roadsides were places of beauty, where countless birds came to feed on the berries and on the seed heads of the dried weeds rising above the snow. The countryside was, in fact, famous for the abundance and variety of its bird life, and when the flood of migrants was pouring through in spring and fall people traveled from great distances to observe them. Others came to fish the streams, which flowed clear and cold out of the hills and contained shady pools where trout lay. So it had been from the days many years ago when the first settlers raised their houses, sank their wells, and built their barns.

Then a strange blight crept over the area and everything be-   3
gan to change. Some evil spell had settled on the community:
mysterious maladies swept the flocks of chickens; the cattle
and sheep sickened and died. Everywhere was a shadow of
death. The farmers spoke of much illness among their families.
In the town the doctors had become more and more puzzled by
new kinds of sickness appearing among their patients. There
had been several sudden and unexplained deaths, not only
among adults but even among children, who would be stricken
suddenly while at play and die within a few hours.

There was a strange stillness. The birds, for example—where   4
had they gone? Many people spoke of them, puzzled and
disturbed. The feeding stations in the backyards were deserted.
The few birds seen anywhere were moribund; they trembled
violently and could not fly. It was a spring without voices. On
the mornings that had once throbbed with the dawn chorus of
robins, catbirds, doves, jays, wrens, and scores of other bird
voices there was now no sound; only silence lay over the fields
and woods and marsh.

On the farms the hens brooded, but no chicks hatched. The   5
farmers complained that they were unable to raise any pigs—
the litters were small and the young survived only a few days.
The apple trees were coming into bloom but no bees droned
among the blossoms, so there was no pollination and there
would be no fruit.

The roadsides, once so attractive, were now lined with   6
browned and withered vegetation as though swept by fire.
These, too, were silent, deserted by all living things. Even the
streams were now lifeless. Anglers no longer visited them, for
all the fish had died.

In the gutters under the eaves and between the shingles of the   7
roofs, a white granular powder still showed a few patches;
some weeks before it had fallen like snow upon the roofs and
the lawns, the fields and streams.

No witchcraft, no enemy action had silenced the rebirth of   8
new life in this stricken world. The people had done it themselves.

This town does not actually exist, but it might easily have a   9
thousand counterparts in America or elsewhere in the world. I
know of no community that has experienced all the misfor-

tunes I describe. Yet every one of these disasters has actually happened somewhere, and many real communities have already suffered a substantial number of them. A grim specter has crept upon us almost unnoticed, and this imagined tragedy may easily become a stark reality we all shall know.

Questions for Study and Discussion

1. A fable is a short narrative that makes an edifying or cautionary point. What is the point of Carson's fable?
2. How do comparison and contrast help Carson make her point?
3. Does Carson use a point-by-point or a subject-by-subject method of organization in this selection? How is the pattern of organization Carson uses appropriate for her purpose? Be prepared to cite examples from the text.
4. What is the significance of the "white granular powder" that Carson mentions in paragraph 7? Why do you suppose she does not introduce the powder earlier?
5. Carson uses a great number of specific details to enhance her comparison and contrast. Which details had a particularly strong effect on you? Explain why.
6. In the last paragraph Carson tells us that "this town does not actually exist." What effect did this information have on you? Did it lessen the impact of her warning? Did it give you cause for hope?

Vocabulary

Refer to your dictionary to define the following words as they are used in this selection. Then use each word in a sentence of your own.

migrants (2)   moribund (4)
blight (3)   specter (9)
maladies (3)

Suggested Writing Assignments

1. Write an essay modeled after Carson's in which you show how a particular place or area changed character for some reason (for example, as a result of herbicides, gentrification, urbanization, commercialization, strip mining, highway development, hurricane, etc.). Describe the area before and after the change, and be sure to give your reaction to the change either implicitly or explicitly.

2. Using one of the following "before and after" situations, write a short essay of comparison and/or contrast:

   before and after a diet
   before and after urban renewal
   before and after Christmas
   before and after beginning college
   before and after a final exam

AM I BLUE?

Alice Walker

*Poet, essayist, and novelist Alice Walker was
born in 1944 in Eatonton, Georgia, the eighth
child of African-American sharecroppers. She
attended Spelman College in Atlanta on scholar-
ship, and later graduated from Sarah Lawrence
College, where during her senior year she produced her first book of poetry. In addition to her
many stories, essays, and books of poetry, she
has written three novels, including* The Third
Life of Grange Copeland *(1978), and* The Color
Purple *(1982) for which she is most famous.* The
Color Purple *won both the Pulitzer prize and the
American Book Award for fiction in 1983. The
following essay appeared in the July 1986 issue
of* Ms. *magazine. In it Walker uses comparison
and contrast to make a poignant case for animal
feelings.*

For about three years my companion and I rented a small 1
house in the country that stood on the edge of a large
meadow that appeared to run from the end of our deck straight
into the mountains. The mountains, however, were quite far
away, and between us and them there was, in fact, a town. It was
one of the many pleasant aspects of the house that you never
really were aware of this.

It was a house of many windows, low, wide, nearly floor to 2
ceiling in the living room, which faced the meadow, and it was
from one of these that I first saw our closest neighbor, a large
white horse, cropping grass, flipping its mane, and ambling
about—not over the entire meadow, which stretched well out of
sight of the house, but over the five or so fenced-in acres that
were next to the twenty-odd that we had rented. I soon learned
that the horse, whose name was Blue, belonged to a man who
lived in another town, but was boarded by our neighbors next

door. Occasionally, one of the children, usually a stocky teen-
ager, but sometimes a much younger girl or boy, could be seen
riding Blue. They would appear in the meadow, climb up on his
back, ride furiously for ten or fifteen minutes, then get off, slap
Blue on the flanks, and not be seen again for a month or more.

There were many apple trees in our yard, and one by the fence   3
that Blue could almost reach. We were soon in the habit of feeding him apples, which he relished, especially because by the
middle of summer the meadow grasses—so green and succu-
lent since January—had dried out from lack of rain, and Blue
stumbled about munching the dried stalks half-heartedly.
Sometimes he would stand very still just by the apple tree, and
when one of us came out he would whinny, snort loudly, or
stamp the ground. This meant, of course: I want an apple.

It was quite wonderful to pick a few apples, or collect those   4
that had fallen to the ground overnight, and patiently hold
them, one by one, up to his large, toothy mouth. I remained as
thrilled as a child by his flexible dark lips, huge, cubelike teeth
that crunched the apples, core and all, with such finality, and
his high, broad-breasted *enormity;* beside which, I felt small
indeed. When I was a child, I used to ride horses, and was especially friendly with one named Nan until the day I was riding
and my brother deliberately spooked her and I was thrown,
head first, against the trunk of a tree. When I came to, I was in
bed and my mother was bending worriedly over me; we silently
agreed that perhaps horseback riding was not the safest sport
for me. Since then I have walked, and prefer walking to horseback riding—but I had forgotten the depth of feeling one could
see in horses' eyes.

I was therefore unprepared for the expression in Blue's. Blue   5
was lonely. Blue was horribly lonely and bored. I was not
shocked that this should be the case; five acres to tramp by
yourself, endlessly, even in the most beautiful of meadows—
and his was—cannot provide many interesting events, and once
rainy season turned to dry that was about it. No, I was shocked
that I had forgotten that human animals and nonhuman animals can communicate quite well; if we are brought up around
animals as children we take this for granted. By the time we are
adults we no longer remember. However, the animals have not
changed. They are in fact *completed* creations (at least they

seem to be, so much more than we) who are not likely *to* change; it is their nature to express themselves. What else are they going to express? And they do. And, generally speaking, they are ignored.

After giving Blue the apples, I would wander back to the 6 house, aware that he was observing me. Were more apples not forthcoming then? Was that to be his sole entertainment for the day? My partner's small son had decided he wanted to learn how to piece a quilt; we worked in silence on our respective squares as I thought . . .

Well, about slavery: about white children, who were raised by 7 black people, who knew their first all-accepting love from black women, and then, when they were twelve or so, were told they must "forget" the deep levels of communication between themselves and "mammy" that they knew. Later they would be able to relate quite calmly, "My old mammy was sold to another good family." "My old mammy was ———." Fill in the blank. Many more years later a white woman would say: "I can't understand these Negroes, these blacks. What do they want? They're so different from us."

And about the Indians, considered to be "like animals" by 8 the "settlers" (a very benign euphemism for what they actually were), who did not understand their description as a compliment.

And about the thousands of American men who marry Japa- 9 nese, Korean, Filipina, and other non-English-speaking women and of how happy they report they are, *"blissfully,"* until their brides learn to speak English, at which point the marriages tend to fall apart. What then did the men see, when they looked into the eyes of the women they married, before they could speak English? Apparently only their own reflections.

I thought of society's impatience with the young. "Why are 10 they playing the music so loud?" Perhaps the children have listened to much of the music of oppressed people their parents danced to before they were born, with its passionate but soft cries for acceptance and love, and they have wondered why their parents failed to hear.

I do not know how long Blue had inhabited his five beautiful, 11 boring acres before we moved into our house; a year after we had arrived—and had also traveled to other valleys, other cities, other worlds—he was still there.

But then, in our second year at the house, something hap-   12
pened in Blue's life. One morning, looking out the window at
the fog that lay like a ribbon over the meadow, I saw another
horse, a brown one, at the other end of Blue's field. Blue appeared to be afraid of it, and for several days made no attempt
to go near. We went away for a week. When we returned, Blue
had decided to make friends and the two horses ambled or galloped along together, and Blue did not come nearly as often to
the fence underneath the apple tree.

When he did, bringing his new friend with him, there was a   13
different look in his eyes. A look of independence, of self-
possession, of inalienable *horse*ness. His friend eventually became pregnant. For months and months there was, it seemed to
me, a mutual feeling between me and the horses of justice, of
peace. I fed apples to them both. The look in Blue's eyes was one
of unabashed "this is *it*ness."

It did not, however, last forever. One day, after a visit to the   14
city, I went out to give Blue some apples. He stood waiting, or
so I thought, though not beneath the tree. When I shook the tree
and jumped back from the shower of apples, he made no move.
I carried some over to him. He managed to half-crunch one. The
rest he let fall to the ground. I dreaded looking into his eyes—
because I had of course noticed that Brown, his partner, had
gone—but I did look. If I had been born into slavery, and my
partner had been sold or killed, my eyes would have looked like
that. The children next door explained that Blue's partner had
been "put with him" (the same expression that old people used,
I had noticed, when speaking of an ancestor during slavery who
had been impregnated by her owner) so that they could mate
and she conceive. Since that was accomplished, she had been
taken back by her owner, who lived somewhere else.

Will she be back? I asked.   15

They didn't know.   16

Blue was like a crazed person. Blue *was*, to me, a crazed per-   17
son. He galloped furiously, as if he were being ridden, around
and around his five beautiful acres. He whinnied until he
couldn't. He tore at the ground with his hooves. He butted himself against his single shade tree. He looked always and always
toward the road down which his partner had gone. And then,
occasionally, when he came up for apples, or I took apples to
him, he looked at me. It was a look so piercing, so full of grief,

a look so *human*, I almost laughed (I felt too sad to cry) to think there are people who do not know that animals suffer. People like me who have forgotten, and daily forget, all that animals try to tell us. "Everything you do to us will happen to you; we are your teachers, as you are ours. We are one lesson" is essentially it, I think. There are those who never once have even considered animals' rights: those who have been taught that animals actually want to be used and abused by us, as small children "love" to be frightened, or women "love" to be mutilated and raped. . . . They are the great-grandchildren of those who honestly thought, because someone taught them this: "Women can't think," and "niggers can't faint." But most disturbing of all, in Blue's large brown eyes was a new look more painful than the look of despair: the look of disgust with human beings, with life; the look of hatred. And it was odd what the look of hatred did. It gave him, for the first time, the look of a beast. And what that meant was that he had put up a barrier within to protect himself from further violence; all the apples in the world wouldn't change that fact.

And so Blue remained, a beautiful part of our landscape, very   18
peaceful to look at from the window, white against the grass. Once a friend came to visit and said, looking out on the soothing view: "And it *would* have to be a *white* horse; the very image of freedom." And I thought, yes, the animals are forced to become for us merely "images" of what they once so beautifully expressed. And we are used to drinking milk from containers showing "contented" cows, whose real lives we want to hear nothing about, eating eggs and drumsticks from "happy" hens, and munching hamburgers advertised by bulls of integrity who seem to command their fate.

As we talked of freedom and justice one day for all, we sat   19
down to steaks. I am eating misery, I thought, as I took the first bite. And spit it out.

Questions for Study and Discussion

1. What kinds of evidence does Walker offer to make her point that Blue can communicate his feelings? (Glossary: *Examples*) Were you convinced? Why or why not?

2. Walker was shocked that she had forgotten that animals and humans can communicate. How does she compare this experience to other relationships?

3. Why does Walker refer to the word "settler" as a "benign euphemism"? Locate other words she puts in quotes. What do they have in common?

4. In paragraph 17, Walker writes, "Everything you do to us will happen to you: we are your teachers, as you are ours." Does she intend the sentence literally? What for Walker is the larger implication of the failure to understand animals rights?

5. Walker is an emotional and powerful writer. Cite several examples of the emotional appeals she makes to her readers and explain in what ways they add to the overall effectiveness of her essay. (Glossary: *Diction*)

6. According to Walker, when does an animal become a "beast"? Do you think Walker intends for us to make a comparison between "beasts" and other victims she has described? Explain.

7. What is Walker's purpose in writing this essay? (Glossary: *Purpose*) What, if anything, does she want us to do? How do you know?

Vocabulary

Refer to your dictionary to define the following words as they are used in this selection. Then use each word in a sentence of your own.

aspects (1)	euphemism (8)
succulent (3)	ambled (12)
forthcoming (6)	inalienable (13)
respective (6)	unabashed (13)
benign (8)	image (18)

Suggested Writing Assignments

1. In an essay compare and contrast a perception you held as a child with the way you see it as an adult.

2. In paragraph 18, Walker compares the reality of Blue's, and other animal's lives with our "images" of them. Citing one of the groups Walker names in her essay, i.e., Native Americans, women, African-Americans, or a different minority group of your choosing, make a similar comparison in a brief essay.

17

CAUSE AND EFFECT

Every time you try to answer a question that asks *why*, you engage in the process of *causal analysis*—you attempt to determine a *cause* or series of causes for a particular *effect*. When you try to answer a question that asks *what if*, you attempt to determine what *effect* will result from a particular *cause*. You will have frequent opportunity to use cause and effect analysis in writing that you will do in college. For example, in history you might be asked to determine the causes of the Seven-Day War between Egypt and Israel; in political science you might be asked to determine the reasons why George Bush won the 1988 presidential election; and, in sociology you might be asked to analyze the effects that the AIDS epidemic has had on sexual behavior patterns among Americans; in economics, you might be asked to predict what would happen to our country if we do not address the problem of our national debt.

Determining causes and effects is usually thought-provoking and quite complex. One reason for this is that there are two types of causes: *immediate causes*, which are readily apparent because they are closest to the effect, and *ultimate causes*, which, being somewhat removed, are not so apparent and perhaps even hidden. Furthermore, ultimate causes may bring about effects which themselves become immediate causes, thus creating a *causal chain*. For example, consider the following causal chain: Sally, a computer salesperson, prepared extensively for a meeting with an important client (ultimate cause), impressed the client (immediate cause), and made a very large sale (effect). The chain did not stop there: the large sale caused her to be promoted by her employer (effect).

A second reason why causal analysis can be so complex is that an effect may have any number of possible or actual causes, and a cause may have any number of possible or actual effects. An upset stomach may be caused by eating spoiled food, but it may also be caused by overeating, flu, allergy, nervousness, pregnancy, or any combination of factors. Similarly, the high cost of electricity may have multiple effects: higher profits for utility companies, fewer sales of electrical appliances, higher prices for other products, and the development of alternative sources of energy.

Sound reasoning and logic, while present in all good writing, are central to any causal analysis. Writers of believable causal analysis examine their material objectively and develop their essays carefully. They examine methodically all causes and effects and evaluate them. They are convinced by their own examination of the material but are not afraid to admit other possible causes and effects. Above all, they do not let their own prejudices interfere with the logic of their analyses and presentations.

Because people are accustomed to thinking of causes with their effects, they sometimes commit an error in logic known as the "after this, therefore because of this" fallacy (in Latin, *post hoc, ergo propter hoc*). This fallacy leads people to believe that because one event occurred after another event the first event somehow caused the second; that is, they sometimes make causal connections that are not proven. For example, if students began to perform better after a free breakfast program was instituted at their school, one could not assume that the improvement was caused by the breakfast program. There could of course be any number of other causes for this effect, and a responsible writer on the subject would analyze and consider them all before suggesting the cause.

NEVER GET SICK IN JULY

Marilyn Machlowitz

Marilyn Machlowitz earned her doctorate in psychology at Yale and is now a management psychologist. She contributes a regular column to Working Woman *magazine, has written* Workaholics *(1980), and is at work on a new book dealing with the consequences of succeeding at an early age. Notice in the following selection, first published in* Esquire *magazine in July 1978, how Machlowitz analyzes why it is a bad idea to get sick in July.*

One Harvard medical school professor warns his students to stay home—as he does—on the Fourth of July. He fears he will become one of the holiday's highway casualties and wind up in an emergency room with an inexperienced intern "practicing" medicine on *him*.

Just the mention of July makes medical students, nurses, interns, residents, and "real doctors" roll their eyes. While hospital administrators maintain that nothing is amiss that month, members of the medical profession know what happens when the house staff turns over and the interns take over each July 1.

This July 1, more than 13,000 new doctors will invade over 600 hospitals across the country. Within minutes they will be overwhelmed: last July 1, less than a month after finishing medical school, Dr. John Baumann, then twenty-five, walked into Washington, D.C.'s, Walter Reed Army Medical Center, where he was immediately faced with caring for "eighteen of the sickest people I had ever seen."

Pity the patient who serves as guinea pig at ten A.M.—or three A.M.—that first day. Indeed, according to Dr. Russell K. Laros, Jr., professor and vice-chairman of obstetrics, gynecology, and reproductive sciences at the University of California, San Francisco, "There is no question that patients throughout the country are mismanaged during July. Without the most meticulous supervision," he adds, "serious errors can be made."

And they are. Internship provides the first chance to practice one's illegible scrawl on prescription blanks, a golden opportunity to make lots of mistakes. Interns—who are still known to most people by that name, even though they are now officially called first-year residents—have ordered the wrong drug in the wrong dosage to be administered the wrong way at the wrong times to the wrong patient. While minor mistakes are most common, serious errors are the sources of hospital horror stories. One intern prescribed an anti-depressant without knowing that it would inactivate the patient's previously prescribed antihypertensive medication.* The patient then experienced a rapid increase in blood pressure and suffered a stroke.

When interns do not know what to do, when they cannot covertly consult *The Washington Manual* (a handbook of medical therapeutics), they can always order tests. The first time one intern attempted to perform a pleural biopsy—a fairly difficult procedure—he punctured the patient's lung. When an acquaintance of mine entered an emergency room one Friday night in July with what was only an advanced case of the flu, she wound up having a spinal tap. While negative findings are often necessary to rule out alternative diagnoses, some of the tests are really unwarranted. Interns admit that the results are required only so they can cover themselves in case a resident or attending physician decides to give them the third degree.

Interns' hours only increase their inadequacy. Dr. Jay Dobkin, president of the Physicians National Housestaff Association, a Washington-based organization representing 12,000 interns and residents, says that "working conditions . . . directly impact and influence the quality of patient care. After thirty-six hours 'on,' most interns find their abilities compromised." Indeed, their schedules (they average 110 hours a week) and their salaries (last year, they averaged $13,145) make interns the chief source of cheap labor. No other hospital personnel will do as much "scut" work—drawing blood, for instance—or dirty work, such as manually disimpacting severely constipated patients.

---

*A depressant medicine used to lower high blood pressure.

Even private patients fall prey to interns, because many physicians prefer being affiliated with hospitals that have interns to perform these routine duties around the clock. One way to reduce the likelihood of falling into the hands of an intern is to rely upon a physician in group practice whose partners can provide substitute coverage. Then, too, it probably pays to select a physician who has hospital privileges at the best teaching institution in town. There, at least, you are unlikely to encounter any interns who slept through school, as some medical students admit they do: only the most able students survive the computer-matching process to win the prestigious positions at university hospitals. 8

It may be reassuring to remember that while veteran nurses joke about scheduling their vacations to start July 1, they monitor interns most carefully and manage to catch many mistakes. Residents bear much more responsibility for supervision and surveillance, and Dr. Lawrence Boxt, president of the 5,000-member, Manhattan-based Committee of Interns and Residents and a resident himself, emphasizes that residents are especially vigilant during July. One of the interns he represents agreed: "You're watched like a hawk. You have so much support and backup. They're not going to let you kill anybody." So no one who requires emergency medical attention should hesitate to be hospitalized in July. 9

I asked Dr. Boxt whether he also had any advice for someone about to enter a hospital for elective surgery. 10

"Yes," he said. "Stay away." 11

Questions for Study and Discussion

1. Machlowitz begins her essay with the anecdote of the Harvard medical school professor. Does this brief story effectively introduce her essay? (Glossary: *Beginnings and Endings*) Why, or why not?
2. What, according to Machlowitz, are the immediate causes of the problems many hospitals experience during the month of July?

3. What does she say are the causes of intern inadequacy? Explain how Machlowitz uses examples and quotations from authorities to substantiate the cause and effect relationship.
4. Why, according to Machlowitz, do interns sometimes order unwarranted tests?
5. What suggestions does Machlowitz give for minimizing patient risk during the month of July?
6. How would you interpret Dr. Boxt's answer to the final question Machlowitz asks him?

Vocabulary

Refer to your dictionary to define the following words as they are used in this selection. Then use each word in a sentence of your own.

meticulous (4)   affiliated (8)
diagnoses (6)   prestigious (8)
unwarranted (6)   vigilant (9)
compromised (7)

Suggested Writing Assignments

1. Write an essay in which you argue for changes in the ways hospitals handle the "July" problem. Make sure your proposals are realistic, clearly stated, and have some chance of producing the desired effects. You may wish to consider some possible objections to your proposals and how they might be overcome.
2. There is often more than one cause for an event. Make a list of at least six possible causes for one of the following:

a quarrel with a friend
an upset victory in a football game
a well-done exam
a broken leg
a change of major

Examine your list, and identify the causes that seem most probable. Which of these are immediate causes and which are ultimate causes? Using this material, write a short cause-and-effect essay.

THREE MILE ISLAND

Barry Commoner

Barry Commoner was born in Brooklyn, New York, in 1917 and received degrees from Columbia and Harvard universities. Trained as a biologist, he has taught at a number of colleges and universities and is currently professor emeritus at Queens College in Flushing, New York, and director of their Center for the Biology of Natural Systems. He is an outspoken environmentalist and a highly respected critic of nuclear power. He is a champion of nonhazardous renewable alternative sources of energy. His most recent book Making Peace With the Planet *appeared in 1990.*

In the following essay, taken from his book The Politics of Energy, *Commoner examines the technological difficulties that in 1979 caused a near disaster at the Three Mile Island nuclear facility in Harrisburg, Pennsylvania.*

The high and growing cost of nuclear power plants is due not so much to the difficulties associated with the technology that it has in common with non-nuclear plants—that is, the conversion of energy of steam into electricity—but rather to its unique feature, the use of fission to supply the heat needed to produce steam. The accident at Harrisburg showed that a failure in the steam-to-electricity section of the plant that would have caused very little trouble in a conventional power plant came close to producing a catastrophic disaster in the nuclear one and has shut down the plant for a long time, and possibly permanently.

The Three Mile Island Power Plant produced the steam needed to drive its electric turbines in a pressurized-water reactor. In such a reactor, water is circulated through the reactor's fuel core, where—because it is under pressure—it is heated far above its normal boiling point by the heat generated by the fission reaction. The superheated water flows through the reactor's "primary loop" into a heat exchanger where it brings water, which circulates in a "secondary loop," to the boiling point, and the resulting steam flows into the turbine to generate electricity. The spent steam is recondensed and pumped back to the heat exchanger, where it is again converted to steam, and so on. A third loop of cooling water is used to condense the steam, carrying off the excess heat to a cooling tower where it is finally released into the air. This arrangement is much more complex than the design of a conventional power system, where the steam generated in the boiler passes directly into the turbine. In this type of nuclear plant the water that circulates through the reactor (which is equivalent to the boiler in a conventional plant) becomes intensely radioactive, and the complex successive circulation loops are essential to keep that radioactivity from leaving the reactor.

On March 28, 1979, at 3:53 A.M., a pump at the Harrisburg plant failed. Because the pump failed, the reactor's heat was not drawn off in the heat exchanger and the very hot water in the primary loop overheated. The pressure in the loop increased, opening a release valve that was supposed to counteract such an event. But the valve stuck open and the primary loop system lost so much water (which ended up as a highly radioactive pool, six feet deep, on the floor of the reactor building) that it was unable to carry off all the heat generated within the reactor core. Under these circumstances, the intense heat held within the reactor could, in theory, melt its fuel rods, and the resulting "meltdown" could then carry a hugely radioactive mass through the floor of the reactor. The reactor's emergency cooling system, which is designed to prevent this disaster, was then automatically activated; but when it was, apparently, turned off too soon, some of the fuel rods overheated. This produced a bubble of hydrogen gas at the top of the reactor. (The hydrogen is dissolved in the water in order to react with oxygen that is produced when the intense reactor radiation splits water molecules into their atomic constituents. When heated, the dissolved hydrogen bubbles out of the solution.) This bubble blocked the flow of cooling water so that despite the action of the emergency cooling system the reactor core was again in danger of melting down. Another danger was that the gas might contain enough oxygen to cause an explosion that could rupture the huge containers that surround the reactor and release a deadly cloud of radioactive material into the surrounding countryside. Working desperately, technicians were able to gradually reduce the size of the gas bubble using a special apparatus brought in from the atomic laboratory at Oak Ridge, Tennessee, and the danger of a catastrophic release of radioactive materials subsided. But the sealed-off plant was now so radioactive that no one could enter it for many months—or, according to some observers, for years—without being exposed to a lethal dose of radiation.

Some radioactive gases did escape from the plant, prompting the Governor of Pennsylvania, Richard Thornburgh, to ask that pregnant women and children leave the area five miles around the plant. Many other people decided to leave as well, and within a week 60,000 or more residents had left the area, drawing money from their banks and leaving state offices and a local hospital shorthanded. 4

Like the horseshoe nail that lost a kingdom, the failure of a pump at the Three Mile Island Nuclear Power Plant may have lost the entire industry. It dramatized the vulnerability of the complex system that is embodied in the elaborate technology of nuclear power. In that design, the normally benign and easily controlled process of producing steam to drive an electric generator turned into a trigger for a radioactive catastrophe. . . . 5

Questions for Study and Discussion

1. What is a "meltdown" (3)? What were the causes of the two potential "meltdown" situations at the Three Mile Island nuclear power plant?
2. To what degree does Commoner attribute the problems at Three Mile Island to human error?
3. A causal chain of events occurs when one cause brings about one or more effects which, in turn, can cause other effects and so on. Discuss the causal chain of events in the Three Mile Island accident as described by Commoner.

4. In paragraph 2 Commoner explains how a nuclear power plant works. How does this description of the process function within the context of the essay? (Glossary: *Unity*)

5. In paragraphs 1 and 2 Commoner compares and contrasts the technology of conventional and nuclear power plants. What is the purpose of this comparison and contrast? (Glossary: *Unity*)

6. In paragraph 3 Commoner provides a detailed causal analysis of the events at Three Mile Island. Commoner does more than establish the chronological sequence of these events; his intention is to establish a causal relationship among them. Which words and phrases in paragraph 3 indicate cause-and-effect relationships?

7. In the first sentence of paragraph 5 Commoner uses an analogy. To what does he allude in the first half of the analogy? What is the purpose of the analogy? (Glossary: *Analogy*)

Vocabulary

Refer to your dictionary to define the following words as they are used in this selection. Then use each word in a sentence of your own.

fission (1)   constituents (3)
conventional (1)   benign (5)
turbine (2)

Suggested Writing Assignments

1. Write a cause-and-effect essay in which you discuss the impact of the Three Mile Island accident on the development of nuclear power and alternate energy sources in the United States. In what ways do you think the events at Three Mile Island and the subsequent investigations and reports have changed our attitude toward the risks we are willing to take in order to satisfy our energy needs?

2. Write an essay in which you discuss the effects of television on you or on American society. You may wish to fo-

cus on the specific influences of one of the following aspects of television:

advertising
sports broadcasts
cultural programming
talk shows
national or international news
children's programming
educational television
situation comedies

WHY WE CRAVE HORROR MOVIES

Stephen King

Stephen King's name is synonymous with horror stories. A graduate of the University of Maine in 1970, King had worked in a knitting mill and as a janitor, laundry worker, and high-school English teacher before he struck it big with his writing. Many consider Stephen King the most successful writer of modern horror fiction working in that genre today. His books have sold well over 20 million copies, and several of his novels have been made into popular motion pictures. His books include Carrie *(1974),* Salem's Lot *(1975),* The Shining *(1977),* The Dead Zone *(1979),* Firestarter *(1980),* Christine *(1983),* Pet Sematary *(1983), and* Tommyknockers *(1988). A short story from the collection* Night Shift *(1978) was produced as the movie* Stand by Me. *The widespread popularity of horror books and films attest to the fact that many people share King's fascination with the macabre. In the following selection, King analyzes the reasons we all flock to good horror movies.*

I think that we're all mentally ill; those of us outside the asylums only hide it a little better—and maybe not all that much better, after all. We've all known people who talk to themselves, people who sometimes squinch their faces into horrible grimaces when they believe no one is watching, people who have some hysterical fear—of snakes, the dark, the tight place, the long drop . . . and, of course, those final worms and grubs that are waiting so patiently underground.

When we pay our four or five bucks and seat ourselves at tenth-row center in a theater showing a horror movie, we are daring the nightmare.

389

Why? Some of the reasons are simple and obvious. To show 3
that we can, that we are not afraid, that we can ride this roller
coaster. Which is not to say that a really good horror movie may
not surprise a scream out of us at some point, the way we may
scream when the roller coaster twists through a complete 360
or plows through a lake at the bottom of the drop. And horror
movies, like roller coasters, have always been the special
province of the young; by the time one turns 40 or 50, one's ap-
petite for double twists or 360-degree loops may be considerably depleted.

We also go to re-establish our feelings of essential normality; 4
the horror movie is innately conservative, even reactionary.
Freda Jackson as the horrible melting woman in *Die, Monster,
Die!* confirms for us that no matter how far we may be removed
from the beauty of a Robert Redford or a Diana Ross, we are
still light-years from true ugliness.

And we go to have fun. 5

Ah, but this is where the ground starts to slope away, isn't it? 6
Because this is a very peculiar sort of fun, indeed. The fun
comes from seeing others menaced—sometimes killed. One
critic has suggested that if pro football has become the voyeur's
version of combat, then the horror film has become the modern
version of the public lynching.

It is true that the mythic, "fairy-tale" horror film intends to 7
take away the shades of gray. . . . It urges us to put away our
more civilized and adult penchant for analysis and to become
children again, seeing things in pure blacks and whites. It may
be that horror movies provide psychic relief on this level because this invitation to lapse into simplicity, irrationality and
even outright madness is extended so rarely. We are told we
may allow our emotions a free rein . . . or no rein at all.

If we are all insane, then sanity becomes a matter of degree. 8
If your insanity leads you to carve up women like Jack the Rip-
per or the Cleveland Torso Murderer, we clap you away in the
funny farm (but neither of those two amateur-night surgeons
was ever caught, heh-heh-heh); if, on the other hand, your
insanity leads you only to talk to yourself when you're under
stress or to pick your nose on your morning bus, then you are
left alone to go about your business . . . though it is doubtful
that you will ever be invited to the best parties.

The potential lyncher is in almost all of us (excluding saints, 9
past and present; but then, most saints have been crazy in their
own ways), and every now and then, he has to be let loose to
scream and roll around in the grass. Our emotions and our
fears form their own body, and we recognize that it demands
its own exercise to maintain proper muscle tone. Certain of
these emotional muscles are accepted—even exalted—in civilized society; they are, of course, the emotions that tend to
maintain the status quo of civilization itself. Love, friendship,
loyalty, kindness—these are all the emotions that we applaud,
emotions that have been immortalized in the couplets of Hall-
mark cards and in the verses (I don't dare call it poetry) of
Leonard Nimoy.

When we exhibit these emotions, society showers us with 10
positive reinforcement; we learn this even before we get out of
diapers. When, as children, we hug our rotten little puke of a
sister and give her a kiss, all the aunts and uncles smile and
twit and cry, "Isn't he the sweetest little thing?" Such coveted
treats as chocolate-covered graham crackers often follow. But if
we deliberately slam the rotten little puke of a sister's fingers in
the door, sanctions follow—angry remonstrance from parents,
aunts and uncles; instead of a chocolate-covered graham
cracker, a spanking.

But anticivilization emotions don't go away, and they demand 11
periodic exercise. We have such "sick" jokes as, "What's the
difference between a truckload of bowling balls and a truckload of dead babies? (You can't unload a truckload of bowling
balls with a pitchfork . . . a joke, by the way, that I heard
originally from a ten-year-old). Such a joke may surprise a
laugh or a grin out of us even as we recoil, a possibility that
confirms the thesis: If we share a brotherhood of man, then we
also share an insanity of man. None of which is intended as a
defense of either the sick joke or insanity but merely as an
explanation of why the best horror films, like the best fairy
tales, manage to be reactionary, anarchistic, and revolutionary
all at the same time.

The mythic horror movie, like the sick joke, has a dirty job to 12
do. It deliberately appeals to all that is worst in us. It is morbid-
ity unchained, our most base instincts let free, our nastiest fan-
tasies realized . . . and it all happens, fittingly enough, in the

dark. For those reasons, good liberals often shy away from horror films. For myself, I like to see the most aggressive of them—*Dawn of the Dead*, for instance—as lifting a trap door in the civilized forebrain and throwing a basket of raw meat to the hungry alligators swimming around in that subterranean river beneath.

Why bother? Because it keeps them from getting out, man. It keeps them down there and me up here. It was Lennon and McCartney who said that all you need is love, and I would agree with that.   13

As long as you keep the gators fed.

14

Questions for Study and Discussion

1. What, according to King, are several of the reasons people go to horror movies? What other reasons can you add to King's list?

2. Identify the analogy King uses in paragraph 3, and explain how it works. (Glossary: *Analogy*)

3. What does King mean when he says "the horror movie is innately conservative, even reactionary" (4)?

4. What emotions does society applaud? Why? Which ones does King label "anticivilization" emotions?

5. In what ways is a horror movie like a sick joke? What is the "dirty job" that the two have in common (12)?

6. King starts his essay with the attention-grabbing sentence "I think that we're all mentally ill." How does he develop this idea of insanity in his essay? What does King mean when he says "the potential lyncher is in almost all of us" (9)? How does King's last line relate to the theme of mental illness?

7. What is King's tone in this essay? (Glossary: *Tone*) Point to particular words or sentences that led you to this conclusion.

Vocabulary

Refer to your dictionary to define the following words as they are used in this selection. Then use each word in a sentence of your own.

grimaces (1)	puke (10)
hysterical (1)	sanctions (10)
voyeur's (6)	remonstrance (10)
penchant (7)	recoil (11)
rein (7)	anarchistic (11)
exalted (9)	morbidity (12)
status quo (9)	subterranean (12)

Suggested Writing Assignments

1. Write an essay in which you analyze the most significant reason(s) for your going to college. You may wish to discuss such matters as your high-school experiences, people and events that influenced your decision, and your goals in college as well as in later life.

2. Write an essay in which you analyze, in light of Stephen King's remarks, a horror movie you've seen. In what ways did the movie satisfy your "anticivilization" emotions? How did you feel before going to the theater? How did you feel when leaving?

LEGALIZE DRUGS

Ethan A. Nadelmann

Writer, speaker, and teacher Ethan Nadelmann was born in 1957 in New York City. His many degrees include a B.A. from McGill University, an M.S. in international relations from the London School of Economics, and both a law degree and a Ph.D. from Harvard University. His extensive writings, which focus on international crime and law enforcement in general, and U.S. drug policy in particular, have appeared in journals such as Foreign Policy *and* The Public Interest. *In the following essay, which first appeared as "Shooting Up" in the* New Republic *on June 13, 1988, Nadelmann makes his claim that the legalization of drugs would eliminate the criminal activity associated with drug use.*

Hamburgers and ketchup. Movies and popcorn. Drugs and crime. 1

Drugs and crime are so thoroughly intertwined in the public 2 mind that to most people a large crime problem seems an inevitable consequence of widespread drug use. But the historical link between the two is more a product of drug laws than of drugs. There are four clear connections between drugs and crime, and three of them would be much diminished if drugs were legalized. This fact doesn't by itself make the case for legalization persuasive, of course, but it deserves careful attention in the emerging debate over whether the prohibition of drugs is worth the trouble.

The first connection between drugs and crime—and the only 3 one that would remain strong after legalization—is the commission of violent and other crimes by people under the influence of illicit drugs. It is this connection that most infects the popular imagination. Obviously some drugs do "cause" people to commit crimes by reducing normal inhibitions, lessening the sense of responsibility, and unleashing aggressive and other antisocial tendencies. Cocaine, particularly in the form of "crack," has earned such a reputation in recent years, just as heroin did in the 1960s and 1970s and marijuana did in the years before that.

Crack's reputation may or may not be more deserved than   4 those of marijuana and heroin. Reliable evidence isn't yet available. But no illicit drug is as widely associated with violent behavior as alcohol. According to Justice Department statistics, 54 percent of all jail inmates convicted of violent crimes in 1983 reported having used alcohol just prior to committing the offense. The impact of drug legalization on this drug-crime connection is hard to predict. Much would depend on overall rates of drug abuse and changes in the nature of consumption, both imponderables. It's worth noting, though, that any shift in consumption from alcohol to marijuana would almost certainly reduce violent behavior.

This connection between drugs and antisocial behavior—   5 which is inherent and may or may not be substantial—is often confused with a second link between the two that is definitely substantial and not inherent: many illicit drug users commit crimes such as robbery, burglary, prostitution, and numbers-running to earn enough money to buy drugs. Unlike the millions of alcoholics who support their habits for modest amounts, many cocaine and heroin addicts spend hundreds, maybe even thousands, of dollars a week. If these drugs were significantly cheaper—if either they were legalized or drug laws were not enforced—the number of crimes committed by drug addicts to pay for their habits would drop dramatically. Even if the drugs were taxed heavily to discourage consumption, prices probably would be much lower than they are today.

The third drug-crime link—also a byproduct of drug laws—is   6 the violent, intimidating, and corrupting behavior of the drug traffickers. Illegal markets tend to breed violence, not just because they attract criminally minded people but also because there are no legal institutions for resolving disputes. During Prohibition violent struggles between bootlegging gangs and hijackings of booze-laden trucks were frequent and notorious. Today's equivalents are the booby traps that surround marijuana fields; the pirates of the Caribbean, who rip off drug-laden vessels en route to the United States; and the machine-gun battles and executions of the more sordid drug mafias—all of which occasionally kill innocent people. Most authorities agree that the dramatic increase in urban murder rates over the past few years is almost entirely due to the rise in drug-dealer killings, mostly of one another.

Perhaps the most unfortunate victims of drug prohibition   7
laws have been the residents of America's ghettos. These laws have proved largely futile in deterring ghetto-dwellers from becoming drug abusers, but they do account for much of what ghetto residents identify as the drug problem. Aggressive, gun-toting drug dealers often upset law-abiding residents far more than do addicts nodding out in doorways. Meanwhile other residents perceive the drug dealers as heroes and successful role models. They're symbols of success to children who see no other options. At the same time the increasingly harsh criminal penalties imposed on adult drug dealers have led drug traffick-ers to recruit juveniles. Where once children started dealing drugs only after they had been using them for a few years, today the sequence is often reversed. Many children start using drugs only after working for older drug dealers for a while.

The conspicuous failure of law enforcement agencies to deal   8
with the disruptive effect of drug traffickers has demoralized inner-city neighborhoods and police departments alike. Inten-sive crackdowns in urban neighborhoods, like intensive anti-cockroach efforts in urban dwellings, do little more than chase the menace a short distance away to infect new areas. By con-trast, legalization of drugs, like legalization of alcohol in the early 1930s, would drive the drug-dealing business off the streets and out of apartment buildings and into government-regulated, tax-paying stores. It also would force many of the gun-toting dealers out of the business and convert others into legitimate businessmen. Some, of course, would turn to other types of criminal activities, just as some of the bootleggers did after Prohibition's repeal. Gone, though, would be the unparal-leled financial gains that tempt people from all sectors of society into the drug-dealing business.

Gone, too, would be the money that draws police into the world of crime. Today police corruption appears to be more pervasive than at any time since Prohibition. In Miami dozens of law enforcement officials have been charged with accepting bribes, ripping off drug dealers, and even dealing drugs themselves. In small towns and rural communities in Georgia, where drug smugglers from the Caribbean and Latin America pass through, dozens of sheriffs have been implicated in corruption. In one New York police precinct, drug-related corruption has generated the city's most far-reaching police scandal since the late 1960s. Nationwide, over 100 cases of drug-related corruption are now prosecuted each year. Every one of the federal law enforcement agencies with significant drug enforcement responsibilities has seen an agent implicated.

It isn't hard to explain the growth of this corruption. The financial temptations are enormous relative to other opportunities, legitimate or illegitimate. Little effort is required. Many police officers are demoralized by the scope of drug traffic, the indifference of many citizens, a frequent lack of appreciation for their efforts, and the seeming futility of it all; even with the regular jailing of drug dealers, there always seem to be more to fill their shoes. Some police also recognize that their real function is not so much to protect victims from predators as to regulate an illicit market that can't be suppressed but that much of society prefers to keep underground. In every respect, the analogy to Prohibition is apt. Repealing drug prohibition laws would dramatically reduce police corruption. By contrast, the measures currently being proposed to deal with the growing problem, including more frequent and aggressive internal inspection, offer little promise and cost money.

The final link between drugs and crime is the tautological connection: producing, selling, buying, and consuming drugs is a crime in and of itself that occurs billions of times each year nationwide. Last year alone, about 30 million Americans violated a drug law, and about 750,000 were arrested, mostly for mere possession, not dealing. In New York City almost half of the felony indictments were on drug charges, and in Washington, D.C., the figure was more than half. Close to 40 percent of inmates in federal prisons are there on drug-dealing charges, and that population is expected to more than double within 15 years.

Clearly, if drugs were legalized, this drug-crime connection— which annually accounts for around $10 billion in criminal justice costs—would be severed. (Selling drugs to children would, of course, continue to be prosecuted.) And the benefits would run deeper than that. We would no longer be labeling as criminals the tens of millions of people who use drugs illicitly, subjecting them to the risk of arrest, and inviting them to associate with drug dealers (who may be criminals in many more senses of the word). The attendant cynicism toward the law in general would diminish, along with the sense of hostility and suspicion that otherwise law-abiding citizens feel toward police. It was costs such as these that strongly influenced many of Prohibition's more conservative opponents. As John D. Rockefeller wrote in explaining why he was withdrawing his support of Prohibition:

> That a vast array of lawbreakers has been recruited and
> financed on a colossal scale; that many of our best citizens,
> piqued at what they regarded as an infringement of their
> private rights, have openly and unabashedly disregarded
> the 18th Amendment; that as an inevitable result respect
> for all law has been greatly lessened; that crime has in-
> creased to an unprecedented degree—I have slowly and
> reluctantly come to believe.

Questions for Study and Discussion

1. What are the four connections Nadelmann makes between drugs and crime? According to Nadelmann, what changes would occur if drugs were legalized? Would anything remain unaffected? How does he explain this?

2. Nadelmann insists that the connection between drugs and crime is not inevitable. What kinds of evidence does he offer to support this argument? Which kinds of evidence did you find the most convincing? (Glossary: *Evidence*) The least convincing? Explain.

3. Nadelmann identifies several groups of people associated with the criminal aspects of drug use. What role does each group presently play? According to Nadelmann, how would that role change if drug use were made legal?
4. What is the analogy Nadelmann draws in paragraph 10? (Glossary: *Analogy*) Is it effective? Why or why not?
5. What is the "tautological connection" between drugs and crime that Nadelmann describes in paragraph 11? Is this connection clearly stated?
6. What exactly is Nadelmann's purpose in writing this essay? (Glossary: *Purpose*) Does he expect his readers to endorse the legalization of drugs or does he want something else? How do you know?

Vocabulary

Refer to your dictionary to define the following words as they are used in this selection. Then use each word in a sentence of your own.

inevitable (1)
illicit (2)
inhibitions (3)
imponderables (4)
inherent (5)
bootlegging (6)
sordid (6)
futile (7)

deterring (7)
conspicuous (8)
implicated (9)
demoralized (10)
predators (10)
tautological (11)
cynicism (12)

Suggested Writing Assignments

1. In a brief essay, respond to Nadelmann's assertion that "any shift in consumption from alcohol to marijuana would almost certainly reduce violent behavior." What reasons do you have for agreeing or disagreeing? What is the relationship between alcohol and violent behavior? Marijuana and violent behavior?

2. Write an essay in which you establish the cause and effect relationship that exists in one of the following pairs.

winter and depression
poverty and crime
wealth and power
health and happiness
old age and wisdom
good looks and popularity
drugs and sex

18

ARGUMENT

Argumentation is the attempt to persuade a reader to accept your point of view, to make a decision, or to pursue a particular course of action. Because the writer of an argument is often interested in explaining a subject, as well as in advocating a particular view, argumentation frequently adopts other rhetorical strategies. Nevertheless, it is the attempt to convince, not to explain, that is most important in an argumentative essay.

There are two basic types of argumentation: logical and persuasive. In *logical argumentation* the writer appeals to the reader's rational or intellectual faculties to convince him or her of the truth of a particular statement or belief. In *persuasive argumentation*, on the other hand, the writer appeals to the reader's emotions and opinions to move the reader to action. These two types of argumentation are seldom found in their pure forms, and the degree to which one or the other is emphasized in written work depends on the writer's subject, specific purpose, and intended audience. Although you may occasionally need or want to appeal to your readers' emotions, most often in your college work you will need to rely only on the fundamental techniques of logical argumentation.

There are two types of reasoning common to essays of argumentation: induction and deduction. *Inductive reasoning*, the more common type, moves from a set of specific examples to a general statement. In doing so, the writer makes what is known as an *inductive leap* from the evidence to the generalization. For example, after examining enrollment statistics, we can conclude that students do not like to take courses offered early in the morning or late in the afternoon. *Deductive reasoning*, on the other hand, moves from a general statement to a specific conclusion. It works on the model of the *syllogism*, a simple three-part argument that consists of a major premise, a minor premise, and a conclusion, as in the following example:

a. All women are mortal. (major premise)
b. Judy is a woman. (minor premise)
c. Judy is mortal. (conclusion)

A well-constructed argument avoids *logical fallacies,* flaws in the reasoning that will render the argument invalid. Following are some of the most common logical fallacies:

1. *Oversimplification.* The tendency to provide simple solutions to complex problems. "The reason we have high unemployment today is the war in the Middle East."

2. *Hasty generalization.* A generalization that is based on too little evidence or on evidence that is not representative. "The movie was very popular. It should get an Academy Award."

3. *Post hoc, ergo propter hoc* ("After this, therefore because of this"). Confusing chance or coincidence with causation. Because one event comes after another one, it does not necessarily mean that the first event caused the second. "Ever since I went to the hockey game, I've had a cold." The assumption here is that going to the hockey game had something to do with the speaker's cold when, in fact, there might be one or more different causes for the cold.

4. *Begging the question.* Assuming in a premise that which needs to be proven. "Conservation is the only means of solving the energy problem over the long haul; therefore, we should seek out methods to conserve energy."

5. *False analogy.* Making a misleading analogy between logically unconnected ideas. "Of course he'll make a fine coach. He was an all-star basketball player."

6. *Either/or thinking.* The tendency to see an issue as having only two sides. "There are good judges and there are bad judges."

7. *Non sequitur* ("It does not follow"). An inference or conclusion that does not follow from established premises or evidence. "She is a sincere speaker; she must know what she is talking about."

As you write your argumentative essays, you should keep the following advice in mind. Somewhere near the beginning of your essay, you should identify the issue to be discussed, explain why you think it is important, and point out what interest you and your readers share in the issue. Then, in the body of your essay, you should organize the various points of your argument. You may move from your least important point to your most important point, from the most familiar to the least familiar, from the easiest to accept or comprehend to the most difficult. For each point in your argument, you should provide sufficient appropriate supporting evidence—facts and statistics, illustrative examples and narratives, quotations from authorities. In addition, you should acknowledge the strongest opposing arguments and explain why you believe your position is more valid.

Be sure that you neither overstate nor understate your position. It is always wise to let the evidence convince your reader. Overstatement not only annoys readers but, more importantly, raises serious doubts about your own confidence in the power of your facts and reasoning. At the same time, no writer persuades by excessively understating or qualifying information with words and phrases such as *perhaps, maybe, I think, sometimes, most often, nearly always,* or *in my opinion.* The result sounds not rational and sensible but indecisive and fuzzy.

HATE, RAPE, AND RAP

Tipper Gore

Tipper Gore was born in Washington, D.C., in 1948 and grew up in Arlington, Virginia. She graduated from Boston University with a degree in psychology in 1970 and pursued graduate studies in psychology at George Peabody College in Nashville, Tennessee. In 1983, Gore helped establish the Parents' Music Resource Center (P.M.R.C.) a group which addresses issues of obscenity and pornography in modern rock lyrics. In "Hate, Rape, and Rap," which first appeared in the Washington Post *in January 1990, Gore contends that the lyrics in some modern rap music inspire feelings of hatred among its listeners.*

Words like "bitch" and "nigger" are dangerous. Racial and sexual epithets, whether screamed across a street or camouflaged by the rhythms of a song, turn people into objects less than human—easier to degrade, easier to violate, easier to destroy. These words and epithets are becoming an accepted part of our lexicon. What's disturbing is that they are being endorsed by some of the very people they diminish, and our children are being sold a social dictionary that says racism, sexism, and antisemitism are okay. 1

As someone who strongly supports the First Amendment, I respect the freedom of every individual to label another as he likes. But speaking out against racism isn't endorsing censorship. No one should silently tolerate racism or sexism or antisemitism, or condone those who turn discrimination into a multimillion-dollar business justified because it's "real." 2

A few weeks ago television viewers saw a confrontation of depressing proportions on the Oprah Winfrey show. It was one I witnessed firsthand; I was there in the middle of it. Viewers 3 heard some black American women say they didn't mind being called "bitches" and they weren't offended by the popular rap music artist Ice-T when he sang about "Evil E" who "f---ed the bitch with a flashlight/pulled it out, left the batteries in/so he could get a charge when he begins." There is more, and worse.

Ice-T, who was also on the show, said the song came from the 4 heart and reflected his experiences. He said he doesn't mind other groups using the word "nigger" in their lyrics. That's how he described himself, he said. Some in the audience questioned why we couldn't see the humor in such a song.

Will our kids get the joke? Do we want them describing them- 5 selves or each other as "niggers?" Do we want our daughters to think of themselves as "bitches" to be abused? Do we want our sons to measure success in gold guns hanging from thick neck chains? The women in the audience may understand the slang; Ice-T can try to justify it. But can our children?

One woman in the audience challenged Ice-T. She told him his 6 song about the flashlight was about as funny as a song about lynching black men.

The difference is that sexism and violence against women are 7 accepted as almost an institutionalized part of our entertainment. Racism is not—or at least, it hasn't been until recently. The fact is, neither racism, sexism nor antisemitism should be accepted.

Yet they are, and in some instances that acceptance has 8 reached startling proportions. The racism expressed in the song "One In A Million" by Guns N' Roses, sparked nationwide discussion and disgust. But, an earlier album, that featured a rape victim in the artwork and lyrics violently degrading to women, created barely a whisper of protest. More than 9 million copies were sold, and it was played across the radio band. This is only one example where hundreds exist.

Rabbi Abraham Cooper of the Simon Wiesenthal Center, who 9 also appeared on the Oprah Show, voiced his concerns about the antisemitic statements made by Professor Griff, a non-singing member of the rap group, Public Enemy; statements that gain added weight from the group's celebrity. "Jews are wicked," Professor Griff said in an interview with The Washington Times. ". . . [Responsible for] a majority of wickedness that goes on across the globe."

The Simon Wiesenthal Center placed a full-page ad in Daily   10
Variety calling for self-restraint from the music industry, a
move that prompted hundreds of calls to the center. Yet Rabbi
Cooper's concerns barely elicited a response from Oprah Winfrey's audience.

Alvin Poussaint, a Harvard psychiatrist who is black, believes   11
that the widespread acceptance of such degrading and deni-
grating images may reflect low self-esteem among black men in
today's society. There are few positive black male role models
for young children, and such messages from existing role
models are damaging. Ice-T defends his reality: "I grew up in
the streets—I'm no Bryant Gumbel." He accuses his critics of
fearing that reality, and says the fear comes from an ignorance
of the triumph of the street ethic.

A valid point, perhaps. But it is not the messenger that is so   12
frightening, it is the perpetuation—almost glorification—of the
cruel and violent reality of his "streets."

A young black mother in the front row rose to defend Ice-T.   13
Her son, she said, was an A student who listened to Ice-T. In her
opinion, as long as Ice-T made a profit, it didn't matter what he
sang.

Cultural economics were a poor excuse for the South's con-   14
tinuation of slavery. Ice-T's financial success cannot excuse the
vileness of his message. What does it mean when performers
such as Ice-T, Axl Rose of Guns N' Roses and others can enrich
themselves with racist and misogynist diatribes and defend it
because it sells? Hitler's antisemitism sold in Nazi Germany.
That didn't make it right.

In America, a woman is raped once every six minutes. A ma-   15
jority of children surveyed by a Rhode Island Rape Crisis Center thought rape was acceptable. In New York City, rape arrests
of 13-year-old boys have increased 200 percent in the past two
years. Children 18 and younger now are responsible for 70 percent of the hate crime committed in the United States. No one
is saying this happens solely because of rap or rock music, but
certainly kids are influenced by the glorification of violence.

Children must be taught to hate. They are not born with ideas   16
of bigotry—they learn from what they see in the world around
them. If their reality consists of a street ethic that promotes and
glorifies violence against women or discrimination against mi-

norities—not only in everyday life, but in their entertainment—then ideas of bigotry and violence will flourish.

We must raise our voices in protest and put pressure on those   17
who not only reflect this hatred but also package, polish, promote and market it; those who would make words like "nigger" acceptable. Let's place a higher value on our children than on our profits and embark on a remedial civil rights course for children who are being taught to hate and a remedial nonviolence course for children who are being taught to destroy. Let's send the message loud and clear through our homes, our streets and our schools, as well as our art and our culture.

Questions for Study and Discussion

1. What is Gore's thesis? Where is it best stated? (Glossary: *Thesis*)

2. In paragraph 1 Gore says that words like "bitch" and "nigger" are dangerous. Does she say why? How do you respond to her charge?

3. Does Gore use inductive or deductive reasoning to argue her point? You may find it helpful to outline the essay so as to more easily see the logic of her development.

4. Gore makes the claim that performers such as Ice-T and Guns 'n' Roses are like Hitler. In what ways does she say they are similar? Is she convincing? Why or why not? Does she include the ways in which they are dissimilar? Explain.

5. What solutions does Gore offer as a means of minimizing children's exposure to objectionable music? In your opinion, is she advocating a form of censorship? Explain.

6. In paragraph 16 Gore says "Children must be taught to hate." What does she mean? How does her statement relate to her thesis?

7. What is the relationship among the words "hate," "rape," and "rap" in Gore's essay? How well do these words serve as a title for this essay? (Glossary: *Title*) Explain.

Vocabulary

Refer to your dictionary to define the following words as they are used in this selection. Then use each word in a sentence of your own.

epithets (1)	misogynist (14)
lexicon (1)	diatribes (14)
antisemitism (7)	remedial (17)

Suggested Writing Assignments

1. Based on what you have just read, write an essay in which you argue either for or against the labelling of music albums. Discuss the extent to which you believe such labelling would or would not constitute censorship.
2. Gore says "Children must be taught to hate," and she insists that they can learn hatred by listening to some modern rap music. Do you think Gore has made a good case for the harmful effects of rock music or has she oversimplified the issue? In an essay, address this question while discussing your own opinion as to why hatred, bigotry, and prejudice still exist in America.

TELEVISION INSULTS MEN, TOO

Bernard R. Goldberg

Journalist and CBS news correspondent, Bernard R. Goldberg was born in 1945 in New York City. Goldberg began his news career at the Associated Press in New York City just four days after graduating from Rutgers University with a degree in journalism. In 1972 he joined the CBS news team. From 1981 through 1987 he served as a correspondent with Dan Rather on the CBS Evening News. Since its debut in 1988, Goldberg has worked as a correspondent with "48 Hours," a CBS news magazine program. The following essay first appeared on the Op-Ed page of the New York Times *on March 14, 1989. In it Goldberg enters the ring to defend men against the new double standard in television programming which encourages sexist humor as long as it is directed against men.*

I t was front page news and it made the TV networks. A   1
mother from Michigan single-handedly convinces some of America's biggest advertisers to cancel their sponsorship of the Fox Broadcasting Company's "Married . . . With Children" because, as she put it, the show blatantly exploits women and the family.

The program is about a blue collar family in which the hus-   2
band is a chauvinist pig and his wife is—excuse the expression—a bimbo.

These are the late 1980's, and making fun of people because   3
of their gender—on TV no less, in front of millions of people—is déclassé. Unless, of course, the gender we're ridiculing is the male gender. Then it's O.K.

Take "Roseanne." (Please!) It's the season's biggest new hit   4
show, which happens to be about another blue collar family. In this one, the wife calls her husband and kids names.

"Roseanne" is Roseanne Barr who has made a career saying 5
such cute things as: "You may marry the man of your dreams,
ladies, but 15 years later you are married to a reclining chair
that burps." Or to her TV show son: "You're not stupid. You're
just clumsy like your daddy."

The producer of "Roseanne" does not mince words either: 6
"Men are slime. They say they're going to do 50 percent of the
work around the house, but they never do."

I will tell you that the producer is a man, which does not les- 7
sen the ugliness of the remark. But because his target is men,
it becomes acceptable. No one, to my knowledge, is pulling
commercials from "Roseanne."

In matters of gender discrimination, it has become part of the 8
accepted orthodoxy—of many feminists and a lot of the media
anyway—that only women have the right to complain. Men have
no such right. Which helps explain why there have been so
many commercials ridiculing men—and getting away with it.

In the past year or so, I have seen a breakfast cereal commer- 9
cial showing a husband and wife playing tennis. She is perky
and he is jerky.

She is a regular Martina Navratilova of the suburbs and he is 10
virtually dead (because he wasn't smart enough to eat the right
cereal).

She doesn't miss a shot. He lets the ball hit him in the head. 11
If he were black, his name would be Stepin Fetchitt.

I have seen a commercial for razor blades that shows a 12
woman in an evening gown smacking a man in a tuxedo across
the face, suggesting, I suppose, that the male face takes enough
punishment to deserve a nice, smooth shave. If he hit her (an
absolutely inconceivable notion, if a sponsor is trying to sell a
woman something) he would be a batterer.

I have seen an airline commercial showing two reporters 13
from competing newspapers. She's strong and smart. He's a
nerd. He says to her: I read your story this morning; you scooped
me again. She replies to him: I didn't know you could read.

I have seen a magazine ad for perfume showing a business 14
woman patting a businessman's behind as they walk down the
street. Ms. Magazine, the Journal of American feminism, ran
the ad. The publisher told me there was nothing sexist about it.

A colleague who writes about advertising and the media says 15 advertisers are afraid to fool around with women's roles. They know, as she puts it, they'll "set off the feminist emergency broadcast system" if they do. So, she concludes, men are fair game.

In 1987, Fred Hayward, who is one of the pioneers of the 16 men's rights movement (yes, there is a men's rights movement) studied thousands of TV and print ads and concluded: "If there's a sleazy character in an ad, 100 percent of the ones that we found were male. If there's an incompetent character, 100 percent of them in the ads are male."

I once interviewed Garrett Epps, a scholar who has written 17 on these matters, who told me: "The female executive who is driven, who is strong, who lives for her work, that's a very positive symbol in our culture now. The male who has the same traits—that guy is a disaster: He harms everybody around him; he's cold; he's unfeeling; he's hurtful."

The crusading mother from Michigan hit on a legitimate is- 18 sue. No more cheap shots, she seems to have said. And the advertisers listened. No more cheap shots is what a lot of men are saying also. Too bad nobody is listening to *them*.

Questions for Study and Discussion

1. What is the "accepted orthodoxy" Goldberg refers to in paragraph 8? Do you agree or disagree with his assessment?

2. According to Goldberg, many of today's commercials ridicule men. What examples does he present to support his arguments? Did you find his examples convincing? What commercials, if any, can you add to Goldberg's list?

3. How does Goldberg use the words "nerd," "jerky," and "batterer," as well as other derogatory terms, to make his point that men are treated unfairly on television? (Glossary: *Diction*) Were you surprised by his use of these words? Were they effective in making his point or did it strike you that he was exaggerating? Explain.

4. Cite several examples of Goldberg's use of short sentences and describe their effect on the reader.

5. What is the "emergency feminist broadcast system" and what familiar phrase is it meant to evoke?

6. Goldberg uses the example of the "crusading mother from Michigan" both as his opening and as a conclusion to his essay. (Glossary: *Beginnings and Endings*) Was this an effective opening and closing to his argument? Why or why not?

Vocabulary

Refer to your dictionary to define the following words as they are used in this selection. Then use each word in a sentence of your own.

blatantly (1)   orthodoxy (8)
exploits (1)   perky (9)
déclassé (3)   nerd (13)
discrimination (8)

Suggested Writing Assignments

1. Write a short essay in which you argue for or against the argument, used by some feminists, that it is "fair" for men to take their "licks," that is their share of anti-male sexism after decades of being guilty of sexist attitudes toward women.

2. Goldberg says men are being characterized in a narrow and insulting manner in current television programming. Watch television for a week to see if any other group is being similarly stereotyped. For example, how are parents, African-Americans, teenagers, women, or blue-collar families portrayed on television? Are they depicted as unique individuals or are they cast into caricatures of commonly held beliefs? What are those beliefs? Are they fair? Ask yourself if it is ever "fair" to make generalizations about the members of a socio-economic group, a race, a gender, or an age group. Discuss your findings and present your conclusions in a brief essay.

As They Say, Drugs Kill

Laura Rowley

*Laura Rowley was born in Oak Lawn, Illinois, in
1965 and graduated from the University of Illinois at Champaign-Urbana in 1987 with a degree
in journalism. While in college, Rowley was the
city editor for the* Daily Illini. *After graduation
she worked at the* United Nations Chronicle *in
New York City. Currently the sales director for a
Manhattan dress company, Rowley continues to
work as a free-lance writer and hopes some day
to travel and work in Africa under the auspice of either the United Nations or the Peace
Corps. In the following essay, which first appeared in* Newsweek on Campus *in 1987, Rowley
argues against substance abuse by recounting a
particularly poignant personal experience. As
you read her piece, notice how she attempts to
persuade without preaching.*

The fastest way to end a party is to have someone die in the
middle of it.

At a party last fall I watched a 22-year-old die of cardiac arrest after he had used drugs. It was a painful, undignified way
to die. And I would like to think that anyone who shared the experience would feel his or her ambivalence about substance
abuse dissolving.

This victim won't be singled out like Len Bias as a bitter example for "troubled youth." He was just another ordinary guy
celebrating with friends at a private house party, the kind
where they roll in the keg first thing in the morning and get
stupefied while watching the football games on cable all afternoon. The living room was littered with beer cans from last
night's party—along with dirty socks and the stuffing from the
secondhand couch.

413

And there were drugs, as at so many other college parties. 4
The drug of choice this evening was psilocybin, hallucinogenic
mushrooms. If you're cool you call them "'shrooms."

This wasn't a crowd huddled in the corner of a darkened 5
room with a single red bulb, shooting needles in their arms.
People played darts, made jokes, passed around a joint and listened to the Grateful Dead on the stereo.

Suddenly, a thin, tall, brown-haired young man began to gasp. 6
His eyes rolled back in his head, and he hit the floor face first
with a crash. Someone laughed, not appreciating the violence
of his fall, thinking the afternoon's festivities had finally caught
up with another guest. The laugh lasted only a second, as the
brown-haired guest began to convulse and choke. The sound of
the stereo and laughter evaporated. Bystanders shouted frantic
suggestions:

"It's an epileptic fit, put something in his mouth!" 7

Roll him over on his stomach!" 8

"Call an ambulance; God, somebody breathe into his mouth." 9

A girl kneeling next to him began to sob his name, and he 10
seemed to moan.

"Wait, he's semicoherent." Four people grabbed for the tele- 11
phone, to find no dial tone, and ran to use a neighbor's. One
slammed the dead phone against the wall in frustration—and
miraculously produced a dial tone.

But the body was now motionless on the kitchen floor. "He 12
has a pulse, he has a pulse."

"But he's not breathing!" 13

"Well, get away—give him some f———ing air!" The three or 14
four guests gathered around his body unbuttoned his shirt.

"Wait—is he OK? Should I call the damn ambulance?" 15

A chorus of frightened voices shouted, "Yes, yes!" 16

"Come on, come on, breathe again. Breathe!" 17

Over muffled sobs came a sudden grating, desperate breath 18
that passed through bloody lips and echoed through the
kitchen and living room.

"He's had this reaction before—when he did acid at a concert 19
last spring. But he recovered in 15 seconds . . . ," one friend
confided.

The rest of the guests looked uncomfortably at the floor or 20
paced purposelessly around the room. One or two whispered,

"Oh, my God," over and over, like a prayer. A friend stood next to me, eyes fixed on the kitchen floor. He mumbled, just audibly, "I've seen this before. My dad died of a heart attack. He had the same look. . . ." I touched his shoulder and leaned against a wall, repeating reassurances to myself. People don't die at parties. People don't die at parties.

Eventually, no more horrible, gnashing sounds tore their way   21
from the victim's lungs. I pushed my hands deep in my jeans pockets wondering how much it costs to pump a stomach and how someone could be so careless if he had had this reaction with another drug. What would he tell his parents about the hospital bill?

Two uniformed paramedics finally arrived, lifted him onto a   22
stretcher and quickly rolled him out. His face was grayish blue, his mouth hung open, rimmed with blood, and his eyes were rolled back with a yellowish color on the rims.

The paramedics could be seen moving rhythmically forward   23
and back through the small windows of the ambulance, whose lights threw a red wash over the stunned watchers on the porch. The paramedics' hands were massaging his chest when someone said, "Did you tell them he took psilocybin? Did you tell them."

"No, I . . ."   24

"My God, so tell them—do you want him to die?" Two people   25
ran to tell the paramedics the student had eaten mushrooms five minutes before the attack.

It seemed irreverent to talk as the ambulance pulled away.   26
My friend, who still saw his father's image, muttered, "That guy's dead." I put my arms around him half to comfort him, half to stop him from saying things I couldn't believe.

The next day, when I called someone who lived in the house,   27
I found that my friend was right.

My hands began to shake and my eyes filled with tears for   28
someone I didn't know. Weeks later the pain has dulled, but I still can't unravel the knot of emotion that has moved from my stomach to my head. When I told one friend what happened, she shook her head and spoke of the stupidity of filling your body with chemical substances. People who would do drugs after seeing that didn't value their lives too highly, she said.

But others refused to read any universal lessons from the   29 incident. Many of those I spoke to about the event considered him the victim of a freak accident, randomly struck down by drugs as a pedestrian might be hit by a speeding taxi. They speculated that the student must have had special physical problems; what happened to him could not happen to them.

Couldn't it? Now when I hear people discussing drugs I'm haunted by the image of him lying on the floor, his body straining to rid itself of substances he chose to take. Painful, undignified, unnecessary—like a wartime casualty. But in war, at least, lessons are supposed to be learned, so that old mistakes are not repeated. If this death cannot make people think and change, that will be an even greater tragedy. 30

Questions for Study and Discussion

1. What is Rowley's purpose in this essay? What does she want us to believe? What does she want us to do? (Glossary: *Purpose*)

2. Rowley uses an extended narrative example to develop her argument. How does she use dialogue, diction choices, and appropriate details to enhance the drama of her story?

3. What does Rowley gain by sharing this powerful experience with her readers? How did Rowley's friends react when she told them her story?

4. Why do you think Rowley chose not to name the young man who died? In what ways is this young man different from Len Bias, the talented basketball player who died of a drug overdose after signing a contract with the Boston Celtics?

5. What in Rowley's tone—her attitude toward her subject and audience—particularly contributes to the persuasiveness of the essay? Cite examples from the selection that support your conclusion. (Glossary: *Tone*)

6. How did Rowley's opening paragraph affect you? What would have been lost had she combined the first two paragraphs? (Glossary: *Beginnings and Endings*)

7. For what audience do you suppose Rowley wrote this essay? In your opinion, would most readers be convinced by what Rowley says about drugs? Are you convinced? Why, or why not? (Glossary: *Audience*)

Vocabulary

Refer to your dictionary to define the following words as they are used in this selection. Then use each word in a sentence of your own.

ambivalence (2)	gnashing (21)
stupefied (3)	irreverent (26)
convulse (6)	unravel (28)
semicoherent (11)	speculated (29)
audibly (20)	tragedy (30)

Suggested Writing Assignments

1. Write a persuasive essay in which you support or refute the following proposition:

   Television advertising is in large part responsible for Americans' belief that over-the-counter drugs are cure-alls.

   Does such advertising in fact promote drug dependence and/or abuse?

2. Write an essay in which you argue against either drinking or smoking. What would drinkers and smokers claim are the benefits of their habits? What are the key arguments against these types of substance abuse? Use examples from your personal experience or from your reading to document your essay.

3. What is the most effective way to bring about social change and to influence societal attitudes? Concentrating on the sorts of changes you have witnessed over the last ten years, write an essay in which you describe how best to influence public opinion.

What's Wrong with Black English

Rachel L. Jones

Rachel L. Jones was a sophomore at Southern Illinois University when she published the following essay in Newsweek *in December 1982. Jones argues against the popularly held belief of both her fellow African-American students and African-American authorities that speaking "white English" is a betrayal of her blackness.*

William Labov, a noted linguist, once said about the use of black English, "It is the goal of most black Americans to acquire full control of the standard language without giving up their own culture." He also suggested that there are certain advantages to having two ways to express one's feelings. I wonder if the good doctor might also consider the goals of those black Americans who have full control of standard English but who are every now and then troubled by that colorful, grammar-to-the-winds patois that is black English. Case in point—me.

I'm a 21-year-old black born to a family that would probably be considered lower-middle class—which in my mind is a polite way of describing a condition only slightly better than poverty. Let's just say we rarely if ever did the winter-vacation thing in the Caribbean. I've often had to defend my humble beginnings to a most unlikely group of people for an even less likely reason. Because of the way I talk, some of my black peers look at me sideways and ask, "Why do you talk like you're white?"

The first time it happened to me I was nine years old. Cornered in the school bathroom by the class bully and her sidekick, I was offered the opportunity to swallow a few of my teeth unless I satisfactorily explained why I always got good grades, why I talked "proper" or "white." I had no ready answer for her, save the fact that my mother had from the time I was old enough to talk stressed the importance of reading and learning, or that L. Frank Baum and Ray Bradbury were my closest companions. I read all my older brothers' and sisters' literature textbooks more faithfully than they did, and even lightweights like the Bobbsey Twins and Trixie Belden were allowed into my bookish inner circle. I don't remember exactly what I told those girls, but I somehow talked my way out of a beating.

I was reminded once again of my "white pipes" problem while apartment hunting in Evanston, Ill., last winter. I doggedly made out lists of available places and called all around. I would immediately be invited over—and immediately turned down. The thinly concealed looks of shock when the front door opened clued me in, along with the flustered instances of "just getting off the phone with the girl who was ahead of you and she wants the rooms." When I finally found a place to live, my roommate stirred up old memories when she remarked a few months later, "You know, I was surprised when I first saw you. You sounded white over the phone." Tell me another one, sister.

I should've asked her a question I've wanted an answer to for years: how does one "talk white"? The silly side of me pictures a rabid white foam spewing forth when I speak. I don't use Valley Girl jargon, so that's not what's meant in my case. Actually, I've pretty much deduced what people mean when they say that to me, and the implications are really frightening.

It means that I'm articulate and well-versed. It means that I can talk as freely about John Steinbeck as I can about Rick James. It means that "ain't" and "he be" are not staples of my vocabulary and are only used around family and friends. (It is almost Jekyll and Hyde-ish the way I can slip out of academic abstractions into a long, lean, double-negative-filled dialogue, but I've come to terms with that aspect of my personality.) As a child, I found it hard to believe that's what people meant by "talking proper"; that would've meant that good grades and standard English were equated with white skin, and that went against everything I'd ever been taught. Running into the same type of mentality as an adult has confirmed the depressing reality that for many blacks, standard English is not only unfamiliar, it is socially unacceptable.

James Baldwin once defended black English by saying it had added "vitality to the language," and even went so far as to label it a language in its own right, saying, "Language [i.e., black

English] is a political instrument" and a "vivid and crucial key to identity." But did Malcolm X urge blacks to take power in this country "any way y'all can"? Did Martin Luther King Jr. say to blacks, "I has been to the mountaintop, and I done seed the Promised Land"? Toni Morrison, Alice Walker and James Baldwin did not achieve their eloquence, grace and stature by using only black English in their writing. Andrew Young, Tom Bradley and Barbara Jordan did not acquire political power by saying, "Y'all crazy if you ain't gon vote for me." They all have full command of standard English, and I don't think that knowledge takes away from their blackness or commitment to black people.

I know from experience that it's important for black people, stripped of culture and heritage, to have something they can point to and say, "This is ours, *we* can comprehend it, *we* alone can speak it with a soulful flourish." I'd be lying if I said that the rhythms of my people caught up in "some serious rap" don't sound natural and right to me sometimes. But how heartwarming is it for those same brothers when they hit the pavement searching for employment? Studies have proven that the use of ethnic dialects decreases power in the marketplace. "I be" is acceptable on the corner, but not with the boss.

Am I letting capitalistic, European-oriented thinking fog the issue? Am I selling out blacks to an ideal of assimilating, being as much like white as possible? I have not formed a personal political ideology, but I do know this: it hurts me to hear black children use black English, knowing that they will be at yet another disadvantage in an educational system already full of stumbling blocks. It hurts me to sit in lecture halls and hear fellow black students complain that the professor "be tripping dem out using big words dey can't understand." And what hurts most is to be stripped of my own blackness simply because I know my way around the English language.

I would have to disagree with Labov in one respect. My goal is not so much to acquire full control of both standard and black English, but to one day see more black people less dependent on a dialect that excludes them from full participation in the world we live in. I don't think I talk white, I think I talk right.

Questions for Study and Discussion

1. What is Jones's purpose in this essay? (Glossary: *Purpose*) For what is she arguing?
2. What purpose is served by Jones's title? Does the title indicate that she will be arguing for or against black English?
3. What, according to Jones, is the attitude of many African-Americans toward standard English? What does Jones find wrong with their thinking and the resulting state of affairs?
4. What is black English? Where does Jones provide a definition of the term? (Glossary: *Definition*)
5. What examples does Jones use to argue that a knowledge of standard English does not diminish a person's blackness or commitment to African-American people? Do you find them convincing?
6. How has Jones used narration to help her case? (Glossary: *Narration*)

Vocabulary

Refer to your dictionary to define the following words as they are used in this selection. Then use each word in a sentence of your own.

linguist (1)   deduced (5)
patois (1)   staples (6)
doggedly (4)   dialect (10)
rabid (5)

Suggested Writing Assignments

1. Much has been written since the late sixties on how black English should be regarded linguistically, socially, educationally, and personally. The subject is sometimes called bidialectalism or bilingualism. Review some aspect of this controversy as presented in newspapers and popular mag-

azines, and come to some conclusions of your own regarding the issues. You may find it helpful to consult the *Reader's Guide to Periodical Literature* in the reference section of your school library. Finally, write an argument based on your own views. Be sure to provide as much evidence as possible to support your conclusions.

2. The title of Rachel Jones's essay suggests a formula for other possible arguments. Using the "What's Wrong with _____" as a title, write an argumentative essay on any one of the following topics:

the sale of over-the-counter tranquilizers
using animals in medical experiments
diets
gun control
cheating
college sports
the English-only movement
state-run lotteries

BIG FAMILIES CAN BE HAPPY, TOO

Sara L. Smith

Sara L. Smith was busy raising her family in Manassas, Virginia when this column appeared in the January 14, 1985 issue of Newsweek. *She wrote the essay to dispel the commonly held myths about large families.*

Last week I dressed my children in their Sunday best and took them to a photographic studio. 1

"How many kids do we have here?" the photographer asked. 2 "One, two, three, four, five—wow!" She regarded me with a mixture of derision and disbelief. "I really feel *sorry* for you."

It wasn't the first time something like that had happened—or 3 the second. With the advent of the Pill and women's lib, large families are out and subject to ridicule. Society has stereotyped families with a lot of children: they belong to certain religious or ethnic groups, they're on welfare, and they aren't too bright.

My husband has also been mortified, and in front of a group 4 of coworkers. After congratulating him on the birth of our daughter, his supervisor asked, "Is this your first or second?"

"My fifth." 5

"You sure are a slow learner," the supervisor remarked. 6

Why doesn't it ever occur to anyone that my husband and I 7 might have *chosen* to have five children?

As I see it, the decrease in large families has gone hand in 8 hand with the weakening of the family in general. Children are now looked upon as liabilities. There have been other times, too, when they were not valued—usually when a society was deteriorating.

To those who claim that large families deplete natural re- 9 sources and stymie conservation efforts, I can only point to statistical fact. With about 5 percent of the world population, the United States uses 24.7 per cent of its energy. Life-styles, not people drain resources. One advantage of raising a big family

on a limited income is that children learn conservation first-hand. They know the hot-water supply is not unlimited. They know food is not to be wasted. Toys and clothing are recycled. Overpopulation? Our school principal was one person who   10
was happy to see me pregnant. "If it weren't for you, I'd be out of a job," he told me, only half jokingly. The baby boom is over, and the United States is in no danger of becoming the next India.

Sure, we take our $7,000 exemption, but contrary to conven-   11
tional wisdom, we are not a drain on the public treasury. We pay more than most in sales taxes, and one day, when our five children begin to work, they will help support those of the current generation who choose to remain childless.

"Oh," people say. "Parents with one or two children can give   12
them so many more benefits." What benefits? Each of my children does not have his or her own room, TV, and stereo. But I think there is such a thing as too much privacy and too many possessions. My children appreciate what they do have. Little things mean a lot. A trip to McDonald's (which costs us close to $25) is an *event*, an excursion that is enjoyed far more because we go twice a year instead of twice a week.

Caring: Then there is the claim that children raised in big   13
families are deprived of their parents' love and attention. It seems to me that my children get not one-fifth as much love as an only child, but five times as much! True, they have to learn at a tender age that the world doesn't revolve around them—a valuable lesson. But they also learn compassion and caring.

Back in the days when large families were desired for their   14
labor, at least children knew they were really needed. Today's child, overwhelmed with possessions and catered to endlessly by parents, is struggling with feelings of worthlessness. Even with labor-saving devices, big families are a lot of work. My children know they have to pitch in, and they know we appreciate their help. Maybe I don't have time to read to the three-year-old, but the eight-year-old does—to the benefit of them both.

My children have also developed an excellent sense of respon-   15
sibility, particularly since I can't possibly keep track of everyone's schoolbooks and projects. They feel responsible for each other, too. My husband and I hope that our emphasis on setting

a good example will hold during their teen-age years. My own feeling is that teen-agers from large, close-knit families have fewer difficulties dealing with peer pressure.

In fact, children from big families are under less pressure in   16
general. The give-and-take in a large family can help enhance a child's self-assurance and tolerance. No, we aren't "The Waltons," and big families have problems. *All* families have problems. There are times when the bills, dishes, chauffeuring, and laundry seem endless (I've had 13 solid years of diapers), and I wonder then if it's all worth it. Some days the bickering alone is enough to make me long for a vacation in the Bahamas—alone.

Fun: But then I remember how much the kids enjoyed the   17
ocean on our last trip to the beach and the fun we all had, even when it rained, and I realize no amount of glamour could replace the satisfaction of watching my children grow and develop.

Many people don't want to deal with the effort and expense   18
involved in rearing a lot of children. But just because large families aren't for everyone, we shouldn't conclude that they aren't for *anyone*. Our society has given us abundant freedom to choose our life-styles, and my husband and I are very happy with our choice. So the next time you see our large family, please laugh with us and not at us.

Questions for Study and Discussion

1. What is Smith's thesis? Where is it best stated? (Glossary: *Thesis*)

2. What are some of the ways Smith explains the decline in large families? Do you agree or disagree with her reasons? Explain.

3. Smith uses several quotes in her essay. What do these quotes have in common? What purpose do they serve in the context of her essay?

4. Smith asks a question in paragraph 7. Does she ever answer it? How would you answer it?

5. Smith has organized her essay as a rebuttal to each of several objections to having large families. What are the

objections she addresses? To which one does she devote
the most space? Why do you suppose she did this? Are
there any objections to large families that she has left
out?

6. What is Smith's purpose in writing this essay? (Glossary:
Purpose) Does she wish to persuade us to her point of
view? Is there something she wants us to do? Or does she
have another purpose altogether? What is her tone and
how effective is it for her purpose? Explain.

Vocabulary

Refer to your dictionary to define the following words as they
are used in this selection. Then use each word in a sentence of
your own.

derision (2)	excursion (12)
advent (3)	compassion (13)
mortified (4)	enhance (16)
liabilities (8)	bickering (17)

Suggested Writing Assignments

1. In her concluding paragraph Smith says "Many people
don't want to deal with the effort and expense involved in
rearing a lot of children." Is Smith guilty herself of stereotyping the "other side," by only allowing the possibility
of a kind of selfishness as a reason for not having a large
family? In a brief essay based on your own experience
discuss some other reasons that might discourage people
from having a large family.

2. Write an essay in which you defend a personal choice that
might be viewed as unwise in your particular social circle. For example, joining a fraternal organization, quitting
school, taking up smoking, becoming engaged, or living at
home. What kinds of evidence will you need to convince
an audience of your peers?

THE BURDEN OF BEARING ARMS

Adam Smith

*Adam Smith is the pen name for George Good-
man, Harvard graduate and Rhodes Scholar.
Smith earned his reputation as a writer on
business and financial issues for both* Time *and*
Fortune *magazines. His popular and topical
books* The Money Game *(1968),* Supermoney
(1972), and Paper Money *(1981) only enhanced his
fame as a financial analyst. In recent years,
Smith's column "Unconventional Wisdom" has
been a mainstay in the pages of* Esquire. *In the
following essay, one of his columns for* Esquire
*in 1986, Smith argues for stronger handgun
controls.*

One night last winter someone shot the prime minister of 1
Sweden. Olaf Palme and his wife were walking home from
a movie in Stockholm when the gunman killed him. The prime
minister had no security guards or secret-service men with
him.

I was struck the next day by points in two stories that ap- 2
peared in the same issue of the *New York Times*. The first, from
Stockholm, reported that this crime "would have been regarded
as highly unusual in Sweden even if the victim had not been the
prime minister." The reason, said Hans Wranghalt, head of the
Stockholm police's criminal-investigation division, is that there
are only twenty to twenty-five murders a year in Stockholm,
and only five or six of those involve handguns. No one could
recall a previous case in which someone had been shot on the
street in Stockholm. In Sweden your chances of walking around
to a ripe old age without being struck by a bullet are extremely
high.

Then—on a back page instead of page one—another point 3
from another policeman, Sergeant Mike Thomas of Houston. In

Houston, there may be five or six shootings a year by children, said Sergeant Thomas, but 1986 was unusual—in a two-month period, twelve children had shot each other, and six of those had died. Guns in Houston are a common household item.

In two months, more *children* had murdered each other in a   4
Texas city with guns than adults did in the course of a year in Stockholm. "In most cases," said Sergeant Thomas, "it's a parent's gun or a friend's gun." Texas officials said it was impossible to estimate the number of guns in Houston because gun sales are recorded only by the dealers who sell the firearms.

The contrast among nations in annual gun deaths is quite   5
striking.

It looks like this: 6

Great Britain—4

Canada—6

Japan—92

West Germany—17

United States—9,800

If death by gunfire were a disease, we would have a national   7
commission working on its eradication. Giant drug companies would be racing to see which could first come up with the cure. Visions of Nobel Prizes would dance in the heads of professors in their labs late at night. Dinners and benefits would be given by leading socialites, with proceeds going to research for the noble cause. Brave little victims—the ones that survived— would appear with the President, and their appearances would become posters.

Gunfire is not a disease, so we roll right along, ten thousand   8
or so dead a year, maybe a couple of hundred thousand injured.

I have written before about handguns and their use, because   9
I am always struck by the casualness with which we take death by gunfire—statistically, that is. "Right to life" inspires violent emotions, but it does not refer to escaping death by gunfire. Yet, as a country, we haven't set the goal of getting the numbers down to single digits in the gunfire death column: Canada—6; England—4.

Anyone who writes on this subject can expect an immediate   10
response from the National Rifle Association. The NRA is the

organization that runs the sleek magazine ads that wave red, white, and blue. It must have a computer that scans for the words "gun control," and then generates ten thousand letters whenever those words appear together.

After a previous column, I was on a radio talk show. Some 11 callers said: "Nobody is going to take my gun away, especially not you, you commie-faggot-wimp." Then I said, "No one is talking about *long* guns. Anyone can have as many shotguns as they like, rifles too. And we are not going to have any huge magnet that sweeps across the sky and picks up the sixty million or so handguns we already have stashed." I even ingratiated myself a bit with the callers. I said, "When I was in the Army Special Forces, we had to take apart and put back together all kinds of guns—Kalashnikovs and Uzis and Mausers and exotica you don't even know about." The callers got interested. Special Forces? Uzis? Mausers? Wow! Then how can *you—they* must have gotten to you. *They* got to you, didn't they? (For the record, I should say that the Army course we had was brief, and when we sat at the tables taking those weapons apart, I always seemed to have a couple of parts left over when I had put them back together, and needed help from the instructors.)

But we do—I said to the callers—have to start to work on this 12 problem of violent death and injury by gunfire. What is surprising—if you haven't followed the annual fracas on gun-control legislation—is that the International Association of Chiefs of Police and other national police organizations have been on the opposite side from the NRA. After reading dozens of documents, I surmised that what most annoyed the police chiefs was the resistance of the gun lobby to banning armor-piercing ammunition. This is one point that really did confuse me. Why would anyone *need* armor-piercing ammunition? Deer and rabbits do not wear armor. Even casual burglars do not wear armor. Armor—bulletproof vests—is worn by one main target: police. Richard Boyd, national president of the Fraternal Order of Police, wrote as follows: "Every day, officers risk their lives protecting citizens from criminal attack, and yet the NRA refuses to support these officers by working to ban the sale of such [armor-piercing] bullets. In fact, NRA lobbyists have blocked the bill for nearly four years. As officers . . . we want armor-piercing bullets banned. We need the continued prohibition on interstate handgun sales. We want a national waiting period and background check for handgun purchases."

Why does the NRA support virtually all forms of handgun sales and ammunition? Robert Torricelli, a New Jersey congressman and a supporter of handgun legislation, said this: "There is more money being made in selling guns than there is in a good cause to prevent their abuse. . . . For all the virtues of our system of government, it often responds more to those who are loudest or the best financed, rather than to those who represent the greatest numbers." The lobbying budget of the NRA is said to be $60 million a year. 13

If one looked only to Congress as a reflection of the American people, it would seem that we were totally a nation of gun lovers: good old boys with the gun racks in our pickup trucks, determined homeowners with handguns in our night tables, ready to wake up and waste the masked intruder. So it is a bit surprising to find that in 1985 the Gallup Poll found that a large majority of Americans want *tougher* handgun controls. Why do we not see this in Congress? 14

The NRA, for its part, says that honest sportsmen are being punished—are even having their constitutional rights abridged. Criminals aren't deterred by bureaucratic rules—they steal most of their guns anyway. The NRA papers say that it is the criminal who should be punished, not the gun dealer or the gun owner. Crime with a gun, no probation, says the NRA. 15

Mandatory sentencing would be a help, said Sarah Brady, but it addresses only part of the problem. Sarah Brady is the wife of James Brady, who is the press secretary to the President. While James Brady still holds that title, he has not really functioned as the press secretary since March 30, 1981, the day he was shot in the head by John Hinckley, who also shot President Reagan in the chest. Brady is still undergoing intensive rehabilitation, his left arm is paralyzed, he has difficulty moving around, and he is able to go to his office only once a week. 16

In her testimony before a House committee considering gun-control legislation, Sarah Brady said: "I ask why it is possible for the John Hinckleys of this world to walk into a store, buy a handgun, and go out and shoot people. . . . He [Hinckley] walked into a Dallas pawnshop, purchased a cheap Saturday night special—no questions asked, no waiting period to see if 17 he had a criminal or mental-illness record—and a few minutes later was on his way, ready to shoot the President of the United States because he thought it would make a popular actress, Jodie Foster, fall in love with him.

"I am a Republican and a conservative. Many people whose 18 political views are similar to mine oppose what they call gun control. As they define it, so do I. . . . What I am for is finding ways to keep handguns out of the wrong hands—licensing handgun owners so that law-enforcement agencies can trace the owner as easily as they can the owner of an automobile."

Sarah Brady is the daughter of an FBI agent and grew up 19 being familiar with guns. She says that an incident in Centralia, Illinois—her husband's hometown—made her active in the gun-control movement. "An old friend invited my son Scott and me to go for a ride in his pickup truck. [Scott was six.] We got in. Scott picked up what looked like a toy pistol and pointed it toward himself. My father taught us from an early age to have a very healthy respect for guns, so I said, 'Scott, don't ever point a gun at anyone, even if it's only a toy.' Then, to my horror, I realized it was no toy. It turned out to be a fully loaded Saturday night special that our friend kept on the seat of his truck for what he called 'safety' reasons."

"I wondered how many other careless adults left handguns 20 lying around for children to pick up. My mind went back to the day Jim was shot, and then further back to the day one of my best friends was murdered—with a handgun—by her enraged boyfriend."

Sarah Brady has become one of the directors of Handgun 21 Control Inc., a lobbying group that is gaining in numbers but still has nothing like the three million members of the NRA. Sarah Brady's group can reel off one horrifying statistic after another:

> Someone is injured by a handgun every two and a half minutes.
> Each year more than two hundred thousand handguns are stolen.
> Each year we spend $500 million treating people who have been shot by handguns.
> Every day, on the average, one child under fourteen is killed with a handgun.

"Women are frequently accused of being emotional," Sarah   22
Brady told me. "But I've never seen greater emotionalism than
the NRA produces. Any restriction proposed at all, and the NRA
sends 'Legislative Alerts' to its members, and tells them to flood
Congress with mail. Not just about armor-piercing bullets and
submachine guns—even *silencers.* Why would a sportsman—or
a homeowner—need a silencer? The NRA says, 'Well, maybe
collectors would like to have silencers.' It's always 'collectors.'"

"Seventy percent of the American people want stronger hand-   23
gun controls, but each congressman is wary because the NRA
can throw all its weight into a campaign. Congressmen are
afraid of the power of these single-issue groups."

I asked Sarah Brady what the most common reaction she got   24
on talk shows was. "The callers say, 'Why do you hate us gun
lovers?'" she said. "'We'll defend you when the time comes.
Why don't you go after the communists?' But I think younger
people are realizing the dangers of gun stores selling Saturday
night specials to anyone off the street. Blue-collar workers will
be some of the hardest to convince—they do like to hang on to
that macho image. It's going to take a long time, but eventually
we will have a grass-roots turn against the random sale of guns."

Many Americans like the adrenaline rush that comes with   25
swift retribution, so Charles Bronson is a hero not only in
Death Wish I but *II* and *III,* and there are posters of Ronald
Reagan as Rambo. Yet Americans do want tougher handgun
legislation. Times are good, and much of the country is enjoying itself. We have a lull in inflation, and the stock market has
made those in it feel rich. But the pleasures of wealth require
peaceful and stable communities. You may be the richest man
in Beirut, but if you can't walk out of your house and down to
the corner in safety, you are poorer than the poorest citizen in
Sweden.

Questions for Study and Discussion

1. Where does Smith stand on guns? Gun control? Gun ac-
   cessories? The N.R.A.?

2. Smith relies on statistics to support his argument. What kinds of numbers does he cite, and in what way are they effective? (Glossary: *Evidence*)
3. What do the personal experiences of Sarah Brady add to Smith's argument? Explain.
4. According to Smith, why do the police object to certain N.R.A. principles? Do their objections seem reasonable? Why or why not?
5. What limits on guns, if any, does Smith propose?
6. Who are the members of Smith's audience, and what does he want from them? How do you know?

Vocabulary

Refer to your dictionary to define the following words as they are used in this selection. Then use each word in a sentence of your own.

eradication (7)	retribution (25)
ingratiated (11)	inflation (25)
bureaucratic (15)	

Suggested Writing Assignments

1. Write an essay in which you outline your own gun control policy. What kind of restrictions would you suggest, and why do you think these restrictions would be important? Use examples from the news or experiences you have heard about to support your plan.
2. Write an essay in which you discuss why individuals such as Tipper Gore and members of the N.R.A. are willing to take a stand on controversial issues even at the risk of being perceived as radical. What do you think motivates them? In what ways are extreme positions useful or harmful in a free society?

ABORTION IS TOO COMPLEX TO FEEL ALL ONE WAY ABOUT

Anna Quindlen

Columnist Anna Quindlen was born in 1952, and after graduating from Barnard College, she began her newspaper career at the New York Post. *Later she moved to the* New York Times *where she wrote the column "About New York," then was made deputy metropolitan editor at the age of thirty-one. Quindlen has contributed to the "Hers" column and for several years wrote the column "Life in the Thirties," in which she reflected on marriage, motherhood, secret desires and self-doubt, drawing on her own family for inspiration. The best of these columns were selected for her book* Living Out Loud *(1988). Currently Quindlen writes the "Public and Private" column for the* Times *in which she comments on global topics from a personal point of view. In the following essay, which first ran in the* Times *as a "Life in the Thirties" column, Quindlen shares her struggle to come to some definite position on the issue of abortion.*

1   It was always the look on their faces that told me first. I was the freshman dormitory counselor and they were the freshmen at a women's college where everyone was smart. One of them could come into my room, a golden girl, a valedictorian, an 800 verbal score on the SAT's, and her eyes would be empty, seeing only a busted future, the devastation of her life as she knew it. She had failed biology, messed up the math; she was pregnant.

2   That was when I became pro-choice.

3   It was the look in his eyes that I will always remember, too. They were as black as the bottom of a well, and in them for a

few minutes I thought I saw myself the way I had always wished to be—clear, simple, elemental, at peace. My child looked at me and I looked back at him in the delivery room, and I realized that out of a sea of infinite possibilities it had come down to this: a specific person born on the hottest day of the year, conceived on a Christmas Eve, made by his father and me miraculously from scratch.

Once I believed that there was a little blob of formless protoplasm in there and a gynecologist went after it with a surgical instrument, and that was that. Then I got pregnant myself—eagerly, intentionally, by the right man, at the right time—and I began to doubt. My abdomen still flat, my stomach roiling with morning sickness, I felt not that I had protoplasm inside but instead a complete human being in miniature to whom I could talk, sing, make promises. Neither of these views was accurate; instead, I think, the reality is something in the middle, And there is where I find myself now, in the middle, hating the idea of abortions, hating the idea of having them outlawed. 4

For I know it is the right thing in some times and places. I remember sitting in a shabby clinic far uptown with one of those freshman, only three months after the Supreme Court had made what we were doing possible, and watching with wonder as the lovely first love she had had with a nice boy unraveled over the space of an hour as they waited for her to be called, degenerated into sniping and silences. I remember a year or two later seeing them pass on campus and not even acknowledge one another because their conjoining had caused them so much pain, and I shuddered to think of them married, with a small psyche in their unready and unwilling hands. 5

I've met 14-year-olds who were pregnant and said they could not have abortions because of their religion, and I see in their eyes the shadows of 22-year-olds I've talked to who lost their kids to foster care because they hit them or used drugs or simply had no money for food and shelter. I read not long ago about a teenager who said she meant to have an abortion but she spent the money on clothes instead; now she has a baby who turns out to be a lot more trouble than a toy. The people who hand out those execrable little pictures of dismembered fetuses at abortion clinics seem to forget the extraordinary pain chil- 6 dren may endure after they are born when they are unwanted, even hated or simply tolerated.

I believe that in a contest between the living and the almost living, the latter must, if necessary, give way to the will of the former. That is what the fetus is to me, the almost living. Yet these questions began to plague me—and, I've discovered, a good many other women—after I became pregnant. But they became even more acute after I had my second child, mainly because he is so different from his brother. On two random nights 18 months apart the same two people managed to conceive, and on one occasion the tumult within turned itself into a curly-haired brunet with merry black eyes who walked and talked late and loved the whole world, and on another it became a blond with hazel Asian eyes and a pug nose who tried to conquer the world almost as soon as he entered it.

If we were to have an abortion next time for some reason or another, which infinite possibility becomes, not a reality, but a nullity? The girl with the blue eyes? The improbable redhead? The natural athlete? The thinker? My husband, ever at the heart of the matter, put it another way. Knowing that he is finding two children somewhat more overwhelming than he expected, I asked if he would want me to have an abortion if I accidentally became pregnant again right away. "And waste a perfectly good human being?" he said.

Coming to this quandary has been difficult for me. In fact, I believe the issue of abortion is difficult for all thoughtful people. I don't know anyone who has had an abortion who has not been haunted by it. If there is one thing I find intolerable about most of the so-called right-to-lifers, it is that they try to portray abortion rights as something that feminists thought up on a slow Saturday over a light lunch. That is nonsense. I also know that some people who support abortion rights are most comfortable with a monolithic position because it seems the strongest front against the smug and sometimes violent opposition.

But I don't feel all one way about abortion anymore, and I don't think it serves a just cause to pretend that many of us do. For years I believed that a woman's right to choose was absolute, but now I wonder. Do I, with a stable home and marriage and sufficient stamina and money, have the right to choose abortion because a pregnancy is inconvenient right now? Legally I do have that right; legally I want always to have that right. It is the morality of exercising it under those circumstances that makes me wonder.

Technology has foiled us. The second trimester has become a 11
time of resurrection; a fetus at six months can be one woman's late abortion, another's premature, viable child. Photographers now have film of embryos the size of a grape, oddly human, flexing their fingers, sucking their thumbs. Women have amniocentesis to find out whether they are carrying a child with birth defects that they may choose to abort. Before the procedure, they must have a sonogram, one of those fuzzy black-and-white photos like a love song heard through static on the radio, which shows someone is in there.

I have taped on my VCR a public-television program in which 12
somehow, inexplicably, a film is shown of a fetus in utero scratching its face, seemingly putting up a tiny hand to shield itself from the camera's eye. It would make a potent weapon in the arsenal of the antiabortionists. I grow sentimental about it as it floats in the salt water, part fish, part human being. It is almost living, but not quite. It has almost turned my heart around, but not quite turned my head.

Questions for Study and Discussion

1. Exactly what is the "ambiguity" of the abortion issue as far as Quindlen is concerned?

2. What kind of language does Quindlen use to describe the different participants in the abortion debate? (Glossary: *Diction*) Citing examples of her diction from the essay, discuss Quindlen's attitudes toward the members of the different groups she names. Who are the "thoughtful" people Quindlen describes? Does she count herself among them? How do you know?

3. Although Quindlen faces the "quandary" of the abortion issue, she has in fact taken a position. What is it? Does she offer any reasons for taking this position? Explain.

4. Cite examples of Quindlen's use of rational and emotional appeals. What is characteristic of each kind of appeal?

Which did you find more convincing? In what ways are her appeals appropriate or inappropriate to her subject? Explain.

5. Quindlen wrote this essay for a liberal, educated, mostly middle-class audience. (Glossary: *Audience*) What risks did she take in writing such an article for this audience? Why do you suppose she was willing to take such risks? What does she want her readers to do?

Vocabulary

Refer to your dictionary to define the following words as they are used in this selection. Then use each word in a sentence of your own.

valedictorian (1)	tumult (7)
elemental (3)	nullity (8)
protoplasm (4)	quandary (9)
unraveled (5)	monolithic (9)
sniping (5)	stamina (10)
conjoining (5)	amniocentesis (11)
execrable (6)	

Suggested Writing Assignments

1. The above column generated more letters to the editor than any other Anna Quindlen has written. In a brief essay, write a letter of your own in which you express your reaction to Quindlen's essay. What kinds of appeals will you use to support your position? Can you make a good argument for your position using only rational or only emotional appeals?

2. Participants on both sides of the abortion debate have objected to the labels the other side uses to describe themselves. They say the press has an obligation not to use terms a group designates for itself, especially if that term makes assumptions about the thinking or attitude of the other side. What is your reaction to the terms "Pro-Life" and "Pro-Choice"? What do these terms imply about the

group so labelling itself, and what do they imply about the opposition? Can you think of other terms to describe the two major positions on legalized abortion that are less loaded? Write an essay in which you argue for or against the use of the labels "Pro-Life" and "Pro-Choice."

ON AIDS AND MORAL DUTY

Willard Gaylin

Born in Cleveland in 1925, Willard Gaylin is professor of clinical psychiatry at Columbia University, and president of the Institute of Society, Ethics, and Life Sciences and the Hastings Center, a New York area public-policy organization. As these last two positions suggest, he is deeply concerned with moral issues in human behavior; a concern reflected in his books In Service of Their Country: War Resistors in Prison *(1970),* Partial Justice: A Study of Bias in Sentencing *(1974), and* Feelings: Our Vital Signs *(1979). In the following essay, which first appeared in the* New York Times *in 1986, Gaylin argues that the horrors of AIDS does not exempt its victims from a responsibility to protect the health of others.*

Potential AIDS victims who refuse to be tested for the dis-   1
ease and then defend their right to remain ignorant about whether they carry the virus are entitled to that right. But ignorance cannot be used to rationalize irresponsibility. Nowhere in their argument is there concern about how such ignorance might endanger public health by exposing others to the virus.

All disease is an outrage, and disease that affects the young   2
and healthy seems particularly outrageous. When a disease selectively attacks the socially disadvantaged, such as homosexuals and drug abusers, it seems an injustice beyond rationalization. Such is the case with acquired immune deficiency syndrome.

Decent people are offended by this unfairness and in the   3
name of benevolence have been driven to do morally irresponsible things such as denying the unpleasant facts of the disease, out of compassion for the victims. We cannot fudge the facts to

440

comfort the afflicted when such obfuscation compounds the tragedy.

Some crucial facts: AIDS is a communicable disease. The percentage of those infected with the AIDS virus who will eventually contract the disease is unknown, but that percentage rises with each new estimate. The disease so far has been 100 percent fatal. The latency period between the time the virus is acquired and the disease develops is also unknown.   4

We now have tests for the presence of the virus that are as efficient and reliable as almost any diagnostic test in medicine. An individual who tests positive can be presumed with near-certainty to carry the virus, whether he has the disease or not.   5

To state that the test for AIDS is "ambiguous," as a clergyman recently said in public, is a misstatement and an immoral act. To state that the test does not directly indicate the presence of the virus is a half truth that misleads and an immoral act. The test correlates so consistently with the presence of the virus in bacteria cultures as to be considered 100 percent certain by experts.   6

Everyone who tests positive must understand that he is a potential vector for the AIDS virus and has a moral duty and responsibility to protect others from contamination. We need not force everyone in high-risk populations to take the test. There is no treatment for the disease. Therefore, to insist on testing serves no therapeutic purpose.   7

Certainly there are those who would prefer ambiguity to certitude. However, a person who is at risk and refuses to have himself tested must behave as though he had been tested and found positive. To do otherwise is cowardice compounding hypocrisy with wrongdoing.   8

Surely an individual has a right to spare himself the agony of knowledge if he prefers wishful thinking to certitude. He must not use his desire for hope as an excuse for denial.   9

We have a duty to protect the innocent and the unborn. Voluntary premarital testing for AIDS is a protection for both partners and for the uncontaminated and unborn children. We know that AIDS is transmissible from male to female, from female to male, from parent to conceived child. We are dealing not just with the protection of the innocent but with an essential step to contain the spread of an epidemic as tragic and   10 as horrible as any that has befallen modern man. We must do everything in our power to keep this still untreatable disease from becoming pandemic.

It may seem unfair to burden the tragic victims with concern for the welfare of others. But moral responsibility is not a luxury of the fortunate, and evil actions perpetrated in despair cannot be condoned out of pity. It is morally wrong for a healthy individual who tests positive for AIDS to be involved with anyone except under the strictest precautions now defined as safe sex.   11

It is morally wrong for someone in a high risk population who refuses to test himself to do other than to assume that he tests positively. It is morally wrong for those who, out of sympathy for the heartbreaking victims of this epidemic, act as though well-wishing and platitudes about the ambiguities of the disease are necessary in order to comfort the victims while they contribute to enlarging the number of those victims. Moral responsibility is the burden of the sick as well as the healthy.   12

Questions for Study and Discussion

1. What is the distinction Gaylin makes in his opening paragraph? What tone does his opening paragraph set for his argument? (Glossary: *Tone*) How well does it serve as an opening for the essay as a whole? (Glossary: *Beginnings and Endings*)

2. What is Gaylin's thesis? (Glossary: *Thesis*) How many times is it stated in the course of his essay? Why do you suppose Gaylin felt obliged to restate his thesis several times? What is the effect on the reader of this repetition?

3. What does Gaylin mean when he says in paragraph 6 that it is an "immoral act" to refer to the AIDS test as "ambiguous"?

4. Gaylin identifies at least three groups of potential AIDS victims in his essay. Identify these different groups and discuss what Gaylin expects from each of them. What kinds of appeals does he make to the members of each group? How effective are his appeals?

5. Given Gaylin's concern over the dangers of the AIDS virus, why doesn't he call for mandatory testing of those in high-risk populations?

6. How would you describe Gaylin's attitude toward the victims of AIDS? (Glossary: *Attitude*) Cite examples of his diction to support your answer. (Glossary: *Diction*)

Vocabulary

Refer to your dictionary to define the following words as they are used in this selection. Then use each word in a sentence of your own.

rationalize (1)	presumed (5)
benevolence (3)	ambiguous (6)
fudge (3)	certitude (8)
obfuscation (3)	pandemic (10)
latency (4)	

Suggested Writing Assignments

1. Write an essay in which you argue the "moral responsibility" attached to another controversial social issue such as sex education in the schools, surrogate mothering, genetic engineering, or single-parent adoption.

2. Argue either for or against Gaylin's assertion that "Moral responsibility is the burden of the sick as well as the healthy."

GLOSSARY OF USEFUL TERMS

Abstract See *Concrete/Abstract.*

Allusion An allusion is a passing reference to a familiar person, place, or thing often drawn from history, the Bible, mythology, or literature. An allusion is an economical way for a writer to capture the essence of an idea, atmosphere, emotion, or historical era, as in "The scandal was his Watergate" or "He saw himself as a modern Job" or "The campaign ended not with a bang but a whimper." An allusion should be familiar to the reader; if it is not, it will add nothing to the meaning.

Analogy Analogy is a special form of comparison in which the writer explains something unfamiliar by comparing it to something familiar: "A transmission line is simply a pipeline for electricity. In the case of a water pipeline, more water will flow through the pipe as water pressure increases. The same is true of electricity in a transmission line."

Anecdote An anecdote is a short narrative about an amusing or interesting event. Writers often use anecdotes to begin essays as well as to illustrate certain points.

Argumentation Argumentation is one of the four basic types of prose. (Narration, description, and exposition are the other three.) To argue is to attempt to persuade a reader to agree with a point of view, to make a given decision, or to pursue a particular course of action. There are two basic types of argumentation: logical and persuasive. See the introduction to Chapter 18 (pp. 401–3) for a detailed discussion of argumentation.

Attitude A writer's attitude reflects his or her opinion of a subject. The writer can think very positively or very negatively about a subject, or somewhere in between. See also *Tone.*

Audience An audience is the intended readership for a piece of writing. For example, the readers of a national weekly news magazine come from all walks of life and have diverse interests, opinions, and educational backgrounds. In contrast, the readership for an organic chemistry journal is made up of people whose interests and education are quite similar. The essays in *Models for Writers* are intended for general readers, intelligent people who may lack specific information about the subject being discussed.

445

Beginnings and Endings   A beginning is that sentence, group of sentences, or section that introduces an essay. Good beginnings usually identify the thesis or controlling idea, attempt to interest readers, and establish a tone.

An ending is that sentence or group of sentences that brings an essay to a close. Good endings are purposeful and well planned. They can be a summary, a concluding example, an anecdote, or a quotation. Endings satisfy readers when they are the natural outgrowths of the essays themselves and give the readers a sense of finality or completion. Good essays do not simply stop; they conclude. See the introduction to Chapter 4 (pp. 70–73) for a detailed discussion of *Beginnings and Endings.*

Cause and Effect   Cause and effect analysis is a type of exposition that explains the reasons for an occurrence or the consequences of an action. See the introduction to Chapter 17 (pp. 377–78) for a detailed discussion of cause and effect. See also *Exposition.*

Classification   See *Division and Classification.*

Cliché   A cliché is an expression that has become ineffective through overuse. Expressions such as *quick as a flash, jump for joy,* and *slow as molasses* are clichés. Writers normally avoid such trite expressions and seek instead to express themselves in fresh and forceful language. See also *Diction.*

Coherence   Coherence is a quality of good writing that results when all sentences, paragraphs, and longer divisions of an essay are naturally connected. Coherent writing is achieved through (1) a logical sequence of ideas (arranged in chronological order, spatial order, order of importance, or some other appropriate order), (2) the purposeful repetition of key words and ideas, (3) a pace suitable for your topic and your reader, and (4) the use of transitional words and expressions. Coherence should not be confused with unity. (See *Unity.*) See also *Transitions.*

Colloquial Expressions   A colloquial expression is characteristic of or appropriate to spoken language or to writing that seeks its effect. Colloquial expressions are informal, as *chem, gym, come up with, be at loose ends, won't,* and *photo* illustrate. See also *Diction.* Thus, colloquial expressions are acceptable in formal writing only if they are used purposefully.

Comparison and Contrast Comparison and contrast is a type of exposition in which the writer points out the similarities and differences between two or more subjects in the same class or category. The function of any comparison and contrast is to clarify—to reach some conclusion about the items being compared and contrasted. See the introduction to Chapter 16 (pp. 346–49) for a detailed discussion of comparison and contrast. See also *Exposition.*

Conclusions See *Beginnings and Endings.*

Concrete/Abstract A concrete word names a specific object, person, place, or action that can be directly perceived by the senses: *car, bread, building, book, John F. Kennedy, Chicago,* or *hiking.* An abstract word, in contrast, refers to general qualities, conditions, ideas, actions, or relationships which cannot be directly perceived by the senses: *bravery, dedication, excellence, anxiety, stress, thinking,* or *hatred.* See also the introduction to Chapter 8 (pp. 165–70).

Connotation/Denotation Both connotation and denotation refer to the meanings of words. Denotation is the dictionary meaning of a word, the literal meaning. Connotation, on the other hand, is the implied or suggested meaning of a word. For example, the denotation of *lamb* is "a young sheep." The connotations of *lamb* are numerous: *gentle, docile, weak, peaceful, blessed, sacrificial, blood, spring, frisky, pure, innocent,* and so on. See also the introduction to Chapter 8 (pp. 165–70).

Controlling Idea See *Thesis.*

Coordination Coordination is the joining of grammatical constructions of the same rank (e.g., words, phrases, clauses) to indicate that they are of equal importance. For example, *They ate hotdogs,* and *we ate hamburgers.* See the introduction to Chapter 7 (pp. 140–44). See also *Subordination.*

Deduction Deduction is the process of reasoning from stated premises to a conclusion that follows necessarily. This form of reasoning moves from the general to the specific. See the introduction to Chapter 18 (pp. 401–3) for a discussion of deductive reasoning and its relation to argumentation. See also *Syllogism.*

Definition Definition is one of the types of exposition. Definition is a statement of the meaning of a word. A definition may be either brief or extended, part of an essay or an entire essay itself. See the introduction to Chapter 14 (pp. 307–8) for a detailed discussion of definition. See also *Exposition.*

Denotation See *Connotation/Denotation.*

Description Description is one of the four basic types of prose. (Narration, exposition, and argumentation are the other three.) Description tells how a person, place, or thing is perceived by the five senses. See the introduction to Chapter 12 (pp. 261–62) for a detailed discussion of description.

Dialogue Conversation of two or more people as represented in writing. Dialogue is what people say directly to one another.

Diction Diction refers to a writer's choice and use of words. Good diction is precise and appropriate—the words mean exactly what the writer intends, and the words are well suited to the writer's subject, intended audience, and purpose in writing. The word-conscious writer knows that there are differences among *aged, old,* and *elderly; blue, navy,* and *azure;* and *disturbed, angry,* and *irritated.* Furthermore, this writer knows in which situation to use each word. See the introduction to Chapter 8 (pp. 165–70) for a detailed discussion of diction. See also *Cliché, Colloquial Expressions, Connotation/Denotation, Jargon, Slang.*

Division and Classification. Division and classification is one of the types of exposition. When dividing and classifying, the writer first establishes categories and then arranges or sorts people, places, or things into these categories according to their different characteristics, thus making them more manageable for the writer and more understandable and meaningful for the reader. See the introduction to Chapter 15 (pp. 323–24) for a detailed discussion of division and classification. See also *Exposition.*

Dominant Impression A dominant impression is the single mood, atmosphere, or quality a writer emphasizes in a piece of descriptive writing. The dominant impression is created through the careful selection of details and is, of course, influenced by the writer's subject, audience, and purpose. See also the introduction to Chapter 12 (pp. 261–62).

Emphasis Emphasis is the placement of important ideas and words within sentences and longer units of writing so that they have the greatest impact. In general, what comes at the end has the most impact, and at the beginning nearly as much; what comes in the middle gets the least emphasis.

Endings See *Beginnings and Endings.*

Evaluation An evaluation of a piece of writing is an assessment of its effectiveness or merit. In evaluating a piece of writing, one should ask the following questions: What is the writer's purpose? Is it a worthwhile purpose? Does the writer achieve the purpose? Is the writer's information sufficient and accurate? What are the strengths of the essay? What are its weaknesses? Depending on the type of writing and the purpose, more specific questions can also be asked. For example, with an argument one could ask: Does the writer follow the principles of logical thinking? Is the writer's evidence sufficient and convincing?

Evidence Evidence is the information on which a judgment or argument is based or by which proof or probability is established. Evidence usually takes the form of statistics, facts, names, examples or illustrations, and opinions of authorities.

Example An example illustrates a larger idea or represents something of which it is a part. An example is a basic means of developing or clarifying an idea. Furthermore, examples enable writers to show and not simply to tell readers what they mean. See also the introduction to Chapter 10 (pp. 213–15).

Exposition Exposition is one of the four basic types of prose. (Narration, description, and argumentation are the other three.) The purpose of exposition is to clarify, explain, and inform. The methods of exposition presented in *Models for Writers* are process analysis, definition, illustration, classification, comparison and contrast, and cause and effect. For a detailed discussion of these methods of exposition, see the appropriate section introductions.

Fallacy See *Logical Fallacies.*

Figures of Speech Figures of speech are brief, imaginative comparisons that highlight the similarities between things that are basically dissimilar. They make writing vivid, interesting, and memorable. The most common figures of speech are:

Simile: An explicit comparison introduced by *like* or *as.* "The fighter's hands were like stone."

Metaphor: An implied comparison that makes one thing the equivalent of another. "All the world's a stage."

Personification: A special kind of simile or metaphor in which human traits are assigned to an inanimate object. "The engine coughed and then stopped."

See the introduction to Chapter 9 (pp. 189–90) for a detailed discussion of figurative language.

Focus   Focus is the limitation that a writer gives his or her subject. The writer's task is to select a manageable topic given the constraints of time, space, and purpose. For example, within the general subject of sports, a writer could focus on government support of amateur athletes or narrow the focus further to government support of Olympic athletes.

General   See *Specific/General.*

Idiom   An idiom is a word or phrase that is used habitually with special meaning. The meaning of an idiom is not always readily apparent to nonnative speakers of that language. For example, *catch cold, hold a job, make up your mind,* and *give them a hand* are all idioms in English.

Illustration   Illustration is the use of examples to explain, elucidate, or corroborate. Writers rely heavily on illustration to make their ideas both clear and concrete. See the introduction to Chapter 10 (pp. 213–15) for a detailed discussion of illustration.

Induction   Induction is the process of reasoning to a conclusion about all members of a class through an examination of only a few members of the class. This form of reasoning moves from the particular to the general. See the introduction to Chapter 18 (pp. 401–3) for a discussion of inductive reasoning and its relation to argumentation.

Inductive Leap   An inductive leap is the point at which a writer of an argument, having presented sufficient evidence, moves to a generalization or conclusion. See also *Induction.*

Introductions   See *Beginnings and Endings.*

Irony   The use of words to suggest something different from their literal meaning. For example, when Jonathan Swift proposes in *A Modest Proposal* that Ireland's problems could be solved if the people of Ireland fattened their babies and sold them to the English landlords for food, he meant that almost any other solution would be preferable. A writer can use irony to establish a special relationship with the reader and to add an extra dimension or twist to the meaning. See also the introduction to Chapter 8 (pp. 165–70).

Jargon   Jargon, or technical language, is the special vocabulary of a trade, profession, or group. Doctors, construction workers, lawyers, and teachers, for example, all have a specialized vocabulary that they use "on the job." See also *Diction.*

Logical Fallacies   A logical fallacy is an error in reasoning that renders an argument invalid. See the introduction to Chapter 18 (pp. 401–3) for a discussion of the more common logical fallacies.

Metaphor   See *Figures of Speech.*

Narration   One of the four basic types of prose. (Description, exposition, and argumentation are the other three.) To narrate is to tell a story, to tell what happened. While narration is most often used in fiction, it is also important in expository writing, either by itself or in conjunction with other types of prose. See the introduction to Chapter 11 (pp. 235–37) for a detailed discussion of narration.

Opinion   An opinion is a belief or conclusion, which may or may not be substantiated by positive knowledge or proof. (If not substantiated, an opinion is a prejudice.) Even when based on evidence and sound reasoning, an opinion is personal and can be changed, and is therefore less persuasive than facts and arguments.

Organization   Organization is the pattern of order that the writer imposes on his or her material. Some often used patterns of organization include time order, space order, and order of importance. See the introduction to Chapter 3 (pp. 56–57) for a more detailed discussion of organization.

Paradox   A paradox is a seemingly contradictory statement that is nonetheless true. For example, "We little know what we have until we lose it" is a paradoxical statement.

Paragraph   The paragraph, the single most important unit of thought in an essay, is a series of closely related sentences. These sentences adequately develop the central or controlling idea of the paragraph. This central or controlling idea, usually stated in a topic sentence, is necessarily related to the purpose of the whole composition. A well-written paragraph has several distinguishing characteristics: a clearly stated or implied topic sentence, adequate development, unity, coherence, and an appropriate organizational strategy. See the introduction to Chapter 5 (pp. 97–99) for a detailed discussion of paragraphs.

Parallelism　Parallel structure is the repetition of word order or grammatical form either within a single sentence or in several sentences that develop the same central idea. As a rhetorical device, parallelism can aid coherence and add emphasis. Franklin Roosevelt's statement, "I see one third of the nation ill-housed, ill-clad, and ill-nourished," illustrates effective parallelism.

Personification　See *Figures of Speech.*

Point of View　Point of view refers to the grammatical person in an essay. For example, first-person point of view uses the pronoun *I* and is commonly found in autobiography and the personal essay; third-person point of view uses the pronouns *he, she,* or *it* and is commonly found in objective writing. See the introduction to Chapter 11 (pp. 235–37) for a discussion of point of view in narration.

Process Analysis　Process analysis is a type of expostion. Process analysis answers the question *how* and explains how something works or gives step-by-step directions for doing something. See the introduction to Chapter 13 (pp. 283–84) for a detailed discussion of process analysis. See also *Exposition.*

Purpose　Purpose is what the writer wants to accomplish in a particular piece of writing. Purposeful writing seeks to *relate* (narration), to *describe* (description), to *explain* (process analysis, definition, classification, comparison and contrast, and cause and effect), or to *convince* (argumentation).

Rhetorical Question　A rhetorical question is asked for its rhetorical effect but requires no answer from the reader. "When will nuclear proliferation end?" is such a question. Writers use rhetorical questions to introduce topics they plan to discuss or to emphasize important points. See the general introduction (pp. 4–17) and the introduction to Chapter 4 (pp. 70–74).

Sentence　A sentence is a grammatical unit that expresses a complete thought. It consists of at least a subject (a noun) and a predicate (a verb). See the introduction to Chapter 7 (pp. 140–44) for a discussion of effective sentences.

Simile See *Figures of Speech.*

Slang Slang is the unconventional, very informal language of particular subgroups in our culture. Slang, such as *bummed, coke, split, rap, dude,* and *stoned,* is acceptable in formal writing only if it is used selectively for specific purposes.

Specific/General General words name groups or classes of objects, qualities, or actions. Specific words, on the other hand, name individual objects, qualities, or actions within a class or group. To some extent the terms *general* and *specific* are relative. For example, *clothing* is a class of things. *Shirt,* however, is more specific than *clothing* but more general than *T-shirt.* See also *Diction.*

Strategy A strategy is a means by which a writer achieves his or her purpose. Strategy includes the many rhetorical decisions that the writer makes about organization, paragraph structure, sentence structure, and diction. In terms of the whole essay, strategy refers to the principal rhetorical mode that a writer uses. If, for example, a writer wishes to show how to make chocolate chip cookies, the most effective strategy would be process analysis. If it is the writer's purpose to show why sales of American cars have declined in recent years, the most effective strategy would be cause and effect analysis.

Style Style is the individual manner in which a writer expresses his or her ideas. Style is created by the author's particular choice of words, construction of sentences, and arrangement of ideas.

Subordination Subordination is the use of grammatical constructions to make one part in a sentence dependent on rather than equal to another. For example, the italicized clause in the following sentence is subordinate: They all cheered *when I finished the race.* See the introduction to Chapter 7 (pp. 140–44). See also *Coordination.*

Supporting Evidence See *Evidence.*

Syllogism A syllogism is an argument that utilizes deductive reasoning and consists of a major premise, a minor premise, and a conclusion. For example,

> All trees that lose leaves are deciduous. (major premise)
> Maple trees lose their leaves. (minor premise)
> Therefore, maple trees are deciduous. (conclusion)

See also *Deduction.*

Symbol   A symbol is a person, place, or thing that represents something beyond itself. For example, the eagle is a symbol of the United States, and the maple leaf, a symbol of Canada.

Syntax   Syntax refers to the way in which words are arranged to form phrases, clauses, and sentences, as well as to the grammatical relationship among the words themselves.

Technical Language   See *Jargon.*

Thesis   A thesis is the main idea of an essay, also known as the controlling idea. A thesis may sometimes be implied rather than stated directly in a thesis statement. See the introduction to Chapter 1 (pp. 21–22) for a detailed discussion of thesis.

Title   A title is a word or phrase set off at the beginning of an essay to identify the subject, to state the main idea of the essay, or to attract the reader's attention. A title may be explicit or suggestive. A subtitle, when used, explains or restricts the meaning of the main title.

Tone   Tone is the manner in which a writer relates to an audience, the "tone of voice" used to address readers. Tone may be friendly, serious, distant, angry, cheerful, bitter, cynical, enthusiastic, morbid, resentful, warm, playful, and so forth. A particular tone results from a writer's diction, sentence structure, purpose, and attitude toward the subject. See the introduction to Chapter 8 (pp. 165–70) for several examples that display different tones.

Topic Sentence   The topic sentence states the central idea of a paragraph and thus limits the content of the paragraph. Although the topic sentence normally appears at the beginning of the paragraph, it may appear at any other point, particularly if the writer is trying to create a special effect. Not all paragraphs contain topic sentences. See also *Paragraph.*

Transitions   Transitions are words or phrases that link sentences, paragraphs, and larger units of a composition in order to achieve coherence. These devices include parallelism, pronoun references, conjunctions, and the repetition of key ideas, as well as the many conventional transitional expressions such as *moreover, on the other hand, in addition, in contrast,* and *therefore.* See the introduction to Chapter 6 (pp. 120–22) for a detailed discussion of transitions. See also *Coherence.*

Unity Unity is that quality of oneness in an essay that results when all the words, sentences, and paragraphs contribute to the thesis. The elements of a unified essay do not distract the reader. Instead, they all harmoniously support a single idea or purpose. See the introduction to Chapter 2 (pp. 38–39) for a detailed discussion of unity.

Verb Verbs can be classified as either strong verbs (*scream, pierce, gush, ravage,* and *amble*) or weak verbs (*be, has, get,* and *do*). Writers often prefer to use strong verbs in order to make writing more specific or more descriptive.

Voice Verbs can be classified as being in either the active or the passive voice. In the active voice the doer of the action is the subject. In the passive voice the receiver of the action is the grammatical subject:

Active: Glenda questioned all of the children.

Passive: All the children were questioned by Glenda.

Acknowledgments (continued from copyright page)

Page 75, "You Are How You Eat" by Enid Nemy. Copyright © 1987 by The New York Times Company. Reprinted by permission.

Page 79, "How to Take a Job Interview" by Kirby W. Stanat. Reprinted from *Job Hunting Secrets and Tactics* by Kirby W. Stanat with Patrick Reardon by permission of Westwind Press, a division of Raintree Publishers Limited. Text copyright © 1977, Kirby Stanat and Patrick Reardon.

Page 85, "Hugh Troy: Practical Joker" by Alfred Rosa and Paul Eschholz. From *The People's Almanac #2* by David Wallenchinsky and Irving Wallace. Copyright © 1978 by David Wallenchinsky and Irving Wallace. Reprinted by permission of William Morrow & Company.

Page 90, "Even You Can Get It" by Bruce Lambert. Copyright © 1989 by The New York Times Company. Reprinted by permission.

Page 100, "Simplicity" by William Zinsser. From *On Writing Well,* Fourth Edition. Copyright © 1976, 1980, 1985, 1988, 1990 by William Zinsser. Reprinted by permission of the author.

Page 107, "Old at Seventeen" by David Vecsey. Copyright © 1987 by The New York Times Company. Reprinted by permission.

Page 112, "Death and Justice" by Edward I. Koch. Reprinted by permission of *The New Republic.* Copyright © 1985, The New Republic, Inc.

Page 123, "Why I Want to Have a Family" by Lisa Brown. From *Newsweek.* Reprinted by permission.

Page 128, "How I Got Smart" by Steve Brody. Original title "Love, With Knowledge Aforethought." Copyright © 1986 by The New York Times Company. Reprinted by permission.

Page 135, "Facing Violence" by Michael T. Kaufman. Copyright © 1984 by The New York Times Company. Reprinted by permission.

Page 149, "Playing to Win" by Margaret A. Whitney. Copyright © 1988 by The New York Times Company. Reprinted by permission.

Page 154, "A Brother's Murder" by Brent Staples. Copyright © 1986 by The New York Times Company. Reprinted by permission.

Page 159, "Salvation" by Langston Hughes. From *The Big Sea* by Langston Hughes. Copyright © 1940 by Langston Hughes. Renewal copyright © 1968 by Arna Bontemps and George Houston Bass. Reprinted by permission of Hill and Wang, a division of Farrar, Straus & Giroux, Inc.

Page 171, "On Being 17, Bright, and Unable to Read" by David Raymond. Copyright © 1976 by The New York Times Company. Reprinted by permission.

Page 176, "Every 23 Minutes" by Linda Weltner. From *The Boston Globe.* Reprinted by permission of the author.

Page 181, "Biting the Bullets" by Gerald Nachman. From *Out on a Limb: Some Very Close Brushes with Life* by Gerald Nachman. Reprinted by permission of the author and the author's agents, Scott Meredith Literary Agency, Inc., 845 Third Avenue, New York, NY 10022.

Page 184, "The Middle-Class Black's Burden" by Leanita McClain. From *Newsweek.* Reprinted by permission.

Page 195, "Conversational Ballgames" by Nancy Sakamoto. From *Polite Fictions* by Nancy Sakamoto. Copyright © 1982 by Kin-Seido, Ltd.

Page 201, "The Barrio" by Robert Ramirez. Reprinted by permission of the author.

Page 207, "The Death of Benny Paret" by Norman Mailer. Reprinted by permission of the author and the author's agents, Scott Meredith Literary Agency, Inc., 845 Third Avenue, New York, NY 10022.

Page 216, "A Crime of Compassion" by Barbara Huttmann. From *Newsweek*. Reprinted by permission.

Page 221, "Darkness at Noon" by Harold Krents. Copyright © 1976 by The New York Times Company. Reprinted by permission.

Page 225, "What Makes a Leader?" by Michael Korda. Copyright © 1987 by Michael Korda. Reprinted by permission of the author.

Page 230, "Rambos of the Road" by Martin Gottfried. Copyright © 1986 by Martin Gottfried. Reprinted by permission of the author.

Page 238, "Shame" by Dick Gregory. From *Nigger: An Autobiography* by Dick Gregory. Copyright © 1964 by Dick Gregory Enterprises, Inc. Used by permission of the publisher, Dutton, an imprint of New American Library, a division of Penguin Books USA, Inc.

Page 243, "38 Who Saw Murder Didn't Call Police" by Martin Gansberg. Copyright © 1964 by The New York Times Company. Reprinted by permission.

Page 248, "The Dare" by Roger Hoffman. Copyright © 1986 by Roger Hoffman. Reprinted with permission of *The New York Times Magazine*.

Page 253, "Momma, the Dentist, and Me" by Maya Angelou. From *I Know Why the Caged Bird Sings* by Maya Angelou. Copyright © 1969 by Maya Angelou. Reprinted by permission of Random House, Inc.

Page 263, "Subway Station" by Gilbert Highet. From *Talents and Geniuses*, copyright © 1957 by Gilbert Highet. Reprinted by permission of Curtis Brown, Ltd.

Page 266, "The Sounds of the City" by James Tuite. Copyright © 1966 by The New York Times Company. Reprinted by permission.

Page 270, "Unforgettable Miss Bessie" by Carl T. Rowan. Reprinted with permission from the March 1985 *Reader's Digest*. Copyright © 1985 by The Reader's Digest Assn., Inc.

Page 276, "My Friend, Albert Einstein" by Banesh Hoffmann. Reprinted with permission from the January 1968 *Reader's Digest*. Copyright © 1967 by The Reader's Digest Assn., Inc.

Page 285, "How to Cram" by Jill Young Miller. Copyright © 1987. Reprinted by permission of *Campus Voice*, a publication of Whittle Communications L.P.

Page 292, "How to Survive a Hotel Fire" by R. H. Kauffman. Copyright © 1976 and 1981 by Jazerant Corporation, 31 Tallman Place, Nyack, NY 10960.

Page 298, "Why Leaves Turn Color in the Fall" by Diane Ackerman. Original title "Where Do Fall Colors Come From." From *A Natural History of the Senses* by Diane Ackerman. Copyright © 1990 by Diane Ackerman. Reprinted by permission of Random House, Inc.

Page 303, "Symbols of Humankind" by Don Lago. From *Science Digest* (March 1981).

Page 309, "A Jerk" by Sydney J. Harris. From "Strictly Personal" by Sydney J. Harris. Copyright © North American Syndicate, Inc. Reprinted by permission of King Features, a division of Hearst Corporation.

Page 312, "Ambition" by Perri Klass. Copyright © 1990 by Perri Klass. First published in *Self* magazine, June 1990. Reprinted by permission of the author.

Page 318, "The Meanings of a Word" by Gloria Naylor. Copyright © 1986 by Gloria Naylor. Reprinted by permission of Sterling Lord Literistic, Inc.

Page 325, "Children's Insults" by Peter Farb. From *Word Play: What Happens When People Talk* by Peter Farb. Copyright © 1973 by Peter Farb. Reprinted by permission of Alfred A. Knopf, Inc.

Page 328, "What's in Your Toothpaste?" by Paul Bodanis. From *The Secret House,* copyright © 1986 by Paul Bodanis. Reprinted by permission of Simon & Schuster, Inc.

Page 333, "The Ways of Meeting Oppression" by Martin Luther King, Jr. From *Stride Toward Freedom* by Martin Luther King, Jr. Copyright © 1958 by Martin Luther King, Jr., renewed 1986 by Coretta Scott King, Dexter King, Martin Luther King, III, Yolanda King and Bernice King. Reprinted by permission of HarperCollins Publishers.

Page 338, "Friends, Good Friends—and Such Good Friends" by Judith Viorst. Copyright © 1977 by Judith Viorst. Originally appeared in *Redbook.*

Page 350, "That Lean and Hungry Look" by Suzanne Britt. From *Newsweek.* Reprinted by permission of the author.

Page 355, "Grant and Lee: A Study in Contrasts" by Bruce Catton. Reprinted with permission. Copyright U.S. Capitol Historical Society, all rights reserved.

Page 361, "What Children Do for Their Parents" by Barney Cohen. Original title "My Son, My Teacher." Copyright © 1990 by *Parenting* magazine, a publication of The Time Inc. Magazine Company. Reprinted by permission.

Page 366, "Fable for Tomorrow" by Rachel Carson. From *Silent Spring* by Rachel Carson. Copyright © 1962 by Rachel L. Carson. Reprinted by permission of Houghton Mifflin Company.

Page 370, "Am I Blue?" by Alice Walker. From *Living by the Word,* copyright © 1986 by Alice Walker, reprinted by permission of Harcourt Brace Jovanovich, Inc.

Page 379, "Never Get Sick in July" by Marilyn Machlowitz. Reprinted by permission of the author.

Page 384, "Three Mile Island" by Barry Commoner. From *The Politics of Energy* by Barry Commoner. Copyright © 1975 by Barry Commoner. Reprinted by permission of Alfred A. Knopf, Inc. Portions of this book previously appeared in *The New Yorker.*

Page 389, "Why We Crave Horror Movies" by Stephen King. Copyright © by Stephen King, 1981, 1988. Reprinted by permission.

Page 394, "Legalize Drugs" by Ethan A. Nadelmann. Reprinted by permission of *The New Republic,* copyright © 1988, The New Republic, Inc.

Page 404, "Hate, Rape, and Rap" by Tipper Gore. Copyright © *The Washington Post.* Reprinted by permission.

Page 409, "Television Insults Men, Too" by Bernard Goldberg. Copyright © 1989 by The New York Times Company. Reprinted by permission.

Page 413, "As They Say, Drugs Kill" by Laura Rowley. From *Newsweek.* Reprinted by permission.

Page 418, "What's Wrong with Black English" by Rachel L. Jones. From *Newsweek.* Reprinted by permission of the author.

Page 423, "Big Families Can Be Happy, Too" by Sara L. Smith. From *Newsweek.* Reprinted by permission of the author.

Page 427, "The Burden of Bearing Arms" by Adam Smith. Copyright © 1986 by Adam Smith (George J. W. Goodman). Reprinted by permission of the author.

Page 434, "Abortion Is Too Complex to Feel All One Way About" by Anna Quindlen. Copyright © 1986 by The New York Times Company. Reprinted by permission.

Page 440, "On AIDS and Moral Duty" by Willard Gaylin. Copyright © 1987 by The New York Times Company. Reprinted by permission.

INDEX

459